The 80th Division in World War I

Volume 1—Camp Lee to Saint Mihiel.

Gary Schreckengost

80thdivision.com

To Our Departed Comrades
And Their Families.
The 80th Division Only Moves Forward!

Copyright © 2016 Gary Schreckengost
All rights reserved.
Unless otherwise noted, all photographs either belong to the 80th Division Veterans'
Association or its members or the U.S. Army Signal Corps.
Frontispiece: 80th Division Advancing to the Front.

80th Division Association
www.80thdivision.com

Preface, 4.

Chapters

1. The War Begins, 14.
2. I Get Selected for Selective Service, 31.
3. America's "Blue Ridge Infantry Division" is Born (Aug.-Sept., 1917), 48.
4. The School of the Soldier, Squad, and Company at Camp Lee (Sept.-Dec., 1917), 86.
5. Infantry Training at Camp Lee (Jan.-May, 1918), 131.
6. Machine Gun Training at Camp Lee (Jan.-May, 1918), 167.
7. Medical Training at Camp Lee (Jan.-May, 1918), 202.
8. Engineer Training at Camp Lee (Jan.-May, 1918), 213.
9. Artillery Training at Camp Lee and Dutch Gap (Jan.-May 1918), 227.
10. *Friedensturm*, Dodging Porpoises, and Over There! (March-June 7, 1918), 259.
11. Training with the Tommies (June 8-July 21, 1918), 301.
12. Up the Line with the British in Picardy (July 22-Aug. 18, 1918), 357.
13. We Join "Black Jack's" American First Army (Aug. 19-Sept. 15, 1918), 393.

Bibliography, 413.

About the Author, 416.

Preface

America's 80th "Blue Ridge" Infantry Division was constituted on August 5, 1917, as part of the National Army (today's Army Reserve), with headquarters at Camp Lee, Virginia. The division itself consisted primarily of drafted men or "Selectees" from Virginia, West Virginia, and Pennsylvania and adopted the now-famous moniker "Blue Ridge Division," as the wondrous Blue Ridge Mountains of the Appalachian chain connected all three states and its peoples. When thrown into combat during the bone-crushing and war-ending Meuse-Argonne Offensive of September-November 1918, the 80th Division was also *the only American division to breach all four of the vaunted German Hindenburg defensive lines during the Meuse-Argonne Offensive* (*HAGEN*, *GISELHER*, *KRIEMHILDE*, and *FREYA*). In fact, the place where it breached *KRIEMHILDE*, the strongest of the lines, there now sits America's largest Soldier cemetery in France, standing as stoic reminder of the 80th Division's desperate and heroic actions. Because of its operations and the operations of many other American divisions, the Associated Powers (the Allies plus the United States) were finally able to smash the near-impregnable German defenses and push north to the outskirts of Sedan, ultimately ending the war with a German defeat. All told, the 80th "Blue Ridge" Division advanced some twenty miles across the most-heavily defended place on the earth at the time, suffered over 6,000 casualties—over half of its infantry strength—and killed or captured thousands of German soldiers in order to achieve ultimate victory. Their actions so inspired their Regular Army division commander, Maj. Gen. Adelbert Cronkhite to loudly proclaim: "The 80th Division Always Moves Forward!"

One of the missions of the 80th Division Association is to try to help Blue Ridge Division Soldiers, family members, and interested parties better understand "what it was like" for its Soldiers in the service of America's Blue Ridge Division.

This book is an effort to fill that need.

As such, *this is the historically accurate story* of a representative Dough Boy who served with America's Blue Ridge Division during World War I: Automatic Rifleman Joe Riddle of Company B, 1st Battalion, 318th Infantry Regiment, 159th Infantry Brigade. In Volume 1, read how and why Joe joined the Army in 1917, what training was like at Camp Lee, Virginia, how he was shipped to France, what it was like serving with the British in Artois and Picardy, France, and what the division did during the American First Army's first offensie of the war: the Saint Mihiel Offensive. In this volume, Volume 2, read what combat was like for Joe and others in the division during the war-ending and bone-crushing Meuse-Argonne Offensive and what it was like when he went home in 1919.

I'd like to acknowledge the people who helped me complete this project. First, I'd also like to acknowledge my 80th Division Association brothers and sisters who helped me with the research, gathering of pictures, and who said "do it Schreck," in no particular order: Capt. Lee Anthony (U.S.N., ret.), the 80th Division Association's "World War I Historian" and editor of Sergeant Stultz's tome about the division's history during the Great War for Civilization, Maj. Gen. John P. McLaren (U.S.A., ret.), commander emeritus of the 80th Division Association and my commanding officer in Iraq, Mr. Ben Jarratt of the Association who meticulously proofed my manuscript and helped improve it, Mr. Andy Adkins, the Association's "World War II Historian" and author of *You Can't Get Much Closer Than This: Combat with the 80th "Blue Ridge" Division in World War II Europe*, Maj. Dean Dominique (U.S.A., ret.), the author of *One Hell of a War: Patton's 317th Infantry Regiment in WWII*, and Mr. Jeff Wignall, the 2015 National Commander of the Association and author of *Farebersviller 1944*.[1]

Maj. Gary Schreckengost (U.S.A., ret.), 80th Division Association
Cold War, Homeland, Bosnia, and Iraq

---

[1] www.80thdivision.com. The Association consists not only of veterans of the division, but also family members of those who served in the division. Lee Anthony's and Ben Jarratt's ancestors, for example, served in the division during World War I.

1-2

HEADQUARTERS EIGHTIETH DIVISION.
AMERICAN EXPEDITIONARY FORCES.

France, 11 November, 1918.

GENERAL ORDER No. 19.
To the Members of the 80th Division:
The 80th Division Only Moves FORWARD.
It not only moves forward against the enemy, but it moves forward in the estimation of all who are capable of judging its courage, its fighting, and its manly qualities.

In the operations for the period of November 1-5, the division moved forward fifteen and five-eighths miles in an air line.

It always led.

It captured two Huns for every man wounded.

It captured one machine gun for every man wounded.

It captured one cannon for every ten men wounded, besides large quantities of munitions and other stores.

It accomplished these results of vast importance to the success of the general operation, with a far smaller percentage of casualties than in any other division engaged.

It has learned from hard training and experience.

The appreciation of the corps and the Army commanders is expressed in the following:

Telegram from the Commanding General, First Army (dated Nov. 1):

"The Army Commander desires that you inform the Commander of the 80th Division of the Army Commander's appreciation of his excellent work during the battle of to-day. He desires that you have this information sent to all organizations of that Division as far as may be practicable this night. He fully realizes the striking blow your division has delivered to the enemy this date."

Telegram from the Commanding General, First Army Corps (dated Nov. 1):

2-2

"The corps commander is particularly pleased with the persistent, intelligent work accomplished by your division today which has borne the brunt of the burden."
Letter from the Commanding General, First Army Corps, A.E.F. (dated Nov. 11):

The corps commander desires that you be informed and that those under your command be informed that in addition to other well deserved commendations received from the Army commander and corps commander, he wishes to express his particular gratification and appreciation of the work of your division from the time it has entered under his command."
It is necessarily a great honor to be allowed to command an organization which earns such commendation.
It is likewise a great honor to belong to such an organization.
I do not know what the future has in store for us.
If it be war, we must and shall sustain our honor and our reputation by giving our best to complete the salvation of our country.
If it be peace, we must and shall maintain our reputation and the honor of our division and the Army, as soldiers of the greatest country on earth, and as right-minded, self-respecting men.
The 80th Division Only Moves FORWARD.

CRONKHITE, Major-General.

1-2

France, 18 March, 1919.

GENERAL ORDERS NO. 12.

The 80th Division, having been instructed to prepare for return to the United States, will pass from the command of this Army Corps on 20 March, 1919.

The 80th Division arrived in France about June 5, 1918. This Division trained with the British Troops and was on active duty with them in the Artois Sector near Arras in July. The Division was in reserve at the battle of ST. MIHIEL, except the 320th Infantry and 315th Machine Gun Battalion, which took part in the operations of the II French Colonial Corps. From September 26 to 29, inclusive, the Division attacked at BETHINCOURT with the III American Corps and advanced nine kilometers in two days. The Division was withdrawn from the line for five days and again attacked on October 4 at NANTILLOIS. In nine days of heavy fighting through the BOIS DE OGONS an advance of four kilometers was made. The Division was withdrawn from the line October 12 for re-equipment and replacements. The Division moved forward on October 29 and 30 and re-entered the line at ST. JUVIN.

The 80th Division passed under the orders of the I Corps on October 23. On November 1, the Division attacked as the right division of the I Corps and in six days advanced a depth of 24 kilometers. The Division was relieved from the line on November 6, with its patrols on the west bank of the Meuse. From 18 November to 1 December, the Division marched 221 kilometers to the 15th Training Area at Auey-le-Franc. The artillery of the Division was part of the time detached from the Division and was in action at all times from September 26-November 11.

2-2

The Division has remained in the 15th Training Area until its present order to prepare from embarkation to the United States.

The 80th Division was given the difficult tasks on the front line and in accomplishing them made a splendid record. The corps commander desired particularly to express his appreciation for the soldierly achievements of this division during the time it served with the I Army Corps. After returning to the training area where living conditions were not easy and often difficult the spirit of the division has been excellent and has been manifest at all times. The division leaves on the first part of its journey with the corps commander's congratulations for its excellent record and his wishes for a speedy return to the United States and a successful future. By command of Major-General Wright.

W.M. FASSETT.
Chief of Staff.

OFFICIAL.
Lt.-Col. A.G.D. Adjutant.

HEADQUARTERS EIGHTIETH DIVISION.

AMERICAN EXPEDITIONARY FORCE.

France, 14 May, 1919.

BULLETIN # 113.

The following letter has been received from Lieut. Gen. Robert Lee Bullard, U.S.A., in command of the III Corps, A.E.F., during the Meuse-Argonne Offensive:

"Under the pressure of great events I, at that time commanding the III Corps to which the 80th Division then belonged, failed to cite the gallant conduct of the division in making three successive assaults with great bravery and finally taking and driving the enemy from Bois Ogons in the great battle of the Meuse-Argonne. I cite it now. It was truly admirable. We see it now more plainly in the light of the results that followed. I ask that this be communicated to your gallant division."

The 80th Division was the only A.E.F. division which went into line in the Meuse-Argonne Offensive three times.

By command of Major General Cronkhite:

W.H. Waldron,

Col., General Staff,

Chief of Staff

The 80th Division officially participated in four campaigns during World War I ("The Great War for Civilization") and suffered 6,101 casualties (217 K.I.A. and 5,884 W.I.A.) out of around 28,000 assigned (22% casualty rate, 2% K.I.A., 20% W.I.A.). We were present at the Saint-Mihiel campaign, too, but the Army didn't officially recognize it as a division battle, as only one regiment, the 320th Infantry, was sent into it. The infantry battalions, of course, suffered far greater casualties. The 3/320th Infantry, for example, suffered 600 casualties out of 840 men (71%), which breaks down to 91 K.I.A. (11%) and 509 W.I.A. (60%). By operation, the casualty figures are as follows:

1918 Somme Offensive: 427 casualties (7 K.I.A., 420 W.I.A.).

1918 Meuse-Argonne (Phase I): 1,064 casualties (27 K.I.A., 1,037 W.I.A.) .

1918 Meuse-Argonne (Phase II): 3,551 casualties (1,154 K.I.A., 2,397 W.I.A.).

1918 Meuse-Argonne (Phase III): 1,059 casualties (44 K.I.A., 1,015 W.I.A.).

As for decorations, citations, and awards, the 80th Division received a total of 619, as follows:

Distinguished Service Crosses: 59

Distinguished Service Medals: 20

General Headquarters, A.E.F. Citation: 41

War Dept. Citations: 31

Division Citations: 35

Brigade Citations: 345

Meritorious Service Certificates: 34

Foreign Citations and Awards: 54

"Sunny Smiles, Virginia Beach." Before the war, life was simple and true.

Woodrow Wilson, President of these United States during "The Great War for Civilization, 1917-18."

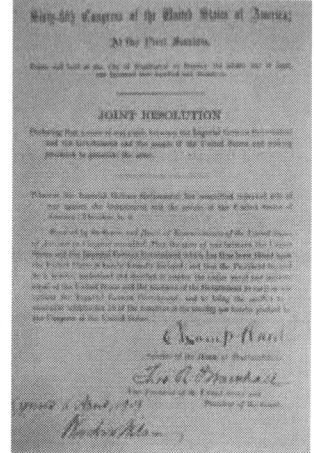

General John "Black Jack" Pershing, commander, A.E.F.; former cavalry officer and decorated for actions in the Old West, in Cuba, the Philippines, and Mexico.

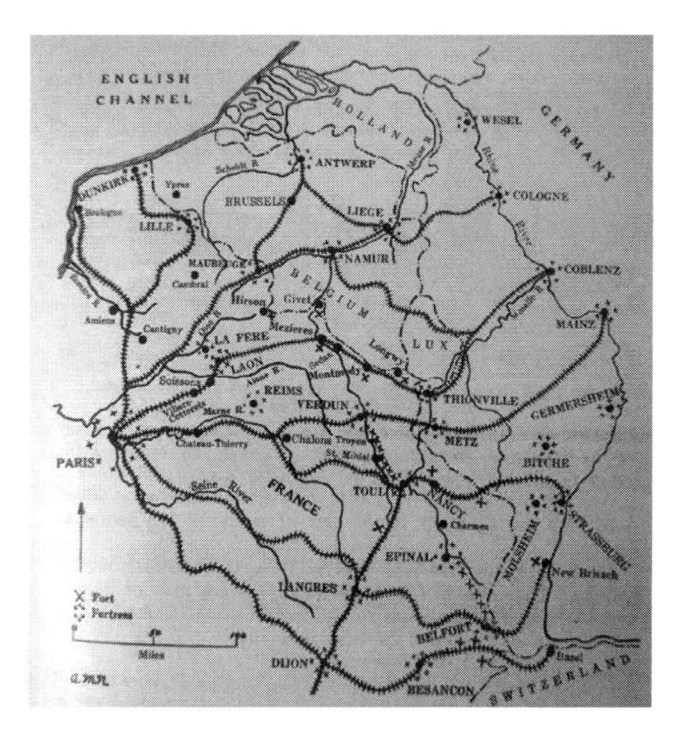

There were several attack axes the French or Germans could have used to attack the other in 1914: (1) Cologne-Liege-Namur-Maubeuge-Paris (2) Thionville-Soissons-Paris, (3) Metz-Verdun-Chateau-Thierry-Paris, (4) Strasburg-Nancy-Toul-Chalons-Thierry-Paris or (5) Belfort-Langres-Paris. While the French chose to attack up the Toul-Nancy-Strasburg corridor (4), the Germans chose to attack down the Cologne-Liége-Namur-Maubeuge-Paris corridor (1). *Mitchell.*

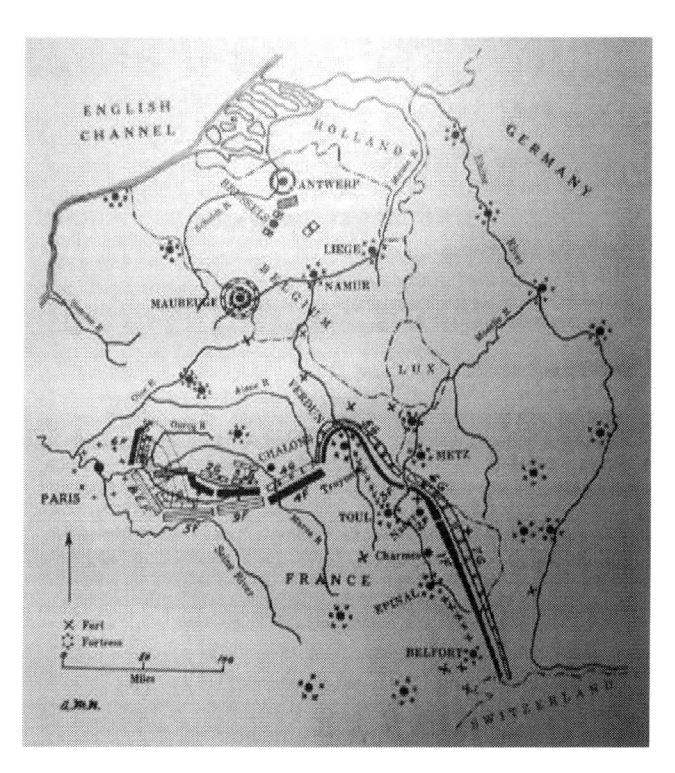

The German strategic plan called for the defeat of France between Paris and Verdun and then turn on the Russians. At the battle of the Marne, however (the line between Paris and Verdun), the Germans failed to break the French and British armies and were forced to fall back along the Maubeuge Line, where they dug-in. For the next three years, 1915-18, the French, British, and other Allied powers tried to break this strong Hun defensive line. They were only able to punch through with the help of U.S. forces in 1918. *Mitchell.*

Chapter 1
The War Begins.

I am Joe Riddle from Petersburg, Virginia. In the summer of 1914, when the war started in Europe, I was but seventeen years old and about ready to enter my senior year in high school. My parents and I lived in a small wood-framed house on West Tab and North Sycamore Streets. My father worked for the Norfolk & Western Railroad and my mother made the best chicken soup in the world.

Aside from spending time with my friends in town or along the banks of the Appomattox River, I sometimes helped my dad on the railroad, checking out cars and such before they rolled out. All was "peace and quiet" (read: boring) until August when most of Europe and her colonial possessions went up in flames. I mean the war didn't come to me in Petersburg, but it did begin a series of events that eventually led me into the Army of the United States (A.U.S.), the 80th (Blue Ridge) Division, and the Meuse-Argonne Offensive of 1918, the biggest battle ever fought by the United States. In short, it was the Austro-Hungarian, German, and Ottoman Empires against the Russian, French, British, and Belgian Empires as well as the Kingdoms of Serbia, Japan, Italy, Greece, and Romania.

On June 28, 1914, Austria-Hungary declared war on Serbia ostensibly for the assassination of its crown prince, Franz Ferdinand, and his wife, in Sarajevo, Bosnia, then part of the Austro-Hungarian Empire (Austria and Hungary were actually two separate kingdoms that had the same head-of state). Russia then mobilized to stop Austria from invading its ally, Serbia, which led Germany, Austria's lone ally, to also mobilize its forces, which led France, Russia's ally, to also mobilize. Germany warned Russia to stand down—it didn't—so on Aug. 1, 1914, Germany declared war on Russia and Russia reciprocated.

This is why most people blame Germany for the war.

With war declared against its ally, France declared war on Germany on Aug. 3 and Germany reciprocated.

According to French and Russian war plans, while France was to invade the German state of Alsace-Lorraine to get it back (*Elsaß-Lottringen* in German—it was taken by Germany from France in 1871 because it had been taken by France from Germany in the 1740s), Russia was to invade German East Prussia and Silesia from the Kingdom of Poland. Crushed in between, Germany would be defeated and its provinces like Alsace-Lorraine, Silesia, and East Prussia would be taken and transferred to France or Russia for the price for peace.

Understanding the perils of fighting a two front war, Germany decided that it had to defeat France first, a country that had a far better army—and far better roads—than Russia. To engage both with the same resources over a long period of time would mean certain defeat. Germany therefore planned to sweep behind France's strong border defenses along the Moselle River near Verdun, Toul, and Epinal by conducting a massive turning movement through Luxembourg and Belgium with five field armies. Once it did so, Germany hoped to destroy France's *armée de manouvre* in a decisive battle of annhiliation near Châlons.[2] In the meantime, the German Sixth and Seventh Armies would defend *Elsaß-Lottringen* against French attack and its Eighth Army would defend East Prussia from Russian attack.

Once France was defeated near Paris, Germany would then turn on Russia, regain East Prussia (which it knew it would lose in the interim), and invade the Russian Empire's Kingdom of Poland.

The plan was as bold as it was revolutionary.

To get at each other, France and Germany had five main avenues of approach (or "axes of advance") into each other's countries, including one that led through neutral Belgium and Luxembourg. From north to south: (1) Cologne-Liège-Namur-Maubeuge-Paris, (2) Thionville-Sedan-Soissons-Paris, (3) Metz-Verdun-Chalons-Chateau-Thierry-Paris, (4) Strasbourg-Toul-Chalons-Chateau-Thierry-Paris, and (5) Belfort-Langres-Paris. While the French chose to attack straight into the German strong defenses in Lorraine using attack axis (4), the Germans conducted their infamous "right hook" through Luxembourg and Belgium using attack axis (1). The Germans did this because they knew that if they attacked up axes two to four, they would be bogged down by the strong French fortifications that were built after the Franco-Prussian War of 1870-71.[3] And if the Germans got bogged down in France, the Russians would eventually be able to generate overwhelming forces in the East, bringing about a decision that would not benefit the German Empire.

When the Belgians refused to allow "safe passage" for the attacking German forces, Germany declared war on them on Aug. 4, invaded, and laid siege to *Liège*, which guarded the main Meuse River crossing between Aachen, Germany, and Paris, France.[4]

Nothing was going to stop their right hook!

With the invasion of neutral Luxembourg and Belgium, Great Britain and its vast imperial holdings (e.g., Canada, Australia, New Zealand, South Africa, India, Kenya, Egypt, etc.)

---

[2] *Armée de manouvre* is pronounced "arm-may day man-oov-rah." It means the "army of maneuver" or the "main army of operations." Defeating it decisively is the key to winning a war and every commander seeks to destroy his opponent's.

[3] Mitchell, Lt. Col. William A. *Outlines of Military History* (Washington, D.C.: National Service Publishing Company, 1931), 639. Hereafter cited as "Mitchell."

[4] *Liège* is pronounced "Lee-age" and Meuse is pronounced "Mooz-ah."

declared war on Germany and the United States, Holland, Switzerland, Sweden, Denmark, Spain, along with many other countries, declared their official neutrality in the war. According to General John "Black Jack" Pershing, the man who eventually became our commanding general in France, Germany was the clear aggressor, not only because it declared war first and attacked first, but also because it attacked neutral countries (Luxembourg and Belgium) in order achieve its political goal of global domination. He writes:

> *The violation of Belgian neutrality afforded Germany the advantage of invading France from the most favorable quarter, yet it was no justification for her to claim that strategic considerations impelled her to take this action. In disregarding the Treaty of London of 1839 Germany presented the strongest kind of evidence of her war guilt. Moreover, this overt act served to give notice to all nations that Germany intended to brook no opposition in her purpose to conquer her ancient enemy once and for all. I cannot escape the conviction that in view of this defiance of neutral rights the United States made a grievous error in not immediately entering a vigorous protest. The argument might be made that as our government was not a signatory to the treaty its violation was none of our business. But one of the stronger members of the family of civilized nations, to which, broadly speaking, we all belong, had committed an outrage against a peaceful neutral neighbor simply because she stood in the way.*[5]

On Aug. 6, Austria-Hungary declared war on Russia and Serbia, Russia's ally, declared war on Germany.

On Aug. 7, the French First and Second Armies invaded German Alsace-Lorraine as planned and drove the defending German Sixth and Seventh Armies back several miles. On that same day, General Sir John French's British Expeditionary Force (B.E.F.), an army-sized command, landed in Flanders to help drive the German First, Second, Third, Fourth, and Fifth Armies out of Belgium.

On Aug. 11, France declared war against Austro-Hungary and it reciprocated.

On Aug. 12, Britain declared war against Austria-Hungary and it reciprocated.

On Aug. 17, the Russians invaded German East Prussia.

On Aug. 23, the German First, Second, and Third Armies defeated the B.E.F. and the French Fifth Army at Mons, Belgium, and the Allies were forced to fall back to the French

---

[5] Pershing, 1:6.

fortress city of Maubeuge. On that same day, Japan, a British ally, declared war on Germany and went after its colonial possessions in China (e.g., Tsingtao) and the Pacific (e.g., the Bismarck Islands).

On Sept. 4, the Germans took Maubeuge, uncoupling the entire Franco-British line in northern France, and it became a race to the Marne River and Paris. If the Germans crossed the Marne east of Paris, they would encircle most of the French army and basically win the war.

The subsequent Battle of the Marne was arguably one of the most important battles in world history because of what did not happen: the Germans did not beat the French and their British allies. The Battle of the Marne started on Sept. 5 and ended on Sept. 12, 1914. The left of the Allied line rested on Paris and their right on Verdun. The battlefront extended some 140 miles. Nearly 2.5 million men were engaged in combat: 1,125,000 Allies versus 1,275,000 Germans. While *Maréchal de France* Joseph Joffre ("Papa Joffre") was in charge of the French armies along the Marne, Sir John French was in charge of the B.E.F.[6]

On account of the decreased strength of the German right flank (*Generalfeldmarschall Helmut von Moltke*, Joffre's counterpart, weakened it to shore up his forces in Alsace-Lorraine, which was a mistake), *Generaloberst Heinrich von Kluck*, commander of the German First Army, was ordered not to encircle Paris from the northwest but to instead drive down to the Marne in a southeasterly direction, echeloned to the rear of the *Generaloberst Karl von Bülows* German Second Army. During the repositioning, however, Kluck pushed too far ahead of Bülow's army, leaving a gap between the two forces.[7]

Spotting this opening, Papa Joffre asked the B.E.F., on Kluck's right, and directed the French Fifth Army, on Kluck's left, to conduct a double-envelopment. These were the same forces that had been defeated by Kluck and Bülow at Mons and Maubeuge and they were out for blood. This go-for-broke counter-attack, which lasted several days, was a resounding success, as not only were Kluck's and Bülow's First and Second Armies driven back, but the German Third, Fourth, and Fifth Armies along with them.

The five German armies fell back in good order, however, and they dug-in a strong (some would say, impregnable) defensive line in northern France and southern Belgium (later to be called "the Hindenburg Line"). From this line, they would hold the Western Allies at bay while they rethought their strategy.

---

[6] Mitchell, 657. *Maréchal de France* Joseph Joffre is pronounced "Mar-she-awl day Frawnz Josef Jof-rah."

[7] Mitchell, 658. *Generalfeldmarschal* Helmut Moltke is pronounced "Gen-er-awl-feld-marsh-all Hel-moot von Molt-kah," *Generaloberst* Heinrich von Kluck is pronounced "Gen-er-awl-ob-erst Hyn-rick von Klook," and Karl von Bülow is pronounced "Carl von Boo-lov." A *Generaloberst* is a four-star (or army) general and a *Generalfeldmarschall* is a five-star (or army group) general.

In German Alsace-Lorraine meanwhile, the German Sixth and Seventh Armies counter-attacked and drove the French First and Second Armies back, pretty much re-establishing the national boundary. By the end of 1914 therefore, the German defensive line in the West was as continuous as it was strong, as it stretched from the Channel Port of Ostend, Belgium, in the north, all the way down to the mountains of neutral Switzerland in the south, with about half of German Alsace in French hands and all of Luxembourg, most of Belgium, and some of France in German hands.

In German East Prussia meanwhile, *Generalfeldmarschall Paul von Hindenburgs* German Eighth Army, in a history-making campaign, actually threw back two Russian armies, freeing the province of Russian forces.

So although the Germans were down, they were not out.

The great "what if" of the campaign is *what if* the Germans would have weighed the main effort more? What if six German armies and not five had been sent on the great turning movement across Belgium and toward the Marne?

As Frederick the Great, the King of Prussia said: "Hit with the fist, don't feel with the fingers."

That's one lesson we in the American Experitionary Force (A.E.F.) would put into action.

-1915-

In 1915, the year of my high school graduation, alliances on both sides grew. The Allies or *Entente Cordiale*, led by France, Russia, and Britain (including its vast imperial possessions of Canada, Australia, New Zealand, South Africa, India, Kenya, etc.), now included Serbia (which was partially occupied by Austria-Hungary), Montenegro (which was partially-occupied by Austria-Hungary), Belgium (which was mostly occupied by Germany), Luxembourg (which was occupied by Germany), Italy (who wanted parts of Austrian Tyrol and Croatia), Greece (who wanted parts of Bulgaria and Turkey), Romania (who wanted parts of Bulgaria and Hungary), Portugal (who wanted some German possessions in Africa), and Japan (who wanted German possessions in Asia).[8] The Central Powers, led by Germany and Austria-Hungary, now included Turkey (who wanted parts of Bulgaria, Greece, and the British and Russian Empires in the southwest Asia), and Bulgaria (who didn't want to get divided up by Serbia, Greece, and Romania). With their defeat at the Marne, the Germans decided to remain on the strategic defensive in the West while they went after the Russians in the East with the Austro-Hungarians and Ottomans.

---

[8] "The Cordial Alliance" or *Entente Cordiale* is pronounced "Awn-tawnt Cord-ee-awl."

As for the Western Allies, in order to regain lost ground, they launched massive counter-attacks against the strongly-held German lines in northern France and got murdered by German machine guns, artillery, and even poison gas. This is when the war in the West or "the Western Front," as it came to be called, became one giant siege campaign (what we blithely called "trench warfare"). Trench or siege warfare is as old as war itself. It is bloody, costly, and slow. The key to victory is to breach the enemy line and then quickly exploit said breach or salient in order to return to open or "maneuver" warfare, which generally brings about decisive results.

In the distant East meanwhile, in Austrian Galicia, German Prussia, and Russian Poland, where the lines weren't nearly as continuous or strong, Germany, Austria, and Hungary drove the Russians back several hundred miles "in open warfare." It was here where the Central Powers now hoped to bring about a decision. Once Russia and its Romanian ally were defeated in the East, then Germany and Austria-Hungary would mass their forces along the Western Front, drive the British into the sea, encircle and destroy the French Army between Paris and Verdun, and win the war.

In order to help prevent this, the Allies invoked a blockade against the Central Powers, which meant that no nation, including the neutral United States, could trade with Germany or its confederates. Starvation would be their weapon! (And it worked.) Of course, the Germans answered the Allied blockade in kind by building a fleet of sleek new submarines (called *Unterseebooten* or "U-Boats"), and the War in the Atlantic really heated up, putting neutral powers, like the U.S., in a real pickle, as it ran against the international law of "Freedom of the Seas." This law states that neutral powers, like the U.S., can trade with anyone, anywhere, anytime. It is a naïve idea, of course, as countries bludgeoning each other into oblivion can not be expected to stand idly by while a neutral party gets rich from the war and strengthens its enemies.

Some Americans, like former President Teddy Roosevelt, understood this and wanted to in fact join the Allies so the U.S. could tip the balance to victory, not only to save thousands of lives, but to also cash in on the peace treaty—like getting some of the German Bismarck Islands in the Pacific, which Japan was eyeing. The vast majority of the American people wanted to stay out of the war, however, and that's what we did, taking a few hits from German U-boats, slowing our trade. Of course, attacking U.S. ships on the high seas was a blatant act of war but the Germans felt they had no choice but to fire on any ship headed for Britain, France, Russia, Portugal, or Italy.

-1916-

In 1916, the year of our presidential election, the Allied nation of Romania was overrun by the Central Powers, the French were bled white at Verdun, the British were slaughtered along the Somme, and British and American shipping were getting rocked by German U-Boat attacks in the North Atlantic. It seemed as if the Central Powers were in fact going to win the war even though Germany had lost most of its African and Asian colonies to French, British, Belgian, Portuguese, or Japanese forces and had failed to knock France out of the war in 1914-15.

The Election of 1916 was essentially between the Democratic President Woodrow Wilson who said, "Stay out and stay neutral" and former Republican Supreme Court Justice Charles Evan Hughes who basically said the same thing about the war but who also wanted to build up our Army and Navy, which Wilson thought would be seen as an act of belligerency and would in fact invite war. Wilson stated in Cincinnati in Oct. of that year:

> *We must have a society of nations, not suddenly, not by insistence, not by any hostile emphasis upon the demand, but by the demonstration of the needs of the time. The nations of the world must get together and say: "Nobody can hereafter be neutral as respects the disturbance of the world's peace for an object which the world's opinion cannot sanction. The world's peace ought to be disturbed if the fundamental rights of humanity are invaded, but it ought not to be distributed for any other thing that I can think of, and America was established in order to indicate, at any rate in one government, the fundamental rights of man. America must be ready hereafter as a member of the family of nations to exert her whole force, moral and physical, to the assertion of those rights throughout the round globe.*[9]

To me, when Wilson said, "exert her whole force, moral and physical," he signaled that he was in fact growing more open to what many called "the Preparedness Movement." Led by people like former President Teddy Roosevelt or the former Army Chief of Staff, Leonard Wood, the leaders of the Preparedness Movement—mostly Republicans but not all—believed that the U.S. should build its land and naval forces in 1915-16 so that we could properly defend ourselves. And if we were drawn into the war, obviously on the side of Britain and France, our entrance would be far more decisive. Then-Brig. Gen. Pershing, in command of the Army's "Southern Department" in Texas in 1916 argued that if we would have deployed just 500,000 trained troops in 1917, when it was "more favorable for the Allies than at any previous time," the Allies

---

[9] As cited in Harbord, James. *The American Army in France, 1917-19* (Boston: Little, Brown, and Company, 1936), 513. Hereafter cited as "Harbord."

plus the U.S. could have in fact won the war by the end of the year, saving hundreds of thousands of lives. He writes:

> *Let us suppose that, instead of adhering to the erroneous theory that neutrality forbade any move toward preparation, we had taken the precaution in the spring of 1916 to organize and equip an army of half a million combatant troops, together with the requisite number of supply troops for such a force . This could have been done merely by increasing the Regular Army and National Guard to war strength. Such action would have given us the equivalent of forty average Allied divisions, ready to sail at once for France upon the declaration of war. Preparation to this extent could have been carried out by taking advantage of the concentration of the Regular Army and National Guard on the Mexican Border in 1916.*
>
> *The actual situation on the Western Front when we entered the war was more favorable for the Allies than at any previous time. The strength of the German forces there had been greatly reduced because of the necessity for supporting the Russian front. Although reports were filtering in regarding the beginning of the revolution, there was little to indicate that Russia was not still a factor to be reckoned with. Actually the Allies had an advantage of something over 20% in numbers, French morale was high, owing to their successful defense of Verdun, and the British armies had reached their maximum power.*
>
> *Under these conditions, it is not extravagant to assert that the addition of 500,000 American combat troops in early spring would have given the Allies such a preponderance of force that the war could have been brought to a victorious conclusion before the end of that year. Even without such aid, the confidence of the Allies led them to undertake a general offensive in April. Although it ended in defeat, especially for the French, the failure can be attributed to a large extent to lack of secrecy of the plans. A well-planned campaign with the assistance of half a million Americans would have told quite another story.*
>
> *Thus, through a false notion of neutrality, which had prevented practically all previous preparation, a favorable opportunity to assist the Allies was lost, the war was prolonged another year and the cost in human life tremendously increased. But, from another viewpoint, it is not improbable*

that if we had been thus prepared, our rights would have been respected and we would not have been forced into the war. We shall see as we proceed how great were the difficulties to be overcome because of our inexcusable failure to do what common reason long before our entry into the war plainly indicated should have been done.[10]

This was one of the more difficult elections for my father to decide (I was too young to vote). He generally agreed with the Progressives of the period who argued that man's condition could be improved through scientific methods and positive governmental action. Wilson was much more of the Progressive candidate than Judge Hughes as he was for the "Eight-hour work day, five days a week" proposal that was floating around Congress. Besides that, he was a native Virginian, and my father, as well at 95% of the voters of Petersburg, was "Yellow-Dog Democrat" (i.e., "he'll vote for anything, even a yellow dog, over a Republican"). There were several points and counter-points to get into the war or to stay out of it, and which side to take.

Foremost was the question of the German U-Boat blockade of Britain, France, Portugal, Italy, and Russia in which American vessels, purposely or not, had been sunk. The most famous was the sinking of the S.S. *Sussex* and *Lusitania* in 1916 in what Germany called "Unrestricted Submarine Warfare." My father and many other people were very concerned about this issue, as it pointed directly to Germany's blatant disregard for "neutral rights." Granted, the Germans stopped the practice of "Unrestricted Submarine Warfare" after the sinking of the *Lusitania*, but would it resume the tactic as the war dragged on and on?

There was also broad concern about the fact that new technology like aeroplanes, submarines, machine guns, tanks, and indirect artillery fire were killing hundreds of thousands of people in the war. How could we face that?

The U.S. Army in 1916 was a joke.

There, I said it.

Our Army was configured to simply defend our coasts and that of Panama Canal and the Philippines or to fight Mexican or Central American "banditti" and had few or none of the new weapons. If the Army couldn't even run down the Mexican rebel General Pancho Villa who had raided into the U.S. to protest the U.S. occupation of Vera Cruz, how was it going to fight dug-in Germans armed with *Maxim Machinen Gewehr 08* (M.G.) that spat out 400 rounds per minute (R.P.M.) in 250-round fabric belts and indirect heavy artillery!? Besides, how would we get our forces "over there" with the German U-Boat cordon?

---

[10] Pershing, 1:8-9.

Not that we *had* to get "over there" with an army. If we actually did go to war with Germany over sinking our vessels, wouldn't it merely be a war on the High Seas against their U-boats?

Our navy against their navy?

So aside from getting into the war, in which Republicans and Democrats generally agreed (stay out), the role of government, on which they differed greatly, the biggest issue on everyone's mind was how the U.S. should "prepare" or "react" to the war. Should we remain "demobilized" with just a small Regular Army and skeleton National Guard and Organized Reserve, or should we totally mobilize to show the combatant nations of the world, especially Germany, to not even think about messing with us. While President Wilson and the Democrats were for the former, Judge Hughes and the G.O.P. were for the latter.

While the presidential candidates debated, President Wilson signed into law the National Defense Act of 1916. It updated the Militia Act of 1903, making the National Guard more in-line with the Regular Army, expanded the Regular Army to 128,000 men and the National Guard to 81,000 men, and, most importantly, created an Officers' and an Enlisted Reserve Corps as well as a Reserve Officers' Training Corps (R.O.T.C). The President was also given expanded authority to federalize the National Guard, with changes to the duration and the circumstances under which it could be called up. The National Defense Act of 1916 finally allowed the Army to stand-up an Aviation arm and the federal government took steps to ensure the immediate availability of wartime weapons and equipment by contracting in advance for production of gunpowder and other materiel.

After much sober contemplation, my father, the State of Virginia, and the country went for Wilson, who promised to keep us out of the war, to not show any acts of belligerency by rearming too much, and to continue with the Progressive agenda. With the reelection of Wilson, we thought that we would stay out of the war and that Europe would be ground into dust, leaving us to be one of the dominant powers in the world with two great seas protecting us.

We were wrong.

-1917-

In February 1917, two events proved key to the war: Germany's renewal of "Unrestricted Submarine Warfare" and Russia's "Revolution of 1917," which led to the abdication of Czar Nicholas II, the Emperor of Russia, Grand Duke of Finland, and King of Poland, etc. Although the Czar's Russian holdings, which were proclaimed "Soviet Socialist Republics," stayed in the war for the rest of the year, the initiative in the East definately turned in the Central Powers' favor.

In the West, in reaction to the Allies' blockade of the Central Powers (which brought famine in Germany and Austria), Germany renewed its unrestricted U-Boat campaign in the Atlantic—targeting any ship headed for Britain, France, or Italy. This meant that any ship headed for Allied waters, including American ones, would be sunk—no questions asked.

In response, on Feb. 3, President Wilson severed diplomatic relations with Germany and over the next few weeks, several U.S. merchant vessels headed for Britain were in fact sunk by German subs.

On March 12, Wilson ordered all merchant vessels to be armed and for the U.S. Navy to protect them.

But still Germany would not relent and the attacks continued.

U.S. naval vessels returned fire.

A few days later, British intelligence intercepted a telegram from the German Foreign Office in Berlin to its embassy in Mexico that instructed the German ambassador there to begin special, secret negotiations with Mexico: that if war broke out between the U.S. and Germany, Germany desired an alliance with Mexico. If accepted, Germany offered to help Mexico recapture all or parts of the Mexican Cession of 1848 (e.g., Texas, New Mexico, Arizona, etc.) if Mexico helped Germany take Puerto Rico and the Panama Canal from the U.S.

Can you believe the gall?

This transmission has come to be known to the world as the infamous "Zimmerman Telegram" because it was drafted by Arthur Zimmerman of the German Foreign Office.

In his Second Inaugural Address in March, Wilson laid out the following principles with which the U.S. would stand upon in world affairs—and he was talking straight to the Prussian King and German Emperor, Wilhelm II:

All nations are equally interested in the peace of the world and in the political stability of free peoples, and equally responsible for their maintenance—that the essential principle of peace is the actual equality of nations in all matters of right or privilege—all nations are equally interested in the peace of the world and in the political stability of free peoples, and equally responsible for their maintenance; That the essential principle of peace is the actual equality of nations in all matters of right or privilege; That peace cannot securely or justly rest upon an armed balance of power; that governments derive all their just powers from the consent of the governed and that no other powers should be supported by the common thought, purpose or power of the family of nations; that the seas should be equally free and safe for the use of all peoples, under rules set up by common agreement and consent, and that, so far as practicable, they should be accessible to all upon equal terms; that national armaments should be limited to the necessities of national order and domestic safety; that the community of interest and of power upon which peace must henceforth depend imposes upon each nation the duty of seeing to it that all influences proceeding from its own citizens meant to encourage or assist revolution in other states should be sternly and effectually suppressed and prevented.

But yet, the attacks continued.

Finally, on April 2, 1917, after all pacific measures had been exhausted, Wilson formally petitioned Congress for a Declaration of War against the "Imperial German Government" as "a state of war already existed." He said:

Gentlemen of the Congress, I have called the Congress into extraordinary session because there are serious, very serious, choices of policy to be made, and made immediately, which it was neither right nor constitutionally permissible that I should assume the responsibility of making. On the 3rd of February last I officially laid before you the extraordinary announcement of the Imperial German Government that on and after the first day of February it was its purpose to put aside all restraints of law or of humanity and use its submarines to sink every vessel that sought to approach either the ports of Great Britain and Ireland or the western coasts of Europe or any of the ports controlled by the enemies of Germany within the Mediterranean. That had seemed to be the object of the German submarine warfare earlier in the war, but since April of last year the Imperial Government had somewhat restrained the commanders of its undersea craft in conformity with its promise then given to us that passenger-boats should not be sunk, and that due warning would be given to all other vessels which its submarines might seek to destroy when no resistance was offered or escape attempted, and care taken that their crews were given at least a fair chance to save their lives in their open boats. The precautions taken were meager and haphazard enough, as was proved in distressing instance after instance in the progress of the cruel and unmanly business, but a certain degree of restraint was observed.

The new policy has swept every restriction aside. Vessels of every kind, whatever their flag, their character, their cargo, their destination, their errand, have been ruthlessly sent to the bottom without warning, and without thought of help or mercy for those on board, the vessels of friendly neutrals along with those of belligerents. Even hospital ships and ships carrying relief to the sorely bereaved and stricken people of Belgium, though the latter were provided with safe conduct through the proscribed areas by the German government itself and were distinguished by and world.

By painful stage after stage has that law been built up with meager enough results, indeed, after all was accomplished that could be accomplished, but always with a clear view at least of what the heart and conscience of mankind demanded. This minimum of right the German government has swept aside under the plea of retaliation and necessity, and because it had no weapons which it could use at sea except these, which it is impossible to employ as it is employing them without throwing to the winds all scruples of humanity or of respect for the understandings that were supposed to underlie the intercourse of the world. I am not now thinking of the loss of property involved, immense and serious as that is, but only of the wanton and wholesale destruction of the lives of non-combatants, men, women and children engaged in pursuits which have always, even in the darkest periods of modern history, been deemed innocent and legitimate.

Property can be paid for—the lives of peaceful and innocent people cannot be.

The present German warfare against commerce is a warfare against mankind. It is a war against all nations. American ships have been sunk, American lives taken, in ways which it has stirred us very deeply to learn of, but the ships and people of other neutral and friendly nations have been sunk and overwhelmed in the waters in the same way. There has been no discrimination. The challenge is to all mankind. Each nation must decide for itself how it will meet it. The choice we make for ourselves must be made with a moderation of counsel and a temperateness of judgment befitting our character and our motives as a nation. We must put excited feeling away.

Our motive will not be revenge or the victorious assertion of the physical might of the nation, but only the vindication of right, of human right, of which we are only a single champion. When I addressed the Congress on the 26th of February last I thought that it would suffice to assert our neutral rights with arms, our right to use the seas against unlawful interference, our right to keep our people safe against unlawful violence. But armed neutrality, it now appears, is impracticable.

Because submarines are in effect outlaws when used as the German submarines have been used against merchant shipping, it is impossible to defend ships against their attacks as the law of nations has assumed that merchantmen would defend themselves against privateers or cruisers, visible craft giving chase upon the open sea. It is common prudence in such circumstances, grim necessity, indeed, to endeavor to destroy them before they have shown their own intention. They must be dealt with upon sight, if dealt with at all.

The German government denies the right of neutrals to use arms at all within the areas of the sea which it has proscribed, even in the defense of rights which no modern publicist has ever before questioned their right to defend. The intimation is conveyed that the armed guards which we have placed on our merchant-ships will be treated as beyond the pale of law and subject to be dealt with as pirates would be.

Armed neutrality is ineffectual enough at best; in such circumstances and in the face of such pretensions it is worse than ineffectual; it is likely to produce what it was meant to prevent; it is practically certain to draw us into the war without either the rights or the effectiveness of belligerents. There is one choice we cannot make, we are incapable of making: we will not choose the path of submission and suffer the most sacred rights of our nation and our people to be ignored or violated. The wrongs against which we now array ourselves are not common wrongs—they reach out to the very roots of human life.

With a profound sense of the solemn and even tragical character of the step I am taking and of the grave responsibilities which it involves, but in unhesitating obedience to what I deem my constitutional duty, I advise that the Congress declare the recent course of the Imperial German Government to be in fact nothing less than war against the government and people of the United States. That it formally accept the status of belligerent which has thus been thrust upon it and that it take immediate steps not only to put the country in a more thorough state of defense, but also to exert all its power and employ all its resources to bring the Government of the German Empire to terms and end the war.

It was one powerful speech.

On April 6, Congress obliged, and we were officially at war with "Imperial German Government," but not with the German people. At Wilson's insistence, the U.S. would be considered as an "Associated Power" with France, Britain, and the rest of "the Allies," working in concert with them, but remaining legally separate from them. He did this, in large part, because he blamed the alliance system for the war itself and wished to protect American sovereignty.

As for whether we should have gotten involved in the war sooner or whether we should have been better prepared, is an on-going debate.

On the one hand, I understand Wilson's desire to stay neutral and not to waste money on a military we didn't need. On the other hand, if most of the rest of the world is at war, especially on the High Seas, wouldn't it have been better if we would have expanded the Army and the Navy starting in 1915? I do agree with General Pershing's premise that if we would have sent just 500,000 trained troops to France in 1917 (about nine divisions with support units—raised, trained, and equipped in 1916), it may have shortened the war by many months, saving hundreds of thousands of lives. On what the war would involve, Wilson was very clear:

What this will involve is clear. It will involve the utmost practicable co-operation in counsel and action with the governments now at war with Germany, and as incident to that the extension to those governments of the most liberal financial credits in order that our resources may so far as possible be added to theirs. It will involve the organization and mobilization of all the material resources of the country to supply the materials of war and serve the incidental needs of the nation in the most abundant and yet the most economical and efficient way possible.

It will involve the immediate full equipment of the Navy in all respects, but particularly in supplying it with the best means of dealing with the enemy's submarines.

It will involve the immediate addition to the armed forces of the United States already provided for by law in case of war at least 500,000 men, who should, in my opinion, be chosen upon the principle of universal liability to service, and also the authorization of subsequent additional increments of equal force so soon as they may be needed and can be handled in training.

It will involve also, of course, the granting of adequate credits to the government, sustained, I hope, so far as they can equitably be sustained by the present generation, by well-conceived taxation. I say sustained so far as may be equitable by taxation because it seems to me that it would be most unwise to base the credits which will now be necessary entirely on money borrowed. It is our duty, I most respectfully urge, to protect our people so far as we may against the very serious hardships and evils which would be likely to arise out of the inflation which would be produced by vast loans. In carrying out the measures by which these things are to be accomplished we should keep constantly in mind the wisdom of interfering as little as possible in our own preparation and in the equipment of our own military forces with the duty—for it will be a very practical duty—of supplying the nations already at war with Germany with the materials which they can obtain only from us or by our assistance. They are in the field and we should help them in every way to be effective there.

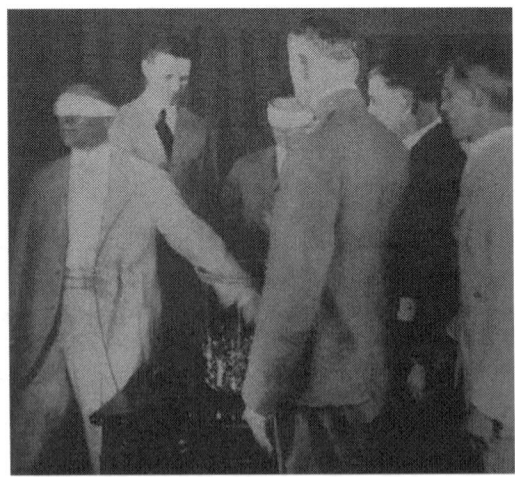

Newton D. Baker, Wilson's able Sect'y of War (L) and "The Greatest Lottery in History. Sect'y of War Baker drawing the first number, 258, in the first draft, July 20, 1917" (R).

Maj. Gen. Leonard Wood, Medal of Honor recipient, Army Chief of Staff 1910-14 (L) and Maj. Gen. Hugh Scott, Army Chief of Staff, 1914-17 (R).

Chapter 2
I Get Selected for Selective Service.

The war for the U.S. against Germany in 1917 (we did not declare war against the Ottoman Empire or Bulgaria—and only declared war against Austria-Hungary on Dec. 7, 1917) was fought almost entirely on the North Atlantic against the German U-Boats with our Navy and Merchant Marine. It was one of the greatest but least remembered campaigns of the war. In Europe, meanwhile, the Allies were getting bled white as they renewed their attacks against the strong German lines in France and Flanders. The British suffered horrendous casualties along Somme River near *Passchendaele* and *Ypres* and it got so bad for France that large parts of its army mutinied and refused to launch another attack against the Germans after their failed and costly offensives that were orchestrated by *Général de France* Robert Nivelle.[11] Even worse for the Allies, in Italy, the Austrians and Germans broke through the Alpine passes near the Vittorio River and in the Soviet Republics, their army had pretty much collapsed and a civil war was brewing between the forces loyal to the Soviets (the "Reds") and the *ancien régime* (the "Whites"). Maybe Pershing was right, if we would have had 500,000 trained troops ready to go right then and there, we probably could have staved off the slaughter if not enabled a breakthrough.

About a month after we declared war, on May 18, President Wilson talked about the "Whole Nation as an Army" and how this would "Not be a Draft of the Unwilling":

The power against which we are arrayed has sought to impose its will upon the world by force. To this end it has increased armament until it has changed the face of war. In the sense in which we have been wont to think of armies there are no armies in this struggle, there are entire nations armed. Thus, the men who remain to till the soil and man the factories are no less a part of the army that is in France than the men beneath the battle flags. It must be so with us. It is not an army that we must shape and train for war—it is a nation. To this end our people must draw close in one compact front against a common foe. But this cannot be if each man pursues a private purpose. All must pursue one purpose. The nation needs all men, but it needs each man, not in the field that will most pleasure him, but in the endeavor that will best serve the common good. Thus, though a sharpshooter pleases to operate a trip-hammer for the forging of great guns, and an expert machinist desires to march with the flag, the The power

---

[11] *Passchendaele* is pronounced "Pash-en-dale," *Ypres* is pronounced "Ee-pra," and *Général de France* Robert Nivelle is pronounced "Jen-er-al day Frawnc Robe-bear Nee-vell."

against which we are arrayed has sought to impose its will upon the world by force. To this end it has increased armament until it has changed the face of war. In the sense in which we have been wont to think of armies there are no armies in this struggle, there are entire nations armed. Thus, the men who remain to till the soil and man the factories are no less a part of the army that is in France than the men beneath the battle flags. It must be so with us. It is not an army that we must shape and train for war—it is a nation.

To this end our people must draw close in one compact front against a common foe. But this cannot be if each man pursues a private purpose. All must pursue one purpose. The nation needs all men, but it needs each man, not in the field that will most pleasure him, but in the endeavor that will best serve the common good. Thus, though a sharpshooter pleases to operate a trip-hammer for the forging of great guns, and an expert machinist desires to march with the flag, the To this end Congress has provided that the nation shall be organized for war by selection, that each man shall be classified for service in the place to which it shall best serve the general good to call him. The significance of this cannot be overstated. It is a new thing in our history and a landmark in our progress. It is a new manner of accepting and vitalizing our duty to give ourselves with thoughtful devotion to the common purpose of us all. It is in no sense a conscription of the unwilling. It is, rather, selection from a nation which has volunteered in mass. It is no more a choosing of those who shall march with the colors than it is a selection of those who shall serve an equally necessary and devoted purpose in the industries that lie behind the battle-lines. The day here named is the time upon which all shall present themselves for assignment to their tasks. It is for that reason destined to be remembered as one of the most conspicuous moments in our history.

On May 26, 1917, General Pershing was once again promoted over the heads of other officers and was given command of the "American Expeditionary Forces" (A.E.F.) that were to serve in France to help defeat the Imperial German Government in conjunction with the Allies. His commission and directive from the Secretary of War, Newton P. Baker, read:

WAR DEPARTMENT.

Washington, May 26, 1917.

From: The Secretary of War.

To: Major General J.J. Pershing, U.S. Army.

The President directs me to communicate to you the following:

The President designates you to command all the land forces of the United States operating in continental Europe and in the United Kingdom of Great Britain and Ireland, including any part of the Marine Corps which may be detached there for service with the Army. In military operations against the Imperial German Government you are directed to cooperate with the forces of the other countries employed against the enemy: but in so doing the underlying idea must be kept in view that the forces of the United States are a separate and distinct component of the combined forces, the identity of which must be preserved. This fundamental rule is subject to such minor exceptions in particular circumstances as your judgment may approve. The decision as to when your command or any of its parts is ready for action is confided to you, and you will exercise full discretion in determining the manner of cooperation. But until the forces of the United States are, in your judgment, sufficiently strong to warrant operations as an independent command, it is understood that you will cooperate as a component of whatever army you may be assigned to by the French Government.

Newton Baker
Secretary of War

The key to Baker's directive to Pershing (in fact, his only directive to Pershing during the entire war) was that the A.E.F. were to remain "a *separate and distinct component* of the combined forces"—it was to fight only in conjunction with the Allies and not under them. This would cause some friction when our forces got over to France later in the year as the British and the French actually expected us to simply roll our battalions into their regiments or brigades and fight under their command, and not ours (fat chance).

As per the National Defense Act of 1916, the U.S. began a mobilization that aligned all facets of our government, economy, and military. This was one reason why Roosevelt had created massive federal government agencies during his tenure as president from 1901-09: to help win a global conflict. With war finally declared against Germany, the U.S. was now confronted with the staggering challenge of converting itself from a land of peace and prosperity into a tremendous military establishment. The most difficult task was the creation of a huge expeditionary army from peace-loving and individualistic (read: soft and selfish) civilians.

Papa Joffre, in his visit to our country in April and May 1917, had impressed upon our government that the Allies needed some of our troops immediately, and that eventually they would need them in great numbers. To supply the first need, two divisions, the soon-to-be famous 1st and 2nd Infantry Divisions, were formed from existing Regular Army and Marine units (the Marine Brigade—4th of the Line—was created to fill out the 2nd Infantry Division). These divisions were rushed to France in December 1917 and January 1918, respectively.

In addition to the 128,000 Regular Army troops at its disposal, the War Department also had 81,000 partially-trained troops from the National Guard. The units of the National Guard were eventually grouped into sixteen divisions, numbered from 26 to 42 and sent to semi-permanent camps (i.e., tents) in the South for further training. These groupings corresponded, roughly, except in the case of the 42nd or "Rainbow Division," with the sections of the country from which the units were recruited (e.g., the 26th Infantry Division was built around National Guard units from New England, the 27th Infantry Division from New York, the 28th Division from Pennsylvania, the 29th Infantry Division from New Jersey, Delaware, Maryland, D.C. and Virginia, etc.). There was to be no distinction between the divisions, however, as all were part of the Army of the United States.

-The Selective Service-

Even with Regular Army and National Guard troops, which were to be fleshed-out by voluntary enlistment, it was obvious to all that our Army would be far short of both what the Allies required and what our population and resources made it possible to furnish. Profiting from Great Britain's experience during the war (it relied upon volunteers at first, then went to universal conscription), it was decided to raise our forces by the "Continental Method of Conscription."

The "Continental Method of Conscription" led to the creation of the "National Army" or the "Army of the United States" (A.U.S.) of which my regiment and division formed a part. The original plan called for sixteen "National Army" divisions, numbered 76 to 92, to be mobilized and trained at sixteen cantonments (i.e., semi-permanent wooden buildings), and to be composed of men chosen by the "Selective Service Act" from 4,500 local draft boards staffed by 125,000 civilians throughout the United States. To lead such an army adequately, approximately 10,000 officers—6,000 more than the entire Regular Army establishment had before the war— were needed. Here again the foresight of the General Staff and especially the former Army Chief of Staff, Maj. Gen. Leonard Wood, saved the political heads of the War Department from the consequences of their own folly.

The Selective Service Act was passed by Congress on May 18, 1917. It gave the President authority to raise the Regular Army from 128,000 to 287,000 men, to mobilize all members of the National Guard and the Organized Reserve, and to draft an additional force of one million men for active duty in the Army of the United States. As such, all male persons aged 21 to 31 years, inclusive, were required to register "in accordance with regulations to be prescribed by the President" or become "liable to imprisonment for one year." This gave the government a pool of some ten million men to choose from. Permitted exemptions from the "Selective Service," as it was called, included national and state officials, ministers of religion, theological students, county and municipal officials, mail and custom house clerks, pilots and mariners, artisans and workmen in armories, arsenals, or navy yards, members of sects whose creeds forbade them to engage in war (e.g., Quakers, Mennonites, Amish, etc.), persons employed in industries and in agriculture necessary to the operations of the armed forces, those physically or mentally deficient, and those with dependents to support.

A presidential proclamation fixed June 5, 1917, as Registration Day, except in Alaska, Hawaii, and Puerto Rico, where a date was named later. Each registrant was given a number, and these numbers, printed on slips of paper and put into black capsules, were to be drawn from a great glass bowl in Washington in July by Secretary of War Newton D. Baker. The rotation in which they were drawn determined the order in which the men whom they represented would be drafted. My number was 258. If that number was called, and every locality, for example, had number 258 (each district was based on population), then I, as well as all of the other 258s across the country, were legally bound to go. I would not be "drafted" per se, but "selected," as if I had won the lottery!

By July, although more than a million men had volunteered for military service, only 558,858 had actually been accepted: 163,633 for the Regular Army, 145,000 for the National Guard, 69,000 for the Navy, and 35,000 for Officers' Training Camps (O.T.C.), which made up the bulk of the Organized Reserve. As such, the Army was still 187,000 short after four months of most intensive recruiting. To gain the rest, President Wilson was forced to draft people into service.

On July 20, 1917, a blindfolded Secretary of War Newton Baker, the former Mayor of Cleveland—a smallish, bespeckled man—drew from a huge glass bowl filled with 10,500 black celluloid capsules, each containing a numbered slip. Baker drew drew the first number for the draft: 258.

258 was my number. Can you believe it!?

I was stunned. We all were. Grandpa had served during the War Between the States with the Virginia Cavalry but my dad hadn't served in the military at all, not even with the Virginia National Guard, and few of us in our neighborhood knew anything about actual war or even the military. We certainly saw the remnants of the 1864-65 Siege of Petersburg all around us, but to us, that's all they were: remnants. The drawn numbers were taken down by three tally clerks and they were recorded on a large blackboard and telegraphed at once to every city, town, and hamlet in the 4,557 registration districts of the country. A total of 1,374,000 men were selected for possible service that day. Because of the weight of the situation, business was practically suspended in many cities and towns. All day and into the night, through the sixteen hours of the drawing, crowds thronged the sidewalks before every bulletin board. That's how we were "selected for military service." Lt. Gen. James Harbord, who commanded the 4th Infantry (Marine) Brigade, the 2nd Division, and the A.E.F.'s all-important Services of Supply (S.O.S.) during the war, stated in his post war reminiscences, *The American Army in France, 1917-19*:

> *With commendable promptness the War Department proceeded to the draft. The preliminary registration for it was accomplished through the local civil authorities, instead of by the military, as in Civil War days. It used the same machinery as the registration for local officials, instead of by the military, as in Civil War days. It used the same machinery as the registration for local*

elections. The registrant was handled by his own friends and neighbors. Without perceptible delay, difficulty or friction, slightly fewer than ten million young Americans between the ages of twenty-one and thirty-one registered for service on June 5...The physical examination and classification of the registered men was done by local examining boards, of which there were nearly 5,000, distributed geographically. District boards considered and disposed of appeals from the local boards. The men examined and certified for service were drawn by lot. The whole draft machinery worked with a smoothness and celerity not always achieved in the processes of democracy. It eventually brought 26 million men either under service or under registration for it. Of every hundred American citizens five found their way to armed service—one male in every ten. The enthusiasm and orderliness with which our citizens accepted the draft in violence to national history and tradition is indisputable evidence of the sincere patriotism with which our people entered the World War...Nor was the draft of military and militant value alone. Medical examination revealed that 27.4 percent of all that were examined were rejected as unfit for military service and another twenty-four percent were defective but were accepted as being able to do partial military service; in other words, 51.4 percent had some physical defect. Examination showed that just under six percent were suffering from venereal diseases. Similarly the tests showed 47.3 percent of the white draft was of a mental age of 13.15 years; while the average mental age of the black draft was 10.1.[12]

The Selective Service Act was later amended on Sept. 12 to include all eligible men from 18 to 45 years, inclusive, yielding an enrollment of some 13 million men, with a total induction of just 2.8 million men once all was said and done. In addition to the nearly 3 million Selectees, there were almost 2 million volunteers in the Army or Navy, with a grand total of 4.8 million American service members during the Great War for Civilization. Thus, 9% of the entire male population of our country entered military service, or approximately one man for every eighteen people.

The volunteer system, although given every opportunity and spurred by the draft, failed to provide the necessary number of recruits. Of the entire A.U.S., the draft furnished 77% of the recruits. Furthermore, there was not a single Regular Army or National Guard formation that

---

[12] Harbord, 27.

did not draw from the draft to complete its strength. In fact, about 25% of their men consisted of drafted men.

-My Draft Notice-

I received my draft notice on Aug. 1 when I returned home from the rail yard with my dad. The document was an imposing-looking epistle entitled an "Order of Induction Into Military Service of the United States," in which the President of the United States bade me a cordial "Greeting" and addressed each of us as follows:

> *Having submitted yourself to a local board composed of your neighbors for the purpose of determining the place and time in which you can best serve the United States in the present emergency, you are hereby notified that you have now been selected for immediate military service.*

After being told to report to the courthouse in Petersburg, I was notified by the concluding sentence: "From and after the day and hour just named you will be a soldier in the military service of the United States," or, as Irving Berlin expressed it: "You're in the Army Now! You're Not Behind the Plow, You'll Never Get Rich, You Son-of-a-B—, You're in the Army Now!"

The last few weeks or so of "freedom" went by like a flash. I don't really remember what I did and it is in fact irrelevant to the story at hand. I knew that my parents were worried and I actually contemplated running away to a place where the government couldn't find me but my dad talked me out of it. "First of all," he said, "there is no where to hide other than Mexico and who wants to go there? You're more likely to get shot there as an American ex-patriot than in the Army fighting Germans in France. Besides," he continued, "it's for a reason. You didn't ask for this war but the country has asked you to go. Because of this, it is your duty to go. If I would have been asked to go like grandpa, I would have gone, too."

-O.T.C.-

Beginning in 1915, the War Department ("the Army") had provided camps where civilians could receive from one to three months of military training by Regular Army officers and at the end of said course would be examined for a commission in the newly-formed "Officers' Reserve Corps." This is generally known as the "Plattsburg Movement," as the first such camp was established at Plattsburg Barracks, New York (along the west bank of Lake Champlain). At the time, it was felt that reliance upon the Civil War Era system of Volunteers would be a ghastly mistake. The promises of some politicians of the day, like Democrat William Jennings Bryan, who stated that "a million Volunteers would spring up overnight," rang a little hollow—esp. to their quality.

Eventually, there were four such "Officer Training Camps" (O.T.C.s), with groups of 2,500 civilian candidates reporting at each. To receive them were ten to twelve Regular Army officers, scattered barracks, and the prospect of three-months of gruelling work. One instructor, as a rule, was allotted 150 candidates, who had to be immediately fed, clothed, and equipped. There were rarely subordinate or non-commissioned officers (N.C.O.s) to aid him. In a number of the camps, the food was insufficient and the clothing often consisted of any cotton khaki that could be collected.

These camps eventually furnished to the Army two colonels, one lieutenant-colonel, 294 majors, 5,429 captains, and 74,842 lieutenants (total of 80,565). Of those commissioned, 48,968 were assigned to the infantry, 20,291 to the field artillery, 1,966 to the engineers, and most of the rest to the quartermaster, ordnance, signal, or coastal artillery branches. Thus almost 61% of the 80,568 officers commissioned in the line went to the infantry, and more than 25% to the field artillery.

According to our company-grade officers (lieutenants and captains), who were graduates of these camps, O.T.C. was a keen, competitive, and rigorous experience, in which both instructor and candidate were subjected to extreme physical pressure. The day began at 5:30 A.M. and ended with instructors and candidates exhausted. On the whole, these candidates were as fine a product as America could turn out. A bank president took his place in the ranks beside a callow college graduate; a prominent lawyer and a grocery clerk used the same pack; the son from a Fifth Avenue home slept beside a naive country-bred youth. Their spirit was magnificent—their patriotism of the highest type.

So we were told.

The manuals or "bibles" they utilized most were the *Plattsburg Manual: A Handbook for Military Training* and Col. James Moss's *Manual of Military Training*.[13] These publications covered every aspect of military training and were found to be very useful for the training of enlisted Selectees, people like me. Col. Moss's Manual included chapters like "Infantry Drill Regulations," "Manual of the Bayonet," "Manual of Physical Training," "Signaling," "Government and Administration of a Company," "Discipline," "General Principles of Company Training and Instruction," "General Common Sense Principles of Applied Minor Tactics," "The Company of Outposts," "The Company in Scouting and Patrolling," "Night Operations," "Field Engineering," "Field Fortifications," "Obstacles," "Trench and Mine Warfare," "Rifle Training

---

[13] Ellis, O.O. and E.B. Garey, Majors, U.S. Army Infantry. *Plattsburg Manual: A Handbook for Military Training* (New York, The Century Company, 1917). Hereafter cited as "*P.M.*" Moss, Col. James. *Manual of Military Training* (Menasha, Wisconsin: Army and College Printers, 1917). Hereafter cited as "*M.M.T.*"

and Instruction," "Marches," "Camps," "Camp Sanitation," "Individual Cooking," "Care of the Health," "Military Deportment," etc.

The outcome of this new, 90-day O.T.C. process was watched anxiously by the War Department and the General Staff considered it to be an astonishing success. Those who failed in the strenuous competition to gain a commission generally confirmed the fairness of their elimination. Of the "just add water officer school," General Harbord wrote:

No officer of a democratic army is completely accepted at the face value of his rank insignia until he has proved his right to leadership in the presence of the enemy. Thus it was that our gallant captains and lieutenants were to fall in disproportionate numbers, even as had other men of their grades in the three years of war that had already been passed. In professional attainments at the time of entrance into the War, the regular officers of neither our Associates nor our enemies were superior to those of our Regular establishment. Our Regular Army measured up grade for grade with any others in the World War. Our untrained officers just entering the service were quick to prove their native gallantry. Their natural adaptability was probably higher than with whom or against whom they were to fight. They were sons of a young and untried nation. The educational level was high among them. These facts to some degree minimized the penalty due our country for its unpreparedness.[14]

On Sept. 14 meanwhile, I reported to the courthouse and was sworn into the U.S. Army by an "Old Army" captain. The oath that we took is as follows:

I [state name], do solemnly swear (or affirm) that I will bear true faith and allegiance to the United States of America—that I will serve them honestly and faithfully against all their enemies whomsoever; and that I will obey the orders of the President of the United States, and the orders of the officers appointed over me according to the Rules and Articles of War.

Once the oath was taken, the old captain said to us: "Welcome to the Army of the United States! Now go that way." After that, we were loaded aboard a Jitney for our short trip to Camp Lee, which was just a few miles east of Petersburg. Going into the service, I wore my least desirable suit of clothes, understanding that I would probably never see them again once things got rolling. I would be amiss if I didn't include Wilson's statement to all of us new "Soldier Boys":

---

[14] As cited in Harbord, 30.

You are undertaking a great duty. The heart of the whole country is with you. Everything that you do will be watched with the deepest interest and with the deepest solicitude not only by those who are dear to you, but by the whole nation besides.

For this great war draws us all together, makes us all comrades and brothers, as all true Americans felt themselves to be when we first made good our national independence.

The eyes of the world will be upon you, because you are in some special sense the soldiers of freedom. Let it be your pride, therefore, to show all men everywhere not only what good soldiers you are, but also what good men you are, keeping yourselves fit and straight in everything and pure and clean through and through.... God keep and guide you! [15]

Army Maj. Gen. James Harbord,
commander of the Marine Brigade, the 2nd
Infantry Division, and then the A.E.F.'s
Service of Supply (S.O.S.)

---

[15] Stultz, Sgt. Russell Lee. *History of the 80th Division, A.E.F.* (80th Division Veterans' Association, N.D.), 10. Hereafter cited as "Stultz."

Maj. Gen. Adelbert Cronkhite, our beloved division commander. He was the Regular Army coastal artillery officer in charge of the Panama Canal Zone before the war.

The division staff. Col. William Waldron, the chief of staff, is top center.

Brig. Gen. Charles S. Farnsworth, Commander of the 159th Inf. Brig. (317th and 318th Inf.). and his principal staff. He was later promoted to command the 37th "Buckeye Division" in France.

Col. George H. Jamerson, Commander of the 317th Inf. Regt. and his principal staff. Most of the 317th Regiment came from western Virginia.

Col. Briant H. Wells, Commander of the 318th Inf. Regt. and his principal staff. Most of the 318th came from eastern Virginia.

Brig. Gen. Lloyd M. Brett, Commander of the 160th Inf. Brig. (319th and 320th Inf.). Arguably the best brigadier in the entire A.E.F. Medal of Honor recipient for actions during the Geronimo Campaign, cited for gallantry during the War with Spain, the Philippines, and the Punitive Expedition under Pershing, Superintendent of Yellowstone Nat'l Park, commander of the 4th Cav. Reg't. when war was declared.

Col. Frank S. Cocheu, Commander of the 319th Inf. Regt. and his principal staff. Most of the 319th Regt. came from Pittsburgh. Maj. Montague's 3/319th was the most engaged and most successful battalion of the division.

Col. Ora E. Hunt, Commander of the 320th Inf. Regt. and his principal staff. Most of the 320th Inf. came from the counties that surrounded Pittsburgh.

Brig. Gen. Gordon G. Heiner, Commander of the 155th Arty. Brig. and his principal staff. Units from the 155th Arty. Brig. spent more days in combat than any other units of the Blue Ridge Division.

Col. Charles D. Herron and 313th Arty. Staff.

Col. Robert S. Welsh and 314th Arty. Staff. Welsh will eventually command the 155th Arty. Brig.

Col. Russell P. Reeder and 315th Arty. Staff. This was the division's "heavy" arty. regiment.

45

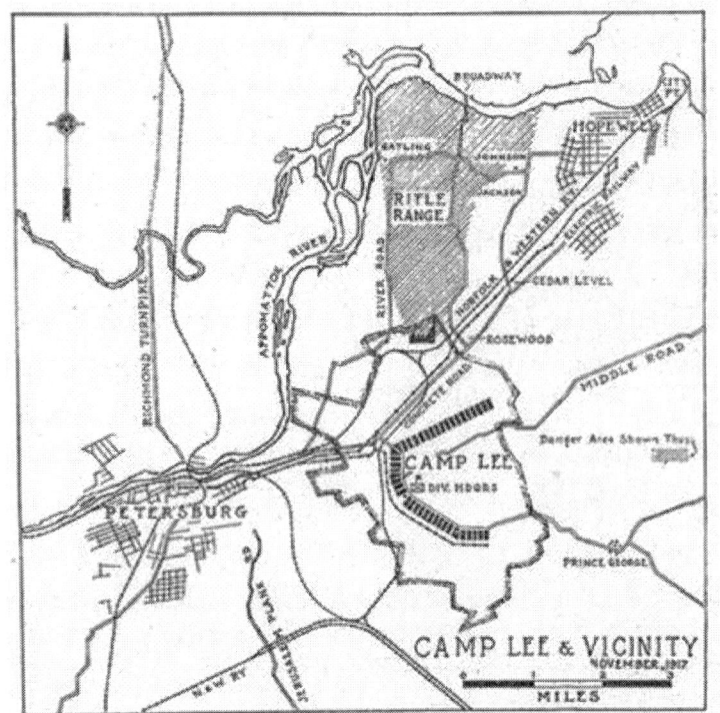

"Camp Lee & Vicinity." Camp Lee, where the 80th Division was assembled, is between Petersburg and Hopewell, Virginia. The camp itself is built in a horseshoe pattern. Note the size of the camp's rifle range, which was constructed along the south bank of the Appomattox River.

The camp's and the division's H.Q. on Camp Lee: "The White House." It was one of the remaining farm houses of the site.

Close-up of "The White House," the H.Q. of Camp Lee and the 80th Division.

Two of the unsung heroes of the war: The intrepid Maj. Charles Sweeny (L), Commander of 2/318th Inf. (later 1/318th Inf.) and Capt. John Crum, Commander of F/318th Inf. IK.I.A. in France) at Camp Lee. They led us through thick and thin from beginning to end. A one-time a student at West Point, Sweeny served as a mercenary officer in Mexico and as a member of the French Foreign Legion, fighting in Flanders during our Great War. Rising from the ranks to captain, he was awarded the prestigious Legion of Honor. Once the U.S. declared war, he joined the U.S. Army as a Major of Infantry. Crum had fought with Pancho Villa in Mexico and with the British in Flanders before he joined the regiment.

Chapter 3
America's 80th (Blue Ridge) Infantry Division is Born.

On the afternoon of Sept. 14 our Jitney pulled up to the main gate of Camp Lee, which was named after the great Virginia general, Robert E. Lee. The camp was being built astride the metalled road between the "Cockade City" (Petersburg), which was famous for its resistance to the Union Army during the War Between the States, and Hopewell, which known as "Virginia's Wonder City"—famous for being the home of one of Dupont's large gun powder works that is located at the confluence of the historic Appomattox and James Rivers.

According to the strategic plan, the Army was to raise, train, and equip sixteen new National Army divisions, numbered 76-91 plus two divisions of Negro (or "Buffalo") Soldiers, numbered 92-93, from the Selectees. As such, it divided the country into sixteen districts and built one training camp for each district. The 76th Infantry Division covered New England, the 77th Division covered New York City, the 78th Division covered New York and New Jersey, the 79th Division covered eastern Pennsylvania, Delaware, Maryland, and D.C., the 80th Division covered western Pennsylvania, West Virginia, and Virginia, and the 81st Division covered the Carolinas, etc. The camp for the 80th Division was located in Virginia, just east of Petersburg, on ground that was known to the locals as "Lakemont." The first official mention of the 80th Division and Camp Lee appeared in the War Department's General Order 95, dated July 18, 1917. Part of the order stated: "The cantonments for troops of the National Army and camps for troops of the National Guard are named, as shown below, in honor of the men named who contributed during their lives to the development of the United States and the acquisition by American citizenship of its present status."[16] One section of the order directed that the cantonment authorized at Petersburg, Virginia, would be the home of the 80th Division, which was to be made up of Selectees from western Pennsylvania, Virginia, and West Virginia. The cantonment was to be known as "Camp Lee," in honor of "Robert E. Lee, General in Chief, C.S.A. Born in Virginia, served in Mexican War and on frontier. Superintendent of U.S.M.A., 1852-1855, commanded the Army of Northern Virginia from June 3, 1862, to Appomattox, April 9, 1865. His last campaign was in vicinity of Petersburg."[17]

Although a number of factors influenced the Army's selection of the site for Camp Lee, the strongest were exceptional transportation facilities and favorable climatic conditions. Situated on an elevated and well drained plateau, the site was two miles east of Petersburg and

---

[16] As cited in Stultz, 1.

[17] *Ibid*, 14.

four miles west of Hopewell and was astride an electric railway that connected the two cities. It was served by the Norfolk & Western Railroad, with nearby Petersburg as an important junction with the Atlantic Coast Line and Seaboard Airline Railroads. It also possessed the east and west facilities of the Chesapeake and Ohio Railway at Richmond, twenty miles distant, likewise those of the Southern Railway and the Virginian Railway at points within fifty miles. Camp Lee was therefore served by all three of the great north and south seaboard railroads and three lines with deep water terminals.

Because of how Camp Lee was being built, we had to come in from the east, disembarking at Rosewood, which is a depot along the Norfolk & Western Railroad.[18] This is where 99.9% of the troops assigned to Camp Lee would come in, as very few of us actually came from nearby Petersburg. From Rosewood, we were directed to walk west up what became known as "Middle Road." Astride Middle Road, in the heart of Camp Lee, Army contractors were still building barracks that were to house companies of 150 men each, which, as we shall see later, wasn't near enough. According to the *Field Service Regulations, U.S. Army 1914 (F.S.R.)*, Camp Lee was a "cantonment":

> *233. When troops are sheltered under canvas, they are in camp. When resting on the ground without shelter, they are in bivouac. When occupying buildings in towns or villages, or huts specially erected, they are in cantonment. Cantonments often develop through improvement of camps—huts or temporary buildings taking the place of tents....*[19]

-Organization-

According to the *F.S.R.*, there were two types of divisions at the time—infantry and cavalry—and fourteen types of battalions: infantry, cavalry, field artillery, coastal artillery, mountain artillery, engineer, pontoon, signal, military police, sanitary (medical), ammunition (ordnance), supply (quartermaster), engineer, and aero squadron:[20]

---

[18] "The Norfolk & Western Railroad had extended their track up into the heart of the great cantonment, and the doubled tracked electric railway connecting Petersburg, Camp Lee, and Hopewell was speedily nearing completion." As cited in Craighill, Edley, *History of the 317th Infantry Regiment, 80th Division* (N.P., N.D.), 14. Hereafter cited as "*317th Infantry.*"

[19] *Field Service Regulations, U.S. Army, 1914. Text Corrections to December 20, 1916.* (New York: Army and Navy Journal, 1916), Paras 233-34. Hereafter cited as "*F.S.R.*" The numbers given are the paragraph numbers.

[20] *Tables of Organization Based on the Field Service Regulations of 1914* (Washington, D.C., War Department), 6, 11. Hereafter cited as "*T.O. 1914.*"

123. Infantry.—The infantry is the principal and most important arm, which is charged with the main work on the field of battle and decides the final issue of combat. The rôle of the infantry, whether offensive or defensive, is the role of the entire force, and the utilization of that arm gives the entire battle its character. The success of the infantry is essential to the success of the combined arms.

125. Cavalry.—The cavalry, preceding contact of the opposing troops of the other arms, is engaged in reconnaissance of the enemy and of the terrain and in accomplishing such a mission as may be assigned it. During combat it directs its activities to the support of the other arms and particularly toward ensuring the success of the Infantry as soon as that arm is fully committed to action. It must not be given a task, nor voluntarily assume one, that will prevent its fullest cooperation with the other arms in the decisive action. The cavalry leader will be given wide initiative in the tactical employment of his command during the decisive combat… The cavalry division is pushed, as independent cavalry, far to the front, often several days' march in advance of the remainder of the field army, to drive back the covering forces of the enemy and to gain accurate information of his dispositions, strength, and movements. This is the most valuable use of the cavalry division in the opening stages of the campaign. the use of the cavalry division as a screen is justified only in exceptional cases, as it is seldom effective in absolutely preventing hostile reconnaissance. Better results can be obtained by using the cavalry as a mass to engage and defeat the enemy's cavalry…

126. Special Troops.—The engineer troops, when not engaged in the special duties of their arm, may be used as infantry, but only in exceptional cases, as part of the attacking line. On the offensive, when used as infantry they form part of the reserve, part of a holding force, or are used for flank protection. On the defensive, they may be used as infantry wherever the development of the action warrants such use.

According to the 1914 Table of Organization (T.O.), each infantry division was to have a headquarters (H.Q.) company, which consisted of a major general (maj. gen.) commanding, a colonel (col.) chief of staff, and four general staff sections: Administration (G-1), Information, Secret Service, Topography, and Censorship (G-2), Operations, Plans, Movement, Artillery Concentration, and Tables of Organization (G-3), Supply, Construction, and Transportation (G-4), and Training and Doctrine (G-5) which were led by lieutenant colonels (lt. cols.) or majors (majs.). Each division was to have three brigades of infantry, one brigade of field artillery, one brigade of support trains, one regiment of cavalry, one battalion of engineers, and one battalion of signal troops, totaling 12,691 men. Each infantry division was also supposed to have some 5,000 mules or horses, around 500 motor vehicles, 48 3-inch field guns (artillery), 224 M1915 Colt-Vickers 30.06 cal. Machine Guns, 8,213 M1903 or M1917 30.06 Rifles, and 4,956 M1911 .45 cal. Automatic Pistols. Each infantry brigade, commanded by a brigadier general (brig. gen.), was to consist of three infantry regiments, each commanded by a colonel, that had a H.Q. company, a supply company, a M.G. company, and three infantry battalions, each commanded by a major, with four rifle companies, each commanded by a captain. Each company was then to have four platoons, each commanded by a lieutenant, with four rifle squads, each commanded by a corporal. Each platoon would also have a *platoon guide* (P.G.) that was a sergeant. By law, an infantry brigade could number no more than 168 commissioned officers and 5,581 enlisted men (E.M.) and each infantry regiment, fifty-five officers and 1,860 E.M. A cavalry division was similarly organized, except it was to have three brigades of cavalry, one regiment of mounted artillery, one battalion of mounted engineers, and one battalion of mounted signal troops with all of the accompanying service of supply (S.O.S.) trains. It was to have 8,021 soldiers and eight civilians, around 17,000 horses or mules, 200 motor vehicles, twenty-four pieces of artillery, twenty-four M.G.s, 5,268 rifles, and 7,546 pistols or revolvers.

According to the *F.S.R.*, one not need say "infantry division" or "infantry brigade" or "infantry regiment" or "infantry company," as it is *implied* to be an infantry organization—the infantry, the "principal and most important arm," was the default setting. This is why people would often simply say "The 80th Division" because, as per regulation, it was *inferred* that it was an infantry outfit. One must, however, designate the units of other branches. e.g., "80th Div." is the proper abbreviation for the 80th Infantry Division, "1st Cav. Div." for the 1st Cavalry Division, "8th Brig. 3d Div." for 8th Infantry Brigade of the 3rd Infantry Division, "2d Cav. Brig. 1st Cav. Div." for the 2nd Cavalry Brigade, 1st Cavalry Division," "4th Brig. F.A." for the 4th Brigade of Field Artillery, "5th Hv.A." for the 5th Heavy Artillery Regiment, "4th M.A." for the 4th Mountain Artillery Regiment, "1st Pon. Bn." for the 1st Pontoon Battalion, and "1st Aero Sq." for the 1st Aero Squadron.[21]

Army doctrine at the beginning of the war, which had been shaped in large part by the Army Chiefs of Staff Maj. Gens. Leonard Wood (1910-14), William Wallace Wotherspoon (1914), and Hugh Scott (1914-17), called for a "Mobile Army" for expeditionary service. With news that cavalry divisions were utterly useless on the Western Front after the open warfare phase of 1914

---

[21] *F.S.R.*, "Appendix 9. List of Abbreviations."

(the British tried a massed cavalry charge at the Somme in 1916 but it was murdered), it was decided to raise only infantry divisions for the A.E.F. According to the *F.S.R.*:

> *3. The Mobile Army.—The mobile army is primarily organized for offensive operations against an enemy, and on this account requires the maximum degree of mobility. The basis of organization for the mobile army is the division. A division is a self-contained unit made up of all necessary arms and services, and complete in itself with every requirement for independent action incident to its ordinary operations. When several divisions are acting together they may be grouped into field armies. To the field army there are attached certain organizations of an auxiliary character, called field army troops.*

For whatever reason, the Army left out "army corps" from its *F.S.R.* A corps or *corps d'armee* is usually commanded by a lt. gen. and it consists of two to four divisions.[22] In France, the A.E.F. did indeed utilize corps H.Q.s, and they acted purely in a tactical capacity (while army, division, and regimental H.Q.s acted as administrative and tactical entities, corps, brigades, and battalion H.Q.s acted purely as tactical entities). Ultimately, the A.E.F. organized three field armies (numbered 1-3) and nine army corps (numbered 1-9). The concept was that each field army would command three corps, which would direct at least three infantry divisions.

In July 1917, the War Department sent the so-called "Baker Commission," headed by Col. Chauncey Baker of the Quartermaster Corps and composed of Regular Army officers from all branches, to France to help the Army determine what Pershing's expeditionary "Mobile Army" should in fact look like. After a quick study, Col. Charles P. Summerall, the commission's artillery representative, believed that the current three infantry brigade/three artillery battalion division structure lacked the combat punch that was neded to conduct offensive operations on the Western Front. If Summerall had it his way, each infantry division would have had twelve battalions of artillery (one per each infantry battalion). He also believed that half of the artillery battalions should be armed with light 3-inch or similar field guns and that the other half should be armed with heavy 6-inch howitzers or their equivalent. Without such firepower, he said, "the experience of the present war shows positively that it is impossible for the infantry to advance." He also argued that, "It may fairly be stated that losses in war today are inversely proportional to the volume and efficiency of friendly artillery fire. If we are to produce a decided effect upon the issue of the war, we must strive to develop some form of a rolling offensive over a very

---

[22] *Corps* is pronounced "core" or "core-dar-may." The "corps" was first made famous by Napoléon and used by the U.S. Army during the War Between the States and the War with Spain.

considerable area and for this purpose; artillery must be furnished in quantities not hitherto contemplated."

The problem with Summerall's position was two-fold: practical and doctrinal. On a practical note, the nations of the Associated Powers did not have the capacity to sustain, let alone fire, that many artillery pieces in France or Flanders. Doctrinally, Pershing believed that too much artillery fire delivered against an objective would render it impossible for the advance of engineer and infantry units, let alone follow-on artillery battalions.[23] According to the *F.S.R.*:

> *127. Heavy Field Artillery.—The limited mobility of heavy field artillery renders its use inadvisable in any position from which the conditions of combat may require its hasty withdrawal. For that reason it has no place in an advance guard; in an outpost, unless occupying a position in which the action is to be fought to a decision...*
>
> *128. On the offensive, heavy field artillery finds it function in firing upon supporting points in the hostile line; upon covered positions occupied by large bodies of the enemy, particularly his reserves; in the destruction of material objects, as buildings, bridges, etc.; and, in general, against a position that has been deliberately taken up and strengthened by the enemy.*
>
> *129. On the defensive, heavy field artillery finds its use in compelling the deployment of the enemy's columns at long distances from the defensive line, against any large formed bodies of the enemy, and against those parts of his materiel or material objects within his lines that offer an important target. Due to its long range, it is profitably used in both offensive and defensive combat in restricting the field of activity of the enemy's shorter range artillery. It can also be used to advantage with the destruction of the enemy's field artillery materiel.*
>
> *130. The use of the heavier types of field artillery presupposes an offensive, where reconnaissance of the enemy's position has been thorough and where the attack has been carefully planned; or a defensive, where the attack has been carefully planned; or a defensive, where there has been time to deliberately select and strengthen a position. Until the use of the heavier field artillery under the conditions given can be clearly foreseen, its position is well to the rear of all the combatant units.*

After a vigorous debate, and with Pershing's blessing, the Army agreed to change the composition of A.E.F.'s infantry divisions to better match the exigencies of the Western Front.

---

[23] Harbord, 100-02.

The new Model 1917 Infantry Division would therefore consist of two infantry brigades (each with two infantry regiments of twelve rifle companies, one H.Q. company, one M.G. company, and one supply company—a total of fifteen companies), one field artillery brigade (two light regiments of two battalions each and one heavy regiment of three battalions—a total of seven artillery battalions per division), three machine gun (M.G.) battalions, as well as engineers, military police (M.P.s), and services of supply (called "S.O.S.") units. The division would total 27,247 soldiers. General Harbord remembered:

The division organization recommended [by the Baker Commission] has been the subject of considerable controversy, particularly as to its size. It has been criticized by some who never fought in it or near it, and generally without consultation of the available official records... The traditional American division, the largest self-sufficient unit, was such a one as, marching on a single road, would not be so long that the rear units would be unable to get up in time to participate with effect before an attack on the leading units could be successful, granted the proper service of security and information. That was for a war of movement, but the World War had ossified into a stalemate of trench [i.e., siege] warfare...Thus we sought to provide a division with sufficient overhead in the way of staff, communication and supplies to permit the deep and very powerful defense developed in the World War, no decisive stroke could be secured in battle without a penetration necessitating several days of steady fighting. It was thus reasoned that the infantry of the division must be of such strength as to permit it to continue in combat for such a number of days that the continuity of battle would not be interrupted before decision was reached.[24]

What General Harbord was saying is that the A.E.F.'s divisions were designed to act as "sledge hammers" against the strong German defensive lines. We knew, for a fact, that we would have to breach at least four strong German defensive lines (code-named *KRIEMHILDE*, etc.). In order to break such lines—to conduct a breach—one has to attack across a narrow front and in depth, with his flanks secured. The 1917 Table of Organization (T.O.) gave us that depth. In France, as you'll see, our division usually attacked with a four-company front, followed by four, followed by four, followed by four, on a two km front. While the first few waves were to act as bullet catchers, the latter would perform the breach, and inititate the pursuit. Once we got into "the open" in October, 1918, as Pershing had promised, we went with two infantry regiments up, one in support, and one in reserve.

---

[24] As cited in Harbord, 102-03.

According to General Order (G.O.) 101, dated Aug. 3, 1917, the composition of the America's 80th Infantry Division was as follows:

Division H.Q.

305th Engineer Regiment

305th Signal Battalion

H.Q., 305th Trains and M.P. Company

305th Sanitary Train

305th Supply Train

305th Engineer Train

313th, 314th, and 315th Machine Gun (M.G.) Battalions

155th Artillery Brigade

313th, 314th, and 315th Artillery Regiments

305th Ammunition Train

305th Trench Mortar Battery (T.M.)

159th Infantry Brigade H.Q.

160th Infantry Brigade H.Q.

317th, 318th, 319th, and 320th Infantry Regiments

-Division Leaders-

Maj. Gen. Adelbert Cronkhite, commander of the important Department of the Panama Canal, was chosen by the Army to command the new 80th Infantry Division. Cronkhite was born in the State of New York on Jan. 5, 1861, just a few months after Lincoln was elected president and South Carolina had seceded from the U.S. He was the son of Col. Henry McLean Cronkhite of the U. S. Army, who was a descendant of a Dutch tradesman who had settled the Mohawk Valley in 1642. Graduated with distinction from the U. S. Military Academy in 1882, Cronkhite was assigned as a lieutenant of Coastal Artillery. After active service in the Indian and Spanish Wars, he was appointed brigadier general in March 1917, assigned to command the all-important Panama Canal Department. Once war was declared against the Imperial German Government, he was promoted to the rank of major general and given command of the 80th Division.

And we were lucky to have him.

Part Dutch, he looked it. Of the swarthy type, only about 5'-8" tall, his head was large and his was hair black, showing no gray; his skin was dark. Broad-shouldered, stockily built and inclined to stoutness, his whole make-up was that of a man of great physical strength and stamina. He actually reminded me of Teddy Roosevelt. Behind a genial, winning manner, it was apparent there was force and decision without harshness. He was a humane man and his battle record later demonstrated that he refused to build a flashy reputation by wasting lives. He was content to have his division, as he put it, "always on the objective—on time."[25]

On Aug. 16, 1917, War Department G. O. 109 directed the commanding general of each of the sixteen National Army cantonments to constitute their commands in accordance with the T.O., Series 1, Aug. 1917, plus one mobile ordnance repair shop, and "In those cantonments where sufficient personnel are available," one infantry regiment of Negro troops to be later assigned to either the 92nd or 93rd Infantry Divisions. The divisional M.G. battalions were to have four firing companies each—two battalions were to be attached to the infantry brigades (giving each infantry regiment three M.G. companies) and one was to remain under the division commander's control. Four battalions of light 3-inch field guns and three battalions of heavy 6-inch howitzers were stipulated for the artillery brigade. The following Regular Army officers were sent to Camp Lee to help Cronkhite command the new 80th Infantry Division:

Brig. Gen. George G. Heiner, to command the 155th Artillery Brigade
Brig. Gen. Charles S. Farnsworth, to command the 159th Infantry Brigade
Brig. Gen. Lloyd M. Brett, to command the 160th Infantry Brigade
Cavalry Lt. Col. William H. Waldron, as colonel to Chief of Staff
Infantry Lt. Col. George H. Jamerson, as colonel to Inspector General
Cavalry Maj. George F. Hamilton, as colonel to command the 305th Trains Brigade
Engineers Maj. George R. Spalding, as colonel to command the 305th Engineers
Artillery Maj. Charles D. Herron, as colonel to command the 313th Artillery
Artillery Maj. Robert S. Welsh, as colonel to command the 314th Artillery
Artillery Maj. Russell Reeder, as colonel to command the 315th Artillery
Infantry Maj. George H. Jamerson, as colonel to command the 318th Infantry
Infantry Maj. Briant H. Wells, as colonel to command the 318th Infantry
Infantry Maj. Frank S. Cocheu, as colonel to command the 319th Infantry
Infantry Maj. Ora E. Hunt, as colonel to command the 320th Infantry

Cronkhite's chief of staff (a very important and difficult position) was Col. William H. Waldron, his opposite in many ways. According to those on the general staff, Col. Waldron "was earnest to the point of intensity in every act, utterly lacking in finesse, given to irascibility, and possessed of a sober sense of humor that bordered on extreme sarcasm. He was endowed with a warm heart but so sensitive that he often appeared cold and at times harsh and indifferent. A

---

[25] Stultz, 35.

human dynamo expecting all about him to work twenty-four hours a day and enjoy it like himself, he was really popular with those who knew him well."[26] Nobody ever questioned his efficiency. A great share of the division's excellent record must be assigned to its chief of staff.

Born in West Virginia, Col. Waldron was commissioned from the ranks as a cavalry lieutenant in the Regular Army in April, 1899. He was a major when war was declared in 1917. Through extensive military writings, he had reputation in the service both as a thinker and worker and especially as an authority on tactics. He had gained valuable experience during service in the Philippine and Chinese Campaigns and had attended the Army Staff College at Fort Leavenworth and the Army War College, from which he was graduated in 1906 and 1911, respectively. He was promoted lieutenant colonel and then colonel in the A.U.S. in 1917.[27]

The commander of the 159th Inf. Brig., Brig. Gen. Charles S. Farnsworth, was born on October 29, 1862 in Lycoming County, Pennsylvania (the county that surrounds Williamsport). He attended local public schools and worked for Western Union and Bell Telephone before being appointed to the United States Military Academy at West Point in 1883. After graduating in 1887, Farnsworth was sent to various posts in the West: Fort Sisseton in South Dakota, Fort Shaw in Montana, and Fort Buford in North Dakota. While at Fort Shaw, he married Laura Galey. They had one son, Robert, and Laura died in 1890. In 1893 Farnsworth became Professor of Military Science and Tactics at the University of North Dakota. In addition to his teaching job, Farnsworth was also head coach of the North Dakota "Fighting Sioux" football team from 1895 to 1896. In 1894, he married Helen Bosard of Grand Forks, North Dakota. They had no children.

During the Spanish-American War, Farnsworth served as a Q.M. in Cuba and was an aide to Brig. Gen. Adna Chaffee. After the war, Farnsworth was sent to Alaska where he directed the building of Fort Gibbon. He was then sent to the Philippines where he was charged with building Fort William McKinley. Later, he expanded the cantonments at the Presidio of San Francisco. In 1909, Farnsworth graduated from the Command and Staff College at Fort Leavenworth Kansas, and, in 1916, from the Army War College, which was in Washington, D.C. During the Punitive Expedition into Mexico, Farnsworth served as an infantry battalion commander and a supply base commander. When war was declared against the Imperial German Government in April 1917, Farnsworth was the Commandant of the Infantry Training School at Fort Sill, Oklahoma.[28]

---

[26] As cited in Stultz, 37.

[27] Stultz, 37.
[28] Stultz, 39.

The commander of the 160th Inf. Brig., Brig. Gen. Lloyd M. Brett, who was arguably one of the best if not the best American infantry brigade commander during the Great War, held the most important position in the division once we were unleashed against the "Hun with the Gun" in France in 1918. He was born in Maine and graduated from West Point in 1879. He served with the famous 2nd Cavalry on the Western frontier until 1897, participating in various Indian campaigns. In the Sioux Campaigns of 1880 and 1881, he was twice mentioned in War Department General Orders and later awarded the Medal of Honor. He was again mentioned in orders by Maj. Gen. Nelson A. Miles for conspicuous gallantry during the "Geronimo Apache Campaign" of 1885-86. During the War with Spain, he commanded a troop of the 2nd Cavalry as a captain and was recommended for brevet to major. From 1899 to 1901, he served as a "Major of Volunteers" during the Filipino Insurrection. From 1910 to 1916, he was Superintendent of Yellowstone National Park, with the rank of lt. col., and then was assigned a cavalry brigade on the Mexican Border. The outbreak of war with Germany in 1917 found him as Colonel Commandant of the 4th Cavalry Regiment in Hawaii. On Sept. 19, 1917, he was appointed brig. gen. after thirty-eight years of service, almost wholly with troops. Maj. Gen. Cronkhite and Brig. Gen. Brett held views closely in agreement (i.e., take care of the men and the men will take care of you).

Those who knew General Brett (I only met him once at a reunion) thought that he was mild, modest, and courteous—the perfect soldier. Loved and almost venerated by his staff and command, Brett reportedly "held the rare gift of remaining a gentleman as well as a soldier under any provocation."[29] The old Indian fighter was perhaps as picturesque a warrior of the "old school" as was to be found in active service in 1917. But there was nothing archaic about him or his soldiering, as he quickly adapted his wide experience to changing methods of warfare. At age sixty (!), he had no superior in military dress or erect bearing. He was handsome. His boots always were the best polished, and he shined them himself. Stories about him multiplied. When we finally made it to the bloody fields of France, it was almost always troops under his command who forced the breach of the strong enemy lines.

The commander of the 80th Division's 155th Arty. Brig. was Brig. Gen. George G. Heiner. Heiner was the youngest brigadier among the first appointments and the only lt. col. of artillery to be made a brig. gen. in August, 1917. Born in the District of Columbia, the son of a Union Army officer who had served under Grant around Richmond in 1865, Heiner graduated from West Point in 1893. After serving in the War with Spain as a lieutenant in the Coastal Artillery, he was promoted to major in 1910, and became a lt. col. in 1916.

---

[29] *Ibid*, 37.

Almost like a younger brother to Cronkhite, under who Heiner had served, it was commonly believed that this association had much to do with his promotion and assignment to the 80th Division. Young and unusually able, he presumably was chosen as the instrument through which Cronkhite, a veteran coastal artilleryman himself, had planned to develop superlative artillery in the Blue Ridge Division. In fact, in the entire coast artillery clique, there probably was not an officer who possessed greater potentialities for carrying out this task and rising even higher than Heiner (or so it was thought). Unfortunately, circumstances often upset even the brightest prospects, and while in France, he will be replaced by Lt. Col. Robert Welsh of the 314th Artillery on Oct. 12, 1918, for reasons that are still not entirely known to us.[30]

-Groupment-

Cronkhite wanted to group the incoming Selectees of our new division into regionally-based units to create a rapid identity, friendly competition, and natural harmony. The division's brigades were therefore formed into a perfect *groupment* for the recruits from the three Blue Mountain states. One of the missions of the 80th Division, like the 29th (Blue and Gray) Division or the 42nd (Rainbow) Division, as well as all of the divisions of the Regular Army, was to in fact enhance national unity. In 1917, the wounds of the late-War Between the States were still relatively fresh and we wanted to prove to ourselves and the world that we could, at least under certain conditions, work together as one nation again—as equals. This was very important to we Virginians, especially, as our state had seen hard service during the War Between the States. We would also be significant players in the new division, working closely with our West Virginia and Pennsylvania brothers—a term we hadn't used since at least since 1848.

Accordingly, Virginians were assigned to Farnsworth's 159th Inf. Brig., which consisted of the 317th and 318th Infantry Regiments and the 314th M.G. Battalion. While the 317th Infantry drew heavily from Piedmont and western Virginia, the 318th Infantry was filled with men from the Tidewater and Shenandoah Valley regions (this was my regiment). The men for the 314th M.G. Battalion mostly came from the Tidewater. Brett's 160th Inf. Brig. was western Pennsylvanian. Its 319th Infantry consisted mostly of men from Pittsburgh, the "Steel City," and its 320th Infantry composed mostly of men from the surrounding counties. Troops from Erie, "the Mistake on the Lake," were assigned to the 313th and 315th M.G. Battalions, and the 305th Engineers drew most of its personnel from the mountainous area east of Pittsburgh. Heiner's 155th Arty. Brig. was West Virginia with a dash of western Pennsylvania. To the 313th Artillery were allocated men from the northern section of the state, the central

---

[30] Stultz, 39.

counties contributed to the 314th Artillery, and the southern districts to the 315th Artillery. The southern area of the state also supplied the personnel for the 305th Trench Mortar (T.M.) Battery. The all-important 305th Ammunition, Motor Supply, and Sanitary Trains were made up of men from throughout the three states, selected in the main because of individual qualifications.

-Officers Arrive to Camp Lee-

The 80th Division's H.Q. building at Camp Lee, which we called "The White House," was a pre-existing farm house that stood on the highest point of the camp. It served as the base for the horseshoe of the brigade barracks. Next to the White House, a water tower was built to give pressure to the indoor plumbing. The camp was very well-planned from a sanitary standpoint. According to Sgt. Russell Stultz of the soon-to-be-organized Company G, 2nd Battalion, 318th Infantry Regiment, 80th Infantry Division:

> *A number of factors influenced the War Department's selection of the site, particularly exceptional transportation facilities and favorable climactic conditions. Situated on an elevated and well-drained plateau, it was two miles east of Petersburg and four miles from Hopewell, connected with the two cities by concrete highway and electric railway. It was served by the Norfolk & Western Railway, with nearby Petersburg an important junction with the Atlantic Coast Line and Seaboard Airline Railroads, north and south truck lines. It also possessed the additional east and west facilities of the Chesapeake & Ohio Railway at Richmond, twenty miles distant.*[31]

Because April to August 1917 did not leave enough time for the construction of a cantonment that was to eventually house over 60,000 men, when commissioned and senior N.C.O.s arrived to Camp Lee in August, they found that most of the structures were still being built. The construction firm of Rinehart & Dennis was being paid by the War Department "cost plus ten per cent" to build Camp Lee and some 14,000 workers were tasked with bringing it to life. But that still wasn't enough. Future-Capt. Josiah Peck, the Intelligence Officer of the 319th Infantry remembered his arrival to Camp Lee from O.T.C., Camp Myer, Virginia:

> *The 27th of August, 1917, was a bright, warm day, which shall long be remembered by those who arrived at Camp Lee for the first time by jitney, trolley car, truck, or any other means of transportation. The scenes presented along the dusty road from Petersburg and in the unfinished camp were those*

---

[31] As cited in Stultz, 14-15.

of unparalleled activity. Some 2,000 officers, dressed in new uniforms— military collars hooked up tight—gray with dust and fine sand, then several inches deep throughout the camp, making their way to the White House to report for assignment. There were Army trucks, piled high with trunk lockers and bedding rolls, long lines of wagons loaded with building materials, straining teams urged on by shouting, sweating, smiling negro drivers, sentinels from the 47th New York Regiment, pacing to and fro, wearing a somewhat bored expression, but working manfully to live up to the letter of the regulations in saluting the officers, combined to make a changing scene of activity both interesting and amusing.[32]

According to Lt. Edley Craighill, the future adjutant of 2/317th Infantry:
It was after the completion of the first Officer Training Camp at Fort Myer, Virginia, and all the newly-minted lieutenants had been given fifteen days leave at home for the first time since their training began, that they fully realized the great task before them. This task was to train and educate in a military sense, the rawest bunch of men, as far as the military was concerned, ever gotten together. On the morning of Aug. 27, 1917, the greater part of these officers reported for duty at Camp Lee and all were anxious and willing to begin their work.[33]

The newly-minted lieutenants reported to division H.Q. where they "passed in single file by a field officer, presenting their orders, on a copy of which he wrote their regimental number." After that, the young officers reported to a "table in the corner of the yard, paid $5 for a meal ticket to one of the messes, and followed an N.C.O. to the area their regiment was to occupy." After that, they were met by their regimental commanding officer, and assigned a job within the regiment. Capt. Peck of the 319th Infantry similarly remembered: "Immediately after the assignment of the officers to the companies, a round of schools began, and thereafter for several days the noise of foot movements on the pine floors of the barrack buildings was added to the general din of construction work."[34]

---

[32] As cited in Peck, Josiah C. *The 319th Infantry A.E.F.* (Paris, France: Herbert Clarke Printing, 1919), 7. Hereafter cited as "*319th Infantry.*"

[33] As cited *317th Infantry*, 12.

[34] *319th Infantry*, 7.

On September 4, 1917, word was received that the first group of Selectees would arrive to Camp Lee the following morning. Lt. Col. James Love was made chief mustering officer for the 318th Infantry and everything was ready to receive the new arrivals, people like me, five months after war had been declared against Germany. The War Department decided that the Selectees would be sent to camp in the approximate rate of 5% the first week, 15% the second, 25% the third, etc. Strenuous efforts had been made to have accommodations ready for the first arrivals. But, in spite of everything, the plumbing was not completed and mess facilities were not installed when the first Selectees arrived, and bedding was received at the same time as the men.

The 318th Infantry Regiment was organized, as per General Order No. 1, as follows:[35]

```
            318th Infantry Regiment.
                 4 Sept., 1917.
                FIELD ORDER NO. 1.


           Col. Briant H. Wells, Commanding
      Lt. Col. James M. Love, Executive Officer
          Capt. Senius J. Raymond, Adjutant
        Capt. Ernest L. Nunn, Supply Officer
      Headquarters Co.: Capt. Paul D. Connor
      Machine Gun Co.: Capt. Robert J. Halpin


       1st Battalion: Maj. Albert B. Dockery
         A Co.: Capt. Clarence E. Goldsmith
           B Co.: Capt. Herbert R. Rising
           C Co.: Capt. Clinton Winant
           D Co.: Capt. Thomas J. Echols


        2d Battalion: Maj. Charles Sweeny
           E Co.: Capt. Edward H. Little
             F Co.: Capt. John Crum
          G Co.: Capt. Charles C. Griffin
            H Co.: Capt. Gulian V. Weir


       3d Battalion: Maj. Albert B. Dockery
            I Co.: Capt. Edward H. Little
           K Co.: Capt. Robert M. Dashiell
          L Co.: Capt. Charles C. Griffin
            M Co.: Capt. Gulian V. Weir
```

---

[35] As cited in *History of the 318th Infantry Regiment of the 80th Division, 1917-1919* (Richmond, Virginia: William Byrd Press, N.D.), 15. Hereafter cited as "*318th Infantry.*"

-N.C.O.s in 1917-

Concurrently, newly-minted sergeants from the Regular Army or National Guard also began to pour into camp and they were assigned to help lieutenants, etc., train the new Selectees. Unlike today (1938), in 1917, the Army only had a few enlisted ranks: Private (Pvt.), Private First Class (P.F.C.), Corporal (Cpl.), Sergeant (Sgt.), First Sergeant (1Sgt.), and Sergeant Major (Sgt.M.). Corporals were generally given command of a squad of ten men. They wore two stripes and were usually selected by the platoon guide (P.G.), the platoon leader (P.L.), the 1Sgt., and the company commander (C.C.). A sergeant, who wore three stripes, generally acted as a platoon guide (P.G.) and was second-in-command of a platoon of forty men. A 1Sgt. was the "top sergeant" of a company. He wore three stripes with a diamond below. He was in charge of all administrative duties of the company and advised whomever was the commander (unlike a P.G., he was never second-in-charge as there were several lieutenants in a company). A Sgt.M. is the highest E.M. in the regiment and he acts in a similar capacity to the regimental commander as a 1Sgt. does for a company commander (C.C.). Sgt.M.s wore three stripes with a star below. In general, while officers command units and are responsible for mission accomplishment, N.C.O.s are in charge of the men. Both jobs are important. In my opinion, the corporal squad leader held the most difficult job of the N.C.O. corps because he was not only relatively new to the Army, but was also responsible not only for the welfare of ten (and later more) E.M., but also mission accomplishment.

From Aug. 27 until Sept. 4, just before the first Selectees arrived to camp, Army contractors were pushing construction work and the officers were bending all of their efforts toward getting the barracks and other buildings ready for the reception of the first contingent of the draft. We "Doughs" would have loved to see our C.C.s, P.L.s, and P.G.s carrying large timbers, pieces of plank, bits of beaverboard, screen wire, etc., into the barracks to be used in constructing heavy meat tables in the kitchens, small tables, fly-proof breadboxes, wastebaskets, etc. In more than one instance, company, regimental, or brigade orderly rooms were built by the officers themselves, laboring with unskilled hands, but doing whatever was necessary to prepare the camp for the arrival of people like me.[36]

---

[36] The term "Dough" or "Doughboy" has some conflicting genesis stories. It was the nick name for we infantrymen. The one that I accept is that while Pershing's division was operating along the Mexican border in 1915-16, his men covered in dust, looked much like the adobe huts that existed in the area—thus the term "Doughboy." Some people say it was because of all the Y.M.C.A. donuts we ate, but I don't buy that one as the nick-name pre-dated the 1917-18 Army and our Y.M.C.A. donut runs. Bottom line: I don't really know why we were called "Doughs" but do know that it was routinely used to identify those who were the the infantry.

-The First Selectees Arrive-

The first group of Selectees arrived to Camp Lee before noon on September 5, 1917. Like me, they were rapidly processed through the division's mustering office. From there, they were sent to a regiment and filled-up Companies A, E, and I. It was decided to flesh out one company per battalion first rather than to distribute the new men throughout the regiment's fifteen companies. This practice was division-wide. Once a company reached 150 E.M., it was officially mustered into federal service. The first company to do so was Company A, 1st Battalion, 318th Infantry Regiment, on September 7, 1917. It is said that A/1/318th Infantry was in fact the first company of the National Army to be mustered into federal service.

When my group reported to the camp *via* the Middle Road a few days later, we were directed to the first building on the left or south. This was the camp's reception station or "recruit depot," also known as the 155th Depot Brigade. It was a large clapboard building. Here the division started our Army file, asked us some questions about our life history, classified us for duty, etc. After that, seven of us were lined up in front of the recruit depot where we met, for the first time, Sgt.M. Guy C. Beale, the highest-ranking N.C.O. of the 318th Infantry Regiment, 80th Division. As per the way the Army does things ("there's the right way, the wrong way, and the Army way"), he read our names off the roster, butchering most of them. Once he did something on his clipboard, regimental Sgt.M.s always seemed to be conjuring something magical on that thing, he said, "Adkins, Getz, Grubbs, Riddle, Schuyler, Stewart, and Tormey, follow me."

As we walked up the line of semi-completed barracks, which were 150' x 50', two stories high. Ben Schuyler actually had the temerity to ask the Sgt.M. a question. Using it as a teaching moment, Sgt.M. Beale froze, turned, got right up into Schuyler's face (Beale was shorter than Schuyler and about twenty years older, too) and barked: "Don't ever speak unless spoken to, recruit! Shut your damned face and do what you're told! You're in the Army now!" The Sgt.M. then backed off and waited for our reaction, which was staid. With that, we continued our short journey past heaps of building material and half-constructed barracks, all to the tune of carpenters' hammers which clattered with M.G.-like precision. We soon learned that the barracks on the left, or south of Middle Road, were for the forming 317th and 318th Infantry Regiments of the 159th Inf. Brig., which were drawing most of their recruits from Virginia. North of the road were the barracks for the newly forming 319th and 320th Infantry Regiments, which were drawing most of their recruits from western Pennsylvania (eastern Pennsylvania was filling the 79th Infantry Division). Also in the camp was the new 155th Arty. Brig., which would consist of the 313th, 314th, and 315th Artillery Regiments. Most of the recruits from this brigade would come from the great state of West Virginia, although many would also come from Pennsylvania or Virginia. Two of my friends, Earl and Henry Schreckengost of the 313th Artillery, for example, came from Armstrong County, Pennsylvania, which is in the big woods just north of Pittsburgh. There were also three new M.G. battalions, the 313th, 314th, and 315th M.G., the 313th and 315th drawing most of its men from western Pennsylvania and the 314th drawing most of its soldiers from Virginia. Many of the recruits for the 319th and 320th Infantry Regiments, coming from the coal fields or steel plants of western Pennsylvania, "no-speak-English-good." Unlike the Virginia units, which consisted mostly of Old English or Scots-Irish stock (i.e., "real Americans"), the Pennsylvania units also consisted of men from Eastern, Southern, or Central Europe—people who spoke Slavic, Latinic, or Germanic languages. There were names like: Aponascevicz, Baldacci, Bugulski, Demkowski, Feighner, Friedlander, Glowicki, Mignoni, Omohundro, Spinosa, Vono, Zucchero, etc.

Before long, we reached the barracks that was assigned to Company B, 1st Battalion, 318th Infantry Regiment, 80th Infantry Division (B/1/318/80). The Sgt.M. lined us up in front of said building and said, "Stand at attention!" We did, or thought we did, with suitcases in hand. Soon after, Sgt. Joseph Brown stepped out and he said: "Alright you men," in his strange (to us) New England accent, "I'm your platoon guide, Sgt. Brown. Just a few months ago I was a corporal in the Regular Army down on the Mexican border. When we declared war, I got promoted to sergeant and was sent here to turn you rag-a-muffin soft civilian sons-a-bitches into soldiers of the United States Army! I am not your buddy—I am not your pal. If you understand that, we'll get along just fine. Any questions?"

Everyone nodded, "no."

With that, we were instructed to file into the unpainted clapboard barrack that had eighty canvas Army cots on each floor, forty to each side. We were told to fill the racks close to the door on the left side, as these belonged to my new unit: the 4th Squad, 2nd Platoon, B Company, 318th Infantry Regiment, 159th Inf. Brig., 80th Infantry Division, American Expeditonary Force (A.E.F.). My "neighbors" were Albert Getz and Ben Schuyler of Norfolk and Richmond, Virginia, respectively.

Afte just a few minutes, Sgt. Brown yelled, "Fall out!"

We all looked at each other, "fall out?"

Almost like clock-work, Brown barked: "That means, get your goat-smelling asses outside and line up at the position of attention, recruits! Now move it!"

So off we moved, scrambling back out of the barracks, registering the distinctive noise of our shoes as they rumbled across the freshly-hewn wooden floor.

"Squad! Atten-shun!"

"Count off by threes—count off!"

Again, we hesitated. I think I was the "Number Three Man."

"When I yell, 'Count off,' that means that you," thumping on Boss Atkins's chest. "Yell 'one!' And you yell, 'Two,' and you yell 'Three!' Once we hit 'three,' we start over! 'One-two-three-one-two-three!' Clear?"

"Count off by threes; count off!"

"One-two-three-one-two-three!"

"Very good. Now, when I command 'squads, right,' each three-man 'squad,' will turn like a door to the right, making a column of three. Squads, right!"

Needless to say, we messed it up twice before we got it right. The term "squads, right" became very representative of our time in the Army and we learned to go from line into column and back again very quickly, and as we saw later, under very harrowing conditions in France against the Hun Germans and their allies.[37]

At "squads, right" we marched over to the regimental supply company, which was run by Sgt. William E. Yoder and each man was issued his first pieces of Army equipment: two olive-drab wool Army blankets, a small pillow, and a metal mess kit that had two oval bowls, a cup, a knife, fork, and spoon.

After that we made our bunks, we filed into the company mess hall with our mess kit and were introduced to Army "chow" in a manner which became painfully familiar to us after just a few days.

Passing through an ever-tedious mess line to a counter, and armed with our newly acquired eating utensils, which we juggled with a difficulty born of inexperience, we made the acquaintance of Army beans and a brackish fluid that too many kind people have called "coffee." The highly conductive metal coffee cup gave us more trouble, perhaps, than anything else, for it seemed to absorb all the heat of its contents. It became so hot, in fact, that it would have blistered our lips had we attempted to drink from it. When it cooled off a bit I confidently grasped the handle, hoping to wash down a few beans, only to find, too late, that the handle catch was loose, and my coffee spilled right into my beans. Falling in on another line, I poured what had now become bean-coffee soup into a garbage pail, washed my mess kit in soupy hot water, and rinsed it in cold water. "Thus endeth the first Army lesson" in the mess hall.

---

[37] "Hun" comes from "Attila the Hun" the Germanic tribal leader of the Huns who defeated several other Germanic tribes and established a kingdom east of the Rhine c. 450, putting the fear of God into the Latin-speaking Gauls and Romans.

Once finished at the mess hall, our platoon, which was not entirely filled, just like our squad (each squad was supposed to have nine pvts. and one cpl.), was ordered by our P.G., Sgt. Brown, to once again "fall in." Brown then barked, "Count off by threes!"

"Squads, right!"

"Forward, march!"

We were marched back to our barracks where were introduced to "police call" (the first of many). Here we lined up in platoon formation as best we could and Sgt. Brown explained to us what we were supposed to do. Police call consisted of picking up anything on the ground that didn't belong there, and that included cigarette butts (which the old Regular Army sergeants, like Brown, sardonically called "buttses," just like they called "people," "peoples," like "sergeant so-and-so, git'cher peoples over 'er!"), match sticks, bits of paper, shafts of straw (!), weeds, etc. The better part of us, unaccustomed to this new duty, felt belittled by it (which was part of the plan, as, little did we know at the time, we would be ordered to do far worse in combat).

After that, we reported to our bunks and were told by Sgt. Brown to "get settled" and that we were "confined to barracks," which wasn't that bad as it actually had an adjoining bath house that had cold running water and flush toilets! For some of us, especially those from the western parts of the state, flush toilets were a luxury that they did not have at home, let alone running water. As for me, it wasn't that big of a deal because although we had an outhouse in Petersburg, we did have indoor cold water plumbing. When I laid down for my first night's rest in the Army, the fact that I was assigned to Lt. Harry Myers's 2nd Platoon, Capt. Herbert R. Rising's B Company, Maj. Albert B. Dockery's 1st Battalion, Col. Briant Wells' 318th Infantry Regiment, Brig. Gen. Charles Farnsworth's 159th Inf. Brig., Maj. Gen. Adelbert Cronkhite's 80th Infantry Division (2/B/1/318/159/80, for short) was just starting to sink in.

-Camp Lee-

Camp Lee ultimately accommodated 60,335 men, becoming the largest of the sixteen National Army cantonments. As originally laid out, it embraced 5,300 acres, exclusive of a rifle range of 3,600 acres, or a total of 8,900 acres. It was arranged in the form of a horse-shoe about one-third of a mile wide and five miles around. The camp comprised 3,000 buildings which required approximately 55,000,000 board feet of lumber and 6,000 square feet of wall board. The roof area alone totalled almost 500 acres. Over 500,000 panes of glass, 380 miles of electric wiring, and 30,000 incandescent lamps were also employed in its construction. Each infantry regiment was to have sixteen unpainted company barracks, 50' x 100', two stories high, and heated by coal stoves.

The camp hospital eventually covered 52 acres, with 2½ miles of connecting corridors and accommodations for a thousand patients, being heated from a central plant. These buildings were the only semi-permanent hospitals erected for the National Army. Camp facilities for recreation and entertainment included twelve Y.M.C.A. buildings, three Knights of Columbus buildings, a 3,000 seat (!) theater, a library building, and a large Youth Male Christian Association hostess house. Other facilities included 21 post exchanges (P.X.), 10 storage warehouses, a bakery with a capacity of 45,000 pounds of bread daily, and a laundry which cost approximately $250,000. Structures at the camp remount stations provided shelter for 20,000 animals. The concrete reservoir had a storage capacity of 1,000,000 gallons, and the steel water tower next to the White House had a capacity of 300,000 gallons. By means of fifteen miles of mains, Petersburg furnished the camp with 3,000,000 gallons of chlorinated and filtered water daily. The waste from the camp was carried off by thirty-five miles of sewer pipe. Eventually, there were three fire stations.[38]

Newly-uniformed "Blue Denim Doughs" with inoculation spots on their arms at Camp Lee.

---

[38] Stultz, 15.

-The Needle-

At 5:30 A.M. the next morning, we were awoken by a bugle call—the first of hundreds. The tune was called "Reveille" and is probably the most famioliar of all bugle calls, aside from "charge!" Irving Berlin wrote the song, "Oh! How I Hate to Get Up in the Morning" to reflect our general attitude of Army life. We'd often hum it as we formed up:

Oh! How I Hate to Get Up in the Morning,
Oh! How I'd love to remain in bed
For the hardest blow of all is to hear the bugler call:
You've got to get up, you've got to get up,
You've got to get up this morning!
Someday I'm going to murder the bugler
Someday they're going to find him dead
I'll amputate his reveille and stomp upon it heavily
And spend the rest of my life in bed!
A bugler in the Army is the luckiest of men
He wakes the boys at five and then goes back to bed again
He doesn't have to blow again until the afternoon
If ev'rything goes well with me I'll be a bugler soon!
Oh! How I Hate To Get Up In The Morning,
Oh! How I'd love to remain in bed
For the hardest blow of all is to hear the bugler call:
You've got to get up, you've got to get up,
You've got to get up this morning!
Oh, boy! The minute the battle is over
Oh, boy! The minute the foe is dead
I'll put my uniform away and move to Philadelphia
And spend the rest of my life in bed!

Sgt. Brown informed us (he slept in a separate room with the other P.G.s of the company—the company first sergeant had his own room) that the bugler was not outside "merely for the sake of exercising his lungs" but that it was the "First Call for Reveille" and that we were already late. If we were in fact late for the top sergeant's morning muster at 5:45 A.M., we may as well just report to the woodpile because that's where we'd spend most of the day: on wood detail.

This here Army doesn't mess around, Getz and I thought.

"Get dressed in ten minutes and line up outside in company front for roll call!" was the first order of the day.

Then followed a few precious moments for washing up in the latrine, which was a large bath house connected to the barracks.

Next came "Mess Call," which was sounded at 7:30 A.M.

After that came our offical physical examinations and the formal muster. As each man entered the medical barracks, a number was stamped on his bare arm—much like the brandling of cattle, we thought. Passing into the first room, where a line of doctors awaited to receive us, we were thoroughly examined. Eyes, ears, heart, lungs, feet, throat, teeth, and other portions of the anatomy all received the careful consideration of Maj. "Doc" Ferdinand Schmitter, the chief medical examiner of the division. Once the location of scars and other physical marks were recorded, we were placed in the hands—none too tender—of the vaccinating surgeon, who passed us on to his partner in crime, the inoculating surgeon. The inoculation was a hypodermic injection of typhoid anti-toxin, administered three times, at ten-day intervals. Few of us will ever forget the effects of "the needle" or the violent dislike we developed for it. The inspectors concluded the examination by taking our fingerprints (apparently, we were to be treated like criminals) and, provided that no physical defects were found, were finally accepted as fit subjects to withstand the privations of military service. As "three shots at ten-day intervals" were required, for more than a month it was a familiar sight to observe a line of men, stripped to the waist, filing by a medical officer who casually jabbed a needle into each man's left arm.

Mustering-in, which took place immediately after the medical examination, consisted of a general survey of the family tree and the refinement of our individual service records. We were happy to oblige the Army with biographical notes, but completely lost courage when some tired clerk irritably and unfeelingly asked us, "Whom do you want to be notified in case you're killed?" Once this question was answered, we were given the all-important "Qualification Card" which served as a guide to those assigning men to various branches of the service. I was cleared to serve in the infantry (yip-ee!), the "principal and most important arm, which is charged with the main work on the field of battle and decides the final issue of combat."[39]

-Regimental Officers-

As was already stated, we boys from eastern Virginia were assigned to the 318th Infantry Regiment, which was constituted on August 5, 1917 in the National Army (today's Organized

---

[39] *F.S.R.*, para. 123.

Reserve) and part of the U.S. Army's 80th Infantry Division. Col. Briant H. Wells of the Regular Army was our regimental commander and Lt. Col. James Love, also of the regulars, was our regimental executive officer (X.O.). My first battalion commander was Maj. Albert Robert B. Dockery and my first company commander was Capt. Herbert R. Rising. Wells and his staff would eventually adopt "Old Virginia Never Tires," from a 19th Century minstrel song, to be our regimental motto. We, as well as the 317th Infantry Regiment and the 313th M.G. Battalion, which drew most of their recruits from western Virginia, made up the 159th Inf. Brig., which was initially commanded by Brig. Gen. Charles S. Farnsworth.

Over the past few months, before our arrival as Selectees, scores of newly-promoted regimental, battalion, and company commanders were trained by Farnsworth. All of the officers assigned to the 318th Infantry, with the exception of Col. Wells, Lt. Col. Love, and Maj. Albert B. Dockery, of the Regular Army, were graduates of O.T.C. at Fort Myer, Virginia, which is just outside of Washington, D.C. The majority of our company-grade officers had received no prior military training other than what they had gained as members of the so-called Provisional Training Regiments at Plattsburg, New York, during the summers of 1915 and 1916. There were, however, a few notable exceptions.

For example, Maj. Charles Sweeny, the intrepid commander of 2/318th Infantry (Companies E, F, G, and H), attended West Point (but did not graduate) and was one of the few Americans who fought for Mexico's liberal president *Francisco González* against the conservative forces of *Général Porfirio Díaz* from 1911-14. After that, Sweeny joined the French Foreign Legion (*Légion Etrangère Français*) and fought in France and Flanders against the hated Hun. During his service in the *Légion Etrangère Français*, Sweeny rose to the rank of infantry captain and was awarded the prestigious *Légion d'honneur* (Legion of Honor), which consists of a beautiful crimson red ribbon with a white Maltese-like Cross as well as the famous *Croix de Guerre* (Cross of War), which is a dark green and red-striped ribbon with a bronze cross and crossed-swords. Maj. Sweeny returned to the States in the spring of 1917 with the mission headed by none other than Papa Joffre, the French Army commander who helped stop the German drive in 1914 along the Marne. In May, Sweeny was commissioned an infantry major in the A.U.S., and assigned to the 80th Division.[40]

Another notable soldier of the 318th Infantry was Capt. John Crum, the commander of Company F. He, like Sweeny, was one of the few Americans who fought for Mexico's liberal president González against Díaz during the aughts, riding with none other than *Général* José *Doroteo Arango Arámbula* ("Pancho Villa") before he crossed into Texas. In 1915, Crum

---

[40] Stultz, 44.

enlisted into the British Army and fought in France and Flanders for two years until the U.S. declared war in April 1917. Sweeny's and Crum's combat experiences proved invaluable to us during training and in combat. In addition to these two officers, there were a few who had served one or more enlistments in the Regular Army and had been commissioned through O.T.C. at Fort Myer, Virginia. Still others had served one or more years in the National Guard, of whom some had seen recent service on the Mexican Border.[41]

In conformity with the policy of assigning officers to serve with men drafted from the same home districts, the 80th Infantry Division's first quota of commissioned personnel was largely drawn from the O.T.C. at Camp Myer, which trained candidates (or cadets) from Pennsylvania, Virginia, and New Jersey. Commissioned on August 15, 1917, most of these newly-minted U.S. Army officers were given leave and instructed to report to Camp Lee on August 27. To hear them tell the story, they "arrived on a fearfully hot, windy day, detraining in a sandy desert, where they were met by Lt. Col. Love, who directed them to the area assigned to the regiment."[42]

It is safe to say that the first impressions of the camp that were formed by these officers were far from pleasing ones. Camp Lee was still in the process of construction and many days were to elapse before it reached completion. As a result, the period between the arrival of the officers and that of the first contingent of the draft, which was to form the nucleus of the division, was spent in helping the carpenters and plumbers. They also attended schools on the *1911 Infantry Drill Regulations* and the *1914 Field Service Regulations* with the fellow officers of Farnsworth's 159th Inf. Brig.

-The Division's *Nomme de Guerre*-

Because the 80th Division consisted primarily of men from Pennsylvania, Virginia, and West Virginia, it was nicknamed the "Blue Ridge Division," as the ancient and indelible Blue Ridge (a portion of the Appalachian Mountains) bound all three states together. Our division's distinctive insignia, which was quickly painted on signs at Camp Lee and later turned into a patch, therefore consisted of three "azure blue" mountain peaks representing the Blue Ridge Mountains of Pennsylvania, Virginia, and West Virginia. Cronkhite adopted the Latin Motto, *Vis Montium* or "Strength of the Mountains." In explaining to us why the 80th Division was named the "Blue Ridge Division," Cronkhite said:

---

[41] Stultz, 44.

[42] As cited in *318th Infantry*, 12-13.

The name of the division was decided upon some months ago, before I sailed for Europe. It was decided, however, to make no announcement of the name until a suitable crest had been selected. During my absence, Capt. Thomas Terry was at work on the matter of the crest. He has consulted the leading authorities in the country, and has had designs submitted by the foremost artists in heraldry. With Lt. Col. Waldron and other officers, he went over the various designs carefully, and selected the one that seemed best to reflect the spirit and geography of the Division. The crest has been approved and formally adopted. I believe it will meet with the enthusiastic indorsement of every officer and enlisted man in the division...

As the men of the division come from the three states of Pennsylvania, Virginia, and West Virginia, it was desired that some name should be decided upon that would apply equally to each of the three commonwealths mentioned. If you will look at a map of the United States, you will notice that the three states are joined by the chain of mountains known as the Blue Ridge... As the Blue Ridge mountains are the inanimate, geographical thread of union, so the Blue Ridge Division, with the best men of the three great states fighting side by side in the same glorious cause, will be the animate, living thread of union...

The slogan selected for the division is "Vis Montium," which, translated from the Latin, is "Strength of the Mountains." I hope and believe that the Blue Ridge Division will live up to the motto. The credit of first suggesting the name Blue Ridge belongs to Lt. Col. Waldron, the Chief of Staff.[43]

[43] As cited in Stultz, 115. To clarify the Latin meaning, "Vis Montium" means "to draw strength from the mountains," meaning that we, the soldiers, drew strength from the Blue Ridge, and not that the Blue Ridge, an inanimate object, is strong. Some people wanted to name the division the "Lee Division" because it was formed at Camp Lee. Cronkhite disapproved, however, not only because he knew that other divisions would also be formed at Camp Lee, but also because he wanted a common symbol to unite all of the soldiers of the division—thus "Blue Ridge Division."

-My Squad-

It took a few days for us to get situated and training did not really start until our entire platoon was filled. I think that was in late-Sept., 1917. By this time, we were already divided into four ten-man squads, each lead by a provisional corporal that Sgt. Brown, our P.G., thought was good enough for the job. In my squad, the 4th Squad, we had Cpl. Oliver Ward from Norfolk, Virginia. He was a little older than most of us and I think that's why he got the job. We also had Earl Andrus, Boss Adkins, Jim Bruce, my good friend Albert Getz, Gerard Long, Richard Grubbs, Joe Riddle (me), Ben Schuyler (pronounced "sky-ler"), and John Spratt. I liked all of them even though a couple talked too much or snored too much. Our P.L. was Lt. Henry Myers, a graduate from the College of William and Mary. Just a few weeks ago, he was a public school teacher in Richmond. The funny thing with him was that he knew about as much as we did. Brown was the most experienced of us all, and he had only been in the Army for a couple of years before he ended up with us.

Scary thought, I know.

Over the next several days, we recruits were rapidly introduced to the rigors and intricacies of Army life. Men were detailed to install kitchen equipment, to go considerable distances in search of water, which, prior to the completion of the plumbing system, was very scarce, and to receive, store, and issue quartermaster (Q.M.) and ordnance (Ord.) items (Q.M. and Ord. supplies embrace practically every item of equipment needed to convert a civilian into a soldier). While Q.M. supplies were usually items made of cloth or felt, Ord. items had metal attached.

Every regiment has "that" unit—the unit that seemed to always have problems in garrison, the unit that had some toxic personalities, the unit in the cantonment area that was an absolute nightmare to deal with, but when unleashed in combat, usually (but not always) did well. I'm not going to say what unit that was in my regiment, but for the 314th Artillery, "that" unit was Battery B. One of my friends who I met after the war at one of the reunions was Henry Schreckengost, who belonged to Capt. D.S. Beebe's B/1/314th Artillery. We talked a few times about the "what fer" of that unit. The battery even admitted it in its official book: "During our eight months of training we received the reputation of being the toughest battery in the regiment—our representation in the guard house was not to be excelled by any organization and although we were sometimes ordered off the field on preliminaries we were always in the lead when the big things came off."[44] If you're a neighbor of that particular unit, it can be a real pain. If you're in that unit, it can either be heaven or hell.

---

[44] *History of 314th Artillery* (314th Artillery Veterans' Association, N.D.), 49. Hereafter cited as "*314th Artillery*.

After morning drill on the regimental parade ground, we were given a 15-minute rest period, followed by another half-hour or so of lecture from the *Infantry Drill Regulations, 1917 (I.D.R.)*.[45] After that, we conducted more physical activities, and at around 11:30 A.M., we were marched back to our barracks, cleaned up and got ready for dinner, which we began to relish more and more. At 1:00 P.M. we usually fell in for the afternoon fun—and it was fun. All we did was play games, run races, compete in broad-jumping, and other forms of Olympic-style events. They all helped us build our minds, bodies, and souls. Recall was sounded at 4:30 P.M. when the sun was at its hottest (although Sept.-Oct.1917, was quite pleasant in good ole Camp Lee) and we returned to our barracks for police call, etc. The general topic of discussion in the bays usually revolved around how much we'd be sore and stiff the next morning. We had our supper at 5:00 P.M. and stood "Retreat" on the parade ground like Old Army Regulars. At first, many of us were still in civilian clothes as we did not get our uniforms for almost three weeks after arriving in camp (and boy did we reek, as most of us only brought one set of civvies—those on our backs upon enlistment—fully expecting to be kitted-out the first day of our enlistment). We had no trouble sleeping at night, I can assure you, as we were all exhausted from the day's training. After a few weeks of this routine, the notes of "Reveille"—that famous bugle tune in the morning—at first received with inherent aversion, soon became no more abhorrent to us than the music of the familiar alarm clock and it was not long before the slouch of the civilian gave way to the erect bearing of the soldier.

I would be amiss not to mention that the majority of the men of Farnsworth's 159th Inf. Brig. had been brought up and spent most of their lives on farms and during the second week they were given an opportunity to put their experience to good use. The drill field which had been assigned to the brigade was pretty much covered with fully grown corn, and, to those officers who had not had the benefit of a farming career, it presented almost insurmountable difficulties in preparing for drill purposes. But someone on the staff had a bright idea. "Tell the farmers to have at!" With that, the "farmer army" was unleashed upon the field and within 24 hours there was not a stalk in sight. The cutting time would have been appreciably less had it not been for the great number of rabbits whose dens were destroyed in the process. It should, be recorded as a matter of history, however, that the rabbit stood as much chance as the proverbial snowball in summer, and rabbits and corn disappeared simultaneously. Thereafter it was a matter of only a few days until the steady "tramp, tramp, tramp" of drilling hosts levelled the furrows and gave us a first-class drill field.

---

[45] *Infantry Drill Regulations, 1917.* (Washington, D.C.: Government Printing Office, 1917). Hereafter cited as "I.D.R."

Over the next several weeks, the division was fleshed out by more Selectees, drawn almost exclusively from the three Blue Ridge Mountain states. In addition to basic training, we carried bricks, laid walks, built woodbins, potato bins, and fixed up the barracks in general. In order to make our quarters safer in case of fire, wooden ladders were erected on the outer front wall of our two-story wooden barracks and a small shed was built alongside where a small hose reel was mounted on an axle and wheels.

That first month in the Army was therefore a strenuous one for all. Squad drill on the parade field continued steadily from 7:30 in the morning until 4:30 in the afternoon, Saturdays and Sundays excepted. Activities, such as marching in step, taking long hikes, learning to don and take care of our gear, building up the camp, and the like, did not cease with the sounding of "Recall." In the evenings there were schools for the officers, schools for the N.C.O.s, schools for the illiterates, etc. Q.M. and ordnance gear, as it became available, was also usually issued after hours, accompanied by talks and demonstrations on its use and care.

At all times company commanders and 1Sgts. were busy training supply sergeants, mess sergeants, or company clerks, the elements of personal hygiene and of first-aid treatment, or explaining the Articles of War and the principles of military discipline and courtesy. In fact, it appeared to most company commanders and 1Sgts. that sleep had been suppressed to being a "non-issue item." There was also mounds of paper work, unceasing, endless, and inexorable. Officers, fresh from civil pursuits, often wondered why all commissions were not reserved for accountants or other bean counters. But order gradually came out of chaos. Material for N.C.O.s was plentiful and was not long in being discovered and after the first month or so the men could be relied upon not to put on our leggings upside down. It was more difficult to catch an entire platoon out of step as each day passed. It was also remarkable how rapidly the men gained in weight and health by reason of the well-ordered lives we led, the vigorous exercise we took, and the enormous meals we consumed three times a day.

-Uniforms-

By about Week Three, we received our first complete uniform issue. The uniform itself is called the "M1910 Summer Uniform." It consisted of an olive drab cotton tunic with standing collar, cotton breeches that reached down to our calves, two cotton shirts, and a M1912 "Campaign Hat" (also called a "Montana," "Lemon Squeezer," "Doughboy," or "Pershing" Hat) with sky blue hat cords (sky blue for infantry, yellow for cavalry, and red for artillery, engineers, etc.). We were also issued white cotton under-shirts and under-drawers, russet leather low-top boots, and M1910 Pea Green Canvas Leggings (officers were issued brown leather leggings). The reason why some men did not get the M1910 Summer Uniform issued to them in a timely fashion was because the Army simply ran out—they were instead issued blue denim overalls, which was the Army's answer to out-fitting mechanics.

Later we were issued the M1912/17 Uniform (wool), the one we wore in France, the M1910 Canvas Cartridge Belt, the M1910 First Aid Pouch, the M1910 Intrenching Tool with Cover, the M1910 Canteen with Cover, the M1910 Canvas Field Pack that is long and narrow, and I.D. tags (Camp Lee numbers started with 8-1-1). The drab wool tunic had four pockets and dark bronze buttons bearing the national eagle. The standing collar or "choker" had a hole punched in each front for the attachment of two dark bronze insignia disks (one that said "U.S." and one that had crossed muskets for infantry, crossed cannons for artillery, etc.).[46]

In the top-left pocket we would generally carry a copy of the all-important (and all-knowing) *I.D.R.* (which was crafted to indeed fit in said pocket). In the other pockets, we would carry, in combat anyway, rations, a notebook and pencil, toilet paper, tobacco, pipe, matches, sometimes and extra bullet or two, etc. I tended to stuff my pockets with as much toilet paper and chocolate that I could. The thought of me wiping with my left hand or starving was not appealing.

-Daily and Weekly Inspections-

Every day, our 1Sgt. inspected our barracks. Before we answered the first drill formation each morning, for example, we cleaned up. Everything had to be spick and span. There was a specific place for everything and everything had to be kept in its place. With mops and brooms and plenty of water the barracks were given a good scrubbing on Friday afternoons and things were put in shape for the Saturday morning inspection, which was conducted by the company commander. Besides the cleanup, clean toilet articles and uniform parts had to be displayed like they were going to be sold in a local five and dime. When the 1Sgt. made his inspection, each bunk had to show a clean towel, tooth brush, soap, comb, pair of socks, and suit of underwear. The articles had to be displayed on the bunk in a specific manner.

Equipment "show down inspections" were also a big feature of the routine. This occasional inspection required the soldier to produce all of his wares and equipment for inventory and to lay them out a certain way on his bunk. The regimental supply officer and company supply sergeant made many rounds taking account of equipment that was short, and several "show-downs" usually transpired before the lacking equipment was actually supplied. There was also a field inspection every Saturday morning, where the general appearance of the

---

[46] Too many people call the infantry device "crossed rifles." They are not rifles, but M1792 Muskets—the first muskets made in the U.S. Government Arsenal at Springfield, Massachusetts, for military use.

soldier was thoroughly scrutinized. We had to be clean-shaven, have neatly polished boots, and a clean uniform with buttons all present and utilized.

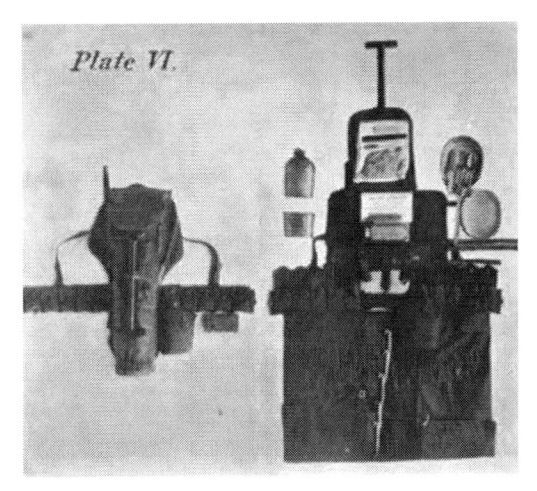

"Show Down Inspection." We were to lay out our gear on our bunks as noted on the right. Everything was to be present, clean, and in good working order.

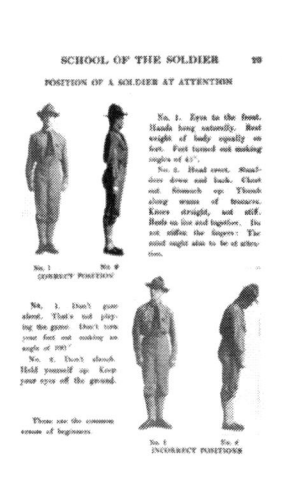

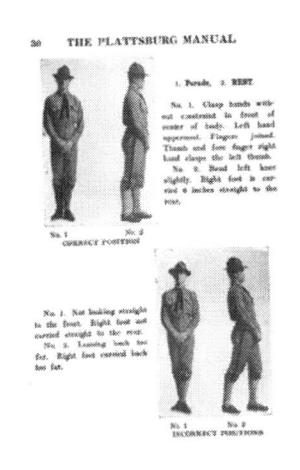

"Instructing the Latest Arrivals, Camp Lee."

80th Division recruits practiced drill with wooden sticks rather than rifles at Camp Lee during the first few weeks of training. Until supplies of weapons and equipment arrived, instructors had to make do with substitutes. Constant drill taught teamwork and taught soldiers to respond quickly to orders.

K/3/317th Inf. recruits with old Krag-Springfield M1892s, used for training purposes during the first several weeks at Camp Lee.

Typical soldier pack with canvas pistol belt (L). We'd stuff our shelter half, three aluminum tent pins, three wooden tent poles, poncho, blanket, overcoat, and extra shirt, underwear, and socks into this pack, as well as a few personal and sundry items. School of the Squad, (R).

"Shelter halves" or "pup tents." Each Dough was issued one canvas shelter half, one three-part wooden pole, three aluminum tent pins, and one guy rope. He was paired with another Dough and together, they constructed a "pup tent." While in combat, we rarely set these up, usually wraping ourselves in the shelter helf.

Typical company formation at Camp Lee. Note the barrack and the adjoining bathhouse.

Close order drill at Camp Lee. "Squads, right! Hut, two, tree, four, what we need the Marines for?"

With full pack, marching through Petersburg.

TROOPS FROM CAMP LEE PARADING IN THE STREETS OF PETERSBURG, VA

Some of the British (L) and French (R) instructors who helped train us at Camp Lee, 1917-18.

Maréchal de France Joseph Joffre "Papa Joffre" (L), *Général de France* Charles Mangin "the Butcher" (C), and U.S. Maj. Gen. Robert Lee Bullard, commander, 1st Inf. Div. and III Corps, A.E.F. (R).

Chapter 4
The Schools of the Soldier, Squad, and Company at Camp Lee.

"The Army" has a very complete and time-tested training system to turn soft civilians—people like me—into hardened, combat-ready soldiers who are able to take the lives of enemy soldiers without batting an eye. This system is called the "Schools of the Soldier, the Squad, and the Company." Although each branch had its own training manuals (e.g., *Manual for N.C.O.s and Privates of Infantry, Manual for N.C.O.s and Privates of Cavalry,* and *Manual for N.C.O.s and Privates of Artillery*), they all shared the same general Schools of the Soldier and Squad drills and exercises. Our officers and N.C.O.s also used *Infantry* or *Artillery Drill and Service Regulations, 1917, The Manual for Military Training, 1916,* and *The Plattsburg Manual: A Handbook for Military Training, 1917*. The "School of the Soldier" basically taught us how to be private soldiers in the U.S. Army. How to stand, walk, act, etc. For example, according to the *Artillery Drill Regulations* (A.D.R.):

> 62. This instruction has for its object the training of the individual recruit and afterwards that of the squad. It must be given with the greatest attention to detail.
>
> 63. In the instruction of the recruit frequent short rests should be given, in order that the men may not be unduly fatigued. The instructor will take advantage of these rests to instruct the recruits in the customs and courtesies of the service, the duties of the orderlies, the proper manner of receiving messages from and delivering them to officers, etc., so that when the recruit is finally reported for duty he will not only know his prescribed drill thoroughly but will know how to conduct himself out of ranks as a trained soldier.
>
> 64. From the beginning the instructor will insist on a smart appearance of the recruits and will require that their clothing be clean and neatly adjusted.
>
> 65. The instructor explains briefly each movement, first executing it himself, if practicable. He requires the recruits to take the proper positions unassisted and does not touch them for the purpose of correcting them, except when they are unable to correct themselves. He avoids keeping them too long at the same movement, although each should be understood before passing to another. He exacts by degrees the desired precision and uniformity.
>
> 48. Commands are of two kinds: Prepatory commands and commands of execution. The preparatory command, such as forward, indicates the movement that is to be executed. The command of execution, such as MARCH, HALT,

causes the execution. Preparatory commands are distinguished in the text by small black type; those of execution by CAPITALS.

50. To permit of the preparatory command being understood, a well-defined pause should be made between it and the command of execution. The duration of this pause depends in a measure upon the size of the body of troops under command...

51. Each preparatory command is pronounced in an ascending tone of voice, but always in such a manner that command of execution may be more energetic and elevated.

The first position we learned was the "Position of the Soldier at Attention" and how to properly salute. According to the *A.D.R.*:

68. Heels on the same line and as near each other as the conformation of the man permits. Feet turned out equally and forming an angle of about 45°. Knees straight without stiffness. Hips level and drawn back slightly; body erect and resting equally on hips; chest lifted and arched; shoulders square and falling equally. Arms and hands hanging naturally, thumbs along the seams of the trousers. Head erect and squarely to the front, chin drawn in so that the axis of the head and neck is vertical; eyes straight to the front. Weight of the body sustained principally upon the balls of the feet, heels resting lightly on the ground.

69. The instructor must insist that the men accustom themselves to the position of attention. It may be so exaggerated that it becomes not only ridiculous but positively harmful. Instead of that, the men must be taught to assume a natural and graceful position, one from which all rigidity is eliminated and from which action is possible without first relaxing muscles that have been constrained in an effort to maintain the position of attention...

According to Col. Moss's *Manual of Military Training* (M.M.T.):

1. Prelude. We will first consider the object and advantages of military training, as they are the natural and logical prelude to the subject of military training and instruction.

2. The object of all military training is to win battles. Everything that you do in military training is done with some immediate object in view, which, in turn, has in view the final object of winning battles. For example:

3. Setting-up exercises. The object of the setting-up exercises, as the name indicates, is to give the new men the set-up—the bearing and carriage—of the military man. In addition these exercises serve to loosen up his muscles and prepare them for his later experiences and development.

4. Calisthenics. Calisthenics may be called the big brother, the grown-up form, of the setting-up exercise. The object of calisthenics is to develop and strengthen all parts and muscles of the human body,—the back, the legs, the arms, the lungs, the heart and all other parts of the body. First and foremost a fighting man's work depends upon his physical fitness. To begin with, a soldier's mind must always be on the alert and equal to any strain, and no man's mind can be at its best when he is handicapped by a weak or ailing body. The work of the fighting man makes harsh demands on his body. It must be strong enough to undergo the strain of marching when every muscle cries out for rest; strong enough to hold a rifle steady under fatigue and excitement; strong enough to withstand all sorts of weather, and the terrible nervous and physical strain of modern battle; and more, it must be strong enough to resist those diseases of campaign which kill more men than do the bullets of the enemy. Hence the necessity of developing and strengthening every part and muscle of the body.

5. Facings and Marchings. The object of the facings and marchings is to give the soldier complete control of his body in drills, so that he can get around with ease and promptness at every command. The marchings—the military walk and run—also teach the soldier how to get from one place to another in campaign with the least amount of physical exertion. Every man knows how to walk and run, but few of them how to do so without making extra work of it. One of the first principles in training the body of the soldier is to make each set of muscles do its own work and save the strength of the other muscles for their work. Thus the soldier marches in quick time—walks—with his legs, keeping the rest of his body as free from motion as possible. He marches in double time—runs—with an easy swinging stride which requires no effort on the part of the muscles of the body. The marchings also teach the soldier to walk and run at a steady gait. For example, in marching in quick time, he takes 120 steps each minute; in double time, he takes 180 per minute. Furthermore, the marchings teach the soldier to walk and run with others,—that is, in a body.

6. Saluting. The form of salutation and greeting for the civilian consists in raising the hat. The form of salutation and greeting for the military man consists in rendering the military salute—a form of salutation which marks you as a member of the Fraternity of Men-at-Arms, men banded together for national defense, bound to each other by love of country and pledged to the loyal support of its symbol, the Flag. For the full significance of the military salute see paragraph 1534.

7. Manual of Arms. The rifle is the soldier's fighting weapon and he must become so accustomed to the feel of it that he handles it without a thought—just as he handles his arms or legs without a thought—and this is what the manual of arms accomplishes. The different movements and positions of the rifle are the ones that experience has taught are the best and the easiest to accomplish the object in view.

8. School of the Squad. The object of squad drill is to teach the soldier his first lesson in team-work—and team-work is the thing that wins battles. In the squad the soldier is associated with seven other men with whom he drills, eats, sleeps, marches, and fights. The squad is the unit upon which all of the work of the company depends. Unless the men of each squad work together as a single man—unless there is team-work—the work of the company is almost impossible.

9. Company Drill. Several squads are banded together into a company—the basic fighting unit. In order for a company to be able to comply promptly with the will of its commander, it must be like a pliable, easily managed instrument. And in order to win battles a company on the firing line must be able to comply promptly with the will of its commander. The object of company drill is to get such team-work amongst the squads that the company will at all times move and act like a pliable, easily managed whole.

10. Close Order. In close order drill the strictest attention is paid to all the little details, all movements being executed with the greatest precision. The soldiers being close together—in close order—they form a compact body that is easily managed, and consequently that lends itself well to teaching the soldier habits of attention, precision, team-work and instant obedience to the voice of his commander. In order to control and handle bodies of men quickly and without confusion, they must be taught to group themselves in an orderly arrangement and to move in an orderly manner. For example, soldiers are grouped or formed in line, in column of squads, column of files, etc. In close order drill soldiers are taught to move in an orderly manner from one group or formation to another; how to stand, step off, march, halt and handle their rifles all together. This practice makes the soldier feel perfectly at home and at ease in the squad and company. He becomes accustomed to working side by side with the man next to him, and, unconsciously, both get into the habit of working together, thus learning the first principles of team-work.

11. Extended Order. This is the fighting drill. Modern fire arms have such great penetration that if the soldiers were all bunched together a single bullet might kill or disable several men and the explosion of a single shell might kill or disable a whole company. Consequently, soldiers must be scattered—extended out—to fight. In extended order not only do the soldiers furnish a smaller target for the enemy to shoot at, but they also get room in which to fight with greater ease and freedom. The object of extended order drill is to practice the squads in team-work by which they are welded into a single fighting machine that can be readily controlled by its commander.

12. Parades, reviews, and other ceremonies. Parades, reviews and other ceremonies, with their martial music, the presence of spectators, etc., are intended to stimulate the interest and excite the military spirit of the command. Also, being occasions for which the soldiers dress up and appear spruce and trim, they inculcate habits of tidiness—they teach a lesson in cleanliness of body and clothes. While it is true it may be said that parades, reviews and other ceremonies form no practical part of the fighting man's training for battle, they nevertheless serve a very useful purpose in his general training. In these ceremonies in which soldiers march to martial music with flags flying, moving and going through the manual of arms with perfect precision and unison, there results a concerted movement that produces a feeling such as we have when we dance or when we sing in chorus. In other words, ceremonies are a sort of "get-together" exercise which pulls men together in spite of themselves, giving them a shoulder-to-shoulder feeling of solidity and power that helps to build up that confidence and spirit which wins battles.

13. Discipline. By discipline we mean the habit of observing all rules and regulations and of obeying promptly all orders. By observing day after day all rules and regulations and obeying promptly all orders, it becomes second nature—a fixed habit—to do these things. Of course, in the Army, like in any other walk of life, there must be law and order, which is impossible unless everyone obeys the rules and regulations gotten up by those in authority. When a man has cultivated the habit of obeying—when obedience has become second nature with him—he obeys the orders of his leaders instinctively, even when under the stress of great excitement, such as when in battle, his own reasoning is confused and his mind is not working. In order to win a battle the will of the commander as expressed through his subordinates down the line from the second in command to the squad leaders, must be carried out by everyone. Hence the vital importance of prompt, instinctive obedience on the part of everybody, and of discipline, which is the mainspring of obedience and also the foundation rock of law and order. And so could we go on indefinitely pointing out the object of each and every requirement of military training, for there is none that has no object and that answers no useful purpose, although the object and purpose may not always be apparent to the young soldier. And remember that the final object of all military training is to win battles.

14. Handiness. The average man does one thing well. He is more or less apt to be clumsy about doing other things. The soldier is constantly called upon to do all sorts of things, and he has to do all of them well. His hands thus become trained and useful to him, and his mind gets into the habit of making his hands do what is required of them—that is to say, the soldier becomes handy. Handy arms are a valuable asset.

15. Self-control. In the work of the soldier, control does not stop with the hands. The mind reaches out—control of the body becomes a habit. The feet, legs, arms and body gradually come under the sway of the mind. In the position of the soldier, for instance, the mind holds the body motionless. In marching, the mind drives the legs to machine-like regularity. In shooting, the mind assumes command of the arms, hands, fingers and eye, linking them up and making them work in harmony. Control of the body, together with the habit of discipline that the soldier acquires, leads to control of the mind—that is, to self-control. Self-control is an important factor in success in any walk of life.

16. Loyalty. Loyalty to his comrades, to his company, to his battalion, to his regiment becomes a religion with the soldier. They are a part of his life. Their reputation is his; their good name, his good name; their interests, his interests—

so, loyalty to them is but natural, and this loyalty soon extends to loyalty in general. When you say a man is loyal the world considers that you have paid him a high tribute.

17. Orderliness. In the military service order and system are watchwords. The smooth running of the military machine depends on them. The care and attention that the soldier is required to give at all times to his clothes, accouterments, equipment and other belongings, instill in him habits of orderliness. Orderliness increases the value of a man.

18. Self-confidence and self-respect. Self-confidence is founded on one's ability to do things. The soldier is taught to defend himself with his rifle, and to take care of himself and to do things in almost any sort of a situation, all of which gives him confidence in himself—self-confidence. Respect for constituted authority, which is a part of the soldier's creed, teaches him respect for himself—self-respect. Self-confidence and self-respect are a credit to any man.

19. Eyes trained to observe. Guard duty, outpost duty, patrolling, scouting and target practice, train both the eye and the mind to observe. Power of observation is a valuable faculty for a man to possess.

20. Teamwork. In drilling, patrolling, marching, maneuvers and in other phases of his training and instruction, the soldier is taught the principles of team-work—coöperation—whose soul is loyalty, a trait of every good soldier. Teamwork—coöperation—leads to success in life.

21. Heeding law and order. The cardinal habit of the soldier is obedience. To obey orders and regulations is a habit with the soldier. And this habit of obeying orders and regulations teaches him to heed law and order. The man who heeds law and order is a welcome member of any community.

22. Sound body. Military training, with its drills, marches, and other forms of physical exercise, together with its regular habits and outdoor work, keeps a man physically fit, giving him a sound body. A sound body, with the physical exercise and outdoor life of the soldier, means good digestion, strength, hardiness and endurance. A sound body is, indeed, one of the greatest blessings of life.

-School of the Squad-

The "School of the Squad" basically taught us how to act as a member of a team. This is the real essence of being a soldier: to be a productive member of a team. According to the *A.D.R.*:

> *57. Formations are habitually in double rank—the men always fall in at attention.*
>
> *58. The interval between men in ranks is four inches and between ranks in flank column is thirty inches, measured from elbow to elbow. The distance between ranks is fourty inches, measured from the back of the man in front to the breast of the man in rear.*
>
> *59. To secure uniformity of interval between files when falling in and in the alignments, each man places the palm of the left hand upon the hip, fingers pointing downward, thumb to the front. In falling in, the hand is dropped by the side as soon as the man next on the left has his interval; in the alignments, at the command front.*
>
> *60. Unless otherwise announced, the guide of a battery or subdivision of a battery is right.*

In early September, we trained with wooden sticks (for lack of a better term) in place of actual rifles. In October, however, we received Spanish-American War-era M1892 Krag-Springfields to train with, although we did not shoot them. While we marched here and there with our Krags, our P.G.s would teach us various marching songs, many of which should not be repeated here. We also drew heavily from the official *Army Song Book*. We in the 318th Inf. adopted "Carry Me Back to Virginny" as our favored song.

> *Carry me back to old Virginny.*
> *There's where the cotton and the corn and taters grow;*
> *There's where the birds warble sweet in the spring-time.*
> *There's where this old darkey's heart am long'd to go.*
> *Carry me back to old Virginny,*
> *There let me live till I wither and decay.*
> *Long by the old Dismal Swamp have I wandered,*
> *There's where this old darkey's life will pass away.*

One song that I heard (and liked) actually came from the Pittsburgh Boys of the 320th Infantry. After the war, then-Capt. Ashby Williams, the commander of E/2/320, stated that he was the author of this particular ballad, which is song with the melody, "Auld Lang Syne":

In Germany the Rhine River is flowing to the sea.
Filled to the brim with German beer as good as can be.
We come from Pennsylvania and old Virginia, too.
We'll drink the damned old river dry and let the army through![47]

By October, as the weather started to turn colder, sufficient opportunity having been given to know the men, the majority of the N.C.O.s were selected and the division gradually assumed the aspect of an actual organization led by General Cronkhite, general staff and all. I, for one, was happy with my chain-of-command, and looked forward to our real training phase before we were sent off to France to help win the war.

-"The Bayonet" Publication-

On Oct. 5, the first issue of "The Bayonet," the official weekly newspaper of the 80th Division, appeared with an initial edition of 15,000 copies. With Lt. Guy T. Visknisski of the 320th Infantry as editor, the enterprise was organized and promoted wholly within the division. Although Visknisski had no staff and no office, the first and subsequent editions would have done credit to a small city. From the first it was popular and attained a paid circulation, at five cents a copy, of 17,000 a week.

In those days there were neither public relations nor special service staffs, although there was a section in the *F.S.R.* entitled "Public Relations." The general consensus was that "The Bayonet" was neither a propaganda organ for the troops nor an attempt to "inform" the public. Its writers were usually private soldiers and they never were given a "line" to follow—they never were told by anybody how to handle the news. Aside from Lt. Visknisski, Lt. Arthur Hornblow, who later became a celebrated motion picture producer, and Lt. Barratt O'Hara, a former lieutenant governor of Illinois, also served as editors. The privates who wrote the copy were their own censors. Eventually "The Bayonet" had a business and editorial staff of nine or ten, including one officer. From its profits on advertising and circulation donated about $2,000 to the Red Cross to care for soldiers' dependents when the division sailed.

From time to time the paper printed a direct statement from the division commander or the chief of staff. As an illustration of the spirit of the times, a message issued by General

---

[47] Williams, Ashby. *Experiences of the Great War: Artois, St. Mihiel, Meuse-Argonne* (Roanoke, Virginia: Press of the Stone Printing and Manufacturing Company, 1919), 168. Hereafter cited as "*1/320th Infantry.*"

Cronkhite for the paper's first number, is interesting. It is addressed as much to the home folks as to the division:

To the Eightieth Division, National Army:

In extending greetings to you in this, the first issue of THE BAYONET, I wish to bring to your attention the fact that this is to be our means of placing before the various elements of the command the many things which shall prove of personal and general interest, not only to us, but to our home folks, for THE BAYONET is to be our mouthpiece both in our home land and in that foreign land where duty calls us to enforce those principles which are the very basis of the freeman's existence.

You are assembling at Camp Robert E. Lee from Pennsylvania, West Virginia and Virginia to form the 80th Division of the Army of the United States. I have known most of your senior officers for many years; I have served with them under varying conditions both in the United States and in its outlying possessions—I can assure you that there are none better... You have come on a serious mission, but your intelligence, your earnestness of conduct, your application to every detail of instruction indicate a full realization of the obligation which you have assumed.

No greater honor may fall to any man than the development of such a fine body of men into a fighting unit, a unit which must redound to the credit of its States and the country, and a unit of which they will be the more proud when it displays its prowess against the enemy.

Let us not forget, however, that our preparations contemplate stern, serious war—that much suffering must be the part of these young sons, and that even greater suffering must come to those who are left behind in anxiety and ignorance of what is happening, now knowing what additional sorrow the day may bring forth.

We are entering into a conflict with the most cruel enemy in the history of the world, an enemy whose means of encompassing death and destruction are so barbaric as to be unimaginable in warfare by civilized beings. We are entering into the most gigantic struggle which ever fell to the lot of man, a struggle which involves the safeguarding of all that makes life worth living; a struggle to enforce again, the principles for which our forefathers fought, to suffer and possibly die in a strange land, that the horrors of war may not be brought to our very doors.

Let every father, every mother, every sister and brother so imbue and support us, in the honor of this duty, that we may go forth only to conquer, glorified in the effort we are to make for the welfare of the world. [48]

On Oct. 6, the third contingent of Selectees arrived to Camp Lee, which further fleshed out America's Blue Ridge Division. By this time, most of the men from the first two contingents had been uniformed and began to feel comfortable with the "new look." As the number of incoming recruits increased, however, a corresponding demand for equipment gave the Q.M. and ordnance sergeants a great deal of worry, as the new Selectees could not be properly outfitted because the Army plum ran-out ran out of uniforms and equipment. Then, too, we heard that the physical size the men making up the new Army averaged larger proportions than those of the Old Army. The sizes of the uniforms therefore ran too small for the larger men, and as a result the latter had to wait until the proper sizes of equipment could specifically be requisitioned.

-Oct. 11, 1917 Richmond Parade-

Another noteworthy event in October was when the people of Richmond expressed a desire to see a parade of Blue Ridge Division soldiers after one month's training. A provisional battalion, under the command of Maj. Jennings C. Wise from the 159th Inf. Brig. and composed of a company from each of the infantry regiments, was sent to the Virginia State Fair Grounds in Richmond on Oct. 11 where it made a credible showing. Most people were astonished by the progress that had been made in such short time, a progress which would have not been possible, had not the men entered heart and soul into the spirit of being a soldier from the very beginning. Cronkhite noted the parade in "The Bayonet":

I wish to thank you for the success attained by the composite battalion which went to Richmond under your command on October 11, 1917. With various members of the division staff, I was present during the drill executed on the Virginia State Fair Grounds, and I can assure you that throughout my military career I have never been more deeply impressed than by the efforts of these men who, but a month before, had never taken arms in hand. I wish to congratulate

---

[48] As cited in Stultz, 54.

both the commissioned and enlisted personnel. It is a matter of special gratification on my part that their conduct conformed to their military bearing.[49]

-The A.E.F. Division-

By far, the biggest event in October 1917 for us was when the War Department changed the Tables of Organization and Equipment (T.O.E.) for all infantry divisions. The Army increased the authorized strength of infantry companies from 150 to 250 men, with the officer personnel increased to one captain, three first lieutenants, and two second lieutenants (usually we started with five second lieutenants and the more senior ones were promoted to first lieutenant). From here on out therefore, each infantry platoon was supposed to have 60 men, each infantry company 250, each infantry battalion to a little over a thousand, each infantry regiment 3,832, each infantry brigade 8,500, and each infantry division around 27,500 with about 12,000 actual rifle-carrying infantrymen.

We doubled over night!

Because the barracks were built under the old T.O. of 150-man companies, we needed a reassignment of barracks. As such, 2/318th Infantry was moved to a new section of the post while the 1st and 3rd Battalions remained in their old barracks, cascading their expanded platoons into the ones vacated by 2/318. It actually made a lot of sense. Our squad would now number fourteen private soldiers and one corporal. Although the 80th Division only listed 851 officers and 16,041 E.M. at the time—well under its new ration strength—that would soon change with the arrival of new recruits over the next several months.[50]

In contrast, French and British divisions operating on the Western Front had divisions of about 12,000 men that consisted of three infantry regiments with three battalions each (i.e., nine battalions per division), an artillery regiment with three battalions each, and a M.G. regiment with three battalions each. The A.E.F. division would be almost double that, with some 27,500 men organized into two Infantry brigades (twelve large infantry battalions per division), one artillery brigade, and one service of support (S.O.S.) brigade. Despite the fact that it would difficult to plan the movement and integration of British, French, and American divisions, as each had different numbers, Baker, Scott, and Pershing insisted that A.E.F. divisions have *offensive punch and staying power on the battlefield.*

---

[49] As cited in Stultz, 55.

[50] *Ibid*, 52.

What I mean by "offensive punch and staying power on the battlefield" is that our general staff was not interested in simply manning the defenses along the border with German Alsace-Lorraine, but was *bound and determined to attack straight into Germany—alone if need be—to show the world that America was not to be toyed with lightly.* To do so, Pershing envisioned advancing infantry brigades with two regiments abreast, with battalions stacked in successive waves (attack, support, and reserve) and then flip-flopping the brigades to maintain a continuous attack up the axis of advance.

In the 80th Division, the infantry regiments were numbered 317, 318, 319, and 320. While the 317th and 318th Infantry Regiments were in the 159th Inf. Brig., the 319th and 320th were in the 160th Inf. Brig. (80 times 2 equals 160, that's how they came up with the numbers). Our artillery regiments and new M.G. battalions were numbered 313, 314, and 315, and our ordnance, quartermaster, sanitary, transportation and engineer regiments were all numbered 305. It was that simple; it was very mathematical. I know that the bigwig pre-war planners like President Teddy Roosevelt (who led the 1st Volunteer Cavalry, the famous "Rough Riders" up San Juan Hill in 1898) and Maj. Gen. Leonard Wood (Roosevelt's superior during the War with Spain) and envisioned it this way. While the new Regular Army divisions would number 1-25, the new National Guard divisions, once mobilized into federal service, would number 26-75, and the brand-spanking new National Army divisions, made up of draftees (us), would number 76 to infinity. That said, the Regular Army would have infantry regiments 1-99, the National Guard 100-299, and the National Army 300 to infinity. Granted, the Regular Army only filled up 7 of its 25 divisions and the National Guard outfits only filled divisions 26-42, but you get the picture. That's why there are "gaps" in the division numbers because each component of the Army, the Regulars, the Guardsmen, and the Selectees of the National Army could only fill in certain numbers. When all was said and done, the highest division number we raised during the war was 93 and the National Army boys (us) and the National Guard actually provided the most divisions with seventeen each. If the war would have gone on into 1919, there is no doubt that we would have had over eighty divisions in Europe, going up to division number 105. But to be clear—every division in Pershing's A.E.F. consisted of Selectees.

-Our Brigades-

In my brigade, General Farnsworth's 159th Inf. Brig., the 317th Infantry Regiment drew most of its men from western Virginia, especially the Shenandoah Valley. As was already stated, my very own 318th Infantry Regiment drew most of its men from Tidewater Virginia, especially from around Richmond. Included in the brigade was the 313th M.G. Battalion, which had five companies, H.Q., A, B, C, and D. In battle, the 313th M.G. Battalion H.Q. was to co-locate with the brigade H.Q. and Companies A and B were sometimes attached to the 317th Infantry (bringing its M.G. companies to three) and C and D Companies were sometimes attached to the 318th Infantry. If the brigade commander wanted all guns forward (which was the norm), he'd give the leading or "attack" battalions more guns.

The 314th M.G. Battalion was the "division M.G. battalion" and it had but two firing companies, A and B, and was motorized.

The 315th M.G. Battalion was usually attached to the 160th Inf. Brig. and like the 313th M.G., was similarly divided. While in France, we, as well as several other A.E.F. divisions, like the 79th Division, massed all of our M.G. battalions under one officer, Lt. Col. Oscar Foley, the late commander of the 313th M.G. Battalion. Foley was called the Division M.G. Officer (D.M.G.O.), and was expected to deploy as many guns forward. The mantra was "M.G.s are never in reserve."[51]

Our sister brigade, General Brett's 160th Inf. Brig., consisted of the 319th and 320th Infantry Regiments and the 315th M.G. Battalion, which drew most of its men from western Pennsylvania, especially from around Pittsburgh.

The division's 155th Arty. Brig., which was commanded by Brig. Gen. George Heiner of the Regular Army, had a brigade H.Q., the 305th Trench Mortar (T.M.) Battery, the 305th Ammunition Trains Battalion, and the 313th, 314th, and 315th Artillery Regiments. Most of the men of the 155th Arty. Brig. came from West Virginia, followed by Pennsylvania. While the 313th and 314th Artillery had two battalions of 75mm field guns in France (Batteries A-D and E-H), the 315th Artillery had three battalions of 155mm French Schneider howitzers. Generally, the artillery brigade H.Q. was co-located with division H.Q. with the 315th Artillery, 314th M.G., and 305th T.M. close-by. Depending on the mission, the division commander would attach and detach his artillery battalions to better weigh the main effort. It was a very practical, sensible, and flexible system. The 313th Artillery was commanded by Col. Charles D. Herron ("Uncle Charley"), the 314th Artillery was commanded by Col. Robert S. Welsh, who took over the brigade from Heiner in France, and the 315th Artillery was commanded by Col. Carroll I. Goodfellow.

Our extremely important 305th Trains Brigade (a combination of quartermaster, ordnance, ammunition and transportation companies) was commanded by Col. George F. Hamilton, a cavalry officer from the Old Army. Its subordinate units were usually attached to

---

[51] *314th M.G. Battalion History, Blue Ridge (80th) Division. Published as a Matter of Record by the Officers and Men of the Battalion* (N.P., 1919), 27, 41. Hereafter cited as "*314th M.G.*"

the infantry or artillery brigades at the division commander's prerogative. Other division units included an M.P. company, the 305th Engineers, which contained construction, sapper, and demolition companies, the 305th Signal Battalion, which provided critical wire and wireless communication among the chain of command, the 305th Transportation Battalion, which will eventually include some 900 motor vehicles and 2,500 draft animals (if all lined up, it is said that their column would take up over ten km of road space), the 305th Quartermaster Battalion, and the 305th Sanitary Battalion, which is a medical unit. The 305th Sanitary Battalion had four field hospital companies, numbered 317, 318, 319, and 320, as well as four ambulance companies, also numbered 317, etc. At first, the concept was for each field hospital and ambulance company to be attached to equally-numbered infantry regiments. As the war went on, however, each field hospital specialized and operated with similar units from other divisions, acting in concert with the corps medical support plan. Examples of specialization were triage, gas, psychic, sick, dressing, etc.

Like I said before, each infantry regiment had fifteen companies: a headquarters company, a M.G. company (of three platoons with two M.G. sections per platoon), a supply company, and three rifle battalions with four rifle companies each. Companies A, B, C, and D made up the 1st Battalion, Companies E, F, G, and H made up the 2nd Battalion, and Companies I, K, L, and M made up the 3rd Battalion. Why they skipped "J" and went right on to "K" I'm not really sure. One old-timer told me that "J" sounded too much like "G." Another told me that "J" stood for Jesus and we can't use His initial. Those are as good reasons I guess there are out there. Who knows?

By late-October, Camp Lee was brought to a state of general completion (although no Army cantonment is ever finished), and the advisability of preserving spare lumber, nails, etc., for a future rainy day had become apparent to all, the result being that an investigation underneath any of the barracks would have disclosed a most remarkable collection of paraphernalia. Before long, General Cronkhite issued an order that nothing must be kept under the barracks and that that all lumber and other material then stored there must be neatly piled at the end of and ten feet from the buildings. The result was most astonishing and each company vied with the others to see which one would have the biggest pile.

-Psychological Tests, Life Insurance, and Liberty Bonds-

The last big event of October 1917 for us at Camp Lee was when Army psychiatrists, led by Lt. Clarence Yoakum, were given the opportunity to amuse themselves as officers and men alike of the division underwent the "Sanity Test." The Sanity Test consisted of placing a dot in that part of the triangle which was in the square (but not in the circle) and deciding that very important question of "how many legs has a Korean?" I heard one man in B/1/318 said: "I don't know, but it must be four, otherwise the man wouldn't be such a damn fool as to ask!"

If you answered all of the questions correctly, you got a 414, which proved you insane—if you didn't answer any of them you got zero, which proved that you didn't have enough brains to be insane.

Intermediate ratings showed intermediate degrees of insanity.

I think that I got a 220.

Fortunately, none of the officers or men were emotionally scarred by ordeal.

Soon after we recovered from the effects of the insane Sanity Test, the War Department created a new game for us, known as the "War Risk Allotment," or the "Survivor's Benefit Insurance." It proved to be a most worthy act of the greatest benefit to all members of the Armed Forces, but one which, unfortunately, was launched before anyone could be found who understood how it actually worked. Because of this, the spare hours of the evening were spent in trying to decide whether one came under Class A, B, or C, if one had a stepmother, two sisters, and a step-brother, etc.

Practically everybody was "War Risked," that is, covered by the life insurance, when the "Liberty Loan" people came to take even more of our pay away. It was expected that we not only gave our service (maybe even our lives?) but also our money (isn't indentured servitude under "due process of law" great?). And in spite of the fact that most members of the division came from parts of the country where money was not plentiful, the "Liberty Loan" people succeeded in three days' time in raising a most gratifying sum (we always found it ironic/infuriating that we were forced to buy "Liberty" bonds). A large portion of this represented the purchase by we individual Doughs who agreed to allot to the government a portion of our pay each month.

To add to our financial distress, our Army-issue low quarter boots (or "Pershing Boots") were already starting to wear out, and we had trouble getting replacements. We therefore created a system of sending shoes away to get them repaired (with our own money).

"You're in the Army now! You're not behind a plow! You'll never get rich, you son-of-a bi—ch, your'e in the Army now!"

To better spur the Liberty Loan campaign, General Cronkhite, on Oct. 9, named a committee consisting of Lt. Col. Ora Hunt of the 320th Infantry to manage the bond-selling drive. The camp was subsequently divided into teams teams, each consisting of one brigade and attached smaller units. The adjutant of each regiment and a designated officer in each special unit was placed in charge of the campaign in his organization, with a committee of three men formed in each company to solicit subscriptions. All soldiers were urged to make allotments of pay for the purchase of bonds. The camp's goal was half a million dollars in ten days, the national quota being $3 million.

A number of men were granted furloughs home to boost Liberty Loan sales. A detail from the 319th Infantry, for example, sold bonds totaling $3 million in their home district around Pittsburgh. It is believed that the 319th Infantry led all cantonments in the country in this particular type of Liberty Loan sale and Camp Lee ranked high in the nation-wide cantonment contest, again adding to its growing record of excellence. The Division Bulletin of Oct. 10, which was not "The Bayonet," announced first sales totaling $66,150. Daily reports were published and reached the climax with $1,783,250 at the conclusion of the campaign Oct. 24. Three and a half times the original goal of $500,000, the subscriptions represented per capita of $63.96 for Camp Lee. The four leading units in sales were the 319th Infantry, $229,350; 320th Infantry, $216,800; 155th Depot Brigade, $193,050; 317th Infantry, $176,150; followed by the 318th Infantry with $151,000. Division H.Q. and other units grouped in the report were credited with sales of $173,850. Only subscriptions by soldiers and by civilians in the permanent employ of the United States and stationed at Camp Lee were included in the camp sales total.

In conformance with a War Department order, the success of the Liberty Loan sale was celebrated at Camp Lee Oct. 24, with a full day of special events. The observance opened in the morning with an exhibition drill by a composite battalion representing the four Infantry regiments and formed from A/1/317th Infantry, A/1/318th Infantry, E/2/319th Infantry, and I/3/320th Infantry, commanded by the experienced Maj. Jennings Wise. Wise, after serving as a lieutenant in the 9th Infantry, subsequently served in the National Guard of New York and Virginia and had recently been Commandant of Cadets at Virginia Military Institute with the rank of "Colonel of Virginia Volunteers." Wise was in fact selected by Col. (and former President) Theodore Roosevelt to recruit a regiment for his proposed "Volunteer Division" to France until President Wilson, with urgings from the War Department, refused to accept it. In May, 1917, Wise was promoted to the rank of infantry captain in the A.U.S. After serving as Assistant to the Department Adjutant, Southern Army, he was promoted to major, organized an infantry battalion in the 90th "Tough Hombre Division" at Camp Travis, Texas, and then, at his request, was transferred to Cronkhite's forming 80th Division.[52]

---

[52] Stultz, 62-63.

-First American Units Deploy to France and Detachments from the 80th Division-

While we were busy selling Liberty Bonds, disaster struck the Allies when the Austro-Hungarians and Germans broke the Italian lines at Trento and Trieste and took Caporetto, threatening Venice and capturing some 275,000 Italian troops in the process. The American writer, Ernest Hemingway, was a volunteer ambulance driver during the Caporetto Campaign and he penned his now-famous *A Farewell to Arms* (published in 1929) to help explain what he experienced. In a panic, the Allies, needing the Italians to stay in the war, dispatched some 100,000 French and British troops to northern Italy, and drove the forces of the Central Powers back. We did not know it at the time that the new (and last) Austro-Hungarian Emperor, Karl I, actually wanted to discuss peace with the Allies after this reversal, but that his senior partner, the German Emperor Wilhelm II, would have none of it. "Kaiser Bill" was convinced that once Russia was taken out of the war by hook or crook in 1918, the Germans could deliver the *coup de grâce* against the hated British, driving them into the sea once and for all. And once the meddling British were driven out of France, the French and Belgians would be faced with a *fait accompli* and surrender.[53]

Because of the desperate situation in Europe, Wilson decided to rush the 1st, 2nd, 3rd, 26th, and 42nd Divisions to France. In order to bring them up to full strength, the War Department called for detachments from all of the other divisions in the East, with the result being that the 80th Division had to send thousands of men to help fill those divisions. It was, of course, very discouraging to the officers and men of America's Blue Ridge Division to see their organizations broken up and scattered to the four winds, and from this time until early in April, training was carried on with the companies greatly reduced in strength, averaging approximately 175 men each (250 was the requisite number).[54]

-Virginia and West Virginia Governors Visit Camp Lee-

On Oct. 22, 1917, as part of the Liberty Loan Campaign, Gov. Henry C. Stuart of Virginia and Gov. John J. Cornwell of West Virginia visited Camp Lee to review the troops from their respective states (which I always hated, as this was supposed to be a national, and not a state war). Gov. Stuart was met at the camp limits by Maj. Wise's provisional full-strength battalion of

---

[53] *Fait accompli* means "accomplished fact" or "something that has already happened and is thus unlikely to be reversed—a done deal"; pronounced "fate ack-awmp-lee."

[54] *319th Infantry*, 10.

Virginia troops that consisted of Companies A and E, 317th Infantry and Companies F and G, 318th Infantry. Once the review was complete, Stuart addressed the 7,000 men of the 159th Inf. Brig. on its parade ground. Gov. Cornwell's reception by the members of the 155th Arty. Brig. was met with similar enthusiasm as the brigade's three regiments, numbering nearly 5,000 men, mostly from West Virginia, marched in review before the "Mountain State's" chief magistrate, each regiment led by its band.

After the reviews and speeches, more than 3,000 soldiers and civilians greeted the visiting state executives when they joined Generals Cronkhite, Brett, Farnsworth, and Heiner in officially dedicating Camp Lee's new Y.M.C.A. Auditorium. Both governors lauded the division and the activities of the Y.M.C.A. During the festivities, the 320th Infantry Band played and wartime songs were sung by 400 members of my very own 318th Infantry, led by Capt. Senius J. Raymond, regimental adjutant. I was among the singers. I mean, why not? I was looking to grub some food.

The governors and other prominent visitors from the area gave very favorable reports of our division upon their return home. Growing recognition developed, and a group of Richmond citizens sponsored a movement to present stands of colors to the 317th and 318th Infantry Regiments. All of this "war propaganda" stuff is all well and good, but doesn't play well with the troops who "know the real deal." For example, the newspapers reported that we were "filled and fully-equipped." We weren't—not by a long-shot. For this particular occasion, brigade provisional battalions were formed, each company having the requisite 250 men, it being the first time any of that any officers or men of this camp had ever seen a company of that size pass in formal review. The *ad hoc* company was in fact comprised of men from two different companies of the brigade. And due to the fact that not all of the men of the companies were fully equipped, other men from other companies acted as fillers to the base companies. What the civilians knew or didn't know from the newspapers really didn't bother us, as we knew that the enemy read our papers, too. As far as we were concerned, we were fully trained, equipped, and ready for war.

-Enemy Aliens-

On Nov. 2, the division received an order to "segregate enemy aliens" from the other troops. An "enemy alien" was regarded as any soldier who was born in Germany and who had yet to become a U.S. citizen. To do so, Cronkhite appointed a board composed of Col. Hunt, Lt. Col. Lee, and Maj. Goodwyn to investigate the matter and to make recommendations concerning the disposition of such personnel. The board recommended that the identified "enemy aliens" be transferred to the post's 155th Depot Brigade until the War Dept. figured out what it wanted to do with them.

The transfers took place early in December, when nearly 1,000 soldiers of German birth were sent to the camp's depot brigade and assigned labor duty, pending final disposition by the War Dept. After Dec. 7, when the U.S. declared war against Austro-Hungary, soldiers who were born in that country were added to the list (Germany and Austro-Hungary were the only two countries the U.S. was a war with).

None of these men caused any trouble and many protested vigorously to the segregation. Even appeals from their officers that they be permitted to remain with their commands were fruitless.[55] We native-borns had mixed feelings about the whole sorted affair because they were, by-and-large, good men. We did not feel that they were "Fifth Columnists," but then again, where we were headed, we didn't have the luxury of understanding the "big picture." Had they been naturalized citizens, I think we would have rioted. We were angry at the fact that the German-born men were even "selected" in the first place. If they were suspect, we thought, then why were they drafted in the first place? We were even more frustrated with the fact that those who had been born in Austro-Hungary could not help that they entered the Army before war was declared against their native country.

It was not until May 15, 1918, just before we headed for France, that Congress passed and the President signed a Naturalization Bill that allowed for the naturalization of practically all aliens in military service, including so-called "enemy aliens" who produced satisfactory evidence of loyalty. Arrangements were thus made to have nearby federal judges hold court in Camp Lee and most of the men who had been transferred to the 155th Depot Brigade as "enemy aliens" were in fact reassigned to the division.

It's a good thing, too, esp. for the 160th Inf. Brig., which had a lot of soldiers who born in the mysterious and ramshackle Austro-Hungarian Empire.

Soonafter, Cronkhite was ordered by the War Department to segregate the seventy-five men of the camp who had proclaimed conscientious objector status because of religious beliefs. Like the "enemy aliens," these men were assigned to 155th Depot Brigade, where they enjoyed a period of relative inactivity pending President Wilson's determination of what constituted non-combatant service. Later in March 1918, in compliance with instructions, they were assigned duty with the sanitary, quartermaster, ordnance, or engineer corps. The most-famous conscientious objector of the war was of course Alvin York of the 325th Infantry, 82nd Division,

---

[55] Stultz, 72.

who earned the Medal of Honor as an infantryman during bloody but decisive Meuse-Argonne Offensive.

-Passes to Petersburg and the Y.M.C.A.-

In November, weekend passes were becoming a regular custom and Petersburg, with a population of around 25,000, and less than half of it being white, was inundated with "Blue Ridge Men." Cronkhite, who held ultimate authority, granted his regimental commanders the ability to distribute passes to Petersburg as they saw fit. Being from Petersburg, I was of course a "V.I.P." to my fellow soldiers who were not and I helped many of them, at least at first, understand where to go and what to avoid. By and large, the townspeople at first were a little uncertain as to the potentialities of the great new camp, but they soon learned they had no cause for alarm. Almost uniformly they were gracious and hospitable. Many threw open their homes for the entertainment of the men and their families. In both Petersburg and Richmond, the officers were extended the privileges of all the clubs and in Richmond a system of week-end visits was arranged for entertainment of groups of the enlisted personnel in private homes. In fact, the 80th Division soon came to be known as "The Petersburg Division" by the locals.

"The Army Club," equipped with a hundred single beds, was soon opened in Petersburg. All Masonic members of the division were guests of the three Masonic Lodges of Petersburg at a mammoth banquet. As I was not a Mason, I was neither interested in nor invited to the revelry. The weekly dances staged at the officers' club at "Lakemont" drew their quota of feminine visitors (another place from which I was barred). All Presbyterians at Camp Lee were tendered a banquet at the Jefferson Hotel in Richmond by the Sixth United Presbyterian Church of Pittsburgh. More than 1,200 soldiers enjoyed a smoker at the Knights of Columbus' Central Hall. Many soldiers from the division were also entertained by the Jewish Welfare Association of Richmond at a dance at the Jefferson Clubhouse. The "Army and Navy Club" was also opened in Richmond, being made possible by public subscription, with accommodations for three hundred men.[56]

We weren't allowed to go just anywhere, however. For example, all Army personnel were forbidden to patronize any restaurant, cafe, soda fountain, or barber shop in Petersburg that failed to display a certificate of approval from the U. S. Public Health Service. Only twenty-three of the one hundred eighteen such places met the health requirements on first inspection. M.Ps were stationed in front of each unsatisfactory establishment to bar soldiers until conditions were

---

[56] Stultz, 46-47.

corrected. Various welfare organizations also provided authorized recreation and education on post. The illiterates found opportunity to learn in the classes formed by the Y.M.C.A., the foreign-born, mostly from the 319th Infantry, profited likewise, as they were taught English. These agencies included also the Knights of Columbus, the Jewish Welfare Board, the American Red Cross, the Fosdick Commission on Training Camp Activities, and others. The Y.M.C.A., with its central auditorium and area huts, was the most widely established and patronized. Nightly entertainments, from song services to boxing matches, were held in each of the "Y" buildings, and on Sunday religious services were conducted in them for Catholics, Christians, and Jews by Army chaplains or by denominational clergymen from nearby cities.

Provided by the Y.M.C.A., "Hostess House" was opened at Camp Lee in November, equipped with a full-service restaurant, lounging room, writing rooms, and other conveniences, and was staffed by women representatives of the organization. With its curtains and chairs, it radiated cheer both to the soldiers and to the numerous visitors who flocked in each weekend. For many it was a retreat from the bare board benches and tables of the barracks. The Knights of Columbus, Jewish Welfare Board, and American Library Association also erected buildings and contributed materially to camp contentment. During the autumn, the Liberty Theater was erected. Its nightly entertainment ranged from motion pictures to professional stage shows by some of the nation's leading theatrical talent, all at a nominal fee.

-Pennsylvania Governor Visits Camp Lee-

In mid-Nov., not to be outdone by the governors of Virginia or West Virginia, the Governor of Pennsylvania, Martin G. Brumbaugh, visited the troops of the 160th Inf. Brig., the 305th Engineers, and the 315th M.G. Battalion. He and his large official party were met at the camp entrance by Maj. Gen. Cronkhite, Brig. Gen. Brett, Col. Cocheu, and Col. Hunt, and was escorted by an ad hoc battalion of brigade troops. He later reviewed the entire brigade on its drill field and addressed the men. At first, I think we liked these visits because it made us feel "important." There was no way in civilian life we would have ever met a state governor—not that most of us wanted to—but it was all part of the "pageantry of the service." After a while, however, we grew to despise these visits. Somebody labeled them "horse and pony shows." We felt that they were there mostly for the visiting officials and not us. Granted, they were in a difficult position. If they didn't visit us to "check" in on us, they'd get political heat from the opposition (the never-ending battle). I know that they knew that we weren't really excited to see them, esp. since we had to do all the work, standing and marching, etc. Nevertheless, it's part of being an American soldier. You will get visited by elected leaders. If they ask you a question (they usually won't because they don't know what to ask), keep it short, because they're really not that interested. If you have a complaint, offer an issue. If you have an issue, give a solution. We Doughs will admit that even though they really don't care that much about a soldier personally, they do care about losing their next election.

-Thanksgiving at Camp Lee-

Shortly before Thanksgiving Day, the War Dept. sent out instructions that 30% of the men would be given leaves to go home for the holiday. Those not included in this percentage were promised to fare well in camp, as the company funds (even more money out of our pockets) of all organizations were called upon to provide a real Thanksgiving meal. For some, a special train carried several hundred football fans to Washington for the gridiron battle between the teams of the 319th Infantry and the U. S. Marine Corps. Heading the Camp Lee adherents were Generals Cronkhite and Brett, Col. Cocheu of the 319th Infantry, and Col. Hunt of the 320th Infantry. The 319th Infantry's band also accompanied the team and played during the game. Although defeated 27-1, the "Camp Lee Eleven" battled savagely. Also at the game were the Secretary of War, the Secretary of the Navy, and the Commandant of the Marine Corps. Since the traditional Army and Navy Game had been suspended because of the war, the 319th Infantry-Marine Corps contest was heralded as its substitute. Other divisional units also sponsored football teams.[57]

For other Thanksgiving Day entertainment, many units formed acting troupes or jazz bands. In our regiment, for example, the 318th Infantry, our energetic and talented adjutant, Capt. Raymond, had been working quietly but efficiently to turn out from the members of the regiment a credible Vaudeville-like show. He had two purposes in mind: entertainment for the members of the regiment and a means of building up a regimental fund with which to purchase instruments for a jazz band (remember, there was no radio back then and phonographs were few and far between) and athletic equipment for the men. On Thanksgiving, he announced that he was prepared to prove to the people of Richmond and Petersburg that Virginians were not only good fighters, but also good actors. The "318th Infantry Minstrels" performed in Richmond on Thanksgiving night to a crowded and most enthusiastic house. It was voted a great success by all and accomplished its objects, proving financially profitable and helping to bring the various elements of the regiment together.

---

[57] Stultz, 78.

-Division Command Group Goes to France-

On Nov. 27, the 80th Division Command Group, led by General Cronkhite, left Camp Lee for New York to hop a troop transport to France in order to conduct a reconnaissance of the battlefront. The command group boarded the ocean liner *Adriatic* at Hoboken, N.J., on Dec. 11, 1917, and sailed next morning for Halifax, Nova Scotia, where it joined a British convoy. The ship's company included Maj. Gen. Leonard Wood (ret.), the former Army Chief of Staff. Only the usual submarine scares marked the voyage, which ended at Liverpool, England, on Christmas Day. When the party entrained for London the following morning, a private car was provided for Generals Wood and Cronkhite. In London, the group called on the American ambassador, Walter Hines Page, and received numerous courtesies from British officers. After a rough channel crossing to Boulogne, France, the group arrived in Paris on Dec. 30.[58]

Once they learned about "the big picture," Wood's and Cronkhite's entourage traveled to the H.Q. of the British 37th Division at Scherpenberg, just southeast of historic *Ypres*, in the dead of winter.[59] There Cronkhite, etc., were met not only by a hospitable welcome, but also by continuous thunder of the big guns across the entire Ypres sector. The commander of the British 37th Division was more than eager to show Cronkhite all that he could. Under his personal guidance, almost every foot of his sector was visited and the Americans came face to face with Ypres, Vimy Ridge, and other bitterly contested battlefields. According Sgt. Stultz of 2/318th Infantry: "Everywhere they found officers and men all smartly turned out even under most adverse conditions; quick to salute, grim and determined, but cheerful."[60] This visit was a precursor to come, as the 80th Division would be matched up with British Divisions in this sector during the summer of 1918.

-Secretary of War Baker Visits Camp Lee-

On Dec. 5, 1917, Newton Diehl Baker, Wilson's able Secretary of War, came to Camp Lee and reviewed the entire division. Baker, a former mayor of Cleveland, was appointed secretary just before war was declared. He had been instrumental in planning and implementing the nation's draft and chose John Pershing to be the commanding general of the A.E.F. Major Sweny's 2/318th Infantry was chosen as Baker's honor guard at Camp Lee. I remember that it was an extremely cold day with a high wind blowing, which made standing around rather trying.

---

[58] *Boulogne* is pronounced "Boo-long."

[59] *Scherpenberg* is pronounced "Sher-pen-berk" and *Ypres* is pronounced "Ee-pra."

[60] As cited in Stultz, 85.

Although the 319th Infantry led the parade, the horseless and gunless artillery and the "Blue Denim Buffalo Soldier Battalion" of the post's S.O.S. and depot brigade. It must be remarked, as a matter of interest, that the papers stated that when Secretary of War Baker reviewed the 80th Division, it "filed by with perfect ranks and with all men fully equipped."[61] That was not an accurate statement, as we were still not yet fully equipped. But then again, newspapers are also read by the enemy and that's exactly what we wanted them to think: that the 80th Division ready to go "Over There" like the 1st, 2nd, 3rd, 26th, and 42nd Divisions. To quote Irving Berlin:

Over there, over there
Send the word, send the word over there
That the Yanks are coming, the Yanks are coming
The drums rum-tumming everywhere
So prepare, say a prayer
Send the word, send the word to beware
We'll be over, we're coming over
And we won't come back till it's over, over there!

-Training in the Cold-

Due to the cold and wet weather, training was carried out with great difficulty from December 1917-March 1918. To better appreciate our struggles, context is needed. One must understand three challenges that confronted us: our own colossal ignorance of all military matters, the lack of ordnance and other material commensurate with our requirements, and the inexperience of our officers. Of the three, the first was the most prominent. We are free to admit, indeed proud to state, that at the time of our induction we knew little, most of us nothing, about military life and the duties of a soldier. We were accustomed to absolute freedom of mind and deed, decidedly unaccustomed to dictatorial treatment at the hands of men who democracy had taught us were no better than ourselves. To turn such independence into obedience and to supplant utter ignorance with knowledge of the exacting requirements of military life, were the tasks confronting our officers. That they succeeded, we will prove once we got "Over There." But we are also content to believe that they never truly succeeded—if they ever planned to—into converting us into that type of perfect soldier prescribed by military regulations, an individual without individuality, a mere mechanism manipulated by simply issuing a command.

---

[61] Stultz, 87.

As for the material with which to train us, it was so woefully inadequate that even the most optimistic quailed in apprehension. Without sufficient rifles, M.G.s, mortars, field guns, tanks, or even gas masks, it seemed impossible that we would learn enough to be able to stand against veteran troops who were dug-in as thick as fleas on a mangy dog. Indeed, it was not until we participated in intensive training with the British in Picardy near or at the front, did we gain a real insight into the nature of our work, though our experiences at Camp Lee gave us the necessary foundation in disciple, drill, and military etiquette.

The inexperience of most of our company-grade officers (captain and below) was a circumstance of tremendous importance and well-beyond their control. The fact that we used to call them "Ninety-Day Wonders" indicates our attitude toward them at the time. It is a temptation to exaggerate their inexperience just as it is a temptation to over-rate many of their accomplishments. It may be said, however, that they were hastily-trained—like we were—and trained in the American Way of War. Clearly, the vast majority of junior officers in the Army were young men fresh from college, or even with unfinished education. Some were less-experienced in the ways of life than many of the men they commanded. In fact, they were men whose enthusiasm and spirit far out-ran their military learning and, at times, their powers of discretion. It is casting no aspersion on their characters or abilities to say so. On the contrary, it is a miracle that they accomplished so much with so little.

-Christmas at Camp Lee-

Before anyone realized it, Christmas was at hand and 30% of the troops were permitted to go home. The balance, esp. those who were not allowed to go home during Thanksgiving, were naturally greatly disappointed in having to remain. Nevertheless, they displayed a splendid spirit of "playing the game," which paid off later on the muddy and bloody fields of France. All except essential duty was suspended on Christmas Day. Every barracks and mess hall was decorated and gifts and food packages from home were distributed. Accumulated company funds were spent lavishly and mess sergeants and cooks determined to surpass all previous achievements. As on Thanksgiving Day, several thousand men were guests in Petersburg or Richmond homes, one Richmond citizen alone entertained some one hundred Doughs. With the Yuletide spirit gripping the entire cantonment, the celebration began on Christmas Eve, when an immense tree was illuminated with thousands of electric lights as men from the 319th Infantry, 314th Artillery, and the 155th Depot Brigade joined in singing carols. A non-denominational church service was held in the Y.M.C.A. Auditorium on Christmas morning and special entertainment was offered the troops at every Y.M.C.A., Knights of Columbus, and Jewish Welfare Center. Featured by a huge tree in Central Park, the citizens of Petersburg welcomed hundreds of the men to their community celebration of Christmas Eve and were presented with candy and cigarettes. At the base hospital, the patients were cheered by the "Godmothers' League of Richmond" with thirty decorated and gift-laden trees and by the "Council of Jewish Women" with their offering of 1,100 bags of candy. Gifts of 13,000 Red Cross packets helped rout homesickness.

The pleasure of this holiday season was considerably dampened for the officers and men of the regiment when we learned that our colonel, Briant Wells, had been ordered to Washington to be a member of the Army General Staff, which was currently led by General Tasker Bliss. Wells's transfer was considered just another of the regiment's many sacrifices in which it was called upon to make for the benefit of the Army. Wells was replaced by Col. Ulysses G. Worrilow, who was born in Rockdale, Pennsylvania, on June 5, 1866. Worrilow enlisted into the Army at Philadelphia on March 12, 1889, and was commissioned an infantry lieutenant from the ranks in 1894. He had seen active service during the Spanish-American War in Cuba, during the Philippine Insurrection with the famous Brig. Gen. Arthur MacArthur, and in Mexico with then-Brig. Gen. "Black Jack" Pershing. When Worrilow was promoted to take command of the 318th Infantry, he was commander of Camp Lee's 155th Depot Brigade, which acted as a feeder organization for the 80th Division and other units of the Army.

-Negro Soldiers at Camp Lee-

On Dec. 27, to assure continued good relations at Camp Lee, General Brett, as acting division and post commander in Cronkhite's absence, issued a G.O. which acquainted the Negro soldiers of Camp Lee, especially those drafted (i.e., forced into service) from the Northern states about Virginia's laws governing the segregation of white and colored persons on street cars and railroads. He pointed out that the law did not permit discrimination against Negroes in accommodations or treatment (as long as they stayed away from "Whites Only" areas), and directed that charges involving discrimination be reported to the soldier's commanding officer. He paid the following tribute to the Negro troops' deportment:

The conduct of the colored soldiers in this camp has been very commendable. Coming into a new life and strange surroundings, they have been, practically without exception, well-treated by the civilian population in this community and by their white fellow-soldiers. They have been prompt to respond to this fair and considerate treatment. A continuance of such relationship will prove a great blessing for the future of the colored people. In order, however, that no friction may arise, it is necessary that colored soldiers, as well as all other men, conform to the laws of the locality in which they are placed.[62]

Under their isolation in a section of the cantonment set aside for them and the severities of the winter weather, there was ample reason for the 7,000 or so Buffalo Soldiers to be discontented. But they rarely complained. Their white officers were quick to praise their discipline and their invariable amiability. Their sense of loyalty frequently shamed less conscientious persons. Most of them were assigned to the Army's S.O.S. and as such, would be among the first American soldiers to serve in France as longshoremen, stevedores, etc.

-French and British Advisors-

Great Britain and France sent to the United States a number of officers and N.C.O.s to assist in the American training program at the end of 1917. All had seen active service (and most had been wounded). The 286 sent by France were distributed among the various divisions as instructors in artillery, automatic rifles (A.R.s), hand and rifle grenades, minor tactics, fortifications, and command and staff duties. The British sent 261 instructors, about 25% of whom were gas and bayonet instructors. The rest were experts in M.G.s or mortars. Accompanying the British officers were some 226 N.C.Os. Of this total, four British and five French officers were assigned to the 80th Division at Camp Lee, together with a number of N.C.O.s. The British instructors were Maj. J. K. Dunlop and Capts. C. K. Wilkie, K. A. J. McClure, and E. K. B. Peck, with bayonet, gas, and mortar instruction their specialities. Composing the French contingent were Capt. Jerome Toujan and Lt. Paul Schloesing of the artillery, Lts. Domezon and Bogrand of the infantry, and Lt. Bosc of the engineers, who were detailed for grenade, A.R., artillery, engineering, and liaison instruction. They were later joined by three additional artillery specialists: Lts. Jacques Bellanger, Jean Sordoillet, and Reille de Soult.[63]

---

[62] As cited in Stultz, 92.

[63] *Ibid*, 68.

With the arrival of these Western Front veterans, renewed energy was injected into the winter training program, which became far-more specialized and mostly in-door. Several schools were organized: bomber (i.e., hand grenade), bayonet, small arms, M.G., A.R., engineer, intelligence; gas defense, signalling, artillery, first aid, sanitation, etc. There were also schools for stable sergeants and teamsters, for mess sergeants, bakers, and cooks, for mechanics, chauffeurs, and horse-shoer, and for saddlers and harness makers. In fact, schools for every thing were everywhere!

On Jan. 5, 1917, another O.T.C. (Officer Training Camp) at Camp Myer was opened and many N.C.O.s were sent as candidates to this school. Once they graduated from the course, which was both academically and physically rigorous, they became newly-minted Army lieutenants (mostly infantry).

As a citizen of Petersburg, I could attest that winters in this locality, while at times cold, were practically free from snow, and that snow, if it fell, never remained on the ground for more than a day or two. It may be said, however, that from about the middle of December 1917 until the end of January 1918, there was at least a foot of ice and snow on the ground. The New Year was heralded in camp by the freezing of nearly all of the water mains, with the thermometer not far from zero.

It was just our luck. The Army ordered it to make our lives even more miserable!

Although it was cold and wet, we still embarked on some road marches during this time period. Road marches are extremely important to build soldiers and units, physically and mentally. According to the *I.D.R.*:

> *623. Marching constitutes the principal occupation of troops in campaign and is one of the heaviest causes of loss. This loss may be materially reduced by proper training and by the proper conduct of the march.*
>
> *624. The training of infantry should consist of systematic physical exercises to develop the general physique and of actual marching to accustom men to the fatigue of bearing arms and equipment. Before mobilization troops should be kept in good physical condition and so practiced as to teach them thoroughly the principles of marching. At the first opportunity after mobilization the men should be hardened to cover long distances without loss.*
>
> *625. With new or untrained troops, the process of hardening the men to this work must be gradual. Immediately after being mustered into the service the physical exercises and marching should be begun. Ten-minute periods of*

vigorous setting-up exercises should be given three times a day to loosen and develop the muscles. One march should be made each day, with full equipment, beginning with a distance of two or three miles and increasing the distance daily as the troops become hardened, until a full day's march under full equipment may be made without exhaustion.

626. A long march should not be made with untrained troops. If a long distance must be covered in a few days, the first march should be short, the length being increased each succeeding day.

627. Special attention should be paid to the fitting of shoes and the care of feet. Shoes should not be too wide or too short. Sores and blisters on the feet should be promptly dressed during halts. At the end of the march feet should be bathed and dressed; the socks and, if practicable, the shoes should be changed.

628. The drinking of water on the march should be avoided. The thirst should be thoroughly quenched before starting on the march and after arrival in camp. On the march the use of water should, in general, be confined to gargling the mouth and throat or to an occasional small drink at most.

629. Except for urgent reasons, marches should not begin before an hour after daylight, but if the distance to be covered necessitates either breaking camp before daylight or making camp after dark, it is better to do the former. Night marching should be avoided when possible.

630. A halt of fifteen minutes should be made after the first half or three-quarters of an hour of marching; thereafter a halt of ten minutes is made in each hour. The number and length of halts may be varied, according to the weather, the condition of the roads, and the equipment carried by the men. When the day's march is long a halt of an hour should be made at noon and the men allowed to eat.

631. The rate of march is regulated by the commander of the leading company of each regiment, or, if the battalions be separated by greater than normal distances, by the commander of the leading company of each battalion. He should maintain a uniform rate, uninfluenced by the movements of troops or mounted men in front of him. The position of companies in the battalion and of battalions in the regiment is ordinarily changed daily so that each in turn leads.

632. The marching efficiency of an organization is judged by the amount of straggling and elongation and the condition of the men at the end of the march.

An officer of each company marches in its rear to prevent undue elongation and straggling. When necessary for a man to fall out on account of sickness, he should be given a permit to do so. This is presented to the surgeon, who will admit him to the ambulance, have him wait for the trains, or follow and rejoin his company at the first halt.

633. Special attention should be paid to the rate of march. It is greater for trained than for untrained troops; for small commands than for large ones; for lightly burdened than for heavily burdened troops. It is greater during cool than during hot weather. With trained troops, in commands of a regiment or less, marching over average roads, the rate should be from 2¾ to three miles per hour. With larger commands carrying full equipment, the rate will be from two to 2½ miles per hour.

634. The marching capacity of trained infantry in small commands is from twenty to twenty-five miles per day. This distance will decrease as the size of the command increases. For a complete division the distance can seldom exceed 12½ miles per day unless the division camps in column.

635. In large commands the marching capacity of troops is greatly reduced by faulty march orders and poor march discipline. The march order should contain such instructions as will enable the troops to take their proper places in column promptly. Delay or confusion in doing so should be investigated. On the other hand, organization commanders should be required to time their movements so that the troops will not be formed sooner than necessary. The halts and starts of the units of a column should be regulated by the watch and be simultaneous. Closing up during a halt, or changing gait to gain or lose distance should be prohibited.

So, throughout the winter of 1917-18, there were very few days when field training was possible, but a full-day of indoor training was followed closely. During this period, the medical officers were especially concerned with keeping fresh air in the sleeping quarters of the men. They were crowded, and to help keep the spread of respiratory diseases down to a minimum, the men were required to sleep alternating head and feet and the windows were cracked open two-inches during the night to ensure proper ventilation. As a guard was always posted in each barrack to ensure that the rules were obeyed, this did in fact occur although most soldiers, especially those close to the windows, protested the cold breezes. Despite our best attempts, however, epidemics of measles and mumps caused the quarantine of several companies, particularly in Farnsworth's 159th Inf. Brig. We attributed it to the fact that most of us were not used to living so close to so many people, unlike the boys from Brett's 160th Inf. Brig., many of whom were from either Pittsburgh or Erie.

It could have been far-worse, but due to the quick action of the division's sanitary corps, we ameliorated our losses. Russell Stoltz's *History of the 80th Division* noted that from Sept. 1 to Jan. 7, a total of 48 deaths were reported at the camp hospital. These represented an annual average death rate of 4.5 per 1,000 troops as against New York's Camp Mills's fourteen per one thousand. A total of 1,805 Blue Ridge Division men were reported sick at this time, with a hospital overflow of 805 cared for by the regimental infirmaries. Of the total, 430 were taken ill from mumps, 193 of measles and 53 of pneumonia.[64]

On Jan. 8, 1918, while we were putting up with the cold, President Wilson introduced his "Fourteen Points for Peace" that were based upon very progressive, liberal principles. The tenor was "peace and honor without victory." He wanted to make this war the "War to End All Wars." While many in the country embraced these principles, others thought that they were Pollyannaish. We soon learned that the Allies thought so, too. But because the Germans would ultimately agree to an armistice or (cease fire) based upon these terms on Nov. 11, 1918, I believe that the reader should be familiar with them and understand the context with which they were introduced. It pretty much called for free trade, open seas, an international tribunal to solve international differences peacefully, the evacuation of occupied territories, returning Alsace and Lorraine to France, and the break-up of the Austro-Hungarian Empire into smaller republics:

> *1. Open covenants of peace, openly arrived at, after which there shall be no private international understandings of any kind but diplomacy shall proceed always frankly and in the public view.*
>
> *2. Absolute freedom of navigation upon the seas, outside territorial waters, alike in peace and in war, except as the seas may be closed in whole or in part by international action for the enforcement of international covenants.*
>
> *3. The removal, of all economic barriers and the establishment of equality of trade conditions among all the nations consenting to the peace and associating themselves for its maintenance.*
>
> *4. Adequate guarantees given and taken that national armaments will be reduced to the lowest point consistent with domestic safety.*
>
> *5. Free, open-minded, and absolutely impartial adjustment of all colonial claims, based upon a strict observance of the principle that in determining all*

---

[64] Stultz, 94.

such questions of sovereignty the interests of the populations concerned must have equal weight with the equitable claims of the government whose title is to be determined.

6. The evacuation of all Russian territory and such a settlement of all questions affecting Russia as will secure the best and freest cooperation of the other nations of the world in obtaining for her an unhampered and unembarrassed opportunity for the independent determination of her own political development and national policy and assure her of a sincere welcome into the society of free nations under institutions of her own choosing; and, more than a welcome, assistance also of every kind that she may need and may herself desire. The treatment accorded Russia by her sister nations in the months to come will be the acid test of their good will, of their comprehension of her needs as distinguished from their own interests, and of their intelligent and unselfish sympathy.

7. Belgium, the whole world will agree, must be evacuated and restored, without any attempt to limit the sovereignty which she enjoys in common with all other free nations. No other single act will serve as this will serve to restore confidence among the nations in the laws which they have themselves set and determined for the government of their relations with one another. Without this healing act the whole structure and validity of international law is forever impaired.

8. All French territory should be freed and the invaded portions restored, and the wrong done to France by Prussia in 1871 in the matter of Alsace-Lorraine, which has unsettled the peace of the world for nearly fifty years, should be righted, in order that peace may once more be made secure in the interest of all.

9. A readjustment of the frontiers of Italy should be effected along clearly recognizable lines of nationality.

10. The people of Austria-Hungary, whose place among the nations we wish to see safeguarded and assured, should be accorded the freest opportunity to autonomous development.

11. Romania, Serbia, and Montenegro should be evacuated; occupied territories restored; Serbia accorded free and secure access to the sea; and the relations of the several Balkan states to one another determined by friendly counsel along historically established lines of allegiance and nationality; and international guarantees of the political and economic independence and territorial integrity of the several Balkan states should be entered into.

12. The Turkish portion of the present Ottoman Empire should be assured a secure sovereignty, but the other nationalities which are now under Turkish rule should be assured an undoubted security of life and an absolutely unmolested opportunity of autonomous development, and the Dardanelles should be permanently opened as a free passage to the ships and commerce of all nations under international guarantees.

13. An independent Polish state should be erected which should include the territories inhabited by indisputably Polish populations, which should be assured a free and secure access to the sea, and whose political and economic independence and territorial integrity should be guaranteed by international covenant.

14. A general association of nations must be formed under specific covenants for the purpose of affording mutual guarantees of political independence and territorial integrity to great and small states alike.

-Cronkhite in France and Former President Taft Visit to Camp Lee-

On Jan. 16, Cronkhite's command group arrived at *Village Roucy*, which is south of *Chemin des Dames* and almost on the Aisne River, where they were assigned to the French 55th Division, commanded by the famous *Général de France Charles Mangin*.[65] Mangin's H.Q. was housed in a *château* set high on a wooded hill, and from its windows field glasses plainly revealed German troops moving inside their lines. Cronkhite and his group remained at *Roucy* for ten days, during which General Mangin devoted most of his valuable time to their questions. Every wish expressed was promptly gratified, including a desire for a trip in an aeroplane. Cronkhite, an artillery officer, especially wished to see French artillery in action. To sate his desire, a small

---

[65] *Village Roucy* is pronounced "Veal-awj Roo-see" and *Chemin des Dames* or "Road of the Women" is pronounced "Lay Shay-mon-day Dam." *Chemin des Dames* acquired its name during the 18th Century when it was the route taken by the two daughters of Louis XV, *Adélaïde* and *Victoire*, who were known as "the Ladies of France." *Aisne* is pronounced "Eye-n" and *Général de France* Charles Mangin is pronounced "Gen-ee-ral day Frawns Char-les Mawn-jawn." Mangin will later be called "The Butcher" (*le Boucher*), right or wrong, by friend and foe alike

patch of woods (or *Bois*) was blown up by a French battery for his benefit. Day trips were also arranged, including one to Rheims, which the Germans bombarded heavily during the visit.[66]

Meanwhile, on Jan 26, thousands of Camp Lee soldiers, augmented by hundreds of civilians, greeted former President William Howard Taft while on a tour of the sixteen National Army camps. In the course of a few hours, he spoke four times. During his chief address at the auditorium, he explained the reasons for our war with the "Imperial German Government, but not its people." At noon, he assisted in the dedication of the new camp library, gift of the American Library Association, which was accepted by General Brett on behalf of the division. Speaking from the steps of the Hostess House later in the afternoon, he received a resounding ovation. His visit was concluded with a stirring address to the Negro troops, who he paid a high tribute to the Buffalo regiments of the Regular Army and challenged the Negro soldiers to emulate the military records of the 24th and 25th Infantry Regiments and the 9th and 10th Cavalry Regiments.

On Jan. 27, 1918, in France, "Cronkhite and Company" left *Roucy* to attend a large M.G. (machine gun) and T.M. (trench mortar) demonstration at a military school near *Fère-en-Tardenois*. There occurred a tragic event. A shell exploded in a British-made Stokes Mortar (Stokes Mortars are 81mm/3-inches), killing two French officers, wounding many soldiers and three American officers, including General Leonard Wood! The inspection group then travelled to *Soissons*, where it was subjected to a violent air raid.[67] Six soldiers were killed in the barracks just opposite General Cronkhite's hotel, while not a window remained in the building.

On Jan. 31, the party arrived at Chaumont, Pershing's H.Q., where Cronkhite was received by General Pershing himself and the mysteries of the the A.E.F.'s H.Q. were explained. Neufchateau, H.Q. of the 26th (Yankee) Division, was visited on Feb. 1, and its commander, Maj. Gen. Clarence R. Edwards, gave the group the benefit of his division's experience in France. Then followed a short stay on Feb. 2 with the soon-to-be-famous American 1st Division (The Big Red One), which was actually holding a sector along the front line. Its H.Q. was at Mesnil-la-Tour, and it was under command of Maj. Gen. Robert Lee Bullard, afterward well-known to the 80th Division as commanding officer of the American III Corps during the Meuse-Argonne. General Cronkhite was especially interested in the American Army schools at Langres and the great French Artillery school at Valdahon.[68]

---

[66] *Rheims* is pronounced "Raams."

[67] *Fère-en-Tardenois* is pronounced "Fair awn Tar-den-wah" and *Soissons* is pronounced "Swa-sons."

[68] Stultz, 85. *Chaumont* is pronounced "Shau-mawn," *Neufchateau* is pronounced "Noof-chaat-oh," *Mesnil-la-Tour* is pronounced "Mez-neel la Tor," *Langres* is pronounced "Long-ruh," and *Valdahon* is pronounced "Val-dawn."

On Feb. 9, "Cronkhite and Company" reached the port city of Bordeaux and was banqueted by the local chapter of the French Chamber of Commerce.[69] The party next boarded the ocean liner *Niagara* and on Feb. 13, 1918, passed through the nets guarding the entrance to the Gironde River. No submarine alarms marred the return voyage and just three weeks after leaving Camp Lee, the group landed at New York, Feb. 25, just in time for "Spring Training at Fort Lee." Cronkhite made a few statements to us, either through G.O. or "The Bayonet," to address our "bearing." For example:

> *We want the 80th Division to be the best division in the Army; it cannot be if it becomes lax and careless in the salute. The British and French services on the Western Front exercise the utmost punctuality in rendering salutes—the guards, the soldiers everywhere…The 80th Division does not want to show up poorly alongside the French and British divisions in the salute or any other military function. The officers must be just as military as the men.*[70]

Commanding officers were also directed to discipline any soldier appearing in improper uniform. The camp's provost marshal (backed by a battalion of M.P.s) was instructed to arrest, in or out of camp, any E.M. not in proper uniform. Names of officers appearing in town without uniform coats and hats were to be sent to the division commander. According to Col. Moss's manual:

> *M.M.T. 1523. Military Deportment and Appearance. The enlisted man is no longer a civilian but a soldier. He is, however, still a citizen of the United States and by becoming a soldier also he is in no way relieved of the responsibilities of a citizen; he has merely assumed in addition thereto the responsibilities of a soldier. For instance, if he should visit an adjoining town and become drunk and disorderly while in uniform, not only could he be arrested and tried by the civil authorities, but he could also be tried by the summary court at his post for conduct to the prejudice of good order and military discipline. Indeed, his uniform is in no way whatsoever a license for him to do anything contrary to law and be protected by the government. Being a soldier, he must conduct himself as such at all times, that he may be looked upon not only by his superior officers as a soldier, but also by the public as a man in every way worthy of the uniform of the American soldier. Whether on or off duty, he should always look*

---

[69] Stultz, 86. *Bordeaux* is pronounced "Bore-dough."

[70] As cited in Stultz, 114.

neat and clean, ever remembering that in bearing and in conversation he should be every inch a soldier—shoes must be clean and polished at all times—no chewing, spitting, gazing about, or raising of hands in ranks—he should know his drill, his orders and his duties—he should always be ready and willing to learn all he can about his profession—he should never debase himself with drink. A soldier's uniform is more than a mere suit of clothes that is worn to hide nakedness and protect the body. The uniform of an army symbolizes its respectability, its honor, its traditions, and its achievements, just as the flag of a nation symbolizes its honor, dignity and history. Always remember this, and remember, too, that the soldier who brings reproach upon his uniform is in the same class as the priest who brings dishonor upon his robes. It is not given to every man to wear the uniform of his country's army—it is an honor and a privilege to do so, and no individual has a right to abuse this honor and privilege by bringing the uniform into disrepute through misbehavior. It should be remembered that the soldiers of a command can make the uniform carry distinction and respect, or they can make it a thing to be derided.

The soldier should take pride in his uniform. A soldier should be soldierly in dress, soldierly in carriage, soldierly in courtesies. A civilian owes it to himself to be neat in dress. A soldier owes it to more than himself—he owes it to his comrades, to his company—he owes it to his country, for just so far as a soldier is slack so far does his company suffer; his shabbiness reflects first upon himself, then upon his company and finally upon the entire Army... The man who misbehaves himself in uniform in public creates a bad impression of the whole command, as a result of which his comrades must suffer. Remember that a man in the uniform of a soldier is conspicuous—much more so than a civilian—and consequently any misconduct on his part is more noticeable than if done in civilian clothes. The man who deliberately besmirches the uniform of his Country's army by appearing in public drunk or by other misconduct, not only fouls his own nest, but he also dishonors the uniform worn by his self-respecting comrades. It is a well known fact that laxity in dress and negligence in military courtesy run hand in hand with laxity and negligence in almost everything else, and that is why we can always look for certain infallible symptoms in the individual dress, carriage and courtesies of soldiers. Should a soldier give care and attention to his dress? Yes; not only should a soldier be always neatly dressed, but he should also be properly dressed—that is, he should be dressed as required by regulations. A soldier should always be neat and trim, precise in dress and carriage and punctilious in salute. Under no circumstances should the blouse or overcoat be worn unbuttoned, or the cap back or on the side of the head. His hair should be kept properly trimmed, his face clean shaven or beard trimmed and his shoes polished, his trousers pressed, the garrison belt accurately fitted to the waist so that it does not sag, his leggins cleaned, his brass letters, numbers and crossed rifles polished, and his white gloves immaculate. Should a man ever be allowed to leave the post on pass if not properly dressed? No—never. The Army Regulations require that chiefs of squads shall see that such members of their squads as have passes leave the post in proper dress. Should a soldier ever stand or walk with his hands in his pockets? No—never. There is nothing more unmilitary than to see a soldier standing or walking with his hands in his pockets. The real soldier always stands erect. He never slouches. Is it permissible, while in uniform, to wear picture buttons, chains, watch charms, etc., exposed to view? No, it is not.

Two rifle squads from 319th Inf. at Camp Lee. They are armed with new M1917 Enfield Magazine Rifles. These are the rifles we took with us to France.

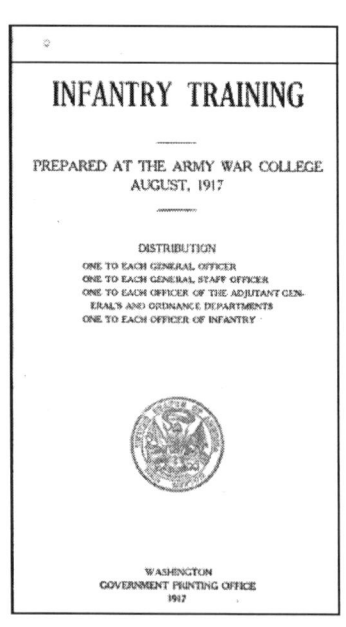

At the Camp Lee Rifle Range with M1917s.

Fire and maneuver at the platoon level at Camp Lee.

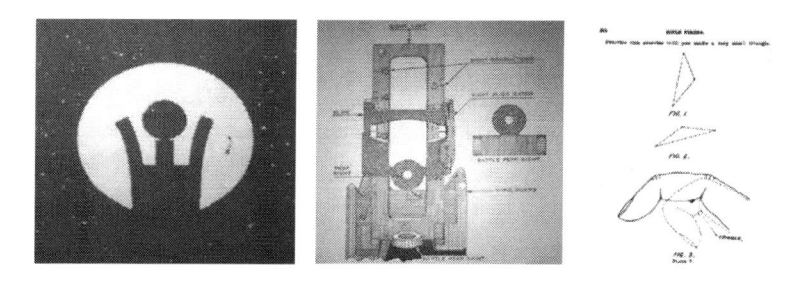

Proper sight picture on an M1917 (L), the rear sight aperature of
an M1917 (C), and the correct trigger squeeze (R).

LOADINGS AND FIRINGS. 91

firmly against the hollow of the right shoulder, right thumb inclined forward and diagonally to the left across the stock, barrel horizontal, left elbow well under the piece, right elbow as high as the shoulder; incline the head slightly forward and a little to the right, cheek against the stock, left eye closed, right eye looking through the notch of the rear sight so as to perceive the top of the front sight and object aimed at, second joint

Pl. 37, Par. 139.   Pl. 38, Par. 139.

Pl. 39, Par. 139.

of forefinger resting lightly against the front of the trigger, but not pressing it.

Each rear rank man aims through the interval to the right of his file leader, and leans slightly forward to advance the muzzle of his piece beyond the front rank.

In aiming kneeling, the left elbow rests on the left knee, point of elbow in front of kneecap.

Kneeling and Lying Down

154. If standing: **KNEEL.**

Half face to the right; carry the right toe about 1 foot to the left rear of the left heel;

kneel on right knee, sitting as nearly as possible on the right heel; left forearm across left thigh; piece remains in position of order arms, right hand grasping it above lower band. (128)

155. If standing or kneeling: **LIE DOWN.**

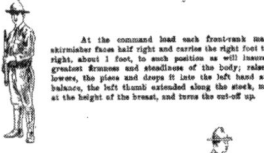

Kneel, but with right knee against left heel;

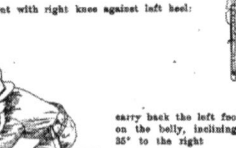

carry back the left foot and lie flat on the belly, inclining body about 35° to the right

piece horizontal, barrel up, muzzle off the ground and pointed to the front; elbows on the ground; left hand at the balance, right hand grasping the small of the stock opposite the neck. This is the position of order arms, lying down. (129)

154 (cont.)

At the command load each front-rank man of skirmisher faces half right and carries the right foot to the right, about 1 foot, to such position as will insure the greatest firmness and steadiness of the body; raises, or lowers, the piece and drops it into the left hand at the balance, the left thumb extended along the stock, muzzle at the height of the breast, and turns the cut-off up.

With the right hand he turns and draws the bolt back,

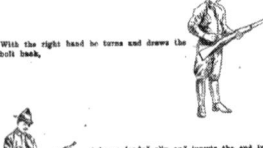

takes a loaded clip and inserts the end in the clip slots, places the thumb on the powder space of the top cartridge, the fingers extending around the piece and tips resting on the magazine floor plate;

forces the cartridges into the magazine by pressing down with the thumb; without removing the clip, thrusts the bolt home, turning down the handle; turns the safety lock to the "safe."

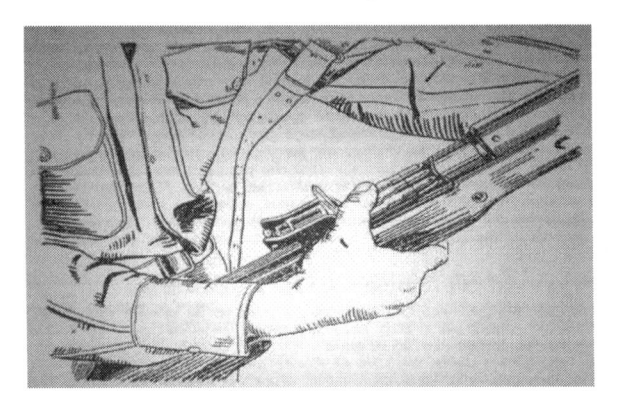

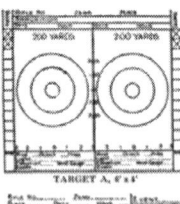

TARGET PRACTICE 269

TARGET A, 4' x 4'

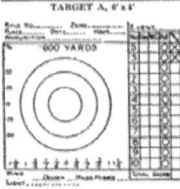

TARGET B, 6' x 6'

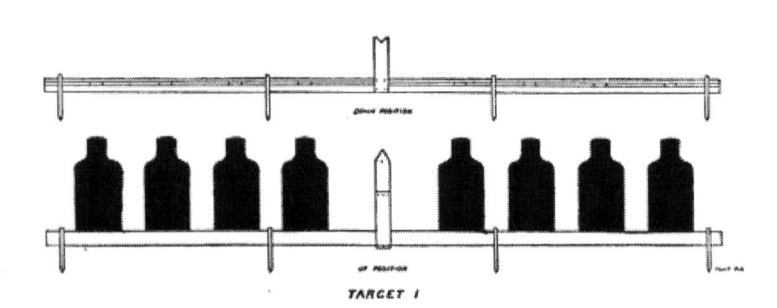

TARGET 1

126

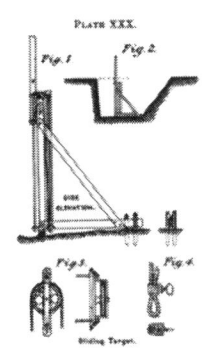

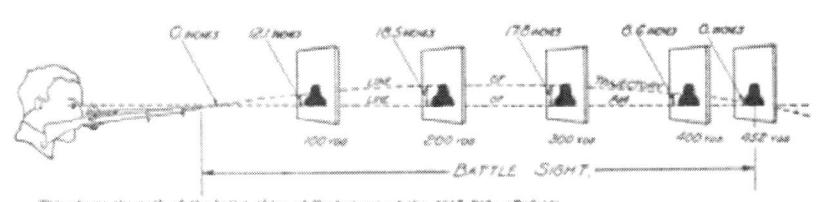

This shows the path of the bullet (Line of Trajectory) of the 1917 Rifle (Enfield).
The Line of Aim, we see, connects the eye, the rear sight, the front sight and the bottom part of the target. It is a straight line.
We see that the Line of Trajectory crosses the Line of Aim at two points. The distance between these points is 452 yards. Therefore, 452 yards is the Battle Sight Range for the 1917 Rifle.

THE BAYONET.

Nomenclature and Description.

11. The bayonet is a cutting and thrusting weapon consisting of three principal parts, viz, the *blade*, *guard*, and *grip*.

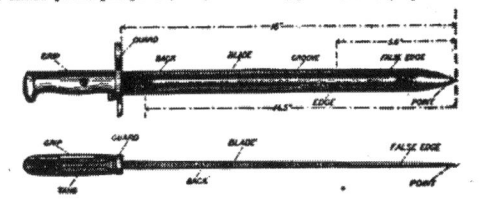

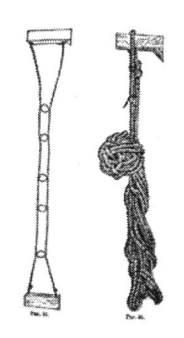

127

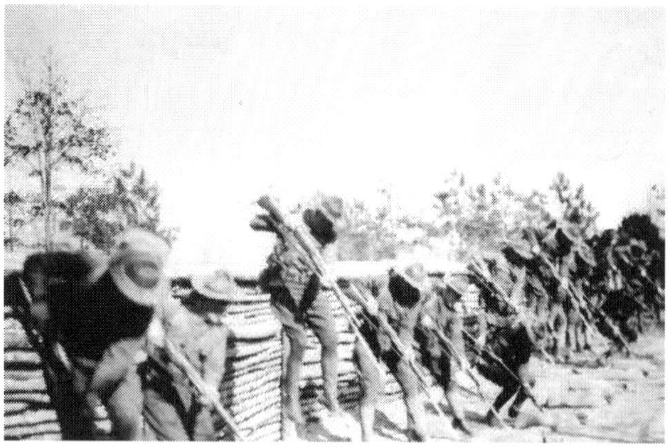

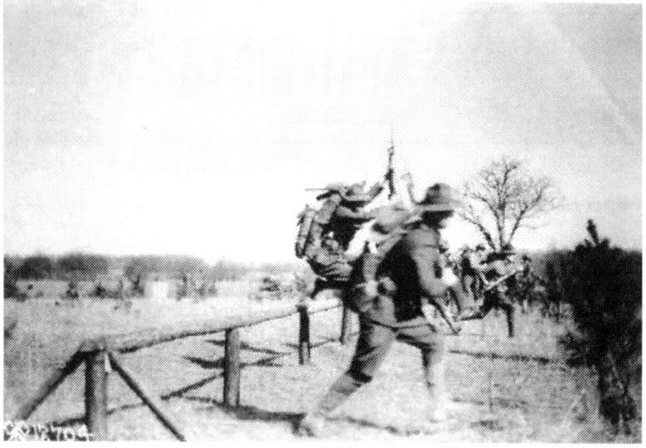

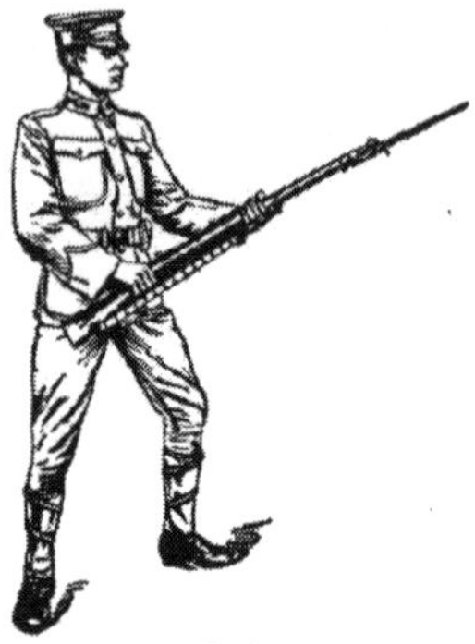

Par. 24.

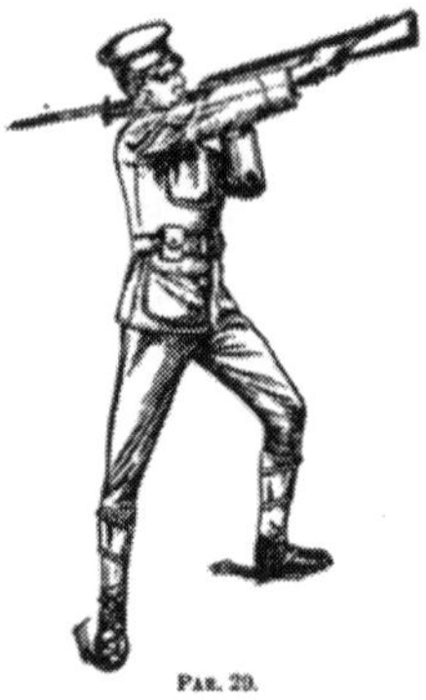

Par. 29.

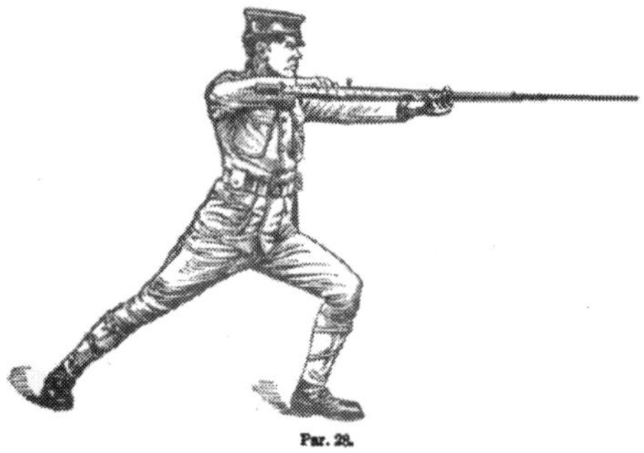

Par. 28.

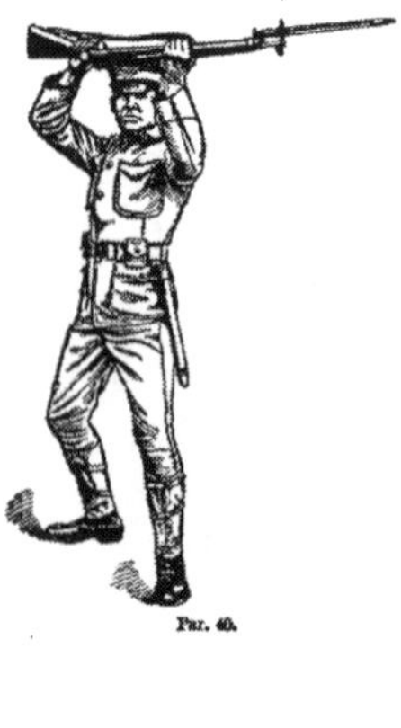

Par. 40.

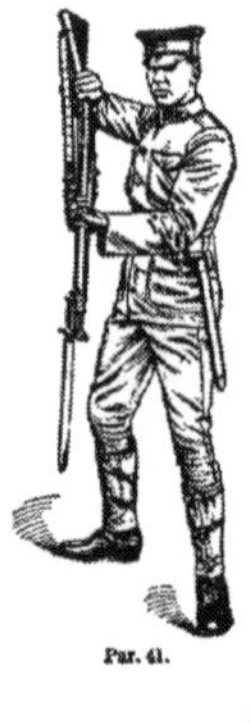

Par. 41.

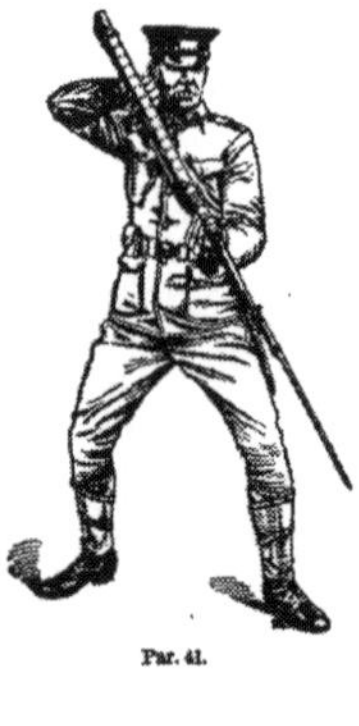

Par. 41.

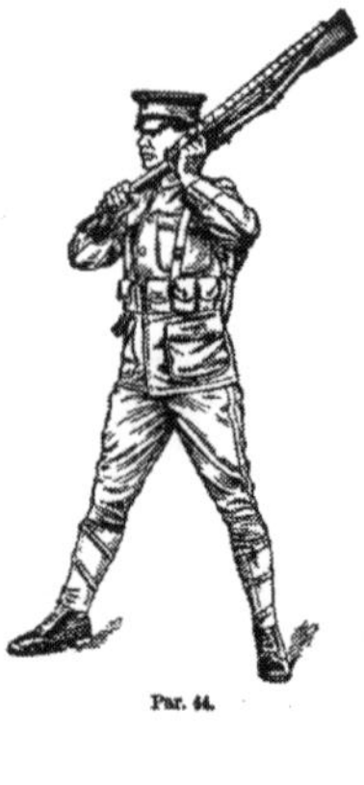

Par. 44.

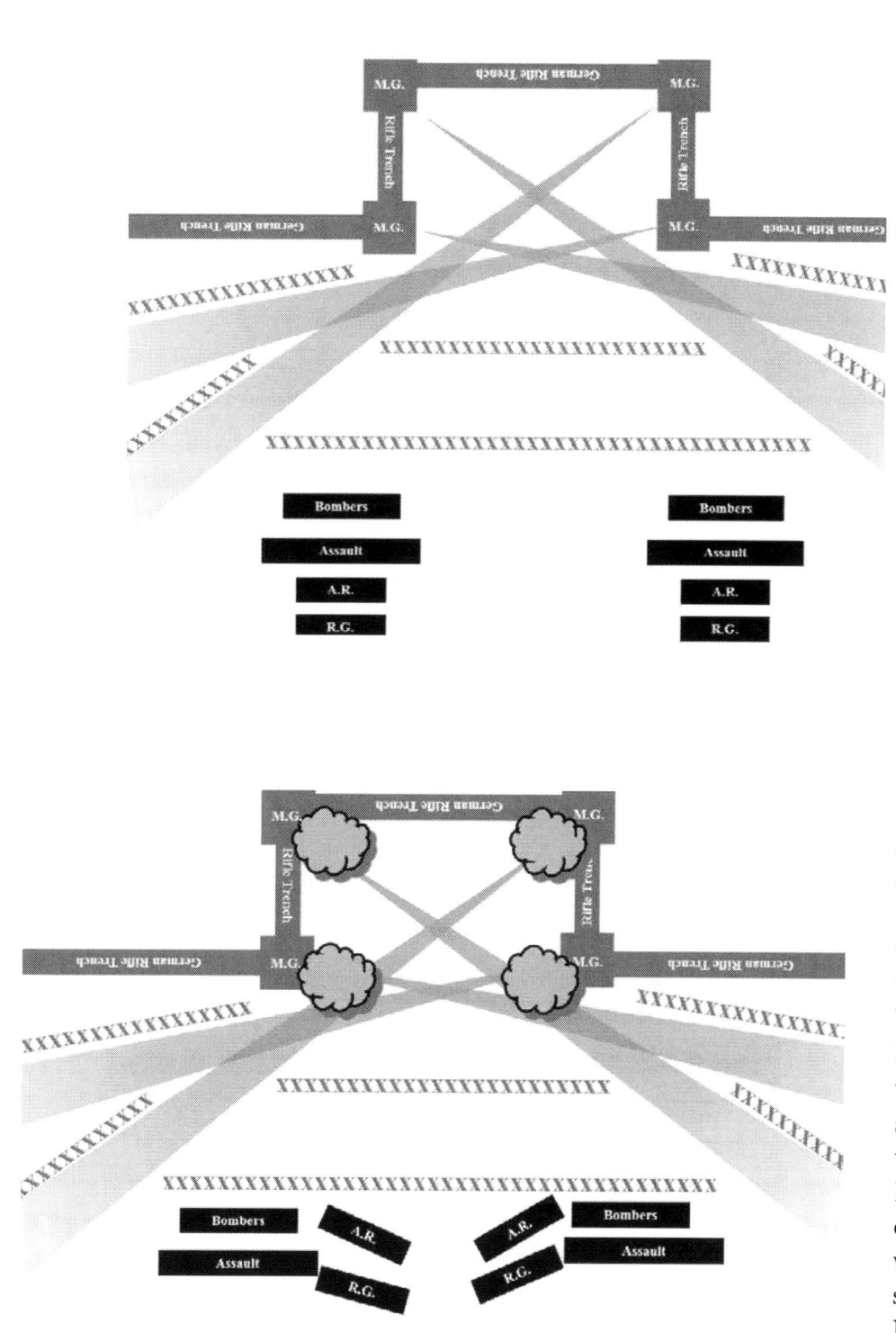

Basic platoon drill to take out German M.G. nests. As the dug-in M.G. nests were protected by interlocking fields of fire, getting shot from the flank or in enfilade was our biggest concern. While the M.G.s fired up a line of barbed wire at an angle, squads of Hun infantry, armed with rifles and hand grenades, would usually fire straight on, protecting the flanks of the M.G.s. On the top, it shows how our infantry companies usually advanced in two platoon columns with squads stacked, one behind the other. On the bottom, as the bombers neared the target and were stopped by well-placed Hun M.G. fire, the A.R.s would maneuver and suppress the M.G.s to their right or left. Behind them would come the R.G.s, who would shoot W.P. smoke grenades at the M.G. nest embrasures.

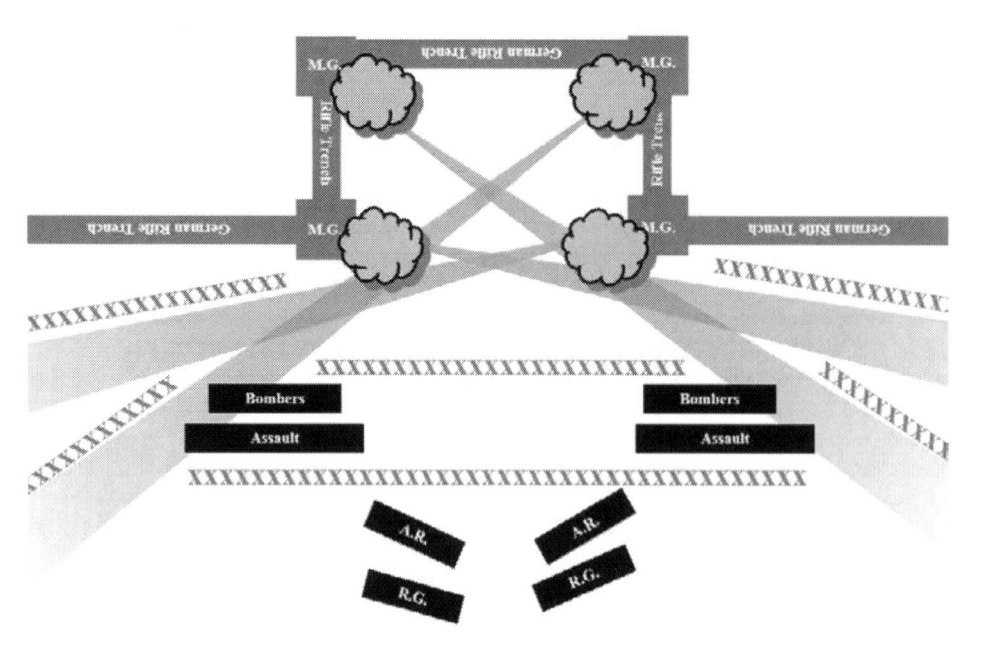

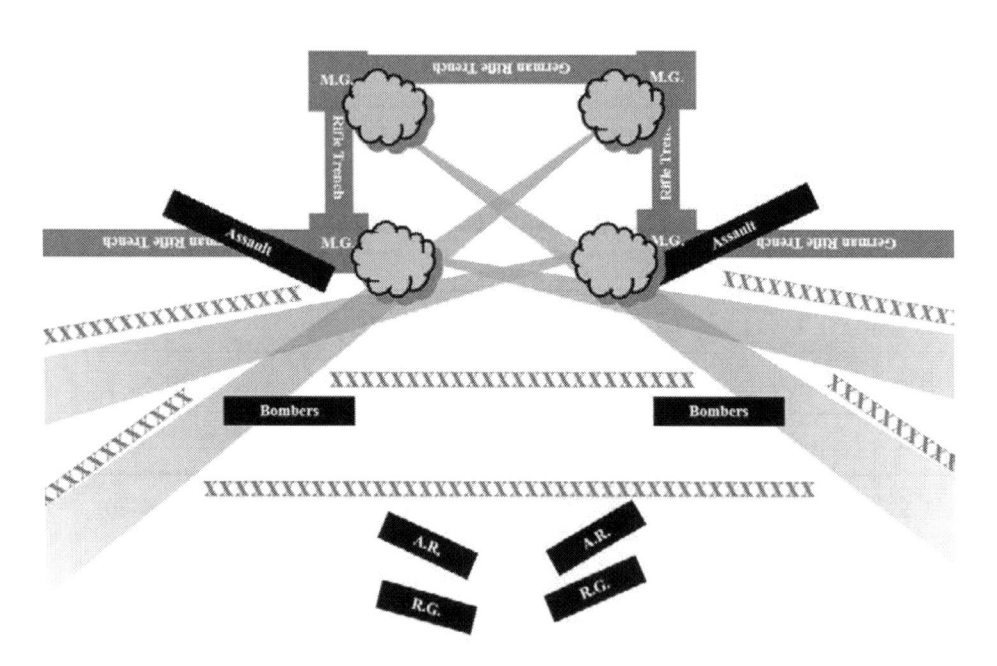

Gaining fire superirority was the key (top). If his platoon was not gaining it, the P.L. would send a patrol back to bring up an M1915 M.G. or an I.G. Once it was determined that the platoon had in fact achieved fire superiority, the P.L. would lead the assault squad through the bombers (bottom) and charge the enemy position, taking the Hun M.G. nest in flank and rear. Once the assault is launched, the P.G. would lead what was left of the bomber, the A.R., and R.G. squads to hold the position. Immediately behind these two platoons were two more platoons from the same company and behind them were four more platoons from another company in the same battalion. The key was to always keep the attack moving forward. The 80th Division Always Moves Forward!"

Chapter 5
Infantry Training at Camp Lee.

According to the *F.S.R.* Para. 123, "The infantry is the principal and most important arm, which is charged with the main work on the field of battle and decides the final issue of combat. The role of the infantry, whether *offensive* or *defensive*, is the role of the entire force, and the utilization of that arm gives the entire battle its character. The success of the infantry is essential to the success of the *combined arms*." As was already stated, the 80th Division consisted of four infantry regiments of three infantry battalions each (twelve total). Each infantry battalion had four infantry companies (forty-eight total per division). The "training bibles" that we used were: *Infantry Training, 1917*, which recommended a multi-week training program, the *Infantry Drill Regulations of 1917*, the *Manual for N.C.O.s and Privates of Infantry of the A.U.S., 1917*, the *Manual for Military Training*, and the *Plattsburg Manual*. According to *Infantry Training, 1917*, the first several weeks of training should consist of the "School of the Soldier," the "School of the Squad," training in orienteering, first aid, military deportment, etc.

We pretty much followed the prescription.

-The Rifle and Bayonet Are The Supreme Weapons of the Infantry Soldier-

On April 9, 1918, from his H.Q. in France, General Pershing sent very specific training guidance to all units in the States that were to join the A.E.F. He stated that "the rifle and the bayonet remain the supreme weapons of the infantry soldier." This pronouncement, although innocuous, was somewhat controversial because according to the French and the British, the rifle and the bayonet were in fact irrelevant on a modern battlefield. In their mind, what now reigned supreme were M.G.s, A.R.s, hand and rifle grenades, mortars, artillery, and tanks. Rifles in fact should be replaced by hand grenades, A.R.s, R.G.s, and automatic pistols. Because Pershing knew that the Allied instructors would say this to us, he published the following training guidance to all A.E.F. divisions:

GENERAL HEADQUARTERS, A.E.F.

April 9, 1918.

The general principles governing the training of troops of the A.E.F. will be announced from these headquarters. Strict compliance with those principles will be exacted and nothing contrary thereto will be taught. Among these principles are the following:

a. The methods to be employed must remain or become distinctly our own.

b. All instructions must contemplate the assumption of a vigorous offensive. This purpose will be emphasized in every phase of training until it becomes a settled habit of thought.

c. The general principles governing combat remain unchanged in their essence. This war has developed special features which involve special phases of training, but the fundamental ideas enunciated in our drill regulations, small arms firing manual, field service regulations, and other service manuals remain the guide for both officers and soldiers and constitute the standard by which their efficiency is to be measured, except as modified in detail by instructions from these headquarters.

d. The rifle and bayonet are the principle weapons of the Infantry soldier. He will be trained to a high degree of skill as a marksman both on the target range and in field firing. An aggressive spirit must be developed until the soldier feels himself, as a bayonet fighter, invincible in battle.

e. All officers and soldiers should realize that at no time in our history has discipline been so important; therefore, discipline of the highest order must be exacted at all times. The standards of the American army will be those of West Point. The rigid attention, upright bearing, attention to detail, uncomplaining obedience to instructions required of the cadet will; be required of every officer and soldier of our armies in France. Failure to attain such discipline will be treated as lack of purpose and willing acceptance of hardships which are necessary to success in battle…

Pershing also stressed the importance of training for "open warfare." Everyone knew that the first phases of combat for the A.E.F. would be in siege warfare—waiting for us to build up strength and then conducting a breach. But one day, the A.E.F. and the Allies were going to actually exploit the breach and conduct what is called a pursuit (or "open warfare"). During this phase, the armies would eventually fight a grand battle of annihilation in the open, winning the war. As Army doctrine stated: "Decisive results are obtained only by the *offensive*. Aggressiveness wins battles."[71] In conducting said offensive operations, however, an army needs to be especially adept at "open" or "maneuver warfare" down to the platoon level, especially given the enhanced killing power of modern weapons, limited visibility, etc. Besides, Pershing noticed, the principles of trench warfare were being taught quickly and well to all of the A.E.F. divisions serving with French or British troops in France or Flanders. As offensive operations are always more difficult to perform and its skills are easily transferable for use in defensive operations, Pershing made it a point for us to get as much offensive or "open warfare" training as possible before we shipped out.

And I'm glad he did.

The British and especially the French advisors who were sent to Camp Lee did not agree with Pershing's prescription, however, as they instead wanted us to train day and night at the trench range practicing trench raids, etc. Their attitude was that we would have to learn how to fight in a siege environment first, then breach, then "open warfare." The problem with this is that once we did in fact conduct the much sought-after breach, there would be no time to train us on open warfare tactics unless we were specifically kept in the rear, training on such tasks, which Cronkhite and all of the old Regulars all knew would not happen. The advisors did yield to Pershing's concerns, however, and helped us wherever they could. Maj. Gen. James G. Harbord, who would serve in the A.E.F. as an infantry brigade and a division commander as well as the commander of the all-important S.O.S. remembered:

> *While [Americans] had traveled far from the old days when with his long-barreled muzzle-loading rifle the hunter "creased" his buffalo or shot the eye out of a squirrel, the tradition of marksmanship still lingered in America, and pioneer history had not yet lost its influence, even in a population where the old stock had been diluted by unrestricted immigration. The authentic story of an Allied soldier with a rifle strapped on his back, chasing an enemy to get close enough to throw a hand grenade would never have been true of any American. Nor were Americans willing to sit down in trenches and*

---

[71] *F.S.R.*, 122.

permanently exchange "dirty looks" with an enemy in another trench but a few yards away... There is no doubt that the firm insistence of General Pershing on training for open warfare had a certain gradual influence on French methods. It quickened the French spirit when the tide turned, supported by their confidence in the energetic intentness of the Americans. In January, 1918, they revised their instruction book to bring back the rifle to its rightful prestige. The emphasis on trench training began to diminish somewhat as our men began to be proficient in that and in the additional training in minor tactics on which we insisted. The difference in methods of training gradually lost first place in correspondence and official conversations. It is fair to say that with the British it had never seemed to be quite the fetish it was with our French comrades.[72]

When we entered combat in France, the primacy of the infantry indeed proved itself, but only in close cooperation with the artillery and the engineers. Although the infantry is the critical or "primary element" of offensive or defensive operations, without artillery or engineer support, it will be ground into a bloody pulp. The basic principles that we trained under were listed under a section called "Combat" in the *F.S.R., I.D.R.*, etc.:

F.S.R. 122. Combat is divided into two general classes, the offensive and the defensive. The defensive is divided into the purely passive defense and the temporary (active) defense, which has for its object the assumption of the offensive at the first favorable opportunity. Decisive results are obtained only by the offensive. Aggressiveness wins battles. The purely passive defense is adopted only when the mission can be fully accomplished by this method of warfare. In all other cases, if a force is obliged by uncontrollable circumstances to adopt the defensive, it must be considered as a temporary expedient, and a change and a change to the offensive with all or part of the forces will be made as soon as conditions warrant such changes.

I.D.R. 351. Modern combat demands the highest order of training, discipline, leadership, and morale on the part of the infantry. Complicated maneuvers are impracticable; efficient leadership and a determination to win by simple and direct methods must be depended upon for success.

---

[72] As cited in Harbord, 185.

I.D.R. 352. The duties of infantry are many and difficult. All infantry must be fit to cope with all conditions that may arise. Modern war requires but one kind of infantry—good infantry.

I.D.R. 353. The infantry must take the offensive to gain decisive results. Both sides are therefore likely to attempt it, though not necessarily at the same time or in the same part of a long battle line. In the local combats which make up the general battle the better endurance, use of ground, fire efficiency, discipline, and training will win. It is the duty of the Infantry to win the local successes which enable the commanding general to win the battle.

I.D.R. 354. The infantry must have the tenacity to hold every advantage gained, the individual and collective discipline and skill needed to master the enemy's fire, the determination to close with the enemy in attack, and to meet him with the bayonet in defense. Infantry must be trained to bear the heaviest burdens and losses, both of combat and march. Good infantry can defeat an enemy greatly superior in numbers, but lacking in training, discipline, leadership, and morale.

I.D.R. 355. It is impossible to establish fixed forms or to give general instructions that will cover all cases. Officers and N.C.O.s must be so trained that they can apply suitable means and methods to each case as it arises. Study and practice are necessary to acquire proper facility in this respect. Theoretical instruction can not replace practical instruction; the former supplies correct ideas and gives to practical work an interest, purpose, and definiteness not otherwise obtainable.

Repeatedly our trainers stressed to us the importance of gaining and maintaining *fire superiority*. This means that we needed to "flood" the enemy with overpowering munitions much like how a water hose would drive away a tribe of ants or put out a fire.

F.S.R. 122. The following principles apply to both offensive and defensive combat:

a. Fire superiority insures success.

b. Unity of command is essential to success. The regiment united in combat has greater force and fighting power than have three separate battalions. A battalion acting as a unit is stronger than are four companies acting independently. All the troops assigned to the execution of a distinct tactical task must be placed under one command.

c. The task assigned any unit must not involve a complicated maneuver. Simple and direct plans and methods are productive of the best results in warfare.

d. All the troops that are necessary to execute a definite task must be assigned to it from the beginning. Avoid putting troops into action in driblets.

e. Detachments during combat are justifiable only when the execution of the tasks assigned them contributes directly to success in the main battle or when they keep a force of the enemy larger than themselves out of the main battle. When combat is imminent all troops must be called to the probable field of battle. A force is never so strong that it can needlessly dispense with the support of any of its parts during combat. Too many troops must not, however, be committed to the action in the early stages, no matter what be the nature of the deployment or the extent of the line held. Some reserves must be kept in hand.

f. Use the reserve only when needed or when a favorable opportunity for its use presents itself. Keep some reserve as long as practicable, but every man than can be used to advantage must participate in the decisive stage of the combat.

g. Flanks must be protected either by reserves, fortifications, or the terrain. Flank protection is the duty of the commanders of all flank units down to the lowest, whether specifically enjoined in orders or not. This applies to units on both sides of gaps that may exist in the combat lines.

h. Reconnaissance continues throughout the action.

The Attack.

F.S.R. 163. In combat, where the force involved is as large as or larger than a division, a simultaneous effective advance against the entire hostile front is out of the question. Modern battles are made up of a number of local combats, where success or failure in any instance may decide the issue of the entire battle. Fronts occupied by field armies [i.e., corps] are but seldom continuous, even in comparatively flat and open country. Some parts of the line will be held much more strongly than others, and the natural defensive features of portions of the front may render part of the line naturally impregnable. It is necessary, therefore, to select the enemy's position limited sections, against which the decisive attacks will be made but to insure success, the attention of the enemy must be held along his entire front. The attack thus develops into two parts: one whose task it is to actually assault the hostile position at selected points, if assault be necessary to drive the enemy out; the other whose task it is to threaten or to actually attack all other parts of the enemy's line, in order to hold the hostile troops in their position and to prevent the strengthening of the points to be assaulted.

F.S.R. 164. As fire superiority is the first and most important requisite to success, it must be obtained at the start and maintained throughout the action. Fire superiority depends mainly upon the volume of the fire. A frontal attack alone against the hostile position may give no opportunity to obtain a greater volume of fire than that of the enemy, unless the latter's lines be unduly extended. Where that condition exists, a combination of a frontal with a flank attack promises the best results. The enemy is attacked in front by part of the force, while the remainder is directed against one of his flanks with a view to enveloping it. A successful envelopment of both flanks of the enemy, simultaneously with the frontal attack, is made possible only by a decided numerical superiority on the part of the attack. An attempt to envelop or to attack both hostile flanks, without an attack in front, entails a dispersion of force so rarely justifiable as to deserve no consideration.

F.S.R. 165. In armies and [corps], only the direct attack is practicable as a whole. But in the local combats of the smaller units into which the entire action is divided envelopment is usually practicable.

F.S.R. 166. The terms "frontal" and "enveloping" attacks have no significance so far as the ultimate relative positions of the contending forces are concerned. Unless the enemy blunders or is decidedly numerically inferior, the enveloping attack finally becomes a frontal attack, so far as the brigade and smaller units involved are concerned. It must be expected, therefore, that all attacks, no matter how initiated, will ultimately be made in a direction normal to the position of the troops opposing them.

F.S.R. 167. Preconcerted plans covering all phases of an attack are objectionable, since it is impossible to determine, until the development of the action makes it manifest, what part or parts of the enemy's line will prove the most attractive for the assault. Both frontal and enveloping attacks will be equally energetic at first, and when the time comes for the decisive attack, the part of the attacking line designated for that purpose is given, by means of the supports or reserves, the added momentum and strength that may be found necessary to a successful assault, while the remainder of the force holds the enemy in its front to his positions.

As has been already stated, most of our officers, especially in the company grades, were products of O.T.C. at Fort Myer. While there, they often utilized the *Plattsburg Manual* (*P.M.*) to not only better understand the requisite skills themselves, but to also better train the recruits during their basic training at Camp Lee. Many E.M., myself included, would often borrow the *P.M.* to better understand said concepts. When our squad leaders, platoon leaders, or company commanders instructed us on the tenants of "the attack," they drew heavily from this particular section of the *P.M.*:

The Theory of Attack.

Decisive results are obtained only by the offensive. Aggressiveness wins battles. If you want to thrash a man go after him—don't wait for him to come to you. When attacking, use every available man. Have every man in the proper place at the proper time and in a physical and moral condition to do his utmost.

Advantages of the Attack.

1. You can elect the point of the attack while the defender must be prepared to resist at all points.

2. The fact that you are advancing in spite of the defender's fire stimulates you and depresses the enemy.

3. You leave your dead behind while the defender must fight among his fallen comrades, which is demoralizing.

4. You usually are conscious of the fact that you have more men on your side than the defender. You have more rifles on the line than the enemy.

5. Your fire is usually more efficacious than that of your opponent because it is usually converging while his is diverging. These advantages alone will not necessarily insure success, but fire superiority, if gained and maintained, does insure success. By gaining and maintain fire superiority you remove all doubt as to the final outcome of the attack.

The Attack.

The European War has demonstrated more clearly than ever before 2 points in attack and defense. First, no people, or group of people, can claim a monopoly on bravery. They all move forward and give up their lives with the same utter abandon. Courage being equal, the advantage goes to him in the attack who possesses superior leaders, greater training, and better equipment. Second, a man's training and courage, his clear eye and steady nerve, his soul's blood and iron, constitute a better defense than steel and concrete. A soldier has little business attacking or defending anything in this day unless he is an athlete, unless he is skilled in the technique of maneuver, unless he is a good shot, unless he knows the value of many features of the terrain (which means the nature of the country—its hills, rivers, mountains, depressions, etc.—considered from a military point of view), unless he is disciplined to a splendid degree, and unless his training has imbued him with an irresistible desire to push forward, to get at his opponent. Assuming, at least, as much as this, we are prepared to consider the subject of the attack (the offensive).

To have your troops superior in number, condition, training, equipment, and morale to that of your enemy; to be at the right place, at the right time, and there to deliver a smashing, terrific blow—this is the greatest principle of the attack. And history shows that victory goes more often to him who attacks.

Initiative in war is no less valuable than in business life. Become at once imbued with the desire to put "the other fellow" defensive. That makes him somewhat dependent upon your own actions. That gives you opportunities to fool him that he does not so fully enjoy. Your commander can elect to attack any point of the defensive line. Your dead and wounded—always a demoralizing element—are left behind. Your target is stationary. Your side is closing in. The enemy is straining every nerve to fire faster and more effectively, and still your side is closing in. There is the thrill of motion.

To attack, you will usually require a greater number of troops than the defense. Why so? Because you will be more exposed. You will have to move forward, however dangerous the ground. Your enemy, for his protection, will be certain to utilize and improve every advantage of cover. Your losses will be greater. You should have a greater number of reserves to fill the depleted ranks. If the defense can maintain a better (superior) fire, that is to say, a fire that kills and wounds a greater number than the opposing fire (we call this fire superiority), he will stop the advance of the attacking force unless that force is so superior in numbers that it can send forward reinforcements after reinforcements as an ocean sends shoreward its series of waves.

Suppose that you were in command of a group of men and that you were ordered to attack. Just what principle points should you weigh? First, you should avail yourself of every opportunity to obtain all information of military value, such as the enemy's strength, his position, and intentions. For this you would have to send out groups of reconnoitering patrols exceptionally skilled in woodcraft, or trained to gather information. As soon as such information as is available is reported to you, you should at once begin the consideration of all the important elements that affect your problem. You must not lose sight of what you were sent out to do (your mission). Consider how this and that fact bear upon your course of action (estimate of the situation). For instance: the enemy's force is reported to be greatly inferior to your own. He is out of supplies. He is greatly fatigued with forced marches. His morale is shattered on account of recent and frequent reverses. His camp is disorganized. It is poorly guarded. Certain roads are in fine condition. Others are very poor. Your troops are in splendid shape and excellent spirits. They believe that they can crush the enemy and want to attack. As you easily see, all such points have great significance in sizing up the case (estimating the situation).

Having estimated the situation, you should investigate and consider all possible courses of attack that are open to you. Don't ask any advice from any one. Select the course that appears to offer the greatest chance of success. Make up your mind what you are going to do (come to a decision).

Having come to a decision, stick to it, right or wrong. Your next and final thing to do is to put your decision into action. To do that, give your subordinates the information they should possess; tell them what you are going to do and how you are going to do it; i.e., issue your orders.

A study of the orders of successful generals in history teaches us that we will be greatly aided in issuing them, if we will observe a system. We understand an order more easily and quickly if it conforms to some plan with which we are familiar.

In order to give your group an opportunity to act with a greater degree of teamwork, and intelligence in case of an emergency, it is necessary to give it data (information) concerning the enemy. Your men should know where there are friendly troops. Now tell them what you are going to do (your plan), whether it be to attack, retire, or assume the defensive. And then order the execution of that plan by assigning to each group its task. Next tell (direct) what is to be done with the wagons (trains), and last, state where you may be found at any time in case of need or where messages may be sent to you.

Having issued the order, let us now observe the progress of the attack. You are probably 1,760 to 3,520 yards (one to two miles) from the enemy. His position is invisible. His artillery has opened fire. Your artillery is replying. The troops must advance within a short distance of the enemy's line as possible, for their ammunition is limited; and after troops are actually launched in the attack, control over them, for ordinary purposes, is practically lost. The farther from the enemy the attack is launched, the longer the exposure of their fire and the greater the number of casualties, so the leaders of the different groups are taking advantage of all the accidents of the ground, of all cover in advancing. They are using one formation here, another there, with a view to minimizing the losses and reaching an advantageous position as soon as possible where they can open an effective fire on the enemy.

Now the enemy's fire is severe. Casualties are becoming heavy. The men are growing restless. It is necessary to return the fire. Fire superiority should be gained at once. Don't move forward until you gain it. If difficult to gain, use every means at your disposal. When you have it, keep it. Part of your men can advance when your side has fire superiority. The remainder of the firing line should fire faster to maintain that superiority. If you lose fire superiority, regain it. If necessary, troops from the rear will generally be sent forward.

Now you are approaching the point where the charge is to be made. Bayonets are fixed; not all at one time, for that would affect the advantage that you possess with your fire. Groups that have been held back in support are advanced. These are to be used at decisive moments. They are held well in hand. The firing line is lost in noise and confusion. Not so the supports; control is exercised over them. If they are not used in the attack they can be used to great advantage to complete the discomfort of the enemy after the clash (shock).

There is at last, if the enemy remains in his position, the clash. Bayonet against bayonet, man against man, nerve against nerve. Apply the great principle of attack and decide for yourself who the victor will be. If successful, then organize your men and prepare for the pursuit of for the return (counter-attack) of the enemy. [73]

In my opinion, the key point of this part of the *P.M.* is that "*Fire superiority should be gained at once. Don't move forward until you gain it. If difficult to gain, use every means at your disposal. When you have it, keep it. Part of your men can advance when your side has fire superiority. The remainder of the firing line should fire faster to maintain that superiority. If you lose fire superiority, regain it. If necessary, troops from the rear will generally be sent forward.*" These were our guiding principles while in combat and they paid off in spades when actually implemented.

In order to gain *fire superiority*, we had to synchronize our indigenous rifles, bayonets, hand grenades, rifle grenades, and automatic rifles with the supporting or combined arms. This sounds easy on paper, but in practice, under stress one can not really fathom, it is extremely difficult. If you are to accomplish the mission with the fewest casualties, *fire superiority* must be gained and kept, like water from a hose, one way or another. You'll note that the regulations allow for flexibility and call for lower echelons to improvise, plan, and problem-solve. Note the sentence: "Having estimated the situation, you should investigate and consider all possible courses of attack that are open to you." According to the *F.S.R.*:

131. Fire superiority must be obtained in the early stages of combat and maintained to the end. Without it, success can be expected either on the defensive or the defensive. It affords the best protection that can be given

---

[73] *P.M.*, 143-49.

troops advancing to the attack, as also the best means of diminishing losses. The artillery must cooperate with the Infantry in obtaining and maintaining fire superiority. Deficiency in the volume of fire on the defensive should be offset by the selection of a position naturally strong, or that can be made strong, in the time available for that purpose.

-Weapon-Specific Squads-

To help achieve *fire superiority* at the lowest level, and with Pershing's blessing, the Army decided to organize each sixty-man Infantry platoon into four weapons-specific squads: bombers, assault, automatic rifle (A.R.)., and rifle grenadiers (R.G.). The bomber squad consisted of one corporal and eleven privates and they carried as many hand grenades or "Mill's Bombs" on their person as possible. Because they often led the attack, they also carried wire cutters or other breeching devices. The assault squad, which usually travelled behind the bombers in combat formation, consisted of one corporal and sisteen privates who were the most fit and the most adept with the bayonet in the platoon The A.R. squad consisted of one corporal, four A.R.-men, four assistant gunners (A.G.), and eight ammo bearers (total of seventeen). It's primary job was to lay down suppressive fire for the bomber and assault squads. The R.G. squad, which usually came up the rear, consisted of one corporal, three R.G.ers (men armed with M1917 Rifles with "R.G. Dischargers" or *Tromblons* attached), and three ammunition bearers (total of eight). The remaining six men of the platoon consisted of the platoon leader (a lieutenant) and platoon guide (a sergeant) and members from the signal and sanitary corps. I was assigned to be A.R.-man #1 in 3/2/B/1/318th Infantry (3rd Squad, 2nd Platoon, B Company, 1st Battalion, 318th U.S. Infantry Regiment, 159th Infantry Brigade, 80th Division, A.E.F.).

With the help of our British advisors, but mostly by utilizing our own Army Regulations and leaning on the service experience of the "old hands," our extended order infantry drill consisted primarily of advancing with the bomber squad, followed by the assault, A.R., and R.G. squads. When contact was reached, the bombers would move forward as best they could, using their wire cutters to full effect. The assault squad would trail behind them while the platoon leader ordered the A.R. and R.G. squads to establish a base of fire either to the left or right of the bomber and assault squads, and gain fire supremacy against the designated target (e.g., an enemy M.G. nest). The platoon leader would then maneuver the bomber squad to within twenty-five yards of the target, where they'd hurl as many hand grenades as possible.

"Boom!"

"Boom!"

"Boom!"

After that, the assault squad would come up to the bombers, and led by the platoon leader, would charge through the bombers with a shout and sweep through the objective with rifle, bayonet, and automatic pistol. The bombers would then follow, followed by the A.R.s and R.G.s. We were also trained to utilize as many "supporting weapons" as possible to in order to gain *fire superiority*, e.g., M.G.s, French-made 37mm direct-fire Infantry Guns (I.G.s), British-made 81mm Stokes Mortars, French-made 75mm cannon, etc. If we didn't get reinforced with supporting weapons, then we would, at Pershing's insistence, move forward "alone and unafraid" on our own. And that's why Pershing emphasized basic rifle marksmanship and bayonet training.

He knew.

The British and French advisors, after attacking for four years—1914-1915-1916-1917—had, of course, pretty much lost their *élan* or attack spirit. They'd attack, but unless supporting weapons gained *fire superiority*, they would not launch the final charge, as they had already suffered far too many casualties at the hands of well-entrenched Huns who were armed to the teeth. To attack a fortified position, which is what they had been doing since 1915, is the most deadly and complicated of all military maneuvers. But because of our newness to the war, Pershing hoped to leverage our native (or naïve?) *élan* to better support our combat associates. Pershing wrote:

The most important question that confronted us in the preparation of our forces of citizen soldiery for efficient service was training. Except for the Spanish-American War, nearly twenty years before, actual combat experience of the Regular Army had been limited to the independent action of minor commands in the Philippines and to two expeditions into Mexico, each with forces smaller than a modern American division. The World War involved the handling of masses where even a division was relatively a small unit. It was one thing to call one or two million men to the colors, and quite another thing to transform them into an organized, instructed army capable of meeting and holding its own in the battle against the best trained force in Europe with three years of actual war experience to its credit...The British methods of teaching trench warfare appealed to me very strongly. They taught their men to be aggressive and undertook to perfect them in hand-to-hand fighting with bayonet, grenade and dagger. A certain amount of this kind of training was necessary to prepare the troops for trench warfare. Moreover it served to stimulate their morale by giving them confidence in their own personal prowess. Through the kindness of Sir Douglas Haig, we were fortunate early in our experience to have assigned to us Lieutenant General R. H. K. Butler and other officers of the British Army in addition to French officers to assist in this individual training. Later, several French and British officers also came to lecture at a number of our schools. We found difficulty, however, in using these Allied instructors, in that the French and, to a large extent, the British, had practically settled down to the conviction that developments since 1914 had changed the principles of warfare. Both held that new conditions imposed by trench fighting had rendered previous conceptions of training more or less obsolete and that preparation for open warfare was no longer necessary. French publications and manuals were generally in accord with this theory. It was, perhaps, logical to expect that the French should take this view as, nationally, unlike the Germans, they had been on the defensive, at least in thought, during the previous half century. It is true that on occasions the French assumed the offensive, but the defensive idea was ever in mind. In the situation that followed the first battle of the Marne, the great armies on the Western Front were entrenched against each other and neither had been able to make more than local gains. The long period during which this condition had prevailed, with its resultant psychological effect, together with the natural leaning of the French toward the defensive, to which should be added the adverse effect of their recent spring experience, had apparently combined to obscure the principles of open warfare. If the French doctrine had prevailed our instruction would have been limited to a brief period of training for trench fighting. A new army brought up entirely on such principles would have been seriously handicapped without the protection of the trenches. It would probably have lacked the aggressiveness to break through the enemy's lines and the knowledge of how to carry on thereafter. It was my opinion that the victory could not be won by the costly process of attrition, but it must be won by driving the enemy out into the open and engaging him in a war of movement. Instruction in this kind of warfare was based upon individual and group initiative, resourcefulness and tactical judgment, which were also of great advantage in trench warfare. Therefore, we took decided issue with the Allies and, without neglecting thorough preparation for trench fighting, undertook to train mainly for open combat, with the object from the start of vigorously forcing the offensive...Intimately connected with the question of training for open warfare was the matter of rifle practice. The earliest of my cablegrams on this subject was in August [1917], in which it was urged that thorough instruction in rifle practice should be carried on at home because of the difficulty of giving it in France...The armies on the Western Front in the recent battles that I had witnessed had all but given up the use of the rifle. Machine guns, grenades, Stokes mortars, and one-pounders had become the main reliance of the average Allied soldier. These were all valuable weapons for specific purposes but they could not replace the combination of an efficient soldier and his rifle. Numerous instances were reported in the Allied armies of men chasing an individual enemy throwing grenades at him instead of using the rifle. Such was the effect of association that continuous effort was necessary to counteract this tendency among our own officers and men and inspire them with confidence in the efficacy of rifle fire. Ultimately, we had the satisfaction of hearing the French admit that we were right, both in emphasizing training for open warfare and insisting upon proficiency in the use of the rifle.[74]

It was therefore Pershing's and the Army's desire that each American infantryman became a little mobile killing machine with his rifle, bayonet, and hand grenades. As stated above, Pershing stressed rifle marksmanship, especially while we were stationed in the States. His recommendations were carried out to the letter in the 80th Division, and we acquired unusually-high proficiency with the rifle. In the March 1918 issue of "The Bayonet" Cronkhite said:

We will follow out exactly the ideas of General Pershing that the men should be made soldiers on this side...The infantryman's weapon is the rifle. It isn't of much account unless the infantryman knows how to shoot. That instruction he must get here. Our rifle range at Camp Lee is probably the finest to be found

---

[74] Pershing, 1:150-53.

anywhere in the world. It is conservative to say that the combined areas of all ranges available to the British Army on the Western Front would not compare in area with the Camp Lee range alone. While we have this advantage, certainly we should avail ourselves of it. [75]

-The M1917 Enfield Rifle-

With this training guidance in hand, especially with the onset of warmer spring weather, lots of time was spent at the shooting range with our new rifles, which were top-of-the-line "U.S. Rifle, Cal. .30, M1917s," also known as "M1917s" or "Enfields." Granted, the division had forty-eight infantry companies and the rifle range only had enough room to accomodate two companies at a time, but somehow we were able to spend a lot of time on the range. As such, the principal part of our remaining training time at Camp Lee was devoted to rifle marksmanship or bayonet training with our newly-issued M1917 Enfield Rifles. The M1917 Rifle shot a .30-06 caliber bullet and held five rounds in its internal magazine. It weighed about nine pounds, which wasn't that bad, but after you figure in everything else and marching for twenty miles, it did get a little heavy. It also had a moose of a bayonet that was over a foot long.

The "United States Rifle, cal .30, Model of 1917" or the "American Enfield" has an interesting story. As it entered World War I, the British Empire had an urgent need for rifles, and contracts for its service rifle were placed with arms manufacturers in the United States (so much for being "neutral"). The Brits directed these companies to produce the rifle in the .303 caliber for convenience of supply. The new rifle was named the "Pattern 14" and the Winchester and Remington gun companies were selected as licensees. A third manufacturer, Eddystone Arsenal, a subsidiary of Remington, was also retooled at the Baldwin Locomotive Works in Eddystone, Pennsylvania (along the Delaware River between Chester and Philadelphia). Thus, three variations of the P14 and M1917 exist, labeled "Winchester," "Remington," or "Eddystone."

When the U.S. entered the war in April 1917, it had a similar need for rifles. The Springfield Armory in Massachusetts had delivered approximately 843,000 M1903 Springfield Rifles, but due to the difficulties in production, rather than re-tool the P14 factories to produce the standard M1903 Springfield, it was decided that it would be much

---

[75] As cited in Stultz, 121.

easier to adapt the British design for the American .30-06 cartridge, for which it was well-suited. Accordingly, Remington Arms Company altered the design for cal. .30-06, under the close supervision of the U.S. Army Ordnance Department, which was formally adopted as the "U.S. Rifle, Cal. .30, Model of 1917." In addition to Remington's factories at Ilion, New York, and Eddystone, Pennsylvania, Winchester produced the rifle at its New Haven, Connecticut plant, a combined total more than twice the M1903s production. Eddystone made an unbelievable 1,181,908 Enfield Rifles, more than the production of Remington (545,541 rifles) and Winchester (465,980 rifles) combined.

Design changes were few but significant. The magazine, bolt face, chamber, and rifling dimensions were altered to fire the .30-06 cartridge and the volley fire sights on the left side of the weapon were removed. The markings were changed to reflect the model and caliber change. A 16.5-inch blade bayonet, the M1917 Bayonet, was produced for use on both the M1903 Springfield and M1917 Enfield. By November 11, 1918, Armistice Day, about 75% of the A.E.F. in France was armed with M1917 Enfield Rifles.

-The Rifle Range-

Exceptional shooting facilities were provided at Camp Lee, which were constructed several miles northwest of our cantonment area by the 305th Engineers, near the concrete road that connected the camp with Hopewell. Equipped with 470 targets, it was one of the best ranges in the Army. Four sets of targets, ranging from 100 to 1,000 yards, provided facilities for two Infantry companies or Artillery batteries at the same time. Battery A/1/314th Artillery was reportedly the first unit to fire at the range.[76] As per the *Small Arms Firing Manual, 1917*, we practiced at 100, 200, 300, 500, and 600 yards with "elective firing" at 800 and 1,000 yards. While some units trained to hit the longer shots, Sgt. Brown said that we needed to focus more on the close ones—to learn to fire quickly and accurately—clank that bolt, reload, and toss another one down range. We were instructed to fire according to the following tactical principles:

---

[76] *314th Artillery*, 47.

Ranges.

I.D.R. 238. For convenience of reference ranges are classified as follows:
    0 to 600 yards, close range.
    600 to 1,200 yards, effective range.
    1,200 to 2,000 yards, long range.
    2,000 yards and over, distant range.

I.D.R. 239. The distance to the target must be determined as accurately as possible and the sights set accordingly. Aside from training and morale, this is the most important single factor in securing effective fire at the longer ranges.

I.D.R. 240. Except in a deliberately prepared defensive position, the most accurate and only practicable method of determining the range will generally be to take the mean of several estimates.

The Range.

I.D.R. 411. Beyond close range, the correct setting of the rear sight is of primary importance, provided the troops are trained and well in hand. The necessity for correct sight setting increases rapidly with the range. Its importance decreases as the quality of the troops decrease, for the error in sight setting, except possibly at very long ranges, becomes unimportant when compared with the error in holding and aiming.

I.D.R. 412. In attack, distance must usually be estimated and corrections made as errors are observed. Mechanical range finders and ranging volleys are practicable at times. In defense, it is generally practicable to measure more accurately the distances to visible objects and to keep a record of them for future use.

Fire.

I.D.R. 232. Ordinarily pieces are loaded and extra ammunition is issued before the company deploys for combat. In close order the company executes the firings at the command of the captain, who posts himself in rear of the center of the company. Usually the firings in close order consist of saluting volleys only.

I.D.R. 233. When the company is deployed, the men execute the firings at the command of their platoon leaders; the latter give such commands as are necessary to carry out the captain's directions, and, from time to time, add such further commands as are necessary to continue, correct, and control the fire ordered.

Discipline.

I.D.R. 416. Discipline makes good direction and control possible and is the distinguishing mark of trained troops.

I.D.R. 417. The discipline necessary in the firing line will be absent unless officers and N.C.O.s can make their will known to the men. In the company, therefore, communication must be made by simple signals which, in the roar of musketry, will attract the attention and convey the correct meaning.

Expenditure of Ammunition.

I.D.R. 418. In attack the supply is more limited than in defense. Better judgment must be exercised in expenditure. Ordinarily, troops in the firing line of an attack can not expect to have that day more ammunition than they carry into the combat, except such additions as come from the distribution of ammunition of dead and wounded and the surplus brought by reinforcements.

I.D.R. 419. When a certain fire effect is required, the necessary ammunition must be expended without hesitation. Several hours of firing may be necessary to gain fire superiority. True economy can be practiced only by closing on the enemy before first opening fire and thereafter suspending fire when there is nothing to shoot at.

The keys to shooting a bolt-action rifle are pretty easy. All you have to do is align the rear sight with the front, let out your breath, and squeeze the trigger. If you "pull" or jerk the trigger, the rifle will shoot to the right and the farther the target is, the more pronounced your mistake will be. After that, you pull up on the bolt lever, unlock the bolt, and pull it back, opening the chamber. This movement ejects the spent casing and brings up a new cartridge. Then simply reverse the movement and you'll be reloaded. Our trainers taught us to reload the rifle while it was still on our right shoulder so we'd stay as much on the target as possible. We were trained to shoot from the prone, kneeling, and standing positions. In combat, we shot from all three positions. Standing, of course, is the most difficult position to hit a target, especially under duress. I mostly liked shooting at the 200 yard target as I seemed to be able to hit that one every single time. I don't know why—I just did. According to the *Manual for Noncommissioned Officers And Privates of Infantry of the Army of the United States 1917 to* be used by Engineer Companies (Dismounted) and Coast Artillery Companies for Infantry Instruction and Training (I.N.C.O.M), the course in small-arms firing consists of:[77]

(a) Nomenclature and care of rifle.

(b) Sighting drills.

(c) Position and aiming drills.

(d) Deflection and elevation correction drills.

(e) Gallery practice.

(f) Estimating distance drill.

(g) Individual known-distance firing, instruction practice.

(h) Individual known-distance firing, record practice.

(i) Long-distance practice.

Preliminary Training in Markmanship.

Effective rifle fire is generally what counts most in battle. To have effective rifle fire, the men on the firing line must be able to hit what they are ordered to shoot at. There is no man who can not be taught how to shoot. It is not necessary or even desirable to begin instruction by firing on a rifle range. A perfectly green recruit who has never fired a rifle may be made into a good shot by a little instruction and some preliminary drills and exercises. Before a man goes on the range to fire it is absolutely necessary that he should know—

1. How to set the rear sight.

2. How to sight or aim.

3. How to squeeze the trigger.

4. How to hold the rifle in all positions. If he does not know these things it is worse than useless for him to fire. He will not improve; the more he shoots the worse he will shoot, and it will become more difficult to teach him.

Coordination.

Good marksmanship consists in learning thoroughly the details of holding the rifle in the various positions.

Aiming.

Squeezing the trigger.

---

[77] *Manual for Noncommissioned Officers and Privates of Infantry of the Army of the United States 1917 to be used by Engineer Companies (Dismounted) and Coast Artillery Companies for Infantry Instruction and Training* (Washington, D.C.: Government Printing Office, 1917), 187-99. Hereafter cited as "*I.N.C.O.M.*"

Calling the shot.

Adjusting the sights.

And, when these have been mastered in detail, then the coordination of them in the act of firing. This coordination consists in putting absolutely all of one's will power into an effort to hold the rifle steadily, especially in getting it to steady down when the aim is perfected; in getting the trigger squeezed off easily at the instant the rifle is steadiest and the aim perfected; in calling the shot at this instant; and, if the shot does not hit near the point called, then in adjusting the sights the correct amount so that the rifle will be sighted to hit where you aim.

Advice to Riflemen.

Before going to the range clean the rifle carefully, removing every trace of oil from the bore. This can best be done with a rag saturated with gasoline. Put a light coat of oil on the bolt and cams. Blacken the front and rear sights with smoke from a burning candle or camphor or with liquid sight black.

Look through the bore and see that there is no obstruction in it.

Keep the rifle off the ground; the stock may absorb dampness, the sights may be injured, or the muzzle filled with dirt.

Watch your hold carefully and be sure to know where the line of sight is at discharge. It is only in this way that the habit of calling shots, which is essential to good shooting, can be acquired.

Study the conditions, adjust the sling, and set the sight before going to the firing point.

Look at the sight adjustment before each shot and see that it has not changed.

If sure of your hold and if the hit is not as called, determine and make full correction in elevation and windage to put the next shot in the bull's-eye. Keep a written record of the weather conditions and the corresponding elevation and windage for each day's firing.

Less elevation will generally be required on hot days; on wet days; in a bright sunlight; with a 6 o'clock wind; or with a cold barrel.

More elevation will generally be required on cold days; on very dry days; with a 12 o'clock wind; with a hot barrel; in a dull or cloudy light.

The upper band should not be tight enough to bind the barrel.

Do not put a cartridge into the chamber until ready to fire.

Do not place cartridges in the sun. They will get hot and shoot high. Do not rub the eyes—especially the sighting eye.

In cold weather warm the trigger hand before shooting. After shooting, clean the rifle carefully and then oil it to prevent rust.

Have a strong, clean cloth that will not tear and jam, properly cut to size, for use in cleaning.

Always clean the rifle from the breech, using a brass cleaning rod when available. An injury to the rifling at the muzzle causes the piece to shoot very irregularly.

Regular physical exercise, taken systematically, will cause a marked improvement in shooting.

Frequent practice of the "Position and aiming drills" is of the greatest help in preparing for shooting on the range.

Rapid firing: Success is rapid firing depends upon catching a quick and accurate aim, holding the piece firmly and evenly, and in squeezing the trigger without a jerk. In order to give as much time as possible for aiming accurately, the soldier must practice taking position, loading with the clip, and working the bolt, so that no time will be lost in these operations.

With constant practice all these movements may be made quickly and without false motions. When the bolt handle is raised, it must be done with enough force to start the shell from the chamber; and when the bolt is pulled back, it must be with sufficient force to throw the empty shell well away from the chamber and far enough to engage the next cartridge.

In loading, use force enough to load each cartridge with one motion. The aim must be caught quickly, and, once caught, must be held and the trigger squeezed steadily.

Rapid firing, as far as holding, aim, and squeezing the trigger are concerned, should be done with all the precision of slow fire. The gain in time should be in getting ready to fire, loading, and working the bolt.

Firing with rests: In order that the shooting may be uniform the piece should always be rested at the same point.

-Bayonet Training-

To augment rifle and physical training and to assist in developing and maintaining our offensive spirit, we infantrymen (especially) practiced bayonet drill. The foundation for bayonet training was found in the *Manual of the Bayonet,* which is in *Appendix C* of the *I.D.R.* and the March 1917 War College publication "Notes on Bayonet Training: Compiled from Foreign Reports." The manual described bayonet training as a progressive program, beginning with stances, then the practice of movements, and capping off with a bayonet assault course. Although training received by the men focused heavily on the use of the bayonet as a weapon, when compared to artillery, M.G.s, and rifles, it actually played a relatively minor role in France. The primary purpose of bayonet training was not to make the men experts of the bayonet, but to in fact *increase physical fitness and cultivate aggression with its use.*

The 305th Engineers constructed the bayonet range at Camp Lee during the fall and winter, with trenches and obstacles of various kinds. The bayonet range was near the trench training area. On the bayonet range, we would practice on dummies that were made of bound up rope or cloth sacks filled with straw. We also practiced on "rope rings" (to increase dexterity and accuracy). In short, most of us felt that bayonet training was a wonderfully efficient means of toughening mind, body, and soul for combat as it helped inculcate the fighting spirit that lies more or less dormant in every man. According to the *Manual of the Bayonet*:

> *1. The infantry soldier relies mainly on fire action to disable the enemy, but he should know that personal combat is often necessary to obtain success. Therefore, he must be instructed in the use of the rifle and bayonet in hand-to-hand encounters.*
>
> *2. The object of this instruction is to teach the soldier how to make effective use of the rifle and bayonet in personal combat; to make him quick and proficient in handling his rifle—to give him an accurate eye and a steady hand; and to give him confidence in the bayonet in offense and defense. When skill in these exercises has been acquired, the rifle will still remain a most formidable weapon at close quarters should the bayonet be lost or disabled.*
>
> *3. Efficiency of organizations in bayonet fighting will be judged by the skill shown by individuals in personal combat. For this purpose pairs or groups of opponents, selected at random from among recruits and trained soldiers,*

should engage in assaults, using the fencing equipment provided for the purpose.

4. Officers and specially selected and thoroughly instructed noncommissioned officers will act as instructors.

5. Instruction in bayonet combat should begin as soon as the soldier is familiar with the handling of his rifle and will progress, as far as practicable, in the order followed in the text.

6. Instruction is ordinarily given on even ground; but practice should also be had on uneven ground, especially in the attack and defense of intrenchments.

We were taught all of the positions in the *Manual of the Bayonet*, including those in a series, which was the entire purpose of the training: to kill an enemy soldier with your bayonet with three moves of less.

46. The purpose of combined movements is to develop more vigorous attacks and more effective defenses than are obtained by the single movements; to develop skill in passing from attack to defense and the reverse. Every movement to the front should be accompanied by an attack, which is increased in effectiveness by the forward movement of the body. Every movement to the rear should ordinarily be accompanied by a parry and should always be followed by an attack. Movements to the right or left may be accompanied by attacks or defenses.

47. Not more than three movements will be used in any combination. The instructor should first indicate the number of movements that are to be combined as two movements or three movements. The execution is determined by one command of execution, and the position of guard is taken upon the completion of the last movement only. Examples:

Front pass and LUNGE.
Right step and THRUST.
Left step and low parry RIGHT.
Rear pass, parry left and LUNGE.
Lunge and cut RIGHT.
Parry right and parry HIGH.
Butt strike and cut DOWN.
Thrust and parry HIGH.
Parry high and LUNGE.
Advance, thrust and cut RIGHT.
Right step, parry left and cut DOWN.

48. Attacks against dummies will be practiced. The approach will be made against the dummies both in quick time and double time.

Practical Bayonet Combat.

49. The principles of practical bayonet combat should be taught as far as possible during the progress of instruction in bayonet exercises.

50. The soldier must be continually impressed with the extreme importance of the offensive due to its moral effect. Should an attack fail, it should be followed immediately by another attack before the opponent has an opportunity to assume the offensive. Keep the opponent on the defensive. If, due to circumstances, it is necessary to take the defensive, constantly watch for an opportunity to assume the offensive and take immediate advantage of it.

51. Observe the ground with a view to obtaining the best footing. Time for this will generally be too limited to permit more than a single hasty glance.

52. In personal combat watch the opponent's eyes if they can be plainly seen, and do not fix the eyes on his weapon nor upon the point of your attack. If his eyes can not be plainly seen, as in night attacks, watch the movements of his weapon and of his body.

53. Keep the body well covered and deliver attacks vigorously. The point of the bayonet should always be kept as nearly as possible in the line of attack. The less the rifle is moved upward, downward, to the right, or to the left, the better prepared the soldier is for attack or defense.

54. Constantly watch for a chance to attack the opponent's left hand. His position of guard will not differ materially from that described in Paragraph 24. If his bayonet is without a cutting edge, he will be at a great disadvantage.

55. The butt is used for close and sudden attacks. It is particularly useful in riot duty. From the position of port arms a sentry can strike a severe blow with the butt of the rifle.

56. Against a man on foot, armed with a sword, be careful that the muzzle of the rifle is not grasped. All the swordsman's energies will be directed toward getting past the bayonet. Attack him with short, stabbing thrusts, and keep him beyond striking distance of his weapon.

57. The adversary may attempt a greater extension in the thrust and lunge by quitting the grasp of his piece with the left hand and advancing the right as far as possible. When this is done, a sharp parry may cause him to lose control of his rifle, leaving him exposed to a counter attack, which should follow promptly.

58. Against odds a small number of men can fight to best advantage by grouping themselves so as to prevent their being attacked from behind.

59. In fighting a mounted man armed with a saber every effort must be made to get on his near or left side, because here his reach is much shorter and his parries much weaker. If not possible to disable such an enemy, attack his horse and then renew the attack on the horseman.

60. In receiving night attacks, the assailant's movements can be best observed from the kneeling or prone position, as his approach generally brings him against the skyline. When he arrives within attacking distance, rise quickly and lunge well forward at the middle of his body.

Back in the fall, when we started learning the basics of bayonet work with our old Krags, the trainer, often on a wooden platform so all could see, would teach us the various bayonet positions like "guard," "thrust," "parry," "lunge," etc. After a few days of that, and with our muscles getting a good work out, we went into a series of moves such as "parry," "head butt," "slash" and "thrust." They mostly taught us how to hook an opponent's rifle with our bayonet at a high parry and then to head butt and slash them. Once the opponent was down, we were taught to thrust the bayonet into his belly (and not his ribs). In general, the separate moves were: guard, thrust, lunge, butt-strike, cut-down, cut-right (or left), parry (right or left), low parry (right or left), to the (left or right) rear parry, club rifle, and swing. The "Combined Movements" or series was our final test.

As we improved, we were taught how to engage an enemy coming from the rear. To so so, one must turn his head to his right shoulder, grasp his rifle at mid-point and then thrust as he turned about. After that, we were taught how to fight in pairs, which was the preferred method. While the first man hooked and parried the opponent with his bayonet, the second was taught to land *le coup de grâce* into the enemy's guts.[78] When this phase was completed, we went through the obstacle course with our rifles and bayonets, jumping over lows walls, climbing over higher ones, jumping ditches, and sticking straw dummies with names like

---

[78] *Le coup de grâce or* "The final blow" is pronounced "Lay coo day graw."

"Hun," "Kaiser," "Wilhelm," "Heinie," or "Kraut."[79] It was an absolute work out—probably the best we ever had.

-Extended Order Drill-

In the Army, there is what is called "extended order drill" and "closed order drill." Closed order drill consists of marching in close order at "Squads, Right!" etc. It is mostly used during the Schools of the Soldier and of the Squad phases. Schools of the Company and Battalion, however, generally consist of extended order drill. Extended order drill reflected how we were supposed to communicate, move, and fight in combat. As such, it was the most important type of training we conducted in order to prepare for combat in France.

As was already stated, "Black Jack" insisted that American Doughs *"attack in irregular formations with scouts preceding the assaulting waves and with a high degree of individual initiative with primary reliance upon the infantry's own firepower to enable it to get forward."* The reason why he emphasized this was to counteract the French advisors who were telling us that our infantry advances should only be covered by massive pre-planned rolling artillery barrages. As we followed the rolling barrages (i.e., blasting a line and moving it forward), all we really needed, they said, were hand grenades and satchel charges (canvas bags stuffed with blocks of T.N.T.). Rifles, in their view, were basically useless on the Western Front. When we were actually thrown into combat in France, however, we discovered that both positions were in fact correct. Nothing beat a motivated infantryman armed with a rifle and bayonet. But he could not advance alone without supporting arms, either.

At Camp Lee, as per Pershing's guidance, we were trained in "open warfare" tactics. The vision was that we'd have to know not only how to survive in the trenches but to also, once the A.E.F. built up enough strength, to conduct breaching operations against the strong German lines, which would then "get us out into the open." Cronkhite's training guidance on this issue is as follows:

> *In trench warfare, nothing is left to chance. Before an advance, even before a small raid, everything, down to the finest detail, is rehearsed time and again...each officer and man is given his part... For example, in preparing the men for a night attack, or other night work, they will first be rehearsed in the*

---

[79] Kaiser Wilhelm II was the King of Prussia and Emperor of Germany during the war until he stepped down in Nov. 1918. We usually called him "Kaiser Bill." Other German monarchs of the German Empire were the Kings of Bavaria, Saxony, and Württemburg. The rest were arch dukes, dukes, or counts.

daylight. Later, they will themselves work under conditions of darkness, while the officers, with the aid of daylight, may closely observe them... The officers and men will live in the trenches, but not for long periods. I can see no advantage in making men unnecessarily uncomfortable. If it rains...and if the mud runs a foot or two deep, they'll stick and like it. But they won't be kept there a week at a time... This will be, however, only one of the forms of instruction, for, pursuant to General Pershing's requirements, orders have been issued to devote by far the greater part of our time to the methods of open warfare... When the men get out in the field, making their own quarters and shifting for themselves under actual field conditions, I feel confident they will enjoy every minute of the experience.[80]

Cronkhite also issued a long training bulletin that limited close-order drill to just one hour a day, trench warfare instruction to just one day a week (explained in a later chapter), and made target practice and open warfare extended order training the main training objectives. The bulletin specified:

Instruction in maneuver operations will embrace:

(1) Service of security and information, patrolling, advance guards, outposts. The principles of the drill regulations and field service regulations will govern.

(2) Combat exercises with particular reference to:

    (a) Reconnaissance prior to engagement; personal reconnaissance of commanders of positions for deployment and of successive firing positions.

    (b) Advance in zone of Artillery fire (Artillery formation).

    (c) Advance by bounds.

    (d) Alternative advance under mutual covering fire(mutual support of units).

(3) Marches (regimental, brigade and divisional) in connection with assumed tactical situation.

(4) Camping (bivouac), camping expedients (construction of improvised field ranges, ovens, etc.).

(5) Night training will involve bayonet fighting, wiring, revetting, intrenching, and tactical exercises (including raids)...

---

[80] As cited in Stultz, 120-21.

(6) Instruction in field fortifications of line troops in general should be principally devoted to: Intensive digging and wire drills.

(7) Pioneer platoons will, in addition, be given thorough instruction in the construction of dugouts. [81]

According to Army Regulations, there were two basic types of attack for an infantry battalion: frontal and enveloping. Either way, an infantry squad, platoon, company, battalion, etc., had to be able to conduct a frontal attack, the most difficult of all military operations. Granted, although we were taught to always establish a base of fire with the R.G. and A.R. squads and "flank" with the bomber and assault squads, in the big picture, this could also be considered as part of a frontal attack. According to the *P.M.*:

The most usual kinds of attack are:

Frontal Attack: This attack is delivered directly against the front of the enemy. It offers little opportunity to bring more rifles against the enemy than he can bring against you. Decisive results can only be expected when your force is larger than your opponent's or when his is unduly extended. It is a dangerous and costly method of attacking.

Enveloping Attack: Cover the front of the enemy with sufficient force to hold his attention and, with the rest of your command, strike a flank more or less obliquely. Since your line is now longer than his, and you have more rifles in action, your fire is converging while that of your enemy's is diverging. Never attempt the envelopment of both flanks unless you greatly outnumber your enemy. Cooperation between the frontal and enveloping attack is essential to success. The fraction of the command that envelops the enemy is generally larger than that part in his front. A wide turning movement is not an enveloping movement. It is dangerous because your troops are separated and can be defeated in detail. In an enveloping movement your line will usually be continuous; it simply overlaps and envelops the enemy. An enveloping attack will nearly always result locally in a frontal attack, for it will meet the enemy's reserve. Let us repeat: do not attempt a wide turning movement. Your forces will be separated, they may not be able to assist each other, and can be defeated in detail. The tendency of a beginner is to attempt a wide turning movement. The error of dispersion is then committed. [82]

---

[81] As cited in Stultz, 109-10.
[82] *P.M.*, 243.

As the weeks passed into late-spring at Camp Lee, our platoon leader and guide would take us further through the *I.D.R.* They'd say things like, "According to Paragraph 449 of the *I.D.R.*, etc." The guiding principles were prescient and it was up to us to take the concepts and apply them to help us solve practical problems on the battlefield. And remember this: terrain dictates all tactical solutions. As such, each tactical problem will have a different solution. But if, during training, every man-jack in the platoon understands basic combat principles, like those outlined in the *I.D.R.*, etc., the better off they will be. According to the *I.D.R.*:

449. Where open terrain exposes troops to hostile artillery fire it may be necessary to make the deployment two miles or more from the hostile position. The foreground should be temporarily occupied by covering troops. If the enemy occupies the foreground with detachments, the covering troops must drive them back.

450. To enable large forces to gain ground toward the enemy, it may sometimes be cheaper and quicker in the end to move well forward and to deploy at night. In such case the area in which the deployment is to be made should, if practicable, be occupied by covering troops before dark. The deployment will be made with great difficulty unless the ground has been studied by daylight. The deployment gains little unless it establishes the firing line well within effective range of the enemy's main position. (See Night Operations.)

451. Each unit assigned a task deploys when on its direction line or opposite its objective, and when it has no longer sufficient cover for advancing in close order. In the firing line, intervals of 25 to 50 yards should be maintained as long as possible between battalions. In the larger units it may be necessary to indicate on the map the direction or objective, but to battalion commanders it should be pointed out on the ground.

452. The reserve is kept near enough to the firing line to be on hand at the decisive stage. It is posted with reference to the attack, or to that part of the attacking line, from which the greater results are expected; it is also charged with flank protection, but should be kept intact. Supports are considered in paragraphs 225 to 228, inclusive, and 298 to 302, inclusive.

Advancing the Attack.

453. The firing line must ordinarily advance a long distance before it is justified in opening fire. It cannot combat the enemy's artillery and it is at a disadvantage if it combats the defender's long range rifle fire. Hence it ignores both and, by taking full advantage of cover and of the discipline of the troops, advances to a first firing position at the shortest range possible.... These and other methods of crossing such zones should be studied and practiced.

454. The best protection against loss while advancing is to escape the enemy's view.

455. Each battalion finds its own firing position, conforming to the general advance as long as practicable and taking advantage of the more advanced position of an adjacent battalion in order to gain ground. The position from which the attack opens fire is further considered in paragraphs 306 to 308, inclusive.

456. It will frequently become necessary for infantry moving to the attack to pass through deployed artillery. This should be done so as to interfere as little as possible with the latter's fire, and never so as to cause that fire to cease entirely. As far as practicable, advantage should be taken of intervals in the line, if any. An understanding between artillery and infantry commanders should be had, so as to effect the movement to the best advantage.

457. In advancing the attack, advanced elements of the firing line or detachments in front of it should not open fire except in defense or to clear the foreground of the enemy. Fire on the hostile main position should not be opened until all or nearly all of the firing line can join in the fire.

The Fire Attack.

458. At the first firing position the attack seeks to gain fire superiority. This may necessitate a steady, accurate fire tor a long time. The object is to subdue the enemy's fire and kneel) it subdued so that the attacking troops may advance from this point to a favorable place near the enemy from which the charge may be made. Hence, in the advance by rushes, sufficient rifles must be kept constantly in action to keep down the enemy's fire; this determines the size of the fraction rushing.

459. To advance without fire superiority against a determined defense would result in such losses as to bring the attack to a standstill or to make the apparent success barren of results.

460. Diminution of the enemy's fire and a pronounced loss in effectiveness are the surest signs that fire superiority has been gained and that a part of the firing line can advance.

461. The men must be impressed with the fact that, having made a considerable advance under fire and having been checked, it is suicidal to turn back in daylight. If they can advance no farther, they must intrench and hold on until the fall of darkness or a favorable turn in the situation develops. Intrenching is resorted to only when necessary. Troops who have intrenched themselves under fire are moved forward again with difficulty.

The key component of the above is to always gain *fire superiority* before you advance, to spilt your unit into a maneuver element and a support by fire element ("sufficient rifles must be kept constantly in action to keep down the enemy's fire") and—and this is important—if pinned down, stay put (unless you're being relentlessly shelled) because "it is suicidal to turn back in daylight." If pinned, wait for the cover of darkness and then pull back with what you have left. We remembered this principle while in combat and it saved many-a-life.

M1915 Colt-Vickers 30.06 cal. M.G.s that the 80th Division used during most of their combat operations in France. Note the condenser hose connected to the condenser box and that the piece loads from right to left.

80th Division soldiers standing behind a M1915 Colt-Vickers M.G. Notice that we called the ammo belt "The Kaiser's Necklace."

37mm Infantry Gun (I.G.) dismounted (L) and mounted (R).

French air-cool Hotchkiss M.G. being used by American Doughs in another division (L) and one of the Ford "Specials" used by the 315th M.G. Battalion (Mot.) (R).

Each Infantry company had several "combat carts" (L) and the 313th and 314th M.G. Battalions, as well as the M.G. companies of the infantry regiments, also had carts. We thus called those M.G. units the "Jackass Artillery" (R).

"Advance Assembled," *M.G.M.* (L). A Blue Ridge M.G. Section "Advancing By Parts." Note all of the ammunition cans being carried, the tripod on one soldier's shoulder, and the gun on the soldier third from the rear. They are advancing up the Meuse-Argonne, fall 1918.

Each company had a horse or mule-drawn field kitchen (L) and a "Water Buffalo" (R). These were the most cherished pieces of equipment for the Doughs.

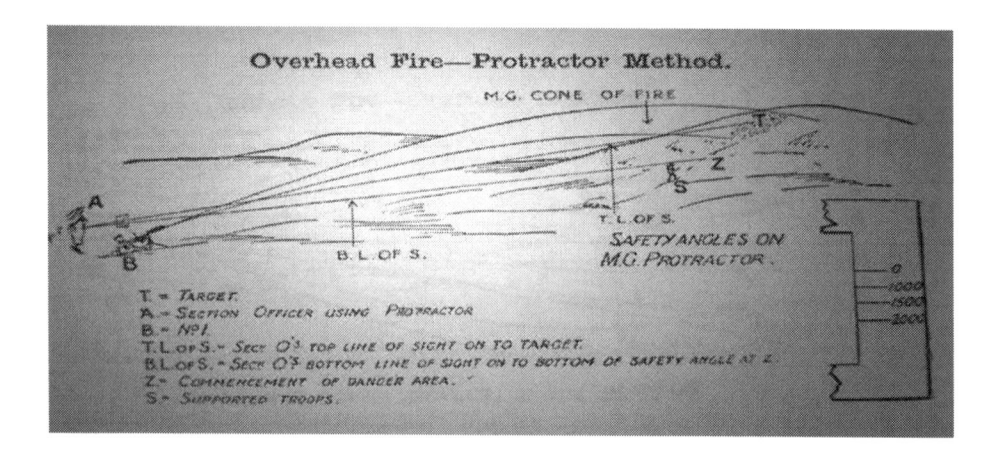

"Overhead Fire—Protractor Method." *B.M.G.M.*

Chapter 6
Machine Gun Training at Camp Lee.

One of the first things the Army did once the U.S. declared war on Germany in April 1917 was to insure that its infantry divisions had enough M.G. sections (one M.G. per section). Under the old 1914 T.O.E., each infantry regiment was apportioned but one M.G. company of four platoons, each platoon consisting of four M.G. sections (sixteen M.G.s per regiment, 144 per division—which wasn't bad). Under the new 1917 T.O.E., however, not only was each infantry regiment provided with a sixteen-M.G. company, but each brigade was also provided with a M.G. battalion of four companies each (total of sixty-four M.G.s) and each division was apportioned a two-company M.G. battalion of twelve guns (total of 224 M.G.s per division—which was even better).

With this in mind, on Sept. 19, 1917, the Army instructed the 80th Division to create the 313th, 314th, and 315th M.G. Battalions from its ranks, each commanded by an infantry major. While men of Maj. Robert Cox's 314th M.G. Battalion, the division's M.G. battalion, were drawn from the 317th and 318th Infantry Regiments, the men for the 313th and 315th M.G. Battalions were drawn from the 319th and 320th Infantry Regiments. According to Lt. Raymond Furr of the 314th M.G. Battalion: "The first recruits arrived about noon Sunday, Sept. 23, practically all of whom came from the cities of Norfolk and Portsmouth and the counties of Norfolk and Princess Anne, eastern Virginia. They were excellent material for M.G.ers."[83]

In Oct., Maj. John Dunlap and Sgt.M. Benjamin A. Fairhurst of the British Army's famed Royal Machine Gun Corps (R.M.G.C.) arrived to Camp Lee to conduct classes at the Division M.G. School. With them, division M.G. officers and N.C.O.s attended a thirty day M.G. course while the E.M. continued to train on the "School of the Soldier." Due to the lack of available water-cooled M1915 Colt-Vickers 30.06 cal. M.G.s, sometimes called "American Vickers," training emphasis was placed upon M.G. teamwork and tactics.[84] As more equipment became available, Cronkhite issued the following training emphasis to the M.G. battalions: range firing, digging and fortification, gun drill, immediate action drill, tactical section drill, tactical handling of the section, company drill, anti-gas training, trench warfare, marching, and inspection.[85] Most of this guidance was manifest and was based on the

---

[83] As cited in *314th M.G.*, 12.

[84] *Ibid*, 13.

[85] Stultz, 119.

Infantry Training Manual of 1917, which actually had a section on training M.G. companies. According to one soldier from the 314th M.G. Battalion:

> *The battalion was sadly lacking in equipment for the latter part of the training. A few old Colt M.G.s were available throughout the winter—that was all—but towards the latter part of April, the American Vickers was issued, and every man had the opportunity of shooting it on the range and learning something of its rather complicated mechanism.*[86]

According to our British M.G. advisors, men who had survived the infamous Somme Offensives of 1915 and 1916, the Maxim M.G. was the lynchpin of the German defenses. They were almost-always masterfully positioned, crewed, and defended. The Germans were the absolute experts of terrain analysis, camouflage, and indirect fire (when a weapon crew can't directly see a target, it fires by map coordinates through a forward observer). They arranged their M.G.s with interlocking fields of fire (i.e., they criss-crossed their fields of fire) and the bullets that would hit you would usually not come from the front, but from the flank. Any fold or dip in the ground that an enemy—like the Belgians, British, French, or Russians took cover in—the Germans more-than-likely had pre-plotted with mortars and indirect M.G. fire. In fact, the British blamed well-positioned and entrenched German M.G.s for the current stalemate/siege on the Western Front as the Allies had yet to find a way to breach the strong German lines with the forces available.

The M.G. was first invented by the American-born inventor Hiram Maxim in 1883 who was, at the time, working in northwest London. Maxim sold his invention to Albert Vickers, an English steel magnate, and together they built and marketed the "Maxim-Vickers M.G." In 1886, the weapon was improved with the invention of new bullets and smokeless powder by the Frenchman Paul Vielle. The subsequent M1886 Maxim-Vickers M.G. fired a .30 cal. round and its barrel is cooled by a water-filled brass cylinder that is called a "water jacket" because it surrounded the barrel with about two gallons of water. This water turned into steam, flowed into a "condenser hose" and then into a "condenser box," which was positioned under the muzzle in order to recycle the water back into the water jacket (empty the liquefied contents from the condenser box into a container and then pour the cooled water back into the jacket).

About ten years later, in 1895, Samuel Browning, a Mormon from Utah, sold his air-cooled M.G. design to the Colt Firearms Company of Connecticut. Called the "M1895 Colt-Browning M.G." (or the "Potato-Digger" because of the shape and sound of its action), it was

---

[86] As cited in *Ibid*, 125.

the first air-cooled and gas-operated M.G. put into service. It fired a .30 cal. round and was used by the 1st U.S. Volunteer Cavalry, "Roosevelt's Rough Riders," in Cuba during the Spanish-American War. Not to be outdone, in 1897, the Hotchkiss Company of Paris, France, invented the air-cooled Hotchkiss M.G. to put the Potato Digger out of business. For better heat dissolution, the Hotchkiss Company designed a huge barrel with "fins" or "shocks" to increase the external surface area, which better dissipated the heat. And instead of fabric belts, which fed bullets for both the Vickers and the Potato Digger, the Hotchkiss was fed by metal strips. In 1907, the Hotchkiss Company manufactured the *Saint-Étienne* 1907 M.G. (*Mitrailleuse* 1907) and this was the weapon they mostly used in 1914-15. In 1909, Hotchkiss invented a lighter air-cooled M.G., the M1909 *Benét-Mercié*, and the U.S. Army purchased several of these, mostly for use by our cavalry regiments. In 1914, Hotchkiss made another upgrade to their product, the *Mitrailleuse 1914,* and this was the weapon that the French mostly used from 1915 forward.[87]

My understanding is that the biggest problem with the air-cooled M.G.s was that the more they shot, the more inaccurate they became because the barrel expanded from the heat. I was told that after only four minutes of steady firing, bullets fired from air-cooled M.G.s failed to grip the rifling inside the barrel and simply began to fling out to and fro. I heard that the Colt Potato Digger was even worse than the Hotchkiss because it simply seized up after firing all but five hundred rounds (one-to-two minutes of steady firing). Our M.G.ers were forced to train with the Potato Diggers for a time, as that's all the Army had available at the time.

In 1915, the British Vickers Company, in an attempt to better fill its order for the war, licensed its M.G. design to the American Colt Firearms Company and Colt manufactured the M1915 Colt-Vickers M.G. for U.S. and Allied Forces. This was the gun that our M.G. companies trained on at Camp Lee and used during our first phases of combat in France. Unlike the original 1883 Vickers, the M1915 M.G. has a lighter, thinner, horizontally-corrogated steel water jacket, a better firing mechanism, and fires 30.06 cal. rounds that are fed by fabric belts. The way it panned out, the first American divisions sent to France in late-1917 and early 1918 (e.g., 1st, 2nd, 3rd, 26th, 28th, and 42nd Divisions) were equipped with M1903 Springfield Rifles, M1914 Hotchkiss M.G.s, and M1915 Chauchat A.R.s. Those that went later, like the 80th Division, fought most of the war with M1917 Enfield Rifles, *Chauchat* A.R.s (and later Browning A.R.s), and M1915 Colt-Vickers M.G.s (and later M1917 Browning M.G.s). Unlike E.M. in the infantry, E.M. in M.G. Companies were assigned M1911 Semi-

---

[87] *Mitrailleuse* or "machine gun" is pronounced "Mit-try-lews."

Automatic Pistols. These little monsters fired seven .45 cal. rounds from a detachable box magazine that was inserted into the grip. Our officers were also assigned these, as well as members from the artillery, cavalry, signal, quartermaster, ordnance, etc. Like the M1895 "Potato Digger," the M1911 Auto Pistol was invented by John Browning.

Machine Guns.

I.D.R. 537. Machine guns must be considered as weapons of emergency. Their effectiveness combined with their mobility renders them of great value at critical, though infrequent, periods of an engagement.

I.D.R. 538. When operating against infantry only, they can be used to a great extent throughout the combat as circumstances may indicate, but they are quickly rendered powerless by efficient field artillery and will promptly draw artillery fire whenever they open. Hence their use in engagements between large commands must be for short periods and at times when their great effectiveness will be most valuable.

I.D.R. 539. Machine guns should be attached to the advance guard. In meeting engagements they will be of great value in assisting their own advance, or in checking the advance of the enemy, and will have considerable time to operate before hostile artillery fire can silence them. Care must be taken not to leave them too long in action.

I.D.R. 540. They are valuable to a rear guard which seeks to check a vigorous pursuit or to gain time.

I.D.R. 541. In attack, if fire of position is practicable, they are of great value. In this case fire should not be opened by the machine guns until the attack is well advanced. At a critical period in the attack, such fire, if suddenly and unexpectedly opened, will greatly assist the advancing line. The fire must be as heavy as possible and must be continued until masked by friendly troops or until the hostile artillery finds the machine guns.

I.D.R. 542. In the defense, machine guns should be used in the same general manner as described above for the attack. Concealment and patient waiting for critical moments and exceptional opportunities are the special characteristics of the machine gun service in decisive actions.

I.D.R. 543. As part of the reserve, machine guns have special importance. If they are with the troops told off to protect the flanks, and if they are well placed, they will often produce decisive results against a hostile turning movement. They are especially qualified to cover a withdrawal or make a captured position secure.

I.D.R. 544. Machine guns should not be assigned to the firing line of an attack. They should be so placed that fire directed upon them is not likely to fall upon the firing line.

I.D.R. 545. A skirmish line can not advance by walking or running when hostile machine guns have the correct range and are ready to fire. Machine-gun fire is not specially effective against troops lying on the ground or crawling.

I.D.R. 546. When opposed by machine guns and without artillery to destroy them, Infantry itself must silence them before it can advance. An infantry command that must depend upon itself for protection against machine guns should concentrate a large number of rifles on each gun in turn and until it has silenced it.

Machine Guns.

M.M.T. 551. Machine guns are weapons of emergency. Machine guns must be considered as weapons of emergency. Their effectiveness combined with their mobility renders them of great value at critical, though infrequent, periods of an engagement.

M.M.T. 552. Machine guns to be used for short periods, when opportunities present themselves. When operating against Infantry only, they can be used to a great extent throughout the combat as circumstances may indicate, but they are quickly rendered powerless by efficient field artillery and will promptly draw artillery fire whenever they open. Hence their use in engagements between large commands must be for short periods and at times when their great effectiveness will be most valuable.

M.M.T. 553. Machine guns attached to advance guard; use in meeting engagements. Machine guns should be attached to the advance guard. In meeting engagements they will be of great value in assisting their own advance, or in checking the advance of the enemy, and will have considerable time to operate before hostile Artillery fire can silence them. Care must be taken not to leave them too long in action.

M.M.T. 554. Use of machine guns with rear guard. They are valuable to a rear guard which seeks to check a vigorous pursuit or to gain time.

M.M.T. 555. Machine guns in attack—fire of position. In attack, if fire of position is practicable, they are of great value. In this case fire should not be opened by the machine guns until the attack is well advanced. At a critical period in the attack, such fire, if suddenly and unexpectedly opened, will greatly assist the advancing line. The fire must be as heavy as possible and must be continued until masked by friendly troops or until the hostile Artillery finds the machine guns.

M.M.T. 556. Machine guns in defense. In the defense, machine guns should be used in the same general manner as described above for the attack. Concealment and patient waiting for critical moments and exceptional opportunities are the special characteristics of the machine-gun service in decisive actions.

M.M.T. 557. Machine guns as part of reserve; use in covering withdrawal. As part of the reserve, machine guns have special importance. If they are with the troops told off to protect the flanks, and if they are well placed, they will often produce decisive results against a hostile turning movement. They are especially qualified to cover a withdrawal or make a captured position secure.

M.M.T. 558. Machine guns not to form part of firing line of attack. Machine guns should not be assigned to the firing line of an attack. They should be so placed that fire directed upon them is not likely to fall upon the firing line.

M.M.T. 559. Effectiveness of machine guns against skirmish line, except when lying down or crawling. A skirmish line can not advance by walking or running when hostile machine guns have the correct range and are ready to fire. Machine-gun fire is not specially effective against troops lying on the ground or crawling.

M.M.T. 560. Silencing of machine guns by infantry. When opposed by machine guns without artillery to destroy them, infantry itself must silence them before it can advance. An infantry command that must depend upon itself for protection against machine guns should concentrate a large number of rifles on each gun in turn and until it has silenced it. In addition to the above, which the Infantry Drill Regulations gives on the subject of machine guns, the following, based on the use of machine guns in the European War, is given:

M.M.T. 561. Machine guns essentially automatic rifles. They are essentially automatic rifles, designed to fire the ordinary rifle cartridge and capable of delivering a stream of small bullets at a rate of as high as 600 per minute. Experience in the European war has determined that the rate of 400 shots per minute is the desirable maximum. Their ranges are the same as for the rifle. The fire of a machine gun has been estimated as equal to that of thirty men.

M.M.T. 562. Mounts. Machine guns are usually mounted on tripods or wheels. The weight of certain types is such that they can readily be carried by the soldier from one point to another.

M.M.T. 563. Methods of transportation. While machine guns are usually designed to be carried or packed, they are easily adapted to various methods of transportation. In the European war we find them mounted on sleds during the winter campaign; on specially designed motor cycles with side cars and accompanied by other motor cycles carrying ammunition; on wheels; on wagons; on armored automobiles; aeroplanes; and finally in the powerful "tanks" of the English.

M.M.T. 564. Concealment. Machine guns while usually considered as weapons of emergency have been used in attack and defense in the European war in all stages. Their mobility and deadly effect have made them of great value. Once their position is discovered they are quickly put out of action by artillery. Owing to this fact the armies in Europe have used alternative positions and have used every means to conceal the guns. Hedges, walls, and pits are used and every effort is used to conceal the flame of discharge. This is usually accomplished by keeping the muzzle well in rear of its cover or loop hole. Machine guns almost invariably betray their positions as soon as they enter into action. The present tendency seems to be to hold them concealed and place them into position in the trenches or emplacements at the moment of combat. Extraordinary means have been resorted to in hiding the guns until they are needed. In the German line, dugouts underground were constructed to conceal the machine guns and crews. Often they permitted the first line of the attack to pass over them and then appeared in rear and opened a deadly fire on the backs of the troops.

M.M.T. 565. Use in villages. In villages, machine guns were used with terrible effect, firing from cellars or windows. The only successful method of destroying them was with hand grenades and even this was costly.

M.M.T. 566. Location on the defense. On the defense machine guns should be mounted in salients and at points where cross fire can be obtained. This makes it more difficult for the enemy to locate the guns. Frontal fire is not so often successful.

M.M.T. 567. Location in attack. In the attack it is accepted that machine guns must cover the Infantry at short and long ranges while other machine guns must accompany the attacking troops to hold the positions or trenches gained. The second or third line would seem to be the best position for machine guns when accompanying troops.

M.M.T. 568. Economy of men. Owing to its rapid and effective fire, and the comparative ease with which it can be concealed, the machine gun permits a great economy of men on a front and the concentrating of the forces thus freed for use in other parts of the field. This was done on a large scale on the Russian front by the Germans in 1915. They constructed miles of wire entanglements in front of positions occupied with an enormous number of machine guns and comparatively few men. The main forces were thus free to be transported wherever danger threatened. In this manner the Germans replaced men by machine guns and wire and were able to cope successfully with the immense Russian armies. The above plate shows a typical machine gun emplacement, constructed in the field. Many elaborate emplacements have been constructed in the European war, using steel and concrete, but for a hasty cover in the field the simple emplacement shown in the figure is recommended.

Weighing their strengths and weaknesses, the Army designated M.G.s as "weapons of emergency" to flesh out/support an infantry firing line (although to never be deployed within an infantry line). The British cautioned us on our over-reliance on the rifle. Shooting on a modern battlefield is far different than shooting on a range at Camp Lee or at a deer in the Blue Mountains, they promised. "In your hands, the rifle is pretty much useless, mate," one said. At least with a tripod-mounted M.G., he argued, you can take the "human element" out of the equation. Tripods, unlike people, don't quiver, they don't breath hard, and they don't freeze. All the M.G.er has to do is squeeze the trigger and his assistant will "walk the cone"

(cone=distribution of bullets) into the target. The key, as we shall see, is in positioning a M.G. in both the offense and defense.

In 1914, the French tactical doctrine of "attack with great vigor" or *attaque à outrance,* relied upon an infantry charge with the bayonet once a target was neutralized by fire superiority.[88] Although rifles and M.G.s would play a role in this neutralization, the main work for the French was to be done by fast-firing 75mm field guns shooting directly at the target. A four-gun battery firing at a rate of twenty rounds/minute could deliver some 20,000 shrapnel balls into an area approximately a hundred yards by four hundred yards. That's twenty times more projectiles than four M.G.s firing at the maximum five hundred rounds per minute (R.P.M.)! The French soon learned, however, that the 75s, if pushed too far forward, were also quickly taken out by enemy fire. They therefore decided to instead push their air-cooled 8mm Hotchkiss M1914 M.G.s and 37mm I.G.s as far forward as possible during an attack.

But then they too were also taken out—usually by well-defended German M.G.s.

After several months of experience on the battlefield, both sides decided to only fire their M.G.s when they had good "enfilade" (or side) shots into an enemy position (much like our own doctrine of "the M.G. is a weapon of emergency"). The general rule of thumb was that a M.G. would not open fire unless ten of the enemy showed itself in flank—all other targets would be handled by rifles, A.R.s, or hand grenades. Despite general perception, a M.G. is not a good side-to-side firing weapon (i.e., traverse). It is, in fact, a great up-and-down (or ranging) weapon. What I mean by this is that a M.G. is best fired at a vertical target (i.e., up and down) by "walking" or "ranging" its "cone of fire" into a target like up a creek bed, or up a road, or into a house, or into an enemy M.G. embrasure. Let the rifles and A.R.s on the M.G.s' flanks do the lateral or traverse firing (i.e., back and forth).

When fired at longer ranges (4,500 yards max.) a M.G.'s "cone of fire" really opens up—much like water spraying from a hose—because not all bullets follow the same trajectory when it leaves the muzzle. The area where the cone of fire hits the ground is called "the beaten zone." This area is usually oval in shape, lengthwise from the barrel of the M.G. For example, a M1915 Colt-Vickers firing at a range of 2,000 yards on flat ground at the same elevation creates a beaten zone of sixty-four yards long and six yards wide. It's not as great as a 75mm cannon firing shrapnel, but is certainly more deadly than rifles, mortars, or I.G.s firing into the same space. The other thing about a M.G. firing at long range, unlike artillery rounds: one doesn't hear the bullets coming in.

---

[88] *Attaque à outrance* is pronounced "attack ah ow-trons."

Seriously.

You'll be walking up an attack axis and then all of the sudden see men being shredded into bacon strips by hundreds of silent killers—little hot and razor-sharp knives falling from the sky. That was a M.G. firing an indirect fire mission onto an identified point on the map!

As was already inferred, American M.G. units were based off the British model in that they were treated much like artillery. The basic tactical unit was the M.G. section. It one corporal and nine privates in three squads: gun squad (four men), ammunition squad (three men), and pack squad (two men). Four M.G. sections made a M.G. platoon and four M.G. platoons made a company (sixteen guns per company). While the M.G. companies from the infantry regiments and the 313th and 315th M.G. Battalions were mule-drawn (in carts), the twelve M.G.s of the 314th M.G. Battalion were motorized, meaning that each section moved its guns, gear, and men in Ford or Packard motor trucks that we called "Specials" or "Mountain Goats." According to the *Drill Regulations for Machine Guns, 1917 (M.G.D.R.)*:[89]

The M.G. Section.

91. The organization of a detachment of men for the service of M.G.s begins naturally with that of a single piece. It is the unit upon which the organization is based and it is called "the Section."

92. With reference to the service of the piece, the section is sub-divided into three elements:

  (a) The gun squad, for the service of the piece.

  (b) The ammunition squad for the service of ammunition and water.

  (c) The pack squad for the care of animals and for service as packers.

To supervise the operations of these three elements as corporal is necessary. He is designated as "Chief of Section."

  The gun squad consists of: four privates, one to who acts as "Pointer."

  The ammunition squad consists of: three privates.

  The pack squad consists of: two packers, privates.

93. The section is composed of one corporal, who is chief of section, one gun squad, one ammunition squad, one pack squad, the necessary mules and equipment, one gun, and its accessories.

94. The chief of section commands the section and is responsible to the chief of platoon for the efficiency of the men and the care of the material and animals assigned to his section. In action, he directs the fire of his piece in accordance

---

[89] *Drill Regulations for Machine Guns: Infantry, 1917* (Washington, D.C., Government Printing Office, 1917). Hereafter cited as "*M.G.D.R.*"

with instructions from higher authority, and, in the absence of instructions, according to his best judgment. He supervises the operations of all the parts of the section, so as they come under his observation, and acts as coach to the Pointer in the conduct of fire.

95. The gun squad serves and cares for the piece and such articles of equipment as may be assigned to its members.

96. The ammunition squad serves and cares for the belt loader, establishes and operates the ammunition station, provides an ample supply of ammunition and water at the gun at all times, assists in loading and unloading the mules, and cares for the articles of equipment assigned to its members.

The Gun Squad.

99. The gun squad is composed of four privates, one of whom acts as "Pointer." They are referred to as "gunmen."

100. The object of the training of the gun squad is two-fold:

> *(a) The gunmen must be taught their individual duties and be practiced in them until their performance becomes a matter of second nature even under the stress and excitement of combat.*
>
> *(b) The individual gun squad must be trained as a unit so that its individual members work together smoothly and quietly for the efficient service of their gun. All privates of the platoon receive this instruction; but the permanent gun squad is composed of men who are selected for their special aptitude.*

Duties of Individuals in the Service of the Piece.

101. <u>Pointer</u>: Commands gun squad, set sights, aims piece, packs and unpacks gun, shifts trail, fires piece, operates roller handle in unloading, reduces jams, if any.

> *<u>No. 1</u>: Leads gun mule, loads piece, unloads piece, assists in packing and unpacking gun, assists pointer to reduce jams, if any.*
>
> *<u>Nos. 2 and 3</u>: Packs and unpacks tripod, serves ammunition and water.*

As stated in the *M.G.D.R.*, the M.G. squad, the majority of the M.G. section, consisted of four privates, a "pointer," who actually fired the gun, chewing up targets, the No. 1 Man, who acted as the assistant gunner (A.G.) and who was posted on the right side of the gun "feeding the beast" with ammunition. No. 2 helped ensure that the gun was properly ejecting rounds down below and the used fabric out the left side. No. 3 brought up ammunition to No.1 with the help of the two-man ammunition squad. No. 3 was positioned next to the pointer and behind No. 1. The key to an effective M.G. Squad, as with all other squads, is teamwork and each man has to not only know his job inside and out, but everyone else's, too. According to the *M.G.D.R.*, the pointer is responsible for:

(a) Laying the piece.

(b) Taking firing commands from the section chief (i.e., target, range, deflection).

(c) Aiming the piece.

(d) Firing the piece.

(e) Loading and unloading the piece.

M.G.D.R. 16. No. 1 of a M.G. squad has the following duties: Load the Piece. The No. 1 Man places an ammunition box on the ground on the right of the piece opposite the feed box, latch toward the piece; opens the ammunition box and, standing in front of the box and facing the rear, passes the belt through the feed box from right to left, drawing it to the left with the right hand until the first cartridge is engaged in the lower feed-box pawls.

M.G.D.R. 17. The duties of No. 1 during firing are:

(a) To see that the belt feeds freely.

(b) To assist the Pointer to reduce jams, if any.

(c) To immediately reload the piece in case of misfire or failure of the mechanism to function properly.

(d) When a belt is exhausted, unless he receives specific instructions to the contrary, to pass the empty ammunition box to the left side of the piece, receive a filled belt and immediately reload the piece.

(e) He observes the action of the roller handle which the piece is actually firing, for, by noting its action he may in nearly every case immediately tell the cause of the minor jams and quickly reduce them.

To explain a little bit more about the duties of No. 1, the "belt" is made of canvas-like white cloth and 30.06 bullets are sleeved in between them. Although the fabric belts were meant to be reused, once we hit the Meuse-Argonne, they were pretty much trashed due to battlefield conditions. On occasion, people used them as bandages or other contingencies.

When wet, the belts were not only a bear to feed through the firing block, but were also even heavier to carry across the shell-scarred battlefield. No. 2 of a M.G. Squad has the following duties:

> *M.G.D.R. 19. The duties of No. 2 are:*
>
> *(a) When the trail is shifted: to see that the tool box is within reach of the Pointer's left hand.*
>
> *(b) At preliminary commands for firing: to see that the wing nuts are screwed fast.*
>
> *(c) During firing: to receive the belt as it is fed through the gun and when it is exhausted to fold it and place it in its box, passing the box to such member of the ammunition squad as comes to receive it or to No. 3.*
>
> *(d) When the Pointer directs No. 2 to "fill water jacket" or at other times when necessary. No. 2 fills the filling cup with water, removes the cap from the filling valve (and condenser tube, if used, from steam escape), places the nozzle of cup in filling valve, handle of cup to the right, cup canted slightly to the right, empties contents of cup into the water jacket and repeats the operation until the water jacket is full. Water can not be introduced into the jacket when there has been sufficient firing to make an appreciable pressure of steam, although it is not essential, per se, that the firing be suspended while the jacket is being filled. The jacket being filled, No. 2 replaces cap on filling valve (and condenser tube, if used in steam escape).*
>
> *(e) When piece is being unloaded: to see that the free end of the belt does not become entangled or twisted before passing through the feed box.*
>
> *(f) When the ammunition squad or gun squad becomes reduced: To supply No. 1 with ammunition and to procure for himself an ample supply of water to cool the barrel.*
>
> *(g) To assist in moving the piece by hand.*

No. 2 is responsible for keeping the water jacket filled with coolant. The gun has a condenser tube that leads from the bottom front of the water jacket into a condenser box. This makes the system self-contained, meaning that the coolant in the water jacket will heat into steam (a gas) and the steam will travel down the tube and into the condenser box where it will cool and return to liquid form. No. 2 can then use the condensed water from the box to refill the water jacket.

Common sense will tell you that the condenser box and tube are very cumbersome in the attack (moving the gun forward is difficult in and of itself). Because they are so cumbersome, the condenser tube and box are sometimes not used in the attack ("condenser tube, if used"). If you choose not to use the box during an attack, steam from the M.G. will simply pour out of the valve of the water jacket as a large steam cloud (which makes target identification even harder and makes the M.G. a very obvious target). Once a M.G. section is moved into the defense, however, the condenser boxes and tubes are absolutely attached, better masking their position and saving the output of water for the gun section. As such, the condenser box, condenser tube, and cans of water were always carried in the gun carts and were brought up when the supported infantry units were ordered to defend. During the war, the British started using canvas "condenser bags" and not the metal condenser boxes for easier transport/deployment. According to the *M.G.D.R.*, on No. 3 and the "Ammunition Squad":

> *20. The duties of No. 3 are:*
> *(a) When the trail is shifted: to replace ammunition within reach of No. 1 and water and filling cup within reach of No. 2.*
> *(b) At preliminary commands for firing: to procure a full box of ammunition, open it, and hand it to No. 1.*
> *(c) During firing: To see that Nos. 1 and 2 have an uninterrupted supply of ammunition and water, No. 3 going to procure this supply himself should the ammunition squad be unable, from any cause, to keep the gun properly supplied.*
> *(d) To assist in moving the piece by hand.*

> *The Ammunition Squad.*
> *64. The ammunition squad is composed of 3 privates. They are designated as ammunition men.*
> *65. The object of the training of the ammunition squad is to familiarize the men with the specific duties that they will perform them quickly, accurately, and without confusion.*

66. To this end they will be carefully instructed all that pertains to the supply of ammunition for the gun, in the nomenclature, care, and operation of the belt-filling machine, and in distribution of the loads.

67. All members of the platoon will receive instructions in the duties of the ammunition squad, but the men who are permanently assigned to this duty will receive the benefit of careful and painstaking individual instruction, and will be impressed with the idea that the gun becomes useless unless their duties are carefully and faithfully performed.

As a soldier, I must tell you that Para. 67 of the *M.G.D.R.* is a gem. Although the terms like "careful and painstaking individual instruction" and "the gun becomes useless unless their duties are carefully and faithfully performed" smack of propaganda or patronage, they are actually appreciated. The bottom line is that although the members of the ammunition squad were not the "brightest bulbs" of the division, their jobs were important. It was they who had to slide the thousands of 30.06 rounds into the cloth sleeves of the ammunition belt with the belt-filling machine, which is a repetitious, thankless job. Thus the term "carefully and faithfully performed." In combat, the ammunition men would ensure that the M.G. kept firing by rotating the ammunition and water boxes and by providing flank and rear security for the M.G. with their rifles. Too many times, however, they would have to fill the positions of the killed or wounded gun squad men.

The Pack Squad.

M.G.D.R. 79. The pack squad is composed of two privates, designated as "off" and "near" packer. The near packer is senior...

M.G.D.R. 83. To keep the personal equipment in order; to feed, water, groom, and care for the animals assigned to the section; to clean out their stalls and space on the picket line; to keep the packs assigned to him in good repair and bring to the attention of the platoon sergeant and deficiencies he himself can not himself supply; to saddle up at the signal for drill, exercise, march, or combat; to assist in herd guard and exercise; to perform his share as watchman; to perform his share of stable police.

While at Camp Lee and later in France, the packers were not trained how to pack a mule as per the 1909 *M.G.D.R.* because standard operating procedure (S.O.P.) at the time was to use horse or mule-drawn "combat carts" in the regimental M.G. companies and the

313th and 315th M.G. Battalions. This is why we oft-times called the M.G. sections "Jackass Artillery." Nevertheless, the Packers still performed a vital function by packing or loading the M.G., ammo, etc. upon the M.G. cart or special motor truck. For a guide, the packers used Para. 168 of the *M.G.D.R.* when it came to loading said carts or trucks of a M.G. section. Upon the cart was loaded: M1915 M.G., M1915 tripod, tool box, spare barrels and water jackets, filling cups, a hatchet, wire cutters, shovels, a pick, a sledge hammer, semaphore kit (signal flags), several water boxes, as many ammunition boxes as could be carried (around twenty), and the blanket rolls of the soldiers of the M.G. section. If the M.G. section had mules (most did), the packers were the primary (but not only) caregivers of the animals and like the ammunition squad, helped secure the flanks and rear of the M.G. while in actual combat.

The most difficult combat task of the M.G. section was in moving forward with the infantry while on the attack. For short distances, under fifty yards, the M.G. squad would simply lift the tripod with the M.G. still attached. While the pointer would carry the toolbox and shovel, No. 2 would grasp the front of the tripod, placing the red-hot water jacket over his right shoulder. No. 3 will grab the rear of the tripod and No. 1 will carry as many ammunition boxes as possible. The commands are: "Forward x-yards!" "Lift!" "Forward, march!" "Squad, halt!" "Emplace!" "Load!" "Fire!"

For longer distances, that over a hundred yards (most frequently used), the M.G. had to be broken down. The commands for that are: "Advance by Parts!" "Move to x!" "Forward, march!" "Squad, halt!" "Emplace!" "Load!" "Fire!" During the war, while we were advancing up through Bois Fontenois, the Army Signal Corps snapped a picture of one of our M.G. crews "advancing by parts." According to Army Regulations:

> *M.G.D.R. 31. The gun is dismounted from the tripod as described in Para. 37 and the equipment is then carried by the squad in column, as follows:*
>
> > *(a) No. 2 at the head of the column carrying the tripod. This is easiest carried by allowing the legs to remain in place, with the wing nuts screwed fast, the trail extending down the back, one leg supported on each shoulder, the hands grasping the legs near their ends.*
> > *(b) No. 1 follows No. 2, carrying the gun on his shoulder.*
> > *(c) No. 3 follows No. 1, carrying two or more boxes of ammunition.*
> > *(d) The Pointer follows No. 3, carrying the tool box and intrenching tools.*

Another critical skill a M.G. squad must master, other than that of actually firing the piece and engaging targets, is in fixing "jams of the first class." According to the *M.G.D.R.*:

196. The M.G. is a delicate piece of machinery. Its moving parts are under pressure of 30,000 lbs. a square inch. To insure the promptness and accuracy on the part of the gun squad in the reduction of jams, their causes and reductions must be thoroughly gone over, both practically and theoretically... The determination of the causes of jams and their repair are simple matters when intelligently and systematically explored. Tinkering ignorantly with the parts of the gun is criminal carelessness; but maladjustment through neglect is inexcusable and liable to cause the consequences in action. The use of too much force, violently removing parts, or forcing the parts to work properly by hammer blows and the like are examples of ignorance or loss of discipline.

198. A jam in a machine gun is the failure of the mechanism to function so that the automatic fire is uninterrupted as there are cartridges in the belt and the trigger is pressed.

199. Jams are classified according to their causes as follows:

    (A) Those whose number may be lessened by reasonable care in:

        (a) Adjustment of the mechanism and the care of the gun.

        (b) Loading of belts and the manner in which the gun is fed.

        (c) Cleaning and oiling of the working parts of the gun before firing.

        (d) Examination of all ammunition before and after it is loaded into belts and the rejection of cartridges that are foul or defective.

        (e) Smoothing (with a fine file or emory) of such projecting surfaces in the mechanism of the gun as it causes undue friction of its working parts.

    (B) Those caused by the wear or breakage of parts because of defective material, long usage, accident, or the enemy's fire. The reduction of jams comprises three steps:

        (a) Determination of the character of the jam by examination.

        (b) Removal of the immediate obstruction.

        (c) Correction or removal of the cause which produces the jam.

The most effective thing a M.G. squad can do to avoid jams, other than keeping the action and ammo clean, is to ensure that the "head-space and timing" are set right. "Headspace" is the space between the face of the bolt and the flat end of the bullet when it's seated in the receiver. Too close, and it will jam. Too far, and it will misfire or misfeed. Add some mud and goo into the mix with messed up headspace, and the M.G. will become another useless block of metal. "Timing" is the setting of the R.P.M. It's supposed to be set at five hundred R.P.M. but each gun is a little different. There's a mechanism on the gun that helps adjust the timing. When a bullet is fired from a Vickers series M.G., it exits the bottom of the gun and the cloth fabric spits out the left side.

In firing the piece, a target is always designated, the firing data announced, and the operation of setting sights, loading, pointing, and firing the piece are habitually performed. According to Paras. 38-41 of the *M.G.D.R.*, the firing commands are:

1. *"Action Front (or Right, Left, or Rear)!"*
2. *"Target, such an object at such o'clock."*
3. *"Range, so many yards."*
4. *"Deflection right (or left), so many points."*

Corrections of Firing Data.

M.G.D.R. 44. After any string of shots the Pointer verifies his aim and calls "Ready." If the shot group was properly placed, the observer then directs the Pointer to "FIRE." If the shot group was off the target, the observer gives the Pointer corrected firing data:

(1) By announcing a new range and deflection as:

    a. Range, so many yards.

    b. Deflection right (left) so many points.

(2) By directing the Pointer to move his sight a certain amount as—

    a. Take fifty yards more elevation.

    b. Take four more points right.

In either case the Pointer corrects his sight as indicated, bringing his aim back onto the target, calls "Ready," and fires the next string of shots when directed to FIRE by the observer.

To Change Target.

M.G.D.R. 45. The command, for example—

    1. Change target.

    2. Door of that white house, at such o'clock.

    3. Range, so many yards.

    4. Deflection right (left) so many points.

At the second command the Pointer shifts the trail to give the piece the general direction and then lays his piece on the new target by the methods prescribed.

As you can see, firing a M.G. is very calculated, very technical, much like artillery. In fact, we in the rifle companies were taught to think of the M.G.s as forms of "baby artillery" or our preferred pegorative "Jackass Artillery" as they performed both direct and indirect fire missions. As such, M.G.s simply did not "spray and pray" much like we A.R. men did because it's not only ineffective, but also wastes pounds of precious ammunition. The pointer was taught to fire five-round bursts, or, as the manual states, a "string of fire." Sometimes we'd call it "squirting." They almost always used their "Traverse and Elevating" tool (T&E, which was also called an "Inclinometer"), that connected the gun with the tripod, as it made the gun far-more accurate. In general, there are seven types of fire missions for the M.G. according to the *M.G.D.R.*, all but one uses the T&E:

1. *Ranging Fire.*
2. *Fire for Effect.*
   a. *Fixed Fire.*
   b. *Traversed Fire.*
   c. *Zoned Fire.*
   d. *Traversed-zone Fire.*
   e. *Fire at Moving Targets.*
   f. *Sweeping Fire.*

1. *Ranging Fire is "walking" or "creeping" fire; it is fire that the Pointer uses to adjust onto a target. Pointers can almost always get the "windage" or left and right of a target (the traverse) on the first shot. Simply point at the target and shoot. The problem comes with the distance, which on the T&E is "elevation" or "range." Pointers are taught to "walk" their bullets into a target. In that way he can make corrections using five-round bursts, or "squirting" the target. Once the target is hit, the Pointer, with the advice of Nos. 1 and 2, will switch over to "Fire for Effect."*

2. *Once the target is hit, the Pointer suppresses or destroys the target with "Fire for Effect." There are six types of "Fire for Effect" missions for the M.G.: Fixed, Traverse, Zone, Traversed-zone, Fire at Moving Targets, and Sweeping Fire.*

a. *"Fixed Fire" consists of dropping the cone of fire onto a small target with a few squirts. The setting of the T&E remains the same throughout the entire fire mission.*

b. *"Traverse Fire" is when the elevation of a target remains the same (e.g., a ridge line) but the target is long (like an Infantry line taken in front or flank) and the traverse, or left or right, needs to be adjusted during the fire mission. The Pointer is taught to aim at one end of the target (hopefully the rear of the target, if available), and then work the cone in the opposite direction, moving the traverse either left or right. The gun will fire a five-round-burst here, then there, then there (squirting), all at the same elevation, but at different locations.*

c. *"Zone Fire" is the same traverse or windage throughout the fire mission, but at different distances or ranges. An example of this is enfilade fire (i.e., firing right down the flank of an infantry squad that is hung-up on a wire) or firing up a trench line. It's the moving the cone up a single axis by squirting the gun.*

d. *"Traversed-zone Fire" is a mixture of the above. It takes the form of a "T." It's when the Pointer moves the cone straight up a compass direction and then traverses it left and right.*

e. *"Fire at Moving Targets" is the hardest of all M.G. fire missions, especially if the target is in the air. If it's a ground target, the Pointer is taught to "Range Fire" and then "Traverse Fire" by firing in front of the target. Once the target has moved beyond the range of the T&E, the Pointer will command "TRAIL RIGHT (or LEFT)" and the Pointer will move the T&E to the extreme right or left to once again squirt the target using Traverse Fire, moving the T&E in the opposite direction.*

f. *"Sweeping Fire" is when the Pointer fires continuously, pausing only to correct the sights or aim. This is often called "free fire" as the T&E is detached from the gun and the Pointer is free to move the gun in any direction. "Sweeping Fire" is only used in an emergency, when enemy infantry is attacking and is within 100 yards of the gun position.*

Another type of mission for a M.G. section is "Night Firing" although it uses the fire techniques listed above.

M.G.D.R. 61. Night Firing.—fixed fire, traversed fire, zone fire, traversed-zone fire, and sweeping fire may be used at night, omitting the readjustment of the sights after each string. When practicable the piece should be laid in daylight on some known element of the target or the ground to be covered and the pointer will endeavor to keep in mind the amount of change made in azimuth and elevation, so that the piece can be returned to approximately the original aiming point as a point of departure. The sights may be illuminated by small electric light-bulbs, if practicable. Night firing is used principally to cover a particular point, as a path, road, defile, or battery, or to cover the ground in front of the gun within point-blank range by sweeping fire. In this case the piece should be laid nearly parallel to the surface of the ground, the elevation clamped, and the traverse cast loose. This method of fire is of particular value on outposts liable to attack or surprise.

The "how many M.G.s versus rifles debate" that the major powers and then the U.S. engaged in was an important one because M.G.s are expensive to build, maintain, and use. The Germans pushed the limit with almost one M.G. per infantry platoon. The U.S. was bound and determined to match or even best that level of commitment and our industrial capacity in fact enabled us to in fact surpass the Germans. In 1915, for example, the British made only 2,772 M.G.s at their lone Vickers factory just outside of London. We all surmised that the famous German Zeppelin raids were specifically targeting this factory. This output gave each British infantry battalion two M.G.s (in the U.S. at the time, each infantry regiment had a M.G. company of six M.G.s, giving each battalion two M.G.s if that's what the regimental commander desired). In 1916, while Pershing was chasing Pancho Villa across northern Mexico with a brigade of cavalry, the British and the French were manufacturing around 1,000 M.G.s a month.

An example of how the British were using their M.G.s was explained to us this way: at Loos, Belgium, the British 9th Infantry Division attached four M.G.s to each of its attack battalions and concentrated fourteen M.G.s to supplement the artillery with *indirect fire*. The British found that M.G.s in indirect fire role actually aided the attack more than the ones attached directly to the infantry attack battalions.

That surprised us.

"Indirect fire with M.G.s? That's stupid!"

The "Indirect Fire with a M.G." was not without controversy because to some, it was seen as a waste of ammunition. One shrapnel round, fired from a British 3-inch-type-gun, for example, packed a far-greater punch than a cone of M.G. bullets. But direct enfilade fire from a M.G. was far-more deadly than a shrapnel round. The Germans, for example, did not use the "M.G. barrage" much even though their P.O.W.s talked about how much they feared the ones delivered by the British. They stated to British questioners that the barrages came in swiftly and silently and almost at a 90-degree angle, splitting men in two, from head to crouch.

In 1915, the British formed the Royal Machine Gun Corps (R.M.G.C.) to improve the killing potential of the M.G. and it worked. As the war continued, the British M.G. sections came to be called "Emma Genes" (M.G.s) or "suicide squads" because once they opened up, the enemy did everything they could do to silence them. But unlike our own infantry divisions, British M.G. platoons, as part of the R.M.G.C., were *not* controlled by the infantry commanders. The section chief alone, or his platoon leader, determined where the M.G. should be emplaced and when and where it should be fired.

Clearly, our own Army Chief of Staff at the time, Tasker Bliss, in organizing three M.G. battalions per A.E.F. division, was impressed by the concept of the R.M.G.C. Bliss even authorized a separate enlisted branch with brass "M.G." collar disks. Officers assigned to the M.G. units, however, were drawn from the infantry and retained their distinctive "crossed muskets" collar pins. But unlike the British, Bliss was not willing to allow the M.G. battalions to operate separately from the infantry commanders. Instead, they would fall under or work closely with the infantry company, battalion, or brigade commanders.

It is my understanding that most of the British M.G. trainers (who were N.C.O.s) sent to Camp Lee in 1917 were coal miners from the Midlands of England or Wales. They had joined "Kitchener's Army" in 1915 to not only help protect their country, but to also get out of those damned cold, damp, and dangerous coal mines. What was ironic is that they went from one mine to another as most of the trenches in Flanders were, in fact, modified mines. The assigned "Emma Gene" trainers emphasized that M.G.ers should be physically fit, be able to carry heavy loads over impossible terrain, be mechanically inclined, fairly well-educated, logical, brave, resolute, and disciplined as they may have to "die in place" to buy time for what was left of a retreating friendly infantry battalion that had just been eviscerated by enemy fire. As such, the British trainers ran all of our M.G. sections through an *ad hoc* "M.G. obstacle course" that consisted of jogging 500 yards from Point A to B with the gun broken down as per regulatons along with several filled ammunition cans (about 25 lbs. each) and then setting up the gun in under a minute.

Needless to say, this Olympic-style feat took some time to master even for the most fit of our gun crews, as body/mind/will can only do so much while under extreme stress. The trainers from the R.M.G.C. warned the Blue Ridge gunners that the barrel of a Vickers M.G. becomes worn and inaccurate after 18,000 rds. fired (72 ammo cans of 250 rds. each). If you fired much beyond that point, the barrel would bend and the gun would explode in the faces of the gun squad. One last point: chlorine or phosgene poison gas actually changes the chemical composition of brass bullets when fired at high temperatures. These tainted bullets pretty much dissolved, totally jamming the M.G. and taking it out of action for about a week. This is why the British strived to make their ammo cans not only water-resistant, but also gas-resistant.

Again and again, our British trainers warned us that the Germans were absolute experts in direct fire M.G. tactics, especially in the defense. The Hun had learned to put their M.G.s in the second or third lines, with murderous interlocking fields of fire with a high probablity of enfilade fire. Generally, they'd run a wire entanglement out the muzzle of a gun and wait until an enemy concentrated in front of it. When ten or so enemy soldiers (e.g., British or French) made their presence known at the wire, the German M.G.ers would open up from the right or left with enfilading fire. The remainder of the guns would to be further back, in concealed and reinforced "nests," preferably in a patch of woods, like *Bois Sepsarges* or *Bois d'Ogons*.[90] The M.G. nests themselves were protected from close-quarter infantry assault by large amounts of hand grenades ("potato masher" or "baseball"-type) hurled by an infantry platoon (the British stated that for all intents and purposes, plan that each German infantry platoon will have at least one M.G. For us in the A.E.F., if reinforced by a M.G. battalion, it was equitable).

In the attack, M.G.s were expected to get as far forward to the advancing infantry as possible with the mule-drawn carts or Ford Specials. Once the terrain became totally impassable for the carts or motor cars, which was easy to do on the Western Front, the M.G. section, reinforced by an infantry ammunition-carrying detail, would "advance in parts." This is why basic orienteering skills, even at the private soldier level, are incredibly important. It is critical to ensure that all soldiers have a compass bearing and a map digit to know where to go because visibility on a modern battlefield is very limited.

Needless to say, when the M.G. British trainers arrived, our M.G. tactics were altered a bit as the British were pushing the tenents outlined in their new *Infantry Machine-Gun Company Training Manual, 1917* (*B.M.G.M.*).[91] In our opinion, the British manual was far

---

[90] *Bois Sepsarges* is pronounced "Bwa Sept-sarj and *Bois d'Ogons* is pronounced "Bwa Doe-gawn." Bois means "woods."

[91] British General Staff. *Infantry Machine-Gun Company Training Manual, 1917*, 71-74. Hereafter cited as "*B.M.G.M.*"

better than ours because it went more into depth about practical, common sense offensive and defensive tactics. The most useful portion of the manual is the chapter entitled "Machine-Guns in Battle," which M.G.ers and A.R.men, people like Getz and I, found to be extremely interesting:

> B.M.G.M. 33. *Characteristics of Machine-guns and Lewis Guns Compared.*
>
> *1. The principal characteristic of the M.G. is its ability to produce rapid and sustained fire. Provided water and ammunition are available, a M.G. is capable of keeping up a rapid fire for a very considerable period. On the other hand the Lewis gun [an A.R.], though capable of extremely rapid fire, is incapable of sustaining this fire for long. This necessitates, therefore, the use of short bursts of fire as the normal practice. Its inability to sustain fire is primarily due to the fact that a water jacket is not provided (in order to economise weight) and the gun consequently becomes hot very quickly. Further, owing to their lightness, the working parts will not stand constant vibration to the same extent as those of the M.G.*
>
> *2. A further difference between the two weapons is in the mounting used. The M.G. is provided with a heavy tripod, which enables the gun to be used for overhead and indirect fire. This mounting also allows of the gun being laid at a fixed point, and fired at any time, by day or night, without further preparation. By this means it is possible to form "bands of fire" through which any enemy attempting to pass must suffer heavy loss. The Lewis Gun is fired from the shoulder, a light bipod providing a support for the barrel; there is no traversing or elevating gear; and aim is taken and altered as when using a rifle. The conditions are, therefore, not suitable for overhead or indirect fire, nor for creating "bands of fire."*
>
> *3. The M.G., owing to its weight, and that of its mounting, is less mobile than the Lewis gun. The latter, being specially provided with a light bipod to increase its mobility, can be carried like a rifle, and fired with very little preliminary preparation, so that after movement its fire can be brought to bear on any object much more rapidly than that of a M.G.*

To add more to the above, it is clear that the "Baker Commission" took the recommendations of the French (and especially) the British seriously when it came to organizing the three new M.G. battalions per each A.E.F. division. The fact that each infantry regiment had an organic M.G. company backed by a pool M.G. sections from an entire M.G. battalion certainly helped us gain *fire superiority* against the Hun. The Army went a step further and ordered that each division appoint a Division Machine Gun Officer (D.M.G.O.) to synchronize the fire power of the M.G. battalions. Our D.M.G.O. was Maj. Oscar Foley of the 313th M.G. Battalion. He was later promoted to lt. col.

To add to M.G.er "suicide squad" survivability, the British trainers drilled into our M.G.ers' heads to advance *in cognito* and to have as few crew members around the gun as possible (i.e., two). Our own M.G. manual called for four men to service the gun. Granted, each gun squad still had a crew of four, but two were kept off to the side and in the prone, just in case one of the other crew members got hit. And although the infantry commander was "in charge" of the M.G.s, he relied upon the M.G.ers and their officers to find the best firing positions in order to help achieve fire superiority in conjunction with his other assigned weapons.

> *B.M.G.M. 68. Command and Control.—The various tasks, which the M.G. company has to carry out, demand the most careful preparation and organization on the part of the company commander. He must ensure that all section commanders fully understand the part they have to play, and he must be always on the watch to regain control, at the earliest possible moment, of any guns temporarily detached, in order to provide a reserve for his [regimental] commander. During action the M.G. company commander will keep in the closest possible touch with the [regimental] commander, and it is important that section officers should keep in close touch with the commanders of units to which they may be attached, and under whose command they come. M.G. officers must carefully observe this principle in order to avoid dual control and consequent misunderstanding. It is unsafe to rely upon telephones, especially in open fighting. Steps must, therefore, be taken to maintain communication by visual signaling and by orderlies.*
>
> *B.M.G.M. 69. Co-operation.—Co-operation is an essential feature in M.G. tactics, both between M.G.s and other arms and between the guns themselves. Grouping M.G.s into companies, by centralizing control, facilities the execution of a comprehensive scheme of M.G. co-operation in accordance with the needs of the tactical situation. When this is to be effected the M.G. company commander must be thoroughly conversant with the situation. He should take every step to ensure co-operation, not only between the guns of his company, but between his company and M.G.s on the flanks.*

Concealment.

B.M.G.M. 70. During movement.—To ensure concealment when on the move, M.G.ers should try to disguise their identity as such by adopting the formation of neighboring troops. This, and any other means of escaping detection, should be constantly practiced. When M.G.s are moving, they should watch and avoid areas that are being swept by shell fire.

B.M.G.M. 71. When in position.—As few men as possible should be near the gun. It will usually be found that two men are quite sufficient. When time, implements &c., are available, guns should be dug in, but, unless it is possible to construct a really satisfactory emplacement, it is better to seek cover from view. A hastily made emplacement will merely serve to draw the attention of the enemy…Every effort must be made to prevent M.G.s being located by artillery. If, however, M.G.s are shelled, their actions will largely depend upon the tactical situation. They may make a change in position of about fifty yards or they may temporarily cease fire, the guns and detachment getting under cover; the latter will often deceive the enemy into thinking that they have been destroyed and enable the guns to obtain a good target later. The careful distribution of the gun numbers will minimize casualties.*

The British also taught the gunners to stay as low as possible when firing the gun. This even included how to even fire the piece while lying on one's back! Although I never saw our gun crews get *that* low, I did see them use the "modified kneeling position" quite often. The key was to stay as low as possible, using any folds in the ground as possible to your advantage.

Machine Guns in the Attack.[92]

1. In order to obtain best results, the M.G. company commander must be thoroughly acquainted with the plan of operations and must take a careful reconnaissance of the ground. By use of maps and study of the ground through a telescope from positions in rear or on the flanks, he should endeavour to make himself familiar with the nature of the ground, the correct use of which may prove of decisive value….

2. Distribution of M.G.s in the attack.—The M.G company commander may divide the guns under his command into groups, some to go forward with the infantry, some to cover their advance, others as a reserve.*

---

[92] *B.M.G.M.*, 73-74.

3. The M.G.s that go forward with the attacking infantry will be placed under the control of the Infantry commander to whom they are attached. The role of these guns will be to:

(a) Assist the infantry in obtaining superiority of fire.

(b) Make good the positions won.

(c) Pursue the enemy with fire.

(d) Cover re-organization of the infantry.

(e) Repel counter-attack.

(f) Cover retirement in the event of the attack proving unsuccessful.

The number of guns to be sent with the infantry will be governed by two factors, viz., the length of the front and the nature of the ground. The time of their advance will be determined by the nature of the ground and progress of the infantry. The progress of the infantry must be carefully watched so that the guns may be brought forward at the earliest possible moment. They should rarely advance with the leading line of Infantry. This is the duty of the Lewis Guns, the fire of which should suffice to hold the position won, until it can be finally consolidated by the M.G.s.

4. The guns detailed to cover the advance of the infantry will normally be under the control of the M.G. company commander, who acts under the instuctions of the [regimental] commander. The role of these guns will be to provde covering fire for the infantry up to the last possible moment in the following ways:

(a) By fire from the flanks, or through gaps in the line.

(b) By overhead fire.

(c) By indirect fire.

Great care must be exercised in (b) and (c) in order to avoid endangering our own troops. Orders to the M.G. detailed for this task may, if necessary, include general instructions to govern their action, after the task has been completed, pending receipt of further orders from the M.G. company commander...

5. Guns kept as a reserve will be under the control of the M.G. company commander, acting under the instructions of the [regimental] commander. Owing to their characteristics, M.G.s are valuable as a reserve of fire power, and when kept in reserve in the hands of the [regimental] commander may prove of the utmost value at the critical moment. It must be remembered, however, that a great development of fire power is most useful in the opening stages of an attack, to cover the advance of the infantry, and it is a mistake to keep the guns in reserve if they can be usefully employed in supporting the advance. These guns may be used for long range searching fire on ground behind the enemy's line, which is likely to hold supports or reserves, but must be available to move forward at once, when required.

6. The great fire power of M.G.s relative to the space they occupy, the rapidity with which they may be brought into or out of action and the ease with which they may be brought into or out of action at the ease with which they can change direction of their fire render them especially suitable for the protection of threatened flanks and for filling gaps which may appear laterally or in depth.

7. During an attack it may be advisable to continue to hold certain tactical points, which have been captured, until the attacking troops have made good their next objective. The characteristics of M.G.s fit them for this duty; their use will avoid diminishing the strength and dash of the attacking Infantry.

Generally, M.G.s were deployed two ways: indirect covering fire ("barrage guns") and those that advanced with the infantry ("direct support guns"). In France, the British taught our gunners how to manipulate their T&Es and move their cones of fire onto a grid on a map, much like artillery. As noted above, these same M.G.s would also guard our flanks with indirect fire and would "contain" an objective by dropping their cones in the rear of or on the flanks of the target, preventing reserves from coming up. Finally, and most importantly, M.G. sections would reinforce the A.R.s in spraying the Bejesus out of a *Son-of-a-Boche* M.G. nest, gaining fire superiority, and allowing our bomber and assault squads to carry the day. Always remember that the most effective fire for a M.G. is "searching fire," which is up and down, near and far, on a particular azimuth.

In the defense, particular attention must be paid to the necessity for sweeping all ravines with enfilading fire. A.R.s like Chauchats, Lewis Guns, or, later, Browning Automatic Rifles (B.A.R.s) should cover areas not covered by the M.G.s. It was also expected that each pointer calculated the necessary firing data, provided limiting stakes and flash arresters (if available—to conceal bursts at night), created a range card (a terrain sketch with T&E coordinates), and familiarized himself with the routes of approach to all other M.G. emplacements, front or rear, which it may become necessary for his crew to occupy. He should also know the locations and the fields of fire of his own and neighboring M.G.s. Furthermore, all pointers were expected to turn over to relieving units all available data which would be necessary for the proper functioning of the crew.

Machine Guns in the Defense. [93]

1. When it has been decided to consolidate a position for defence a reconnaissance should be carried out, the M.G.s being generally allotted on the following principles.

2. Some guns should be posted as soon as possible in accordance with the nature of the ground to form a complete belt of flanking M.G. fire along the front of the position. Important concealed approaches and folds in the ground should be covered by M.G.s. Co-operation must be arranged with the Lewis guns of the battalions, which can cover the less important approaches or small depressions or hollows which the M.G.s cannot sweep.

3. A proportion of M.G.s should be kept in reserve. When the ground is suitable, these may be used for indirect overhead fire if the results are likely to justify the expenditure of ammunition, and the readiness of the guns to take up other tasks is not impaired. It will often be found advisable to prepare M.G. emplacements at important tactical occupation, if necessary. Preparatin in this respect will facilitate a rapid readjustment of the line at any point.

4. Secondary positions and lines of retirement must be reconnoitered, and steps must be taken to ensure that the detachments are familiar with them. In case of a withdrawal becoming necessary, M.G.s in supporting positions will cover the retirement of the infantry and guns in the front line. When the latter have occupied their secondary positions, they, in turn, will cover the movement of the guns originally in support.

You will read in Volume 2 how M.G.s were brought up to solidify our lines of defense, esp. during the night. In the defense, they, as well as the artillery, were our main defensive weapon and the rifles and A.R.s simply supported their flanks or covered their defiaded areas (defiladed areas are places where enemy bullets cannot strike—it's a coveted area that all infantrymen wished to obtain). As much as we could, we would position our M.G.s in a "lazy W" formation where they could shoot enfilading fire across the front of the riflemen. The Germans

---

[93] *B.M.G.M.*, 74-75.

did the same thing, except they would string a line of wire along their cone of fire and wait until a bunch of us gathered at a breach point before they opened up.

Village Fighting. [94]

1. As soon as the infantry have made good one edge of a village, M.G.s should be brought up in close support. They should then search windows, doorways, roofs, &c., likely to be held by the enemy.

2. M.G.s should be used to command cross-streets, &c., so as to guard against attack on the flanks or rear of the infantry. They should also be posted on the edges of the villages to prevent flank attacks, and when possible should be pushed forward well on the flanks, so as to command the exits from the village.

3. During village fighting use may be made of windows, doors, &c., as M.G. positions. If a good field of fire cannot be obtained from existing doors and windows, and time is available, small holes can be made in the outside walls of the upper storeys of buildings, enabling a good field of fire to be obtained.

Occupation of Various Positions.

1. M.G.s may be hidden in almost any position, but it is advisable to avoid places which are either obvious or easy to recognise, such as cross-roads or single objects, or places which can be easily be located on the map. It is important that guns should merge into the surroundings, and straight edges or distinct shadows should not be made.

2. Banks of rivers, canals, and railways, ditches, folds in the ground, hedges, palings or walls, also mounds of earth, may be used either to afford a covered line of approach and supply to a gun position or else a gun position itself. When firing over the top of the cover, greater protection is given if hollows are scooped out for the front tripod legs.

3. Houses may be employed in the following ways: The gun may be placed in rear, firing through windows or doors in line or past the sides of the house. When firing from a window, door, or hole in the roof, the gun should be placed well back for concealment. A damp piece of cloth hung in front of the gun helps to conceal the flash. When firing from a cellar, care should be taken not to cause a cloud of dust to rise and give away the position. A means of

---

[94] *B.M.G.M.*, 78-79.

retirement and alternative emplacements should be arranged. Overhead fire and observation may often be obtained from high buildings.

4. Woods and crops provide cover from view facilities for communication, and good lines of approach or supply. In neither case should guns be placed too near to the front edge. In woods it will often be possible to construct hasty overhead cover.

5. If a barricade has been contructed across a road, M.G.s should not be put in the barricade itself but, if possible, in a concealed position to a flank from which they can sweep the road.

6. Haystacks do not as a rule afford a very satisfactory position, but guns may be placed in a hollow in front, or behind, firing past the side, or else in a hollow on top, firing through the front face of the stack. A M.G. concealed in a field which is covered with cornstalks, manure heaps, or mounds of roots is very hard to locate.

7. Wood stacks, planks, logs of trees, and farm implements may be used to conceal guns; cover from fire can often be obtained by the addition of bricks or sand bags.

8. Trees generally provide better observation posts than M.G. positions.

The last part, "Occupation of Various Positions," is the hardest and most important skill for a M.G. squad to master. All of the above are suggestions or guidelines only, as most of the time, a M.G.er or rifleman doesn't have many choices. He is where he is and has to make the best of it. Sometimes a M.G. was in fact set up in the middle of the woods firing straight on at fifty yards. When our division fought through Gercourt, Dannevoux, and Buzancy, for example, most of the enemy had already been driven out and did not wish to counter-attack to retake them, thus the M.G.s were moved forward into a woodline.[95]

As for the A.R.s, there were four A.R.s per infantry platoon while we fought in France. I was one of those A.R.men and Getz was my assistant gunner (A.G.). While with the British in *Picardy*, we used a Lewis Gun, which we really liked. While operating with Pershing's American First Army in Saint-Mihiel and the Meuse-Argonne, we used either the M1915 Chauchat, which was average (jammed too much because the American 30.06 bullets were too big for it) or the

---

[95] *Gercourt* is pronounced "Geyr-core," *Dannevoux* is pronounced "Dan-ev-voo," and *Buzancy* is pronounced "Booz-an-see."

M1918 Browning Automatic Rifle (B.A.R.), which we loved.[96] What Getz and I realized after we read the above paragraph was the importance of moving and looking like basic riflemen while we advanced so we wouldn't be recognized as A.R. men to the Hun.

B.M.G.M. 34. The Employment of Lewis Guns.

1. Owing to its greater mobility a much greater liberty of action can be allowed to this weapon than to the M.G. It must, however, be clearly understood that the Lewis Gun cannot take the place of the M.G. It is a supplement to, and not a substitute for, the latter type of weapon.

2. It is adapted for even closer co-operation with infantry than the M.G., as the Lewis gunner can move and appear to the enemy as an ordinary rifleman. Its distribution as a battalion and company weapon provides a mobile reserve of fire available for the smallest unit commander wherever the Infantry can go.

3. It is specially adapted for a concentrated enfilade fire on a definite line such as a hedge or wall, or to cover a road or defile where it is not possible to deploy a number of rifles, and for places where it is difficult or impossible to bring up a M.G. unobserved. When wider fronts have to be swept with fire or heavier fire is required at longer ranges M.G.s can be more usefully employed.

4. Although the expenditure of ammunition is not so great as with M.G.s, the difficulty of getting ammunition up to the more exposed positions to which Lewis Guns can go will be much greater. It is important, therefore, to withhold fire as long as possible and to use the power of the gun to develop unexpected bursts of fire against favourable [sic] targets.[97]

To close, in combat we found that although the M.G.s were helpful, they were not as important to us in the rifle platoons during the attack than our own rifles, R.G.s, and A.R.s. I'm not saying that we weren't glad when they came up—we were. But fighting in places like *Bois d'Ogons*, in which fields of fire were actually limited and bomb craters seriously hampered heavier weapons in moving forward, we were, too often, left to our own devices—just like "Black Jack" warned. I think that's what Pershing was trying to tell us: "supporting arms" are nice—in

---

[96] *Saint-Mihiel et la Meuse-Argonne* is pronounced "Sawn Me-hell ae Me-use Ar-goan" and *Chauchat* is pronounced "Chow-chawt."

[97] *B.M.G.M.*, 65-68.

fact essential—but in the end, it comes down to a Dough with rifle, bayonet, intrenching tool, and hand grenade—or in my case, automatic rifle.

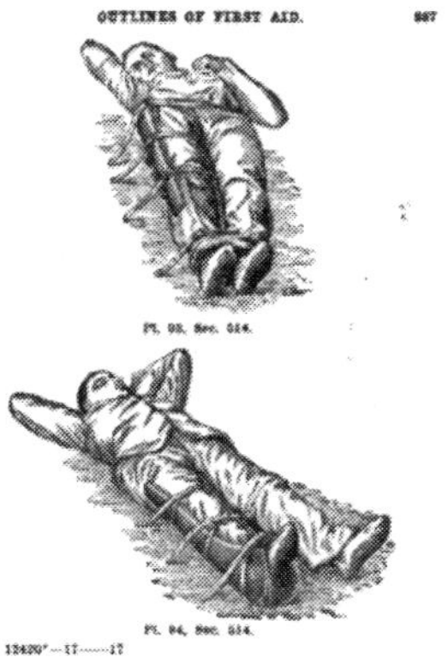

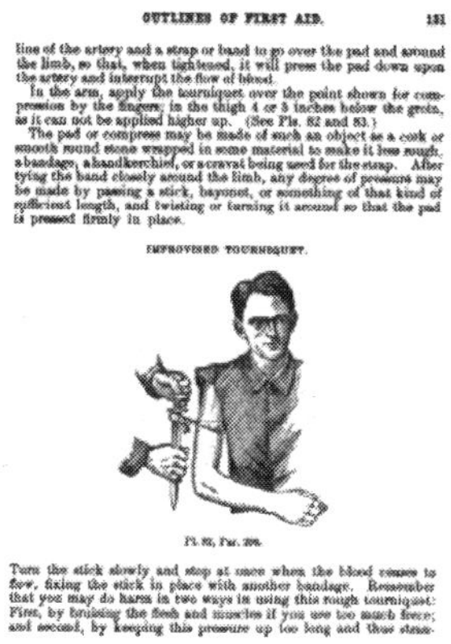

Casualty evacuation carries. *M.S.T, 1917.*

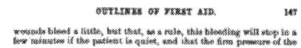

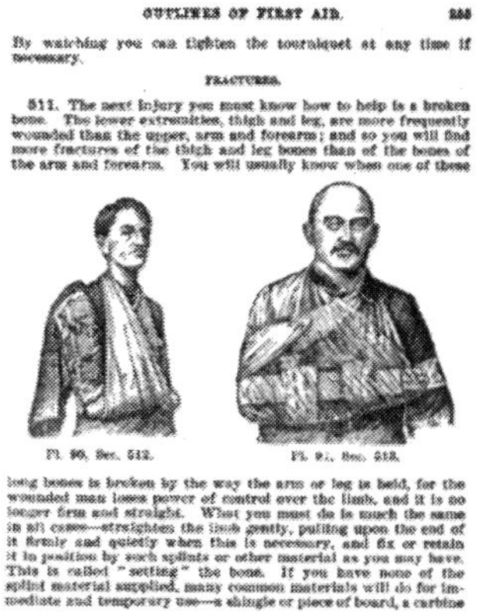

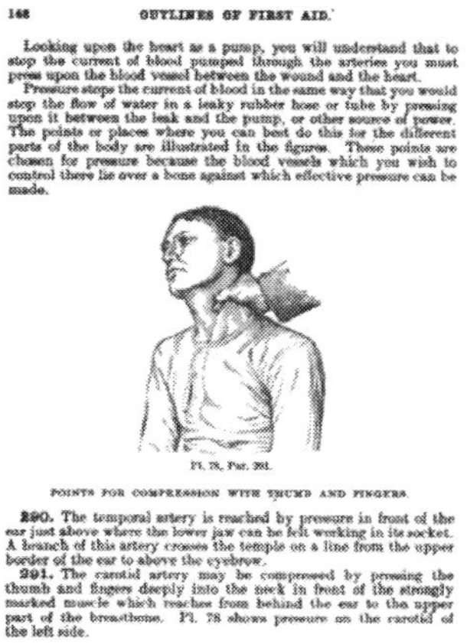

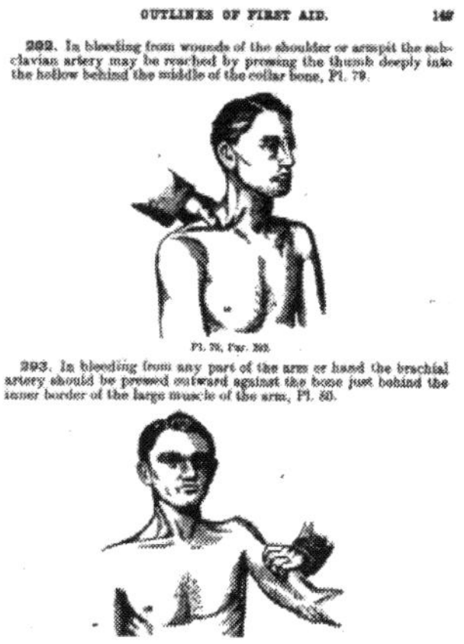

Litter training at Camp Lee, 1918.

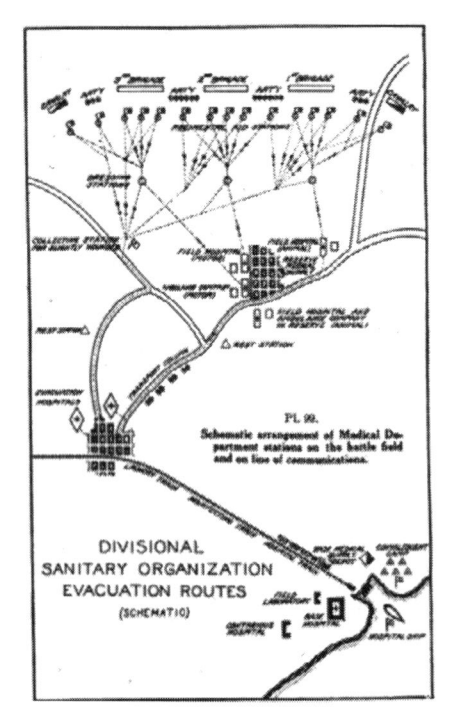

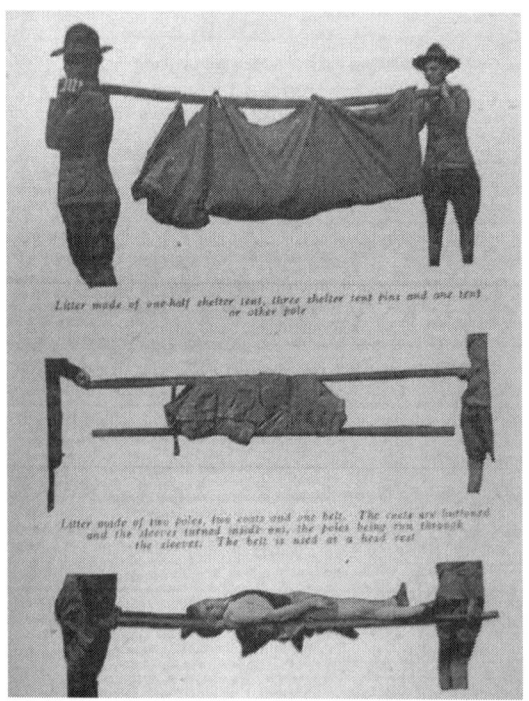

"Divisional Sanitary Organization Evacuation Routes" (L) and the different ways to make ad hoc stretchers using tunics, blankets, or shelter halves with poles.

3
1
2
4

2
II
I
1

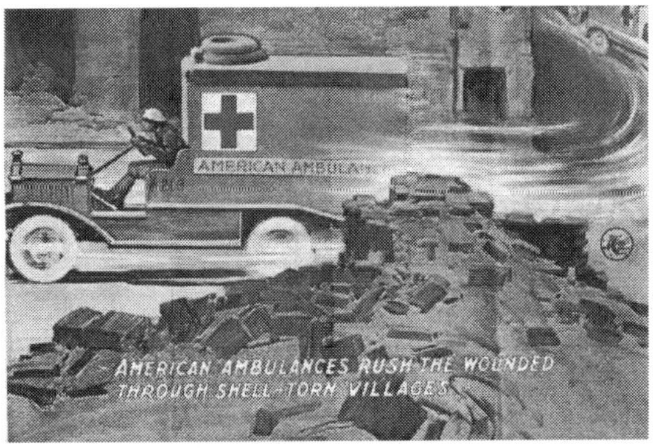
AMERICAN AMBULANCES RUSH THE WOUNDED
THROUGH SHELL-TORN VILLAGES

4
1
2
3

2
3
1

Chapter 7
Medical Training at Camp Lee.

To be honest, we Doughs did not take "First Aid" or "Sanitation" or "Health Care and Kindred Subjects" training seriously at Camp Lee. We paid for that mistake. Any combat veteran will tell you that learning first aid or how to stay healthy in the field is as important as learning about weapons or tactics. As was already stated, each infantry battalion was assigned a "sanitation section" and each brigade a field hospital and an ambulance company. Maybe we took it for granted that the dedicated "sanitation men" or "medics" would handle all of the sick or wounded. Looking back on this ludicrous assumption is almost stunning—especially considering the volume of casualties we knew (but did not fully appreciate) we would suffer. It was even directly stated in Col. Moss's *Manual of Military Training*:

> *1451: Good health is just as necessary to an army as rifles and ammunition. Not only does every sick man take away one rifle from the firing line, but in addition he becomes a care and a burden at the hands of the Army. Indeed, it is fully as important for a soldier to take care of his health as it is for him to take care of his rifle and ammunition. The importance of doing everything possible to look after one's health is shown by the fact that in every war so far, many more men have died from disease than were killed in battle or died from wounds. In our Civil War, for instance, for every man on the Union side who was killed or died of wounds, two died from disease. In the Spanish-American War the proportion was 1 to 5.5.*

General Cronkhite even issued the following directive to his subordinate commanders while we were still training at Camp Lee:

> *Organization commanders will cause their surgeons daily to see and to note the health of every member of his command. The surgeon will go to the men and will anticipate the needs of the men, instead of waiting for the men to come to him.*[98]

Defense from illness or injury is the key to staying healthy in the field and the Army offered several suggestions on how to do it. According to Col. Moss:

> *M.M.T. 1452: Diseases are caused by little, tiny live animals or plants called germs. They are so small that you require a magnifying glass to see them.*
>
> *M.M.T. 1453: There are only five ways to catch disease:*

---

[98] As cited in Stultz, 119.

1. By breathing in the live germs.

2. By swallowing the live germs.

3. By touching the live germs.

4. By having the live germs stuck into the skin by insects that bite.

5. By inheritance from parents.

M.M.T. 1454: *The following are some of the more common diseases caught by breathing in germs: colds, diphtheria, tonsillitis, grippe, scarlet fever, pneumonia, and consumption. The germs that cause these diseases grow well in the dark, warm, moist lining of the nose, throat, windpipe, and lungs, and they are coughed or sneezed out or blown out and float in tiny bubbles in the air or fall to dry into dust which is blown about y the wind, and so are breathed in, or they may be transferred directly by kissing invalids and sick children.*

M.M.T. 1455: *Do not visit sick people or a house where children are sick. Do not let other people cough or sneeze over your food or into your face. Do not allow others to spit on the floor of your squad room or tent. Do put your hand to your face when you cough or sneeze. Do rinse out your nose with hot, weak-salt water at night and especially if you have been inhaling dust. Brush your teeth after every meal and before going to bed. Do not pick your nose with the fingernails, as it makes sore spots in which germs grow. On dusty hikes, tie a handkerchief across the nose and mouth. Never sweep the floor with a dry broom. Use a damp mop and so pick up the germs and carry them out instead of driving them up in the air as dust.*

M.M.T. 1456: *The following are some of the more common diseases caught by swallowing the germs: typhoid fever, dysentery, cholera, and ptomaine poisoning.*

M.M.T. 1457: *Impure water is one of the most common distributors of disease that there is. Therefore, water from sources unknown or soiled by sewage, should be avoided as deadly and should not be used, unless boiled, for drinking, brushing the teeth, or rinsing mess kits. You can not always tell polluted water by its appearance, smell, or taste. Unless from a sewer or drain, it may look clear and sparkling, with no smell and have a pleasant taste, so water that is not known to be pure should not be drunk.*

M.M.T. 1462: Beware of water from wells, farm pumps, or barrels, especially those found in railroad cars, stations, or ferry boats. Do not drink lemonade, soft drinks, or milk from peddlers. Beware of a public drinking cup. Always wash your hands before going to meals and before putting things into your mouth, especially after going to the toilet or handling animals. Do not adopt strange dogs and do not pet dogs. Before eating fruit or raw vegetables, wash and peel them unless picked from the tree yourself. Do not eat food that is spoiled, smells or tastes badly, or is fly-blown or maggoty or full of bugs. Do not eat food which is not sufficiently cooked. All smoked, dried, or salt meats or fish, such as ham, bacon, sausage, dried beef, bloaters, salt mackerel, or codfish, must be well-cooked, as they may contain "Measles" or other worm eggs. Cooking kills the egg. Do not eat food exposed in public stands to dust, flies, dirty hands, dirty water, dirty cans, or dirty glasses and buckets. Do not allow flies to breed in dirt or other filth around your house, nor allow them to walk on your food. This is possible by burning, burying or otherwise removing the dirt or filth and by using fly traps, "swatters," or fly paper. Do not wet your fingers with spit when you turn the pages of books or magazines...

M.M.T. 1463: The following are some of the more common diseases caught by touching the germs: ringworm, mange, barber's itch, sore eyes, boils, earbuncles, lockjaw, small pox, cancroids, syphilis, and gonorrhea (clap).

M.M.T. 1464: Ringworm, mange, and barber's itch are carried from person to person by finger nails and hands from dirty water to those who bathe in it or have their underwear washed in it.

M.M.T. 1465: The germs of lockjaw are found in manure and in soil fertilized with it; hence, a bullet which passes through such soil before wounding carries these germs into the wound. Any wound soiled with such dirt will be infected.

The last point, "a bullet which passes through such soil before wounding carries these germs into the wound," is something that we learned to fully appreciate in combat. It is critical to keep a wound as clean as possible (including keeping a little blood flowing), even under horrendous conditions. Your wounded comrade may survive the wound itself, but not the subsequent fever that was caused by infection. Again, at first, this point did not resonate strongly with us, but as our days in combat increased, we became far more cognizant of it:

M.M.T. 1467: To avoid diseases caught by touching germs, keep your skin clean with soap and water. Do not bathe or wash your clothes in dirty water, have them boiled when laundered. Do not go barefoot, even in the barracks. Do not use towels or toilet articles of other people, especially in public wash-rooms unless they furnish a fresh towel to you. Do not sleep in houses left empty by the enemy, unless ordered to do so... Do not rub the eyes with dirty hands. When dirt gets in have a doctor get it out.

It is imperative that N.C.O.s (especially) model, mentor, and guide the men under their charge to maintain as much "Personal Hygiene in the Field" as possible, especially when conducting what we called "Recovery Operations." The *M.M.T.* lists seven general rules to help maintain personal hygiene in the field:[99]

1. *Keep the skin clean. A dirty body invites sickness. Small troubles such as chafing, sore feet, saddle boils, sore eyes, felons, whitlows, earache, toothache, carbuncles, fleas, lice, and ringworms, are all caused by lack of cleanliness, and they put a man on sick report... Keep your feet clean with soap and water and put on dry socks before sleeping at night. Soiled socks should be washed and hung up to dry overnight.*

2. *Keep the body properly protected against the weather.*

3. *Keep the body properly fed. Your company mess is sufficient for your needs and is wholesome, provided it is well chewed. Large lumps of food take a longer time to digest than small particles do, and so they tire the stomach and cause constipation, gas, and indigestion with headache. Do not eat food left behind in strange houses or by the enemy, nor food that smells or looks badly.*

4. *Keep the body properly supplied with fresh air. The brain, kidneys, and other internal organs require oxygen (a part of the air) continually, and if deprived of it for 5 minutes, the body will die. Therefore, it is easy to see that we must continually get plenty of fresh air into the lungs to supply the blood which carries the oxygen throughout the body. Except in wintertime when steam heated barracks are filled with sleeping men, it is not, as a rule, difficult to get all the fresh air we need. The air in a dormitory should smell sweet and clean, even though warm. Fresh air should be continually admitted in a way that will not throw a draft on any of the sleepers. It is much better to sleep in a cold room with fresh air than in a hot, stuffy one.*

5. *Keep the body well exercised without exhaustion.*

---

[99] *M.M.T.*, 1470-77.

> 6. *Keep the body rested by sufficient sleep. Eight hours of uninterrupted sleep are enough for the average man and you should always have that much in every twenty-four hours....*
>
> 7. *Keep the body free of wastes. Get into the habit of emptying the bowels at certain hours each day. Immediately after breakfast is a good time. This is a habit that can be cultivated just like any other habit. Cultivate it. It will do much to keep you in good health. Always empty the bowels and the bladder, especially the bowels, whenever you have the least desire to do so. Do not allow a little personal inconvenience or laziness to prevent you from doing this. The wastes of the bowels and the bladder, especially the bowels, are poisons that should always be expelled from the body just as soon as possible.*

Beside "Personal Hygiene in the Field," the most important sanitation skills are "First Aid for Wounds." If you are involved in combat, you will not only see casualties, but will also be forced to help care for them. Although medics will probably be present to assist you, you must understand that they can only do so much—they can only handle one casualty at a time. The two biggest injuries will involve bleeding or breathing. After five minutes without a breath of air, a person will die. If an artery is cut, he will bleed to death in five minutes. We were taught to staunch the bleeding first, then work on the breathing. If the patient was still alive after five minutes, we were to continue with the first aid. If not, then move on: he's dead. In staunching or even stopping the bleeding, we were taught how to apply pressure points, bandages, and tourniquets:

> *M.M.T. 1520. Wounds may be made in every degree of size, from the jab of a splinter to the loss of a part of the body from shrapnel. No matter what form of the wound or the cause, we know the following fact to be of the utmost importance: A wound without germs in it will heal rapidly without pain, redness, heat, or pus and the patient will have no fever. He will eat his regular meals and act as though well. Such wounds we see made by surgeons when operating. On the other hand, wounds infected with germs are painful, hot, angry, red, and swollen and form large qualities of pus or matter. Pus is a mixture of germs, blood and the flesh that they have destroyed. This pus prevents wounds from healing and often burrowed under the skin, forming abscesses which cause fever and chills, and the pus enters the blood causing*

delirium and death. Our one aim in treating wounds is to keep out germs, and we accomplish this by means of the first aid packet.

M.M.T. 1521. The first aid packet consist of two gauze compresses sewed to two cotton bandages. They are sealed in waxed paper. There are also two safety pins wrapped in wax paper. These articles are placed in an air-tight metal case which protects them from contamination. Now, the one important fact about this first aid packet is that the bandage compresses and safety pins have been sterilized—that is—they contain no living germs of any kind. It is, therefore, perfectly safe to put on a wound, provided the pad touches the wound before it touches anything else and provided that the wound has not been handled. Therefore, do not wash a fresh clean wound. CAUTION. Have the wound ready before you open the packet. Do not touch the gauze pad with ANYTHING. Do not breathe on it, and be especially careful not to cough or sneeze over it. These things put germs on in which will grow in the wound. By observing these instructions you may save a man's life. By not observing them, you may cause his death, or cause him much pain and suffering. The life of a wounded man is often in the hands of the first one who attends him. It is said that since the adoption of the first aid packet by armies, it has done more than anything else to save the lives of those wounded in battle by preventing the infection of wounds... When a bullet strikes a man first, the wound is clean cut and germ free and will heal rapidly. If, however, it strikes something first, and bounces off (ricochets) and then strikes a man, it will be knocked into an irregular shape and, therefore, cause a ragged wound with much bruising. What is more important, such a bullet will carry germs into the wound from the object struck, and almost surely some shreds of clothing. When a wound is infected it is extremely difficult to kill the germs (disinfect). Such a wound, before applying the first aid dressing should be painted with a tincture of iodine or alcohol or be well washed with boiled salt water.

The other type of wound we had to deal with was the treatment of burns. According to the *Drill and Service Manual for Sanitary Troops, U.S.A., April 15, 1917, (M.S.T.)*:

312. In the treatment of burns, do not pull the clothing from the burnt part, but rip it or cut it off. Do not break the blisters nor prick them, even if large. Protect the burn quickly with a mixture of equal parts of linseed or olive oil and limewater, if you have them, or with the plain oil, covering the whole with lint or cotton bandages. Put nothing on the burn that will be difficult afterwards.[100]

According to the *M.S.T.* (and common sense), the best first aid is one that is rendered quickly, quietly, and gently:

303: You have already been warned to be gentle in the treatment of the wounded and the necessity for not touching the wound must always be in your mind; but there are also some other general directions, which you will do well to remember:

1. Act quickly and quietly.

2. Make the patient sit or lie down.

3. See an injury clearly before treating it.

4. Do not remove more clothing is necessary to examine the injury and keep the patient warm with covering, if needed. Always rip, if you cannot rip, cut the clothing from the injured part and pull nothing off.

5. Give alcoholic stimulants cautiously and slowly, only when necessary. Hot drinks will often suffice when obtainable.

6. Keep from the patient all persons not actually needed to help him.

Once we were able to staunch or even stop the bleeding of a wounded comrade, the next step was to create a "diagnosis tag." Any paper would suffice. It communicated to the official sanitary personnel in the rear what first aid was actually rendered:

M.S.T. 304. The diagnosis tag is very important in preventing unnecessary handling of the wounded man and interference with his dressing on the field. When available, it is to be attached by the person who applied the first aid dressing and is not to be removed until the patient reaches the field hospital. When a patient has a tag on, it is to be carefully read before additional treatment is given, and will usually indicate that no further treatment is needed before reaching the hospital.

Once the tag was completed, the final step was to evacuate the patient to a field ambulance with as few people as possible. Generally, the reserve battalion of a regiment

---

[100] *Drill and Service Manual for Sanitary Troops, U.S.A., April 15, 1917.* Hereafter cited as "M.S.T."

provided said litter teams during an attack. As such, all soldiers had to have a basic understanding on how to evacuate a casualty via a "litter," service or improvised:

Transportation.

M.S.T. 314. The carriage of patients for moderate distances on or from the field is best done with the service litter or, when that can not be procured, by some improvised substitute which secures the comfort and safety of the person disabled.

Improvisation of Litters.

M.S.T. 179. Many things can be used for this purpose: camp cots, window shutters, doors, benches, ladders, etc., properly padded. Litters may be made with sacks or bags of any description, if large and strong enough, by ripping the bottoms and passing two poles through them and tying crosspieces to the poles to keep them apart; two, or even three, sacks placed end to end on the same poles may be necessary to make a safe and comfortable litter.

M.S.T. 180. The usual military improvisation is by means of rifles and blankets...The rifle should be unloaded...At the command, the bearers shall lay their rifles on the ground and face each other. No.2 will slip off his blanket roll, give one end to No. 1 and together they will spread it out on the ground. No. 1 then places his rifle across the center of the blanket, the butt toward the original front of the squad and trigger guard in. Both bearers (No. 1 at left front, No. 2 at the rear left corner) fold the blanket over the rifle. No. 2 then places his rifle over the center of the new fold and the blanket is folded. Owing to the shortness of the present rifle it is of little use in this improvisation but the method may be used with poles, instead of rifles.

Position of Patient on the Litter.

M.S.T. 158: The position of a patient on the litter depends on the character of his injuries. An overcoat, blanket, or other suitable and convenient article should be used as a pillow to give support and slightly raised position to the head. If the patient is faint, the head should be kept low. Difficulty of breathing in wounds of the chest is relieved by a sufficient padding underneath. In wounds of the abdomen, the best position is on the injured side, or on the back if the abdomen is injured, the legs in either case being drawn up, and a pillow or other available object placed under the knees to keep them bent.

Methods of Removing Wounded Without Litter.

M.S.T. 196. A travois consists of two long poles, one end of each is attached to a horse, a mule, or even pulled by men, while the other ends are dragged across the ground. It is a vehicle intended to transport the sick or wounded when the use of wheeled vehicles or other means of transportation is impractical or unavailable.

M.S.T. 184: A good rifle seat may be made by running the barrels of 2 rifles through the sleeves of an overcoat, turned inside out and buttoned up, sleeves in, so that the coat lies back up, collar to the rear. The front bearer rolls the tail tightly around the barrels and takes grasp over them; the rear bearer holds by the butts, trigger guards up.

M.S.T. 186: A single bearer may carry a patient in his arms or on his back.

In combat, we actually used a combination of all the listed transportation methods: service or improvised litter, travois, rifle seat, and man-carry. The key was to get the wounded person back through the blown-up landscape as soon as possible with the greatest care. About a half-mile behind the line, brigade would usually have several of its ambulances waiting. Ambulances were either horse-drawn or motorized:

M.S.T. 196. The ambulance is a four-wheeled vehicle, ordinarily drawn by two animals in garrison and four in the field. It provides transportation for eight men sitting or four recumbent on litters, or four sitting and two recumbent. It is fitted with two hinged seats which, when not used as such, are folded one against each side. The arrangements for supporting the litters consist of two center posts and eight straps. Fastened to each of the center posts is a hanger for the inside handles of the litter and opposite each hanger and attached to the side of the ambulance is a strap to hold the outside handles.

Like other A.E.F. divisions, the Blue Ridge Division had a sanitary (medical) battalion, ours was the 305th Sanitary Battalion. It consisted of doctors, nurses, and personnel from the sanitary corps (planners, medics, litter bearers, hospital stewards, etc.). Our division surgeon was Lt. Col. Thomas L. Rhodes and the commander of the 305th Sanitary Battalion was Maj. Linsly Williams. Williams' battalion had four field hospital companies and four ambulance companies, one for each Infantry regiment of the division.[101]

---

[101] Stultz, 26.

The 305th Engineers laying a pontoon bridge across the Appomattox River.

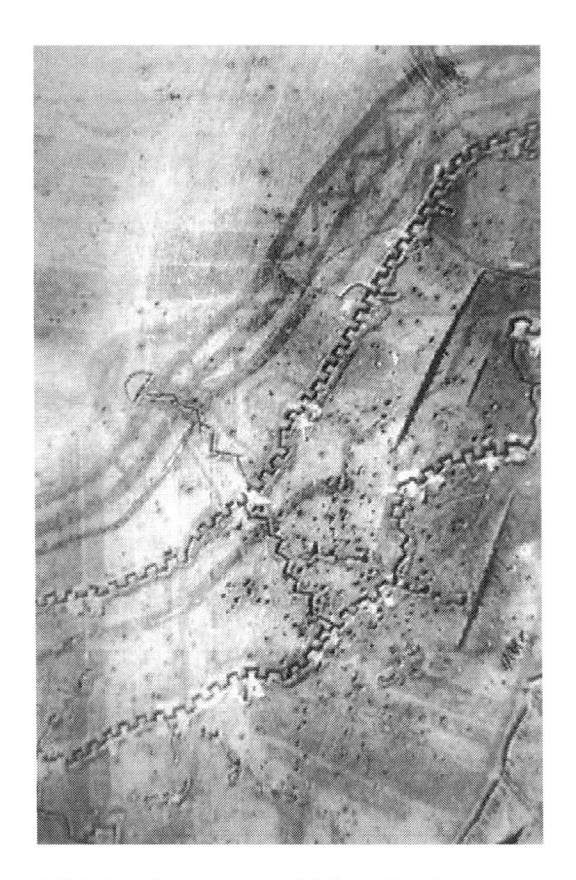

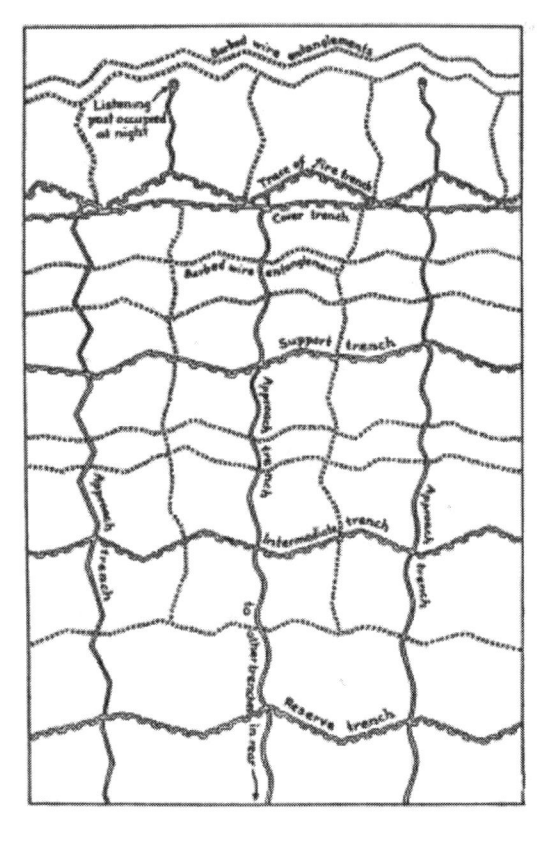

This is what we would face in France: strongly constructed German defenses dug-in with interlocking fields of fire (L). The sketch on the (R) shows what was in the *P.M.* with the multiple layers of defense ("defense-in-depth") with listening posts, firing trenches, approach trenches, etc.

212

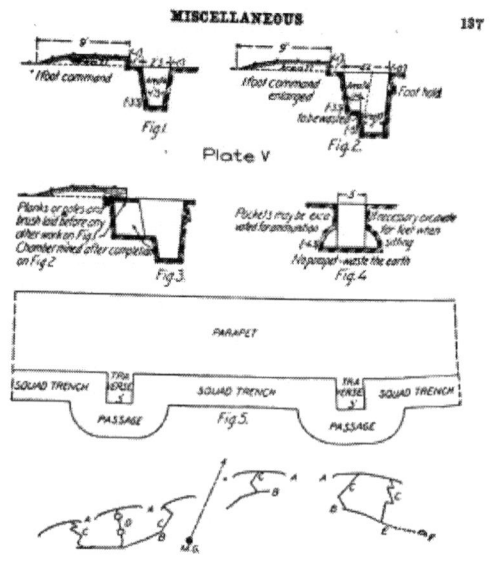

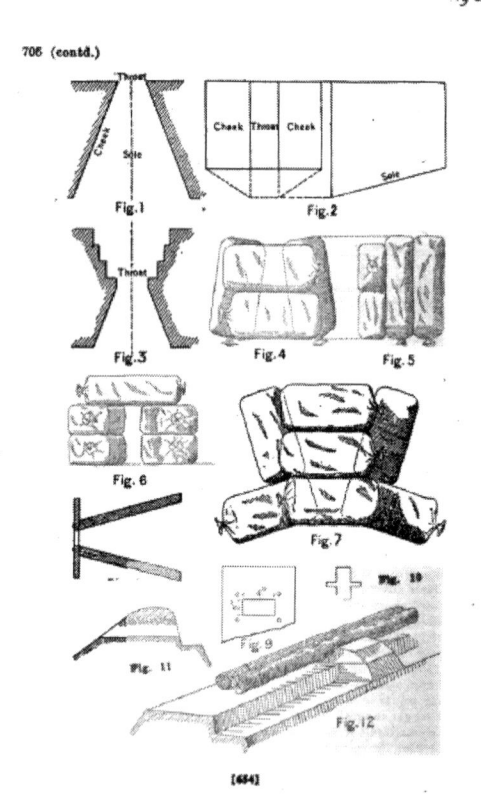

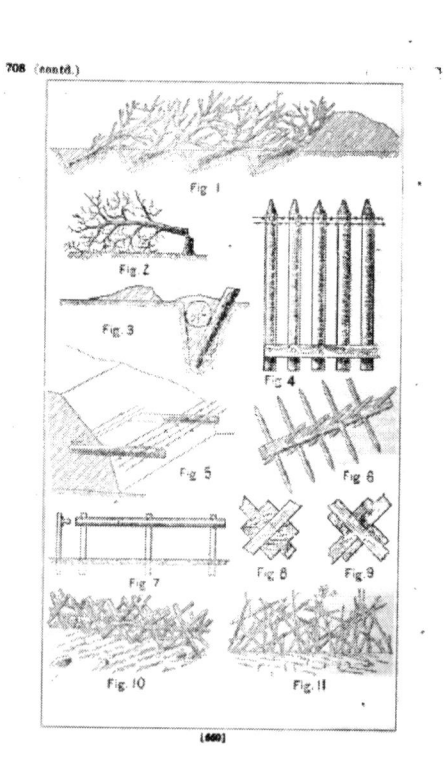

Chapter 8
Engineer and Trench Warfare Training at Camp Lee.

As spring 1918 came on, Col. Spalding's 305th Engineers put the finishing touches on the battalion-sized trench training range on the post, aided by our French and British advisors. The range was complete in every detail, with first and second line trenches linked by communication or approach trenches, listening posts, firing trenches, barb wire, etc. Camouflage was supplied by sod, pine needles, and grass. Dug-outs, equipped with bunks, were large enough to lodge as many as fourty soldiers. In their construction, men from the mining districts of the respective countries showed their prowess.

It must be understood that with the German defeat at the Battle of the Marne in 1914, the war on the Western Front basically became a giant siege. Both flanks were secure, one on the English Channel and the other on the border of neutral (but armed) Switzerland. Portions of this intrenched front were weak, while other sections were strong. The strongest positions of the Western Front were in the *Verdun-Belfort* region and the weakest were along what is called the Chemin des Dames, which is between *Rheims* and *Soissons*, and just northeast of *Paris*.

Neither side had enough forces to exploit a breach—they could conduct a breach—but could not send in enough forces or supplies to exploit it to reach a decision. As such, the war in the West became one of attrition, as each side, especially the Germans, protected itself by trenches and endeavored to wear down the opponent. There were occasional local assaults, however, when one side felt that success would more than counter-balance the losses that were sustained. The key became to break the enemy's morale and power of resistance. While the Germans tried to bleed the French white at Verdun, the Allies tried to starve Germany into submission with a blockade, which, according to the great battle captains Frederick the Great, Napoleon Bonaparte, and Winfield Scott, was the most deadly weapon in war. In siege warfare, engineers are essential; and because the war on the Western Front was one giant siege, engineers were paramount.[102] According to the *Engineer Field Service Manual*:

> *When the advance positions of both sides are close to each other, there ensues a series of conflicts which have been designated by the term "Trench Warfare." In sieges, the forces in closest contact are in the advanced parallels, saps, and mining galleries on the side of the attacker, and in the intrenched position and counter-mines of the defender—in extended intrenched fronts, the forces in closest contact are in the firing trenches, saps, and mines and counter-mines of the two sides. The methods of conflict in trench warfare are practically the same*

---
[102] Mitchell, 662.

as in former wars, with modifications due to the advances of science. Hand grenades, bombs, obstacles, etc., were used at Sevastopal, Port Arthur, and at Verdun.

The essential difference between the capture of an intrenched position and victory over extended intrenched positions lies in the fact that only the garrison of an intrenched position, like a fort, must be subdued. Victory over extended intrenched positions, however, requires that the nation behind said positions must be subdued. As long as the garrison of a fortress still retains numbers, food, ammunition, and morale, it may be possible to capture local strong points, but the garrison will not surrender until its power of resistance is broken; other strong points to the rear will be occupied and the resistance continued. Similarly, as long as the nation still retains numbers, food, ammunition, and morale, it may be possible to capture local strong points and force the abandonment of an extended trench line, but the nation will not cease making war until its physical or moral power of resistance is broken; other extended intrenched lines will be occupied and resistance continued.[103]

We understood that the developments of attack and defense of extended intrenched positions during the Great War were simply an expanded replication of large scale siege operations since time immemorial. There was a general failure during the war to recognize the fact that the tactics of siege warfare must be applied in a large way to the attack and defense of long intrenched fronts. During the first three years, for example, the operations consisted of local, uncoordinated attacks, meaning that the British attacked in their zone at "x" time, the French in theirs at "y," the Russians in theirs at "z," the Italians at "q," etc. This disjunction allowed the armies of the Central Powers to mas at one point and then move to another. It was only in 1917, as we assembled at Camp Lee, that the Allies were finally treating the Western Front as one strategic problem. The greatest difficulty in grasping the broader conception lay in the inability of each side to make adequate concentrations of infantry and artillery, the inability to manufacture and concentrate the enormous amounts of ammunition required, and the difficulties of moving forward with the troops the enormous quantities of ammunition.[104] According to the *I.D.R.* on "Defense: Positions And Intrenchments":

---

[103] As cited in Mitchell, 663. "Sevastopal" was during the Crimean War of 1853-56 and "Port Arthur" was during the Russo-Japanese War of 1904-05.

[104] Mitchell, 663.

489. The first requirement of a good position is a clear field of fire and view to the front and exposed flanks to a distance of six hundred to eight hundred yards or more. The length of front should be suitable to the size of the command and the flanks should be secure. The position should have lateral communication and cover for supports and reserves. It should be one which the enemy cannot avoid, but must attack or give up his mission. A position having all these advantages will rarely, if ever, be found. The one should be taken which conforms closest to the description.

490. The natural cover of the position should be fully utilized. In addition, it should be strengthened by fieldworks and obstacles. The best protection is afforded by deep, narrow, inconspicuous trenches. If little time is available, as much as practicable must be done. That the fieldworks may not be needed should not cause their construction to be omitted, and the fact that they have been constructed should not influence the action of a commander, if conditions are found to be other than expected.

491. When time and troops are available the preparations include the necessary communicating and cover trenches, head cover, bombproofs, etc. The fire trenches should be well supplied with ammunition. The supports are placed close at hand in cover trenches when natural cover is not available.

492. Dummy trenches frequently cause the hostile artillery to waste time and ammunition and to divert its fire.

493. The location, extent, profile, garrison, etc., of fieldworks are matters to be decided by the infantry commanders. Officers must be able to choose ground and properly intrench it.

494. In combat exercises, when it is impracticable to construct the trenches appropriate to the exercise, their trace may be outlined by bayonets, sticks, or other markers, and the responsible officers required to indicate the profile selected, method and time of construction, garrisons, etc.

584. Ordinarily, infantry intrenches itself whenever it is compelled to halt for a considerable time in the presence of the enemy. Infantry charged with a resisting mission should intrench whenever there is any likelihood that the cover constructed will be of use.

585. Except in permanent fortifications or in fortifications prepared long in advance, the infantry plans and constructs the field works that it will occupy.

When performing their duties in this connection officers should bear in mind that profile and construction are simple matters compared with location and correct tactical use.

586. Intrenchments enable the commander to hold a position with the least possible number of men and to prolong his line or increase his reserve. They are constructed with a view to giving cover which will diminish losses, but they must not be so built or placed as to interfere with the free use of the rifle. Fire effect is the first consideration.

587. The trace of a fire trench or of a system of fire trenches depends upon the ground and the proposed density of the entire firing line. The trenches are laid out in company lengths, if possible. Adjoining trenches should afford each other mutual support. The flanks and important gaps in the line should be protected by fire trenches echeloned in rear.

588. To locate the trace, lie on the ground at intervals and select the best field of fire consistent with the requirements of the situation. A profile should be selected which will permit the fire to sweep the foreground, require the minimum of labor and time, and permit the best concealment. No fixed type can be prescribed. The type must be selected with due regard to the terrain, the enemy, time, tools, materials, soil, etc.

589. Hasty cover. With the intrenching tool, troops can quickly throw up a low parapet about three feet thick which will furnish considerable cover against rifle fire, but scarcely any against shrapnel. Such cover is frequently of value to an attack that is temporarily unable to continue. In time, and particularly at night, it may be developed into a deep fire or cover trench.

590. Fire trenches should be placed and constructed so as to give a good field of fire and to give the troops protection behind a vertical wall, preferably with some head or overhead cover. They should be concealed or inconspicuous in order to avoid artillery fire or to decrease its accuracy. They should have natural or artificial communication with their supports, but in establishing the trace this is a secondary consideration. The simplest form of fire trench is deep and narrow and has a flat, concealed parapet. In ordinary soil, and on a basis of two reliefs and tasks of five feet, it can be constructed in about two hours with intrenching tools. This trench affords fair cover for troops subjected to fire, but not actually firing. When it is probable that time will permit elaboration, the simple trench should be planned with a view to developing it ultimately into a more complete form. Devices should be added to increase the security of the trench and the comfort of the men. Where the excavated earth is easily removed, a fire trench without parapet may be the one best suited to the soil and other conditions affecting the choice of profile. The enemy's Infantry, as well as his Artillery, will generally have great difficulty in seeing this type of trench. In very difficult soil, if the time is short, it may be necessary to dig a wider, shallower trench with a higher parapet. Head cover, notches, and loop holes are of value to troops when firing, but many forms weaken and disclose the location of the parapet. Filled sandbags kept in the trench when the men are not firing may be thrown on the parapet to form notches or loopholes when the troops in the trench open fire and concealment of the trench is no longer necessary or possible. By the use of observation stations the maximum rest and security is afforded the troops. Stations are best located in the angles of traverses or at the end of the trench.

591. Where the nature of the position makes it advisable to construct traverses at regular intervals it is generally best to construct a section of trench for each squad, with traverses between squads.

592. Cover trenches are placed as closely as practicable to their respective fire trenches. Where natural cover is not available, each fire trench should have artificial cover in rear for its support—either a cover trench of its own or one in common with an adjoining fire trench. The cover trench is simple and rectangular in profile. Concealment is indispensable. It is generally concealed by the contour of the ground or by natural features, but to guard against hostile searching fire overhead cover is frequently advisable. Cover trenches should be made as comfortable as possible. It will often be advisable to make them extensive enough to provide cooking and resting facilities for the garrisons of the corresponding fire trenches.

593. Communicating trenches are frequently necessary in order to connect fire trenches with their corresponding cover trenches where natural, covered communication is impracticable. They are generally rectangular in profile, deep, and narrow. They are traversed or zigzagged to escape enfilade. Returns or pockets should be provided for use as latrines, storerooms, dressing stations, passing points for troops, etc. Cover from observation while passing through the trench may insure against loss as effectively as material cover from the enemy's fire. Communicating ways, naturally or artificially screened from the enemy's view, sometimes provide sufficient cover for the passage of troops.

594. Dummy trenches frequently draw the enemy's attention and fire and thus protect the true fire trench. Any type is suitable which presents to the enemy the appearance of a true trench imperfectly concealed.

595. When it is uncertain whether time will permit the completion of all the work planned, work should proceed with due regard to the order of importance of the several operations. Ordinarily the order of importance will be: 1. Clearing foreground to improve the field of fire and construction of fire trench. 2. Head or overhead cover; concealment. 3. Placing obstacles and recording ranges. 4. Cover trenches for supports and local reserves. 5. Communicating trenches. 6. Widening and deepening of trenches; interior conveniences.

The trenches on the Western Front were well-known to us at Camp Lee in an academic sense. We often queried "how in the dickens" we were actually going to break through them, especially since the French and British—considered having the second and third best armies of the world at the time, next to the Germans—could not. We were of course told: "Shear numbers, lads—sheer numbers…Fire and maneuver, lads—fire and maneuver." To help us better understand what we would be up against, it was important to teach us the anatomy of a German trench system, which was an absolute Wonder of the World. In general, the Hun defended in depth. At the very front-front, he had wire entanglements and listening posts. Connecting the listening posts to the firing trenches, which were in "skeleton key" or "lazy-w" formations, were perpendicular "approach" or "communication" trenches that were dug in a zigzag formation (to prevent enfilade fire). The firing trench had several M.G. dugouts with mutually supporting and interlocking fields of fire. Between the M.G.s were the firing trenches with bomb proofs where platoons of infantry were located. During the war-ending Meuse-Argonne Offensive, we had to breach four of these strong defensive lines.

M.M.T. 1160. On the battlefields of Europe today there are generally three lines of fire trenches. This permits the defender to fall back to a second or third prepared position in the case he is driven out of his first trench. Generally, the second line is located on the forward slope of a hill and the third line is located on the reverse slope. In many instances the first line of trenches consist of as many as four to five lines of trenches running in a general lateral direction and connected by a deep narrow communicating trenches. The depth between the first and last of these trenches is, in some instances, not over a hundred yards. Sign boards are necessary at short intervals to prevent the soldiers from getting lost. The effect of having so many alternative firing trenches is to make it extremely difficult for an enemy to advance from, or to even hold one of them, even when he gains footing, as he would be swept by fire from the supporting trenches in rear and also by flanking fire from the adjacent trenches.

M.M.T. 1161. Location. There are two things to be considered in locating trenches: (1) The tactical situation, and (2) the nature of the ground. The first consideration requires that the trenches be so located as to give the best field of fire. Locating near the base of hills possesses the advantage of horizontal fire, but, as a rule, it is difficult to support trenches so located and to retreat therefrom in the case of necessity. While location near the crest of hills—on the "military crest"—does not possess the advantage of horizontal fire, it is easier to support trenches so located and to retreat therefrom. Depending upon circumstances, there are times when it will be better to intrench near the base of hills and there are other times when it will be better to intrench on the "military crest," of which is always in front of the natural crest. The construction of trenches along the "military crest" does not give any "dead space"—that is, any space to the front that can not be reached by the fire of the men in the trenches.

In France, we always faced German defensive lines along the forward slope of a ridge line or other elevation. They were zig-zagged and interspersed among fields, woods, and towns. We were taught and learned by experience that in the attack, it is imperative to try to find as much "dead space" as you can to at least be able to catch your breath. The risk you take is that if the enemy has plotted said dead space on a map for an Artillery strike, you're cooked. Just as long as you understand that, you're good. Para. 1161 of Moss's *M.M.T.* continues:

Whether we should construct our trenches on high ground or low ground is a matter that should always be carefully considered under the particular conditions that happen to exist at that particular time, and the matter may be summarized as follows: (1) We can generally see better what is going on to our front and flanks; and the men have a feeling of security that they do not enjoy on low ground. (2) We can generally reinforce the firing line better and the dead and wounded can be removed more easily. (3) The line of retreat is better. The disadvantages of high ground are: (1) The plunging fire of a high position is not as effective as a sweeping fire of a low one. (2) It is not as easy to conceal our position. The advantages of low ground are: (1) The low, sweeping fire that we get, especially when the ground in front is fairly flat and the view over the greater part of it is uninterrupted, is the most effective kind of fire. (2) As a rule it is easier to conceal trenches on low ground, especially from artillery fire. (3) If our trenches are on low ground, our artillery will be able to find good positions on the hill behind us without interfering with the Infantry defense. The disadvantages of low ground are: (1) As a rule it will be more difficult to reinforce the firing line and to remove the dead and wounded from the trenches. (2) On a low position there will usually be an increase of dead space in our front.

The experience of the European war emphasizes the fact that the location of the rifle trenches is today, just as much as ever, a matter of compromise to be determined by sound judgment on the part of the responsible officers. The siting of trenches so that they are not under artillery observation is a matter of great importance, but, it has yet to be proven that this requirement is more important than an extensive field of fire. There are many instances where to escape observation and fire from the artillery; trenches were located on the reverse slopes, giving only a limited field of fire. This restricted field of fire permitted the enemy to approach within a few hundred yards of the trench and robbed them of the concealment they had hoped to gain. The choice between a site in front, and one in rear of a crest, is influenced by local conditions which govern the effectiveness of our own and the enemy's fire. In general, the best location for effective fire trenches lies between the military crest of rising ground and the lowest line from which the foreground is visible. If the position on the military crest is conspicuous, it is inadvisable.

In order to attack the German trench system more effectively, the Allies placed offensive operations against it into three classes: (I) Limited Attack on a Strong Point to Inflict Enemy Casualties, (II) Envelopment of a Strong Point to Inflict Enemy Casualties and to Gain Better Ground, and (III) Envelopment of a Strong Point and Exploitation with Follow-on Forces to Bring About a Decisive Battle of Maneuver. In Picardy with the British, we conducted Class II Attacks. In the Meuse-Argonne, we conducted Class III Attacks. A Class I Attack, so-called, was a "Limited Attack on a Strong Point to Inflict Enemy Casualties." In this attack, the selected point did not follow the military maxim of "attacking weak points with resultant fall of strong points." Both sides generally selected strong points for the attack as at Verdun (German) and the Somme (British). The defender was generally able to delay the enemy by an organization in depth, and succeeded in holding the strong point until he could concentrate troops from adjacent sectors in sufficient strength to beat back the attack. The selected points were too strong, however, and were not taken in spite of great superiority of troops brought against them. By means of fortifications, the defenders held out until enough reinforcements were received to beat off the attack (Verdun was attacked first by the Germans and to try to relieve pressure from it, the British attacked the Germans up the Somme River Valley, which did end the German attack at Verdun, as the Germans rushed troops from Verdun to the Somme). The goal of a Class I Attack is not to take a position, but to inflict as many casualties on the enemy as possible. It is generally believed that this is the worst kind of attack, as it is demoralizing to troops.[105]

A Class II or "Envelopment of a Strong Point to Inflict Enemy Casualties and to Gain Better Ground" attack was the preferred method of war and was utilized by the Allies and Central Powers after Verdun and the Somme in 1916. The purpose of this type of attack is to penetrate the flank (or flanks) of an enemy strong point so that the enemy will be forced to abandon it. During this type of attack, the defender at first finds himself unable to combat the concentration successfully. The weak point has not sufficiently strong enough fortifications to enable the defender to hold his position until he can bring up enough reinforcements. After some experience, both sides devised countermeasures. The first countermeasure consisted of preparing "switch" positions on the flanks of weak points, so that even after the attacker was successful, the defender would not be forced to abandon a strong point. The defender next increased his organization in depth, so that he was able to delay the enemy's advance for a reasonable time until the arrival of his reinforcements. The enormous concentrations of artillery fire rendered necessary this greater organization in depth. A fairly weak force could hold a weak line against an infantry advance—but when the enemy concentrated hundreds of guns, it was not advisable to put all of this force in the front line and subject it to the losses by artillery while awaiting the infantry attack, which incidentally might never come. By organizing in great depth, the defender reduced his losses and was still able to delay somewhat the progress of the attacker. The attacker's progress was generally so rapid that the defender could not bring up sufficient reinforcements in time to prevent the capture of a part of his intrenched front. Hence, the defender next adopted the plan of intrenching a system of outposts some distance in front of his

---

[105] Mitchell, 665.

main line of resistance. It was the duty of this outpost system to give warning of any strong attack, to assist materially in breaking up the attack, and to gain time for the defender to concentrate forces to resist. The defender also established an "artillery barrage zone" in front of his main line. This system worked very well when the defender could concentrate enough artillery to make the barrage zone deadly enough to drive back the attacker.[106]

A Class III Attack or "Envelopment of a Strong Point and Exploitation with Follow-on Forces to Bring About a Decisive Battle of Maneuver," we performed well (and at great cost) in the Meuse-Argonne. With this type of attack, weak points are assailed, as in Class II, on both sides of a strong point, with the object of forcing the abandonment of the strong point by the defenders in order to save themselves from capture or destruction. It's more commonly called a "double envelopment." During the Meuse-Argonne Offensive in fall 1918, for example, while one division, the American 79th (Cross of Lorraine) Division, attacked the German strong point of *Montfaucon* frontally, two other divisions, on the 79th Division's flanks, broke through and enveloped *Montfaucon* from the left, right, and rear. In a weakly defended sector, like along the *Chemin des Dames* (the Meuse-Argonne was considered a strongly defended sector), there were not a great many of these strong points and it often happened that the attacker captured almost all of the weak points before the strong points were attacked in front and rear.

During the German *Friedensturm* or "Peace Offensive" in the spring of 1918, the Hun leveled several Class III attacks against the Allies in northern France, almost driving the British into the sea.[107] When they failed, it was the Associated Powers' turn (i.e., the Allies plus the United States) to unleash Class III attacks against the Germans until they could take no more without losing it all. This type of attack is marked by locating as many weak points as possible by sending platoons, companies, battalions, and even brigades through them. Infiltration is the key. For us in the attacking infantry, the ability to move forward with our own devices was paramount. After that, the key was for the engineers to connect the advancing infantry with the S.O.S. troops so the attack could be continued. And that, dear reader, was the most important job of the engineers—to ensure infantry and artillery forward mobility. Without it, no matter how good our infantry or artillery, our Class III attack would have rapidly devolved into an indecisive Class II or even Class I attack.

As well as learning how to create, improve, or breach fortifications, the men of the 305th Engineers were taught how to build or improve roads from very little and how to build military

---

[106] *Ibid*, 665-66.

[107] *Montfaucon* or "Mount Falcon" is pronounced "Mohn Fal-cone" and *Friedensturm* or "Peace Offensive" is pronounced "Free-den-sterm."

bridges, pontoon or otherwise. The roads were "corduroy" in nature. That means that Engineers would cut down six-inch diameter trees, clear them of their branches, and lay them perpendicular to a ruddy road, allowing units to pass. During the month of March, after completing the trench and rifle ranges, the 305th Engineers even built and rebuilt a pontoon bridge across the Appomattox River.[108]

---

[108] Stultz, 119.

Members of the 155th Arty. Brig. training on range finders at Camp Lee.

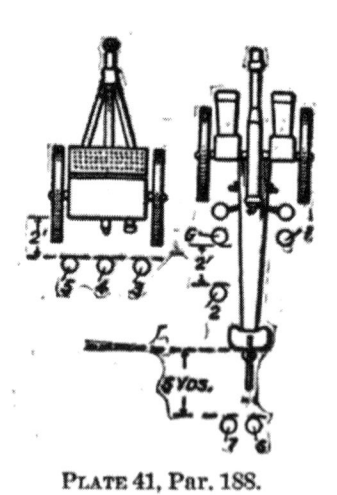

Gun squad positions (left) and caisson, gun carriage, and caisson (below).

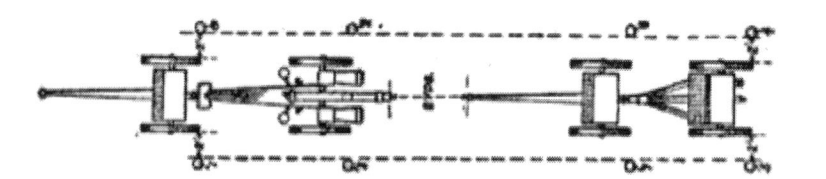

PLATE 41, PAR. 188.

M1902 three-inch Field Gun. In France, the A.E.F. fired French 75mm field guns instead.

A French 75mm Field Gun going into battery.

M1908 six-inch Howitzer.

French *Schneider* 155mm Howitzer in action. The 315th Arty. would fire these monsters in France.

French *Schneider* 155mm Howitzer with the gun in "travel lock" position (meaning pulled back).

Artillery training at Dutch Gap, Virginia, 1918.

Firing the M1902 three-inch Field Gun at Dutch Gap.

Chapter 9
Artillery Training at Camp Lee and Dutch Gap.

F.S.R. 124: The artillery is the close supporting arm of the Infantry and its duties are inseparability connected with those of the infantry. Its targets are those units of the enemy which, from the infantry point of view, are most dangerous to its infantry or that hinder infantry success. The greater the difficulties of the infantry the more powerful must be the artillery support. In order to insure close cooperation of the artillery with the infantry in combat, the leader of each infantry unit to which artillery support has been assigned will, in both the attack and defense, make known to the artillery commander his plans and their expected development and will, throughout the action, keep the artillery representative accompanying him fully informed of the needs of the infantry in the matter of artillery support... The security of the artillery in combat must be provided for either by the distribution of the other arms or specifically in orders. But when such is not the case the necessary protection must be afforded by the nearest unit of infantry or cavalry whose mission will permit it to give such protection.

80th Division artillery officers and N.C.O.s (sometimes called "Red Legs" because the artillery's branch color is red and from the War of 1812 forward, they wore red stripes on their trousers) utilized the following manuals to help train themselves and their units: the Army's *Drill and Service Regulations for Field Artillery, 1917* (A.D.R.), the *Manual for the Battery Commander—75mm Gun*, the *Manual for N.C.O.s and Privates of Field Artillery of the Army of the U.S., 1917* (N.C.O.M.A.). The *A.D.R.* has an amazing 1,864 paragraphs, as the artillery branch, like the engineers, is very a technical field. According to the *A.D.R.*:[109]

A.D.R. 1. The reason for the existence of field artillery is its ability to assist the other arms, especially the infantry, upon the field of battle. The degree to which the field artillery prepares itself to render this assistance is, then, the measure of its training. No refinements of drill-ground instruction or other minor details must be allowed to obscure this definite object or to impede progress toward its attainment.

---

[109] *Drill and Service Regulations for Field Artillery, 1917* (Washington, D.C., Government Printing Office, 1917). Hereafter cited as "*A.D.R.*"

According to the *N.C.O.M.A.*:

The field artillery of the U.S.A. is one of the true rapid-fire type, the principal characteristics of which are (a) control of recoil, by means of which the piece remains practically undisturbed under the shock of discharge, thus facilitating loading, aiming, and firing; (b) sighting apparatus, by means of which the pieces may be directed accurately upon a target which is concealed from view of the guns by intervening obstacles; (c) means for obtaining a considerable angle of elevation for the piece itself without altering the position of the carriage, thus increasing the range; (d) means for changing the direction of the gun, within certain limits, without shifting the whole carriage, thus enabling a quick change from one target to another to be made; (c) fixed ammunition, similar in form to the familiar small-arms cartridge... The carriage consists, in a general way, of the cradle, the rocker, the sighting arrangement, the trail, the shields, and the wheels and axle... It provides means for rendering the carriage stable by controlling the recoil and forcing the piece back into firing position after discharge; for elevating and traversing the piece; for sighting and laying the piece; for protecting the cannoneers against rifle and shrapnel bullets; and for transporting the piece.[110]

This is somewhat of a departure from how artillery was regarded during the preceding century. Napoleon, a famed artillery officer himself reportedly said: "Artillery is more essential to cavalry than to infantry, because cavalry has no fire for its defense, but depends on the saber." But what didn't change, also according to Napoleon, are that: "Great battles are won with artillery," "The worse the troops the greater the need of artillery," and "God is on the side with the best artillery." As an infantryman, I can tell you for a fact that we valued the following supporting units the most: medics, artillery liaison officers, and M.G.ers—in that order.

A.E.F. divisions were assigned three field artillery regiments, two light and one heavy, one trench mortar (T.M.) battery, as well as accompanying ammunition trains, etc. While the light regiments, in our case, Herron's and Welsh's 313th and 314th Artillery, had two battalions of four batteries each (eight heavy batteries total), the heavy regiment, in our case, Reeder's 315th Artillery, had three battalions of three batteries each (nine heavy batteries total). The initial concept was for each light regiment to be assigned to an Infantry brigade while the heavy

---

[110] *Manual for N.C.O.s and Privates of Field Artillery of the A.U.S., 1917* (Washington, D.C., Government Printing Office, 1917), 1: 18-19. Hereafter cited as "*N.C.O.M.A.*

regiment was controlled directly by the division commander in order to reinforce what is called "the main effort." When we got into combat, however, all three artillery regiments supported the Infantry brigade and of all the units of the 80th (Blue Ridge) Division, the artillery spent more days in combat than anybody else.

In other words, the guns were never held in reserve.

According to the *F.S.R.*, a field artillery battery (light or heavy) in 1914 was to consist of four artillery pieces, twelve caissons, sixteen limbers, a battery wagon, a store wagon, a forge limber, and a store limber. Limbers are two-wheeled vehicles that towed a gun or a caisson and a caisson was attached to a limber and it had multiple ammunition chests that were divided into compartments for carrying different types of ammunition. As far as personnel, each battery was to have: one captain, four lieutenants, one 1Sgt., one Q.M. sergeant, one stable sergeant, one mess sergeant, one chief mechanic, four gun sergeants, four caisson sergeant, one signal corporal, two scout corporals, four gunner corporals, two mounted signalmen, seven mechanics, thirteen caisson corporals, sixty cannoneers, and sixty drivers, totaling around one hundred and seventy officers and men.[111]

The other types of artillery organizations were coastal (heavy and fixed) and mountain (ultra-light and highly mobile). An artillery battery itself consisted of a H.Q., which included the officers, the top sergeant, his orderlies, the Q.M., stable, and mess sergeants, the mechanics, and the battery commander's scouts and signalmen, two firing platoons with two guns each (each platoon was commanded by a lieutenant and each gun section was commanded by a sergeant). Each gun section had one field gun or howitzer, a limber with six horses or mules to tow it, and a caisson. While a limber, which towed the gun, had one ammunition chest that stored around thirty rounds for a light piece, a caisson was pulled by a caisson limber and carried two ammunition chests (i.e., about ninety rounds on hand per gun).

> *A.D.R. 132. For technical, tactical, and administrative purposes the enlisted personnel of the battery is assigned by sections. A section dismounted consists of one sergeant, who is chief of section, and all the men assigned to the service of the piece and its caisson, called a gun section (four per battery, Sections 1-4); or to the service of two caissons, called a caisson section (four per battery, Sections 5-8). The leading caisson in a section is called the 1st Caisson; the rear caisson, the 2nd Caisson. Those who are assigned to the service of the battery wagon and the store wagon and to the tools carried in these wagons are*

---

[111] *T.O.E., 1914*, 17 and *N.C.O.M.A.*, 1:19.

called the 9th Section. The section assigned to the service of supply is called the Supply Section.

A.D.R. 133. The first four sections of the battery are gun sections. The remaining sections, except the ninth section and the supply section, are cassison sections. Each gun consists of a gun squad and a driver squad. The 9th Section consists of a mechanic squad and a driver squad. The supply section consists of two squads.

A.D.R. 135. Each gun squad consists of 1 of the corporals and 8 of the privates assigned to the service of the gun section. The corporal is the gunner and should be selected for his qualifications without regard to rank in his section. The privates are cannoneers, numbered from No. 1 to No. 8.

A.D.R. 136. Each caisson squad consists of one of the corporals and seven of the privates assigned to the service of a caisson section. The corporal is the caisson corporal. The privates are cannoneers, three of whom are assigned to the first cassion and numbered from No. 4 to No. 6 and the remaining 4 to the second caisson and numbered from No. 4 to No. 7.

A.D.R. 137. Each driver squad of the gun and caisson sections consists of a caisson corporal and eight drivers of the carriages of the section. The driver squad of the ninth section consists of two of the spare drivers and the eight drivers of the carriages of that section. Movements prescribed for a gun squad apply with obvious modifications to a caisson squad, driver squad, or mechanic squad.

Because I was not a Red Leg, I chose to include large portions of the artillery drill and service manuals with short explanations to instill upon the reader how utterly important and technical the artillery branch is, for without it, we in the infantry could not have moved an inch against the strong German lines in France. Granted, I've talked with several artillery officers, N.C.O.s, and E.M. during our post-war reunions and as a current (1938) serving infantry officer in the Organized Reserves, I have learned far-more about the "black arts" than what I understood in 1917-19, but I still could not fire one of those critters in combat (although I can now direct their fire upon any target with a map, compass, and radio set).

Object of the Instruction.

A.D.R. 2. To enable it to render effective assistance upon the battlefield, field artillery must be able, first, to march rapidly and in good order and to establish itself, promptly and without confusion, in such positions as will best utilize the available terrain; second, to deliver an effective and overpowering fire upon any designated part of the enemy's position. Throughout training in marching, camping, reconnaissance and communication service, fire discipline, conduct of fire and fire direction, carried out over varied coutry, is essential to the attainment of these qualifications.

A.D.R. 3. An additional object of instruction is to develop resourcefulness, initiative, and self-reliance on the part of field artillerymen of all grades.

A.D.R. 11. Officers and N.C.O.s of each grade will be frequently practiced in the duties of the next higher grade or command.

A.D.R. 12. Thorough training of the individual soldier is the basis of efficiency. Great precision and attention to detail are essential in this instruction in order that the soldier may acquire that habit of implicit obedience to orders and of accurate performance of his individual duties which is indispensable in combined training. If all the individuals of a battery, including the officers, are thoroughly trained, a comparatively short period of work in formal battery drills, occupation of positions, marches, etc., with the battery as a whole will suffice to produce an efficient organization for field service. On the other hand, no amount of drill of a battery as a whole is likely to produce an efficient organization if its members are not thoroughly instructed as individuals. Similarly, comparatively little work of a battalion as a whole is necessary if the batteries and the battalion H.Q. detail have been thoroughly trained in their individual duties...

A.D.R. 13. Instuction of the gun squad as a whole will not be taken up to the exclusion of individual training until the men are thouroughly proficient in the nomenclature and operation of all those parts of the guns, instruments, and other matériel which the cannoneers are called upon to handle actual firing. Drivers will be thoroughly instructed in equitation before taking up the drill with pairs. Similarly, they must understand the principles of managing the off horse and be able to handle the pair before taking up a team hitched.

A.D.R. 14. So far as concerns the enlisted personnel, the most important element of a battery's efficiency on the battlefield is its fire discipline. The basis of good fire discipline, as of all other matters, is thorough individual instruction, and it can only be secured and maintained by constant and vigorous drills and other exercises. To this end gun squads will be given daily such exercises as will serve to fix their attention and cultivate their dexterity. Efficient gun squads can not be improvised. The duties of cannoneers and their manual dexterity required for their performance are easily forgotten....

Training of Noncommissioned Officers.

A.D.R. 20. Exceptional care and attention will be devoted by battery commanders to the selection and training of candidates for appointment as corporals and of corporals to fit them for duty as sergeants. In each battery a special course of instruction will be given by one of the lieutenants. This course will be considered the equivalent of the course in the noncommissioned officers' school.

A.D.R. 21. The corporals and privates selected will be instructed according to a schedule submitted by each battery commander and approved by the regimental commander or by the senior artillery officer present with the command...

Training and Inspection of Recruits.

A.D.R. 23. All instruction of recruits will be by battery. When it is possible to do so, recruits will be assigned to batteries in detachments of not less than thirty men.

A.D.R. 24. Every phase of the instruction of recruits will be under the immediate supervision of an officer. After the recruits have been under instruction a sufficient length of time to enable the battery commander to form an idea as to their capability they will be temporarily divided into classes of cannoneers and drivers. This division will be made permanent prior to the second inspection...

A.D.R. 26. To determine whether or not the recruits have been properly trained, two inspections will be held by the regimental commander, the battalion commander being present, or by the battalion commander in the absence of the regimental commander...

A.D.R. 28. The first inspection will be for all the recruits and will consist of a detailed examination and inspection in the following subjects:

1. Dismounted inspection under arms.

2. Manual of the pistol.

3. Setting up exercises, to include all exercises prescribed in "Recruit Instruction, Manual of Physical Training."

4. Swimming, if facilities are available.

5. Running one-half mile.

6. Customs and courtesies of the service.

7. Dismounted drill, to include the execution of each movement prescribed for the squad and for the battery dismounted.

8. Inspection of barracks or camp, the recruits standing by their beds with their equipment displayed.

9. Inspection of all articles included in the field kit.

10. Packing; rolling the mounted and dismounted blanket roll; rolling the slicker.

11. Shelter-tent pitching.

12. Individual instruction as cannoneers, to include sufficient instruction to enable them to qualify as second-class gunners.

13. Drill of the gun squads in all the exercises preliminary to the service of the piece, to include the execution of each movement described.

14. Care of horses.

15. Equitation, to include "Soldier Mounted."

16. Care of leather equipment as demonstrated by actually cleaning a saddle and bridle.

A.D.R. 29. The second inspection will be held not less than five months no more than six months after the recruits have joined the battery.

1. Dismounted inspection under arms.

2. Setting up exercises, to include all exercises prescribed in "Recruit Instruction, Manual of Physical Training."

3. Customs and courtesies of the service.

4. Dismounted drill, to include the execution of each movement prescribed for the squad and for the battery dismounted.

5. Guard duty, to determine whether the recruit understands his duties as a sentinel.

6. First aid; hygiene, care of the person.

7. Care and use of the pistol, to include the firing of two scores, slow fire, at twenty-five yards.

8. Pitching, striking, and packing battery tentage.

9. Inspection of clothing and equipment.

10. Individual cooking, to include the preparation of coffee, bacon, and potatoes.

Battery Administration.

A.D.R. 32. The administrative duties of a battery of field artillery are too numerous for their efficient supervision in detail by one officer. To secure such supervision the battery commander must utilize the services of his lieutenants. The most effective assistance will not be obtained by holding each lietenant responsible for a platoon, which is not a self-sustaining unit but one dependent upon agencies outside itself. The assignment of lieutenants to administrative functions must then be made so as to correspond to the various duties necessary to the daily existence of the battery as a whole. These duties may be classified into 3 departments:

Department A: The care and maintenance of all parts of the wheeled matériel.

Department B: The care of animals, the inspection, care, and issue of forage, the police of stables and picket lines, adjustment and care of harness, shoeing, etc.

Department C: The care and police of quarters, the superintendence of the battery mess, personal equipment and clothing, and the routine office work.

Each of these departments, together with all necessary personnel and matériel, should be under the direct supervision of one of the lieutenants, who should be held reponsble for the work of his department. Except in emergencies the battery commander should give instructions affecting any department through the lieutenant in charge.

This division of administrative duties is also utilized to facilitate the instruction of the battery as follows: The lieutenant in charge of Department A is the executive, and is placed in immediate charge of the individual instruction of the cannoneers and their duties in the gun squads; the one in charge of Department B is placed in immediate charge of the instruction of equitation, in driving, and all duties pertaining to the horses; and the one in charge of Department C is reconnaissance officer and is placed in immediate charge of all dismounted instruction and assist the captain in the training of the battery commander's scout detail.

The fourth lieutenant, when available, is ordinarily the one with the least experience as a battery officer. He should be utilized in assisting the others and should be required to thoroughly familiarize himself with their work.

In time of war the captain assigns his lieutenants to the departments to which they are best fitted, the especial fitness of the executive being the first consideration.

More so than the other regiments of the division, the artillery regiments trained under severe *matériel* and equipment shortages. As such, they and the trench mortar battery resorted to all manner of improvisation. There was only enough equipment to outfit one battery in September, and the batteries rotated using it. At other times, wooden models of both light and heavy cannon were constructed and employed in technical instruction and there was little that was not simulated.

In November, Army ordnance trains arrived to Camp Lee bearing M1885-97 3.2-inch (81mm) Field Guns, M1902 3-inch (76mm) Field Guns, M1903 4.7-inch (118mm) Field Guns, and even a few M1915 3.8-inch (97mm) and M1908 6-inch (152mm) Howitzers that had been made by the Bethlehem Steel Works in Bethlehem, Pennsylvania. Scores of limbers and caissons were also delivered. These would be used for training purposes only as it had already been decided to equip the artillery regiments of the A.E.F. with French 75mm field guns or 155mm Schneider howitzers. This was done for two reasons: to ease ammunition re-supply concerns and availability. If the A.E.F. entered combat with its own field pieces, the logistical tail back to the States, across the big blue Atlantic, would not have been able to fill the need. French industry, however, was producing far-more guns and ammunition than it had troops. The Americans would therefore provide the troops and the French would provide the arms and ammunition.

Clearly, the M1902 and M1908 pieces most closely matched the French 75s and 155s and their use as training aids for the gun crews was good enough. Col. "Uncle Charlie" Herron, commander of the 313th Artillery remembered: "To each battery had been issued a sufficient number of artillery carriages of one sort or another, including even antiquated three-inch relics of the Spanish-American War, to enable the cannoneers to learn the rudiments of standing gun drill and to become familiar with the material they were to handle."[112] Even without exact guns, limbers, or caissons for every section to drill with (four guns, limbers, and caissons for every firing battery, twelve guns and limbers and eighteen caissons for every battalion, seventy-two

---

[112] As cited in Irving, Thomas and Edward Crowell. *A History of the 313th Artillery, U.S.A.* (New York: Thomas Y. Crowell Company, 1920), 4. Hereafter cited as *"313th Artillery."*

guns and limbers and 118 caissons for the division), the men made due as the key was in building an artillery team.

Before we go any further, I think it would help the reader better appreciate what the Red Legs of the division went through during the Meuse-Argonne Offensive by understanding some of the basic parts of a light (3-inch) or heavy (6-inch) artillery piece. Using the M1905 Field Gun as an example, just below the barrel is a hydraulic "recuperator." This is a very important part on the gun as it returns the barrel back into its firing position after it is fired. With a recuperator, the gun barrel recoils within the hydraulic buffer (resistance created by pushing oil through a narrow aperture) and then returns to firing position. As only the barrel moved, there was no need to relay the gun between shots. A recuperator thus allows a gun crew to fire rapidly.

"Boom!"

"Clank."

"Boom!"

"Clank."

The long "tail pole" of a gun is called a "trail" and the shovel at the end of it is called a "spade." The spade helps stabilize the gun during firing (stabilization is key, because you'll see that the farther the range to target, the more exaggerated a correction becomes). The handle above the spade is called a "traversing lever." This lever helps the gunner aim left or right. The metal plate that protects the gun crew is called a "shield." The hole in the shield is where the gunner's "rocking bar" or "panoramic" sight is affixed. The front opening of the barrel is called the "muzzle" and at the rear of it is the "breach." The gun is loaded from the breach. Just below the breach are two small brass elevating and traversing wheels and there are two seats, one for the gunner, on the left, and one for his assistant, on the right.

While the M1902 3-inch artillery piece is a "field gun," the 6-inch M1908 is a "howitzer." A field gun has more of a flat trajectory and can fire both direct (gunner can see the target) and indirect (gunner can't see the target) missions. Howitzers, meanwhile, fire rounds at more of a high angle or arched trajectory. As such, howitzers are the weapons of choice for bombarding narrow targets like trenches or targets that have to be hit from above, like dug-outs. Field guns are the weapons of choice for firing directly at M.G. positions or tanks or in firing shrapnel or gas missions. According to the *N.C.O.M.A*:

Field guns are distinguished from howitzers by their greater range, greater muzzle velocity, flatter trajectory, and somewhat greater rate of fire. The flat trajectory of the field gun renders it very effective against targets not protected by overhead cover of relatively steep masks. But for the latter class of targets, which can be reached only from above, howitzers are necessary... Howitzers are distinguished from field guns by their individual characteristics of curved and zone fire. By firing a projectile at a relatively high angle of elevation, a greater angle of fall is obtained as it strikes the intended object, and this characteristic makes the howitzers especially valuable in penetrating overhead cover or other targets which can only be reached from above. By varying the amount of of powder charge and the angles of elevation at which howitzers are fired, objects at varying ranges may be reached at such an angle of fall as to produce the desired effect... Howitzers are further distinguished from field guns by two distinctive features of design:

(1) In the howitzer, on account of the short trail and high angles of elevation, the gun is placed underneath the cradle with the object of reducing the overturning tendency at the end of the trail and rendering the carriage stable under all conditions of loading and elevation; while in the field gun the gun is placed above the cradle.

(2) In the howitzer the amount of recoil varies for different elevations and is automaticatclly regulated, so that the higher the elevation the shorter the recoil will be; while in the field gun the length of the recoil is practically the same for all elevations.[113]

Light artillery pieces fire what is called "fixed ammunition" and heavy artillery pieces fire what is called "semi-fixed ammunition." Fixed ammunition means that the propellent (i.e., powder) and projectile (e.g., shell) come together in one package, just like a modern bullet. Semi-fixed ammunition when the propelling charge is carried separately from the projectile itself. This is necessary for howitzers because of the varying powder charges used for the different range zones or angles of fire. The powder charge is assembled in the cartridge case in three parts, each in a raw-silk bag. For "outer zone" ranges the full powder charge is used. For the "middle zone" the top bag is removed and discarded before the cartridge is inserted in the chamber and for the "inner zone," the top and middle bags are removed. All field guns, except very heavy types, use fixed ammunition, while howitzers use semi-fixed ammunition.[114]

Ammunition may be further classified into shrapnel, which is designed to explode in the air and rain hundreds of ball bearings downward, smoke, gas, or high explosive (H.E.), which is

---

[113] *A.N.C.O.M.*, 1:20.

[114] *Ibid*, 1:22.

designed to explode upon contact. A three-inch H.E. round has a kill radius of twenty yards. This is why light artillery is positioned no farther than twenty yards from each other so their rounds will land together taking out everything that was above ground.[115] While the 3-inch field guns fired 15 pound shells, 6-inch howitzers fired 120 pound shells. According to the *A.N.C.O.M.*:

> *The projectiles supplied for field artillery are of two general classes, shrapnel and shell. The weight of each projectile is the same for each caliber. A complete round of ammunition consists of the cartridge case, the primer, the powder (propelling) charge, and the projectile. The propelling charge is of smokeless powder...The shrapnel consists roughly of a hollow steel case with a solid base, fitted with a base bursting charge of black powder, a filling of shrapnel balls held in place by a smoke-producing composition, and closed by a combination fuse. The fuse may be so set as to cause the shrapnel to burst in the air at any desired distance from the gun or on impact. When the shrapnel bursts in the air the bursting charge strips off the head of the case and sends the shrapnel balls out of the case with an added velocity and scatters them to the front, somewhat in the same manner that shot is expelled from the shotgun cartridge. The smoke-producing composition is ignited when the shrapnel bursts and produces a white ball of smoke which aids in observation. The velocity of the shrapnel balls is sufficient to disable man or beast at ranges from the point of burst varying from two hundred yards for the longer ranges to five hundred yards for mid and short ranges. The proper height of burst above the line joining gun and target is assumed to be such as will give at least one ball for every square yard of a vertical target. When a shrapnel round bursts on impact the effect is somewhat similar to that of a shell. Shrapnel is used in general against animate objects, such as men and horses.*[116]

To transport the gun, the gun squad retracted the barrel back across its carriage and onto its trail and hooked it to a limber which was like a small tow truck:

> *A.D.R. 193. When prepared for movement the howitzer is always locked by one of the traveling locks, and the pawls are disengaged from the rockers... When locked by the rear traveling lock the howitzer is said to be in traveling position. It is always put in this position for marches of any length... When*

---

[115] *A.D.R.*, Para 945.

[116] *A.N.C.O.M.* 1:23.

locked to the recoil cylinder by means of the cylinder retaining ring, the howitzer is said to be in the firing position. It may be locked by the front traveling lock and moved for short distances while in position.

To unlimber the gun and "place it into battery" (ready to fire alone or in battery with three other guns), the gun squad will:

A.D.R. 198. (1) On account of the extreme difficulty of man handling heavy field materiel, the teams will be used to draw the carriages to the positions they are to occupy in firing unless the necessity for concealment demands the placing of the carriages by hand. In the latter case a sufficient number of cannoneers with picket ropes should be employed at each carriage in turn to move it promptly to its proper position. (2) In order to avoid unnecessary strain on the piece wheels and increased difficulties of draft, the howitzer should usually be left in its traveling position as long as practicable. For moving short distances over smooth ground, however, the piece may be in its firing position. (3) The howitzer is habitually shifted to its firing position before unlimbering. (5) In unlimbering to fire to the front, the caisson establishes the position. (6) In unlimbering to fire to the rear, the piece establishes the position. (7) If necessary to move the carriages by hand to the firing position, they are moved before being unlimbered.

Horses began to reach the brigade in December 1917 and they made possible some training in equitation. The drivers now divided their time between horse exercise and grooming, stable building and policing, and drivers' drill. Before the horses arrived, many a prospective driver could be observed learning to mount and dismount on a dummy animal created out of a barrel and several boards. It was through such expedients that the brigade acquired much of its basic training. "Uncle Charlie" Herron continues:

Horses began to arrive in small lots from the remount station where they had been held in quarantine. The drivers were dividing their time between horse exercise, grooming by detail, stable building and drivers' drill, with the aid of wooden sleds to represent carriages. To the sleds rope traces were attached and the drivers, combining the attributes of man and horse took positions as lead, swing, and wheel pairs, and learned to guide their carriages even before some of them knew how to ride properly. This ingenious arrangement was resorted to because of the temporary lack of horse equipment. In fact, before the horses themselves began to arrive, many a prospective driver might have been seen learning to mount and dismount on a dummy animal made of several lengths of timber and a barrel... The stables required endless attention...as they were situated on low ground which had been heavily wooded and needed much drainage and building up. The blasting of stumps was taken care of in true artillery style, and furnished striking illustrations of the probable error and dispersion of a dynamited stump.[117]

One of the most laborious and important duties for an A.E.F. artillerist (especially the drivers) was in taking care of the horses, without which, the guns would have been immobilized and thus useless in conducting offensive operations. For the average Red Leg, he was given what was called "stable detail" from time to time. When on stable detail, one arose at around 5:45 A.M., quietly dressed, without lights, and went to the stables and breakfasted the animals. If one was a speed artist he might get back in time for his own breakfast. After breakfast he immediately reported to the stable sergeant of the battery. The horses were then led to the corral and the real stable duties of the day commenced. In leading the horses through the stable to the corral, the length of one's life was dependant upon his ability to duck the hoofs of the ones remaining in the stables.

When it came to cleaning the stables, many a "buck" private made a resolve that in the next war he was going to enlist as a mule-skinner. Driving the battery wagon bore the earmarks of being a job of more dignity than loading the wagon. Besides cleaning the stables and "graining-up" for the horses, the day of the stable police was spent in miscellaneous jobs, which the stable sergeant never ran out of. The stable detail underwent changes as time wore on. A permanent stable man was assigned for every stable and the detail was reduced to three privates.

Stable police was of double import on Saturday mornings, preparatory to the weekly inspection. Every branch and department of military life has a variety of inspections to undergo at periodical times. The inspections keep the boys in khaki on the alert—cleanliness becoming second nature. Nowhere can a vast body of men live bachelor-like as soldiers do and maintain the degree of tidiness and general sanitary healthfulness, as the thorough arm of camp inspection and discipline maintains in the Army. According to the *A.D.R.*:

457. Almost any horse can be trained to be an honest and willing puller. Through ignorance, lack of judgment, bad management, or laziness on the part of the driver he can far more easily be trained to be a shirker and a quitter. A horse will not pull freely or willingly if to do so causes him pain. It

---

[117] As cited in *313th Artillery*, 4.

is essential, therefore, that his harness, especially his collar, fit him with absolute comfort; that his shoulders be hardened through careful conditioning and rational work and are therefore not tender or sore; and that he apply his weight in the collar slowly and gradually, without sudden starts or jerks that would pound and bruise his shoulders. Even though all of the above conditions be favorable, a horse will not pull unless he is confirmed in the belief that when he applies his strength the load behind him will yield. Thus an unwilling horse may be hitched to an immovable object and within a few minutes, especially if he be yelled at or whipped, be transformed into a sulker and a balker that only long, patient, and careful handing will cure. To allow repeated trials and failures in pulling is the quickest and most effective method of ruining the draft efficiency of any team. It must be borne in mind that there is a limit to the draft power of any artillery team and that this power, due to the tandem method of hitching, is, even with perfect driving, from twenty to fifty per cent less than the sum of the powers of the individual horses. A team should never be given deliberately a task that is clearly beyond its strength.

Driving Up Steep Slopes and Over Difficult Ground.
458. In order to exert his maximum strength when in a difficult pull, the draft horse must get the greatest possible weight forward and into the collar. By maintaining a low, extended, and advanced carriage of the head and neck he is able to add considerably to his power of traction. He should, therefore, be allowed full freedom of rein when in a heavy pull and not be forced to fight the driver's hand. Because a horse can exert a greater power of traction when ridden, it is often advantageous when in a difficult pull to mount cannoneers on the horses. When pulling up a hill the drivers should lean well forward and should encourage their horses by a low and quiet use of the voice... The most favorable gait for heavy pulling is a steady, uniform walk, with every horse straight in his collar and the team straight from lead to wheel. The tendency to rush a hill or other difficult pull must be avoided. Any increase of speed for such a purpose can not be taken up with perfect uniformity by all the horses of a team and the footing for each horse is renedered more uncertain and difficult.

The 305th Ammunition Train, which was commanded by Lt. Col. Fred E. Buchanan and assigned to Brig. Gen. George Heiner's 155th Arty. Brig., consisted of a three-company horse battalion and a four-company motor battalion. No caissons were issued to the train at Camp Lee, and its first trucks were not received until March 31, 1918. As with the rest of the brigade, preliminary exercises in the "School of the Mounted Soldier" were practiced on wooden horses. As was already stated, most of the train's enlisted personnel came from western Pennsylvania, many of the men being of foreign birth, and during the early training days it was necessary to form some of them into squads of common language. The train did not receive its complete saddle and harness equipment until May, following which members of the "horse battalion" proudly promenaded Sycamore Street, Petersburg, with spurs, chin-straps and riding crops, until higher authority forbade the practice.

By April 1918, there was enough tack among the various batteries to move the four available M1902 3-inch Field Guns per regiment with caissons and limbers full of ammunition to the Camp Lee artillery range for the first "service practices." Each battery, heavy or light, took turns at the firing range performing direct and indirect fire exercises with the field guns in conjunction with the French instructors. (Hey, they really work!) In short, the Gun Squads were rotated to the guns, maps were checked, observation posts (O.P.s) were established with wire communications, the range was cleared, the data was figured and relayed to the gun, and shots were fired with the accompanying warning of "On the way." Once the men saw or learned that their rounds actually hit the target, confidence in their training soared.[118]

From this time on, training went swiftly. There was much to be accomplished by everyone in order to speed up the functioning of the batteries as a whole (remember: the "artillery team"), and the stimulus of frequent target practice where the results of one's labor could be appreciated by the increased accuracy of the fire was a source of great satisfaction. Unlike the infantry, which needed its officers to have strong inter-personal and problem-solving skills, flexibility, and physical fitness, artillery officers were prized for their mathematical/problem-solving skills. Weeks not spent on the range were devoted to the solving of tactical problems, the practice of constructing gun emplacements and bomb proof O.P.s, the mastery of topography, the use of ground panels in working with aeroplanes, the laying of theoretical phone nets and, in the evenings, to the constant practice with maps, buzzers, probabilities, firing tables, and corrections of the moment (i.e., adjusting fire).

To adjust fire, our artillery forward observers (F.O.s) had to instruct the fire direction center (F.D.C.) back along the gun line from what direction in degrees (360) or mils (6400) they

---

[118] *313th Artillery*, 5.

were adjusting. In that way, the F.D.C. would know what "right," "left," "add," or "drop" meant. The O.P. would tell F.D.C. where the target was on an Army topographic map that had been divided into one km squares. From this map, the O.P. gives a "six-digit grid" to the F.D.C., a description of the target (e.g., M.G. nest), where it was (e.g., on a hill), and his direction relative to the target. A description of the location is given to help ensure that the grid coordinates are right because under stressful conditions, as a million things can go wrong and the last thing we want to do is to drop a 75mm or 155mm artillery shell or shells on our own troops.

The most important skill that artillery officers had to master was the ability to plot what were crawled "rolling" and "creeping" barrages. Rolling barrages are set-piece barrages that are to move forward at a set time and at a set distance. They are to suppress enemy targets, allowing the attacking Infantry to come in behind. A creeping barrage is the same as a rolling one, except that it is set at a slower rate.

In order to fire a rolling barrage, each artillery battalion is supposed to create firing data for each of its guns: fire x-rounds at this position at this time, fire x rounds at that position at that time, usually based on an "H-plus" system. All of the guns were to cooperate and a wall of H.E. and shrapnel was supposed to move forward, and sometimes, backward, against a target.

Rolling barrages were extremely effective but had one glaring weakness: they usually outpaced the infantry and the infantry was usually "alone and unafraid" when it came to taking out defensive positions that were not destroyed by the barrage.

Once the basics of gunnery were mastered, French artillery advisors, having learned their lessons in the grim school of war, focused on survivability, and sustainability. To survive, our gunners had to "shoot and scoot" as the Hun air corps had eyes like a hawk. To sustain, our gunners had to protect their ammunition from direct hits.

In April, Heiner's brigade, which was the "red-headed-step-child-of-the-division," moved out to Dutch Gap artillery firing range, which is north of Camp Lee along the James River, to put all of its training to use. All in the brigade agreed that this was the highlight of their training while in the States. The artillery firing range at Dutch Gap, also known as "Camp McLaughlen," was situated in a beautiful pine grove along the south bank of the James River between Richmond and Petersburg—a far-cry from the dust bowl of Camp Lee. In 1611, Sir Thomas Dale of the Virginia Company of London founded the colony of Henricus there and before him were the *Algonquin*-speaking *Arrohateck* Indians. During the failed War for Southern Independence, it was the position of Capt. William Watts Parker's Confederate artillery battery and Brig. Gen. Napoleon B. McLaughlen's Yankee infantry brigade of Maj. Gen. Benjamin "Spoons" Butler's U.S. Army of the James during the Siege of Petersburg, 1864-65 (thus the name "Camp

McLaughlen"). But to most men of the 155th Arty. Brig., this history mattered little. What mattered was that it gave them a break from the swirling dust and small ranges of Camp Lee and the ability to come into their own as real A.E.F. Red Legs.

The Dutch Gap Range was much more extensive than the one at Camp Lee, and being only 12 miles away, was easily assessable. The targets were on an island across the river to the north, where souvenir hunters could pick up, besides the fragments of our own shells, relics of the battles of over fifty years before between the Blue and the Gray. With the three regiments alternating, firing practice was executed by battalions. On March 15, 1/313th Artillery was the first battalion to fire. The 313th Artillery was followed by battalions from the 314th and 315th Artillery, with each battalion spending approximately ten days on the range. Movement to and from the range, where the Red Legs lived in tents, was made by foot march. A wagon train and a motor ambulance with a detachment from the sanitary trains accompanied the troops. One officer from the 313th Artillery remembered:

> *With numerous battery positions and O.P.s and with night firing and the working out of different firing solutions, training progressed with enormous bounds. Scouting parties, those who were assigned to find battery firing positions, dashed across the country mounted. They were followed by caissons, limbers, and gun carriages of the main body, which rumbled across the dirt roads, spitting up dust.*[119]

According to the *A.D.R.*:

> *Reconnaissance and Selection of Positions (R.S.O.P.).*
>
> *1582. The duty of locating the enemy and securing information concerning him devolves in general upon troops of the other arms. It is most essential that the information thus secured should be promptly transmitted to the artillery. As successful cooperative action depends in great measure in great measure upon the maintenance of quick and reliable communication between the different elements of command, artillery commanders should use every means in their power to establish such relations with commanders of the other arms as will insure prompt transmission of information.*
>
> *1583. The artillery must, however, obtain for itself such special information as is needed to insure the proper posting and effective employment of the guns to carry out the tasks assigned it [R.S.O.P.]. For this purpose, reconnaissances are made by the artillery commander and his immediate subordinates, assisted*

---

[119] *313th Artillery*, 5-6.

by their respective reconnaissance officers and scouts. The effective action of artillery is enhanced by (a) selecting at once the most favorable positions; (b) making the necessary preliminary dispositions, such as securing firing data, organizing a suitable information and communication service; (c) preparing concealment and protective cover; (d) posting the guns without the knowledge of the enemy; and (e) opening at the proper time a sudden, unexpected, and overpowering fire upon the designated objectives.

When it is necessary to bring guns into action quickly for the support of other troops, the main consideration is to get them as promptly as possible to a place from which they ca render effective support. In such a case, delay occasioned by the search for technical and tactical advantages is entirely inadmissible. A good eye for ground and skill in making use of available cover may, however, even here permit an artillery commander to post his guns advantageously.

1584. All field artillery commanders habitually precede their commands to the position to be occupied. Every effort should be made to conclude all preliminary arrangements for action prior to the arrival of the firing batteries. Delay in opening fire must not be caused by lack of timely reconnaissance and preparation.

1585. It is essential that the officer commanding the artillery should be in close touch with the officer commanding the troops. The artillery commander should accompany the commander of the troops on the preliminary reconnaissance should be kept constantly informed as to the tactical situation and the plan of action, and should receive early instructions as to the special tasks to be performed by the artillery. Similarly, subordinate artillery commanders should be kept informed of the general plan of action and of the situation, so far as it affects them.

At the earliest opportunity, the officer commanding the Artillery reconnoiters and selects the positions for the Artillery in accordance with the instructions which he has received and the tactical requirements of the situation. He causes his immediate subordinate commanders to accompany him or informs them when and where they are to report to receive their instructions and undertake their own reconnaissance. It is important that they should reach the ground at the earliest practicable moment.

1586. When a commander rides forward on reconnaissance he instructs the officer left in command on the following points, so far as may be desirable and practicable: (1) The tactical situation; (2) whether or not the command is to follow at once; (3) the time and place for subdivision, if such subdivision had not been made; (4) the route to be followed; (5) the rate of march. Additional instructions may be transmitted from time-to-time by markers, who should be left at places where uncertainty as to the route may arise or where difficulties are to be avoided. As soon as the position and the best method of approaching it have been determined upon agents or scouts may be sent to meet battalions or batteries and guide them by the most favorable routes to their respective positions.

1587. In undertaking a reconnaissance, an artillery commander should have a clear idea in his mind of the general plan of action and of the task to be accomplished by the force under his command. Unembarrassed by details, he should study the tactical situation and the lay of the ground, select the position with a view of carrying out his special mission, and arrange for the necessary preparatory dispositions. The details of securing information, etc., should be performed by reconnaissance officers and scouts.

1588. It is advisable to attach artillery reconnaissance officers to advanced troops in order that they may secure early information as to the enemy, and give the artillery commanders detailed information as to the ground available for occupation by the artillery and so as to the location and disposition of the enemy and of friendly troops. To insure effective cooperation, officers generally accompany the commanders of the infantry lines during either offensive or defensive action, in order to keep the artillery commander informed as to the changes in the tactical situation and as to the cooperation desired of the artillery by the infantry.

1589. An artillery reconnaissance officer attached to advanced troops should, as soon as possible after the determination of the enemy's location, submit to the artillery commander a report giving all obtainable information as to the enemy and describing the most suitable position for our own artillery. This report should be accompanied by a sketch, showing the enemy's position, the position selected for our own artillery, the characteristics of the country intervening between the two, and such other important information as may be readily set forth. The report should embrace information such as the following relative to the position selected: (a) The various routes of approach and their relative practicability, stating difficulties, if any; (b) possibility of approach under cover; (c) whether direct or indirect laying is recommended; (d)

1590. Whether in a position thus tentatively selected or in one chosen by an artillery commander, a reconnaissance officer is required in appropriate cases to prepare a sketch of the enemy's position. The known positions of the enemy, and prominent features of the landscape as well, are named or numbered on the sketch; copies of such a sketch being sent to the subordinate Artillery commanders, the indication of objectives may be facilitated. Firing data are also secured by the reconnaissance officer and those pertaining to each important position shown in the sketch are indicated above in the margin.

The duties of key artillery personnel are as follows:

Artillery Brigade Commander.

(a) Informs himself as the enemy's location and dispositions and the general plan of the commander of the troops.

(b) Examines the terrain.

(c) Submits to the commander of the troops recommendations as to the use of and positions for the artillery.

(d) Assigns the regiments, and, if necessary, smaller units, to duties and to areas to be occupied in accordance with the plan decided upon by the commander of troops.

(e) Takes general measures to insure communication between the Field Artillery and the other arms, as well as between the elements of the Artillery itself.

(f) Takes the general measures for the security of the field artillery in combat and its resupply.

(g) Takes definite measures to insure communication between himself and the commander of the troops.

Artillery Regimental Commander.

(a) Informs himself as to the enemy's location and dispositions and as to the location and dispositions of friendly troops.

(b) Examines the area assigned his regiment by means of a reconnaissance which should be as thorough as the situation permits.

(c) Assigns the battalions to areas or positions and duties with as much exactness as the conditions permit.

(d) Takes definite measures to insure communication between his headquarters and the troops which his regiment is to support, as well as between his headquarters and the stations of his battalion commanders.

(e) Supplements the arrangements for the security of his regiment and for the supply of ammunition in accordance with the instructions which he has received.

Artillery Battalion Commander.

(a) Secures by personal observation and by the employment of reconnaissance officers and scouts information as detailed as possible as to the location and dispositions of the enemy; the location and dispositions of friendly troops; the terrain in and about his assigned position or area—the best methods of approaching it advantageously, its freedom from the enemy, etc.

(b) Examines the general positions assigned him.

(c) Assigns the batteries to duties and to positions, indicating the location of their observation stations when such action is practicable and desirable.

(d) Gives such instructions concerning protective cover as may be necessary.

(e) Provides for such auxiliary observing stations as may be needed to secure information as to the effectiveness of our own fire and as to the movements of the enemy and of friendly troops.

(f) Provides for communication with battery commanders and with his auxiliary observers.

(g) Makes sure that the security of the position is provided for by adjacent troops or by scouts.

(h) Selects practicable routes for subsequent possible movements to the front, flanks, or rear.

(i) Provides for the resupply of ammunition, selecting a position for the combat train in case the battery combat trains are united.

Battery Commander.

(a) *Examines the targets or sector assigned him and studies carefully the ground in its neighborhood.*

(b) *Examines the ground assigned him for a position and picks out the most suitable place within the limits imposed for posting the firing battery. If DIRECT laying is to be employed, he makes sure that each gunner will be able to see through the sights the part of the target to be assigned to him. If INDIRECT laying is to be employed, he makes sure that each gun will be able to fire over any intervening obstacle [e.g., tree line or building], and selects an aiming point, verifying the fact that each gunner will be able to see it through its sight.*

(c) *Selects a suitable observing station within the limits imposed by his orders and the situation.*

(d) *Determines the best method of approaching the position, under cover if possible.*

(e) *Selects the place for posting his limbers.*

(f) *Selects position for his combat train whenever the battery combat trains are posted separately.*

(g) *Sends instructions to the executive for posting the battery.*

(h) *Secures such firing data as may be needed.*

The Executive Officer.

(a) *Commands the battery in the absence of the captain.*

(b) *Conducts the battery to the position selected by the captain.*

(c) *Posts the firing battery.*

(d) *Makes all preparations necessary to expedite the opening of fire.*

(e) *Takes his station near the guns where he can best exercise his functions.*

(f) *Verifies the reliability of the communication systems at his station.*

(g) *Forms the sheaf [i.e., angle and spread of the guns to target] as the necessary data comes available.*

(h) *Attends to the preparation of protective cover and to the immediate security of the firing battery.*

The Reconnaissance Officer.

(a) Securing by personal reconnaissance and the assistance of Scouts such information as to the enemy, our own troops, or the terrain as is desirable or ordered.

(b) Supervising the work of scouts, observing parties, etc.

(c) Securing and tabulating firing data, preparing sketches, and securing other information requisite for the direction and conduct of fire.

(d) Observing the field of action, watching for movements of the enemy and of our own troops which may affect the situation, and keeping his commanding officer appraised of changes to the situation.

Training of Scouts.

1529. For scout duty, alert, cool-headed, and intelligent men should be selected; they should be good horsemen and have good eyesight and good hearing. Each Scout should be provided with a good field glass, a compass, a watch, a whistle, a pocket message and sketch book, a pencil, and a combination flag kit [i.e., semaphores].

1530. The training for a scout should have for its object to:

(a) develop his powers of observation.

(b) teach him what to look for and how to recognize it.

(c) teach him how to report intelligently and concisely, both verbal and written.

(d) make route sketches.

(e) use field glasses.

(f) read maps.

(g) make panoramic and position sketches.

(h) signal.

(i) operate telephones.

The scout's powers of observation and description are developed first and of all by simple exercises. Thus he may be required to look at a given section of terrain and describe what he sees in it. The scout is made to appreciate the lay of the land as indicated primarily by its drainage, and secondarily by other natural features, and by the works of man. A good eye for country is thus to be acquired; the scout learns to appreciate the configuration of a terrain which may be only partially visible to him, and thus to deduce the most favorable *routes for traversing it and the most probable positions for hostile occupation. The Scout must also be taught to distinguish troops of the different arms, to recognize their formations and to familiarize himself with their usual methods of action.*

Choice of Position.

1546. The area within which the field artillery must take position is determined by the tactical situation and the plan of action decided upon by the commander of the troops. The field artillery is not free, therefore, to choose its own position, but must make the best use of the terrain within the limits thus imposed.

1547. The commander of troops [i.e., the infantry brigade commander] designates the areas or places near which the field artillery is to take up its positions and influences the distribution of the units by a general indication of the tasks to be performed. The artillery commander then translates those assigned tasks and designates his units to achieve the said tasks... Regimental commanders amplify the orders of the senior artillery commander as may be necessary, particularly with reference to ammunition and other supply and lines of communication. Battalion commanders assign their batteries to positions or areas in which to take position, and assign targets or sectors of attack or observation.

1548. The only invariable rule in the choice of a position are:
(a) obtaining an effective range.
(b) securing a large field of fire.
(c) concealment from view.
(d) facility of movement to the front, flanks, and rear.
(e) proximity of good cover for teams.
(f) favorable conditions for resupply of ammunition.

Positions combining all of the above qualities are seldom or never found. The choice to which consideration carries most weight depends upon the tactical situation.

1549. By a suitable choice of positions and of observing stations the greater part of the terrain within range of the guns may be included within the field of fire. Concealed positions and indirect laying are habitually used. Certain conditions require positions in the open from which direct laying may be used.

1552. Skill in the concealment of guns is to be acquired by the careful study of ground and by extensive experience on a varied terrain. The following suggestions are to be noted:

(a) Positions which, from the enemy's point of view, are on the sky line are usually the most conspicuous. By placing the guns below the sky line, so that they will have a favorable background and by preventing movements of the personnel, a battery may be unrecognized, even though it is in the open. It is important, however, to have a crest, a hedge, or a clump of trees in front so as to increase the enemy's difficulty of observation and of exact location. In the absence of natural cover artificial means may be used to conceal the guns.

(b) A position in rear of a crest [reverse slope], with a parallel crest of about the same height in front and some distance away, offers many advantages. The enemy is apt to mistake the crest nearest him for the one actually occupied and to consider shots falling between the crests as beyond his target. Trees, a hedge, standing grain, etc., four or five hundred yards in front of the guns, and so that the line of sight just passes over them, may similarly serve to deceive the enemy as to the actual position.

(c) When indirect laying is to be employed, a position on a gentle slope just far enough behind the crest to insure the concealment of the flashes best facilitates running the guns up to the crest should direct laying be called for. If the position is covered by the enemy, however, and the crest is plainly seen by him, the guns are in a very vulnerable position, as shrapnel may be employed to search such a reverse slope very effectively.

(d) The most advantageous position, from the point of view of concealment alone, is one more than 400 yards in rear of a covering mask, having flash defilade and hidden from the view of any auxiliary observers whom the enemy may push to the front and flanks. This is called COUNTER-SLOPE.

Ruses.

1553. Ruses.—Dummy emplacements suitably prepared will often serve to deceive the enemy, distract his attention, and cause him to waste ammunition. A few guns may be sent to occupy such faux positions with the view of drawing the enemy's fire to it, leading him to reveal his own position and strength. Such guns should be posted with wide intervals; their rapidity of fire may be utilized to produce the impression of a large force of artillery.

Firing Over Friendly Troops.

1554. Firing Over Friendly Troops.—Firing over our own troops is to be regarded as normal procedure. Freedom is thus gained to post Artillery so as to cover effectively the whole front of the combat and to realize the power of concentrating the fire of widely separated lines. PROJECTILES SHOULD CLEAR FRIENDLY TROOPS AT LEAST ten YARDS. Fire over them should not be conducted with elevations of less than 1,000 yards, or when they are within 400 yards of the guns. These limitations are modified by the relation between positions occupied by the target, the friendly troops, and the guns.

-The Fire Direction Center (F.D.C.)-

For a gun crew to hit targets in *indirect fire* mode (i.e., targets that cannot be seen by a gunner), an F.D.C. needs to know where its guns are relative a target by using a map with exact distances. With this information, the F.D.C. will to calculate two things for the gun: the up or down angle of fire, which determines the distance a particular projectile will travel (called "range"), and how far the target is left or right of the guns (called "deflection"). Once a battery commander, his reconnaissance officer, and the scouts have chosen a battery location, the executive officer will emplace the guns "in battery" facing a cardinal direction—usually the direction of the enemy. Once set, he will either post an aiming stake or designate an aiming point (e.g., church steeple). That point will represent 3,200 mils on a 6,400 mil scale (it does not matter the direction of fire—for whatever it is, the central setting is 3200 mils). If the target is to the right of the guns, the reading will be 3,100 or less; if it is to the left, the reading will be 3,300 or more. If the target is right dead along the axis of the aiming point, it will be 3,200 (which almost never happens).

After receiving a fire mission, the F.D.C. plots the target and the gun or guns on a map. It will then determine the distance and how far left or right the target is to the guns. In most cases, the farther the distance, the higher the angle of the gun (denoted on firing tables). Once the distance is set, the F.D.C. will make adjustments according to the height of the guns relative to the height of the target. This is called "site." e.g., if the guns are at 300' elevation and the target is at 600', this will affect the angle of fire. Once distance plus site is determined, the F.D.C. has calculated what is called "range." The F.D.C. will next determine the "deflection" (i.e., left or right) of the guns. In most cases, the farther the range, the less millage adjustment is needed. e.g., for every 1,000 yards, 1 mil equals 10 yards, for every 2,000 yards, 1 mil equals twenty meters, etc. Finally, the F.D.C. has to compensate for the fact that, due to the rifling of the piece, all projectiles have a "universal twist to the right." The farther the range, the more the round shoots right. Once this is figured in (meaning point the gun a little bit more to the left, depending on how far the target is), the F.D.C. will send the final solution with "range and deflection" that the Gunner will set on his piece.

When in combat, as we shall see, all of these factors will be important. If a gun line is placed on a slope, for example, it must compensate the angle of the gun in order to actually hit the target. Unfortunately, due to the impossibility of quick communication with front-line troops, most fire missions in France were pre-planned "rolling" or "creeping" barrages in which the F.D.C. had time to prepare the firing settings of the pieces long before firing.

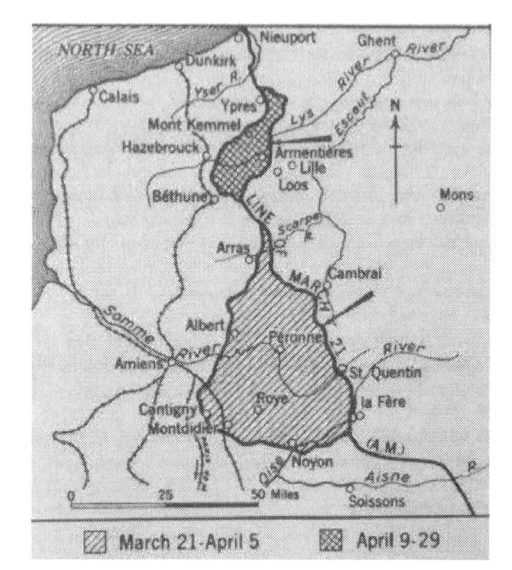

"Ground Gained by German Offensives of March and April, 1918, *A.B.M.C.* (L) and *Maréchal de France* Ferdinand Foch, Supreme Commander of Allied and Associated Forces (R).

Maj. Gen. Robert Lee Bullard, Commander of the 1st Division and later the American III Corps (R).

"Loading 160th Inf. Bde. troops for France on the James, City Point, Virginia, 5-25-18."

"Leaving Newport News with Brett's 160th Inf. Brig." (L) and "U.S. Destroyer at Sea 6-7-18. Our convoy to France. Protection to 13 transports." This would have been the U.S.S. *Huntington*, which escorted the 160th Inf. Bde.

U.S.S. *Siboney,* which transported the 313th Arty. and the 305th Ammunition, Supply, and Transportation Trains from Norfolk to Brest (L) and a typical American convoy headed across the North Atlantic to France, 1918 (R).

Hello France! Brest Harbor with the 319th Inf. (L) and "Disembarkation in France."
We wore our M1911 Campaign Hats well into the summer, until we received new
M1917 Overseas Service Caps (R).

"Newly Arrived Troops Disembarking at Brest" by Jack Duncan.

Army logistical zones in France. The main ports of debarkation for the Doughboys were Brest, St. Nazaire, or Bordeaux. The main A.E.F. supply line ran from Brest to Chaumont, where Pershing's H.Q. was located.

319th Inf. soldiers on their way to Calais, June 14, 1918.

Views of Camp Pontanezen, France.

40 or 8s.

"A car load of Hommes—Good-bye Calais." Blue Ridgers on a 40 or 8.

Chapter 10

Friedensturm, Dodging Porpoises, and Over There! (March 3-June 7, 1918).

On March 3, 1918, the Soviet Republics, led by the Bolshevik leader Vladimir Ilyich Ulyanov (A.K.A. "Lenin"), dropped out of the war against the German, Austrian, and Ottoman Empires with the Treaty of Brest-Litovsk. In the treaty, Germany and Austria kept everything west of Brest-Litovsk (modern-day Poland and parts of the Ukraine and the Baltic States) and the Turks gained some ground in the Caucuses. This was horrible news for the Associated Powers ("the Allies" plus the U.S.) because Germany, Austria, and Hungary would now be able to send hundreds of thousands of men and tons of *matériel* from the Eastern Front to the Western and Southern Fronts. We all understood that most of these forces would be sent against us, if there was anything left of the French, British, or Belgian Armies once we got there, of course. According to the Allies, these reinforcements would give the Germans operating on the Western Front an infantry superiority of some 324,000 men. That meant they could mass at one point along the line—gaining three-to-one odds in favor of the attack—and not only breach the line, but also exploit a breakthrough and fight a decisive battle of annhilation, probably between Calais and Dunkirk, along the English Channel.

In a carefully crafted plan, *Generalfeldmarschall Paul von Hindenburg*, to whom the Kaiser had delegated all strategic authority, hoped to crush the British by a double envelopment toward Amiens and Hazebruck, driving them into the English Channel, and then turn south and take Paris from the west, paralyzing France and more than likely winning the war.

Von Hindenburg's first blow fell on March 21, 1918. Superior to the Allies in strength, morale, training, and experience in mobile warfare, with the added advantage of unity of command, the Germans swept away all resistance and by March 31, had penetrated to *Noyon*, creating a broad salient, 37 miles deep on a base of 65 miles, capturing some 90,000 prisoners and 1,300 guns.

On March 21, 1918, this fear was realized when the Germans, leveraging their 324,000-man superiority, smashed the British lines between Arras and La Fère and drove southwest some forty miles to Cantigny, using new infiltration/*Stosstruppen* tactics, weapons, and units that had been developed by soldiers like *General der Infantrie* (lt. gen.) Oskar von Hutier while fighting the Russians in Prussia and Poland.[120] This was the beginning of what the Germans

---

[120] *Calais* is pronounced "Call-ay," *Arras* is pronounced "Are-ah," *La Fère* is pronounced "La Fair," *Cantigny* is pronounced "Can-tig-nee." These elite attack teams were also called "*Sturm*" or "attack" troops. "*Stoss*" means "impact" and it was this term that was used more by the German Army because they considered all of their soldiers to be "attack" troops. These special shock or impact units were actually pioneer/demolition platoons. Commanded by a lieutenant, they consisted of light and medium M.G. teams, flamethrower teams, grenadiers, explosive experts, and pioneers. *Unternehmen Friedensturm* is pronounced "Ohnter-nay-men Free-den-sterm."

called *Friedensturm* or "Peace Offensive," which intended to drive British, British Commonwealth, Belgian, and Portuguese forces from France before we Americans could make our strength known.

The first phase of the grand offensive, code-named *Unternehmen Michael* (Operation Michael), pitted 64 German divisions in three field armies—George von Marwitz's, Karl von Bülow's, and Oskar von Hutier's—against Sir Douglas Haig's B.E.F., which had but 19 divisions on line and 13 in reserve (64 German versus 32 British divisions). By March 25, the Germans had captured some 90,000 prisoners, succeeded in separating the British from the French, and the British were actually in danger of being driven back into the English Channel! Huge German artillery pieces (e.g., the "Big Bertha" or "Paris Gun") even got close enough to fire on targets in Paris. General James Harbord wrote:

> *General von Hindenburg discussed the possible sectors for the great offensive with his Army Group commanders and his staff. Three sectors were under consideration: between Ypres and Lens, between Arras and La Fère, or on both sides of Verdun, omitting the fortress. He decided for the center attack [i.e., between Arras and La Fère, with the center at Saint-Quentin], with the main effort between Arras and Peronne, toward the coast. If it succeeded, great strategical results were to be hoped for, as it would cut the principal part of the British forces from the French, and possibly roll it up with its back on the Channel... After selecting the divisions and other forces available for the big attack, it was decided to strike between Croisilles, southeast of Arras, and Moeuvres, straddling the Cambrai re-entrant angle, and between Villiers-Guislain and the Oise River south of Saint-Quentin... March 21 was a chill, foggy morning, and the Allied aeroplanes were practically useless through poor visibility. For eight days the attack continued. The British Fifth Army was practically destroyed. The frontage which the Allies were compelled to hold with diminished numbers was tremendously increased. It seriously lowered Allied morale and correspondingly raised that of their enemy. The Germans demonstrated that they could break through highly-organized defenses.*[121]

The Germans also called it the *Kaiserschlacht* or "Emperor's Battle," which is pronounced "Kye-zer Shlawckt." British Commonwealth Forces are Canadian, Australian, New Zealand, and South African troops.

[121] As cited in Harbord, 242.

What shocked (and impressed) the Allies most during *Unternehmen Michael* was the Germans' use of "*Stoss*," "*Sturm*," or "*Hutier*" tactics. These tactics called for highly trained and heavily armed assault troops who were considered as being "super engineers" to breach the British lines and keep going. Avoiding all strong points, acting like water going downhill, the *Stosstruppen* moved hell-bent-for-leather for the British rear and killed as many cooks, clerks, mechanics, and artillerists as possible. One of the weapons most effectively used by the *Stoss* platoons was the M.G. 08/15 or the "Light Maxim." Unlike the standard Maxim, which was mounted on a sled quad-pod, the M.G.15 had a pistol grip, a shoulder stock, a bi-pod, and a drum magazine. On the defense, the Germans generally kept their M.G. 15s in the outpost line or in shell holes while they kept their heavier, sled-mounted M.G.s in the second or third lines, code-named *"SIEGFRIED"* or *"KRIEMHILDE,"* etc. General James Harbord explained our general understanding of German "shock tactics" in this way:

> *In defensive warfare conducted from trenches, the topography had lost much of its significance. The possession of commanding ground was not decisive. It now might easily become so in a war of movement. Its possession must be considered as an incidential objective. In this kind of warfare the lines must be kept thin, but constantly strengthened from behind. In the German conception the light M.G. had been regarded as an auxiliary weapon. They were now to be taught that the soldier with the light M.G. was the true Infantryman, and the man only with the rifle, a mere "rifle carrier." Its power, compared to the rifle, made the light M.G. the principal infantry weapon... The two consitiuted an infantry group which operated as a unit. The heavy M.G. with its longer range would facilitate the advance by keeping down the enemy fire. It accompanied the advance, of course, but really as an auxiliary. A second auxiliary arm was the light trench mortar, now mobile and sighted to be capable of direct fire. The infantry battalion became the tactical unit of the division as the group of rifle, M.G., and T.M. was the unit of the battalion... The massed artillery was expected to prepare the attack. Its mass, however, had to be supplemented by field guns attached to advancing battalions and regiments as I.G.s. Each [German] division had a company of medium T.M.s which were made as mobile as possible and allotted to battalions as needed. With there were flame projectors, principally for close-fighting against men in dug-outs, cellars, and blockhouses. No tanks were contemplated except detachments of tanks captured from the Allies. The Germans started to construct tanks but did not*

get into production on a large scale until the last days of the war. Aircraft support for the infantry was provided by special battle aeroplane flights. Diving from height, they flew at a comparatively low level above infantry lines, artillery, reserves, and advancing columns. They were given tactical tasks. They were reconnasiacce troops and bombers for the far-rear, but took part in the fighting on the ground. Their other activities were incidental to this participation in ground fighting... The fire of massed artillery was considered the most important preparation for the infantry attack. The number of guns was figured as a hundred per km of front to be attacked. The guns were brought close to the most-advanced lines, as otherwise they might have to change position during the battle. They were to be concealed from observation from the front and from above. The old artillery duel had passed out and these guns were not intended for long periods as placed. They no longer considered ranging as practicable and sought effect without ranging. Careful testing of guns behind the front, and the tabulation of the errors of the day as probable from wind, atmospeheric density, and the wearing of the piece, with an artillery meteoriocal service and perfect maps, were available to all batteries. These, with sound-ranging and aerial photography, were the factors that replaced the old-time ranging fire.[122]

The German "Peace Offensive" attacks were summed-up in the following Army flyer:
Surprise: By preserving order of battle until the attack was imminent, the attacking troops making night marches and taking their places under cover.
Short intense artillery preparation: This bombardment came as a tactical surprise. It included wide distribution of gas in back areas...Advance by [what is called] "nutcrackering": The attack was to take place at dawn by groups of successive thin lines of Infantry with their auxiliary arms. [One British officer] described it "as like a thrust with open but steel-tipped fingers." The advance of those lines is covered by gas, smoke, and artillery fire, and in its greatest exemplar—March 21, 1918—the morning was foggy. It was insisted that battalions of front-line units push their attacks without reference to the progress of front units on either side of them. The reduction of strong points was to be accomplished by units in support or reserve, and by passing around in the rear of any opposing units still holding out.

---

[122] Harbord, 239-40.

Constant artillery support: The massed artillery keeps up its fire, and the light artillery closely follows the infantry...No stated objectives: The divisions march on prescribed routes of direction, and when necessary their places are taken by fresh divisions. [123]

As you will soon read, we Americans adopted many of these tactics—except for the last one: "no stated objectives." Granted, the primary mission in war is to scare as many enemy soldiers as possible to make him do what you want him to do (i.e., it's all psychological). However, one helps "put the scare into the foe" or "gains psychological dominance" by taking ground and maneuvering the enemy into a disadvantageous position (check mate). As such, we were always assigned an objective or a rally point for no other reason than to better help us reconsolidate after an engagement. To simply say, "Go that way" will get a unit into a whole-lot-of-trouble.

Faced with the "Peace Offensive Crisis," on March 26, 1918, at the Doullens Conference, the Allies finally relented and agreed to appoint one supreme commander or *"Generalissimo"*: *Maréchal de France Ferdinand Foch.* Up until this time, although the French, British, Italian, and Greek Armies in France, Flanders, Italy, and the Balkans had not fought at cross-purposes, they also had not worked together as well as they could have or should have and, compounding the problem, they operated along exterior lines. The Germans, Austrians, and Hungarians, however, had operated along interior lines and generally worked together (dominated by the German General Staff). To be clear, Foch did not "command" the armies of the Associated Powers *per se*, however. He was empowered to merely better coordinate their efforts—to ask them to attack here or there and when, in conjunction with other armies. For example, only General Pershing commanded the units of the A.E.F. He operated, however, as a part of a larger force that was coordinated by Foch. Everyone who was "Over There" understood that the A.E.F. alone could not have defeated Germany, but neither could the Allies (if they could have, they would have done so already). All of us were needed and all were collectively responsible for the ultimate victory.

From April 9-29, the Germans hit the British again in the vicinity of Ypres. This was to be the phase of the offensive that finally broke the British and took the Belgian and French ports of Nieuport, Dunkirk, and Calais. The Germans slogged their way west until April 29, when they ran out of steam. But as before, "the Hun with the Gun" came close to reaching the English Channel. If they would have, the French Army would have been out-flanked and alone, Paris would have fallen, and Germany would have more-than-likely won the war, formally annexing

---

[123] As cited in Harbord, 240.

Belgium and Luxembourg into their ever-growing empire and even gaining several Belgian and French colonies across the globe. With the recent Treaty of Brest-Litovsk, the Germans had already expanded their empire east by adding several new principalities, late of the Russian Empire. With its flanks secure and its empire enlarged, Germany could then have built up its naval and air forces over the next several years to finally challenge the British Empire for global hegemony. The German *Friedensturm* attacks to date were in fact so destructive that the British were forced to draft eighteen-year-olds to replace their losses. For the Germans, it was even worse, however, as they could no longer replace their losses with draftees. They had reached the tipping point.

And the full power of the A.E.F. was yet to be felt.

On May 27, the Germans struck the weakened French line along the *Chemin des Dames* between Soissons and Rheims and were headed for Paris *via* the Marne River and Chateau-Thierry.[124] There were about 300,000 American troops in France at the time and most of them were not ready for combat (but almost as many as the German superiority of 324,000 troops when the offensive started). In desperation and deference to the Allies, Pershing decided to commit five American divisions to help blunt the German advance. For example, Maj. Gen. Robert Lee Bullard's American 1st Division ("The Big Red One") was dispatched to help the British retake Cantigny from the Germans on May 28.[125] General Harbord remembered:

Pershing told Foch that the Americans were ready and anxious to do their part, and that he was willing to send any troops that he had to any duty that Foch might suggest. He asked the Generalissimo for suggestions as to how we might help. General Foch was much touched, apparently, and taking General Pershing by the arm hurried him across the lawn to where the others still stood, and asked him to repeat to them what he had just said to him...General Pershing's French was not exactly God-given, but it was never misunderstood...He said: "I have come to tell you that the American people would consider it a great honor for our troops to be engaged in the present battle—I ask you for this in their name and my own. At this moment there are no other questions but of fighting. Infantry, artillery, aviation, all that we have is yours—use them as you will. More will come in numbers equal to

---

[124] *La rivière Aisne* is pronounced "la Riv-ee-yair Ayn," *Soissons* is pronounced "Swa-sawn," *Rheims* is pronounced "Raams," *and Chateau-Thierry* is pronounced "Shat-toe Tee-air-ee."

[125] The 1st Infantry Division consisted of the 16th, 18th, 26th, and 28th Infantry Regiments and the 5th, 6th, and 7th Artillery Regiments. Being the first American unit committed to battle, it was generally seen as being the "premier" division in the A.E.F.

> *requirements. I have come especially to tell you that the American people will be proud to take part in the greatest battle of all history.*[126]

At Cantigny, the 1st Division's 2nd Inf. Brig. counter-attacked the strong German defensive lines using all of the skills its men had been taught over the past several months (when an American division attacked during the Great War, it usually did so with one brigade up, with two regiments abreast, using the other as reinforcement). In the subsequent fighting, the "Big Red One" took its assigned objective and repelled several vicious German counter-attacks. This first offensive victory of the Americans cannot be under-estimated. If we would have been repelled, for example, our morale, and that of the Allies, would have dropped and that of the Germans would have risen. From this point forward, the A.E.F., along with the Allies, would be on the attack—all the way up until the Armistice was declared on Nov. 11, 1918.

For Foch, the question of reserves was his primary concern at this point. Britain and France had already drained their available man-power for 1918. But America's resources were virtually untapped. Behind the dozen or so divisions already in France loomed hundreds of thousands of fighting men assembled in our training camps in the States (like the 80th Division at Camp Lee). With these, the Associated Powers would finally possess the preponderance of power. During these dark days for the Allies, the heads of state of France, Britain, and Italy met in Versailles and sent the following telegram to President Wilson:

> *General Foch has presented to us a statement of the utmost gravity, which points out that the numerical superiority of the enemy in France, where 162 Allied divisions now oppose two hundred German divisions, is very heavy, and that, as there is no possibility of the British and French increasing the number of their divisions (on the contrary, they are put to great straits to keep them up) there is a great danger of the War being lost unless the numerical inferiority of the Allies can be remedied as rapidly as possible by the advent of American troops…He places the total American force required for this at no less than one hundred divisions [i.e., 1.4 million men—Allied divisions were about half of the M1917 U.S. Infantry Division], and urges the continuous raising of fresh American levies, which, in his opinion, should not be less than 300,000 a month with a view to establishing a total American force of one hundred divisions at as early a date as can possibly be done.*[127]

---

[126] Harbord, 244.

[127] As cited in Bullard, Robert Lee, Maj. Gen. (U.S.A., ret). *Personalities and Reminiscences of the War* (Garden City, N.Y., 1925), 464. Hereafter cited as "Bullard."

The real question was how to get these American soldiers to France A.S.A.P. Doughs were landing at a rate of 50,000 a month. The War Department had planned to send to France by July 1918 some twenty divisions of 25,000 men each (i.e., 500,000). These numbers fell far-short of General Pershing's request of July 6, 1917, however, which contemplated at least a million troops in France by May 1918. The problem was shipping. We had the troops, but not the ships available to get them "Over There." On Dec. 2, 1917, General Pershing in fact cabled for expansion of the American shipping program: "The Allies are very weak and we must come to their rescue this year, 1918. The year after may be too late. It is very doubtful if they can hold on until 1919, unless we give them a lot of support this year." General James Harbord, who was later put in charge of the entire S.O.S. remembered:

> *Our tonnage allotments did not keep up to our need. In July the A.E.F. asked for 750,000 tons, were allotted 475,000, and actually received 438,000. In August 700,000 tons were allotted but only 511,000 were received. But in this latter month 50,000 tons of Q.M. supplies, of which we already had a surplus, were sent, while there was a deficiency of 50,000 tons for the transportation corps and the motor transport... shipments of ordnance material were short 33% of estimated allotments; of signal material 52%; of chemical warfare requirements 51%; of medical supplies 23%; of railway material, largely rolling stock, 20%.*[128]

To ameliorate the problem, the British, in the wake of *Friedensturm,* agreed to transport and train six American divisions themselves. While command, staff, and the infantry brigades were to be given experience with British divisions, the artillery brigades would be trained under French direction and with French *matériel*. It was planned that this "in country" training would embrace about ten weeks after which the brigades would be ready for front-line duty to at least help hold the line while the more-experienced British and French divisions continued with their counter-attacks across France and Flanders. These sober facts were well-known to Cronkhite when he outlined his views immediately after returning to Camp Lee, declaring that "American soldiers are needed on the Western Front just as much as you would need a pair of shoes if you were barefooted." It was on March 8, 1918, that Cronkhite, interviewed by the camp newspaper, "The Bayonet," revealed the plan for the division's early movement overseas. He said:

> *I cannot emphasize too strongly the sense of personal responsibility I feel that each soldier should be well and thoroughly trained. If I can help it, there will*

---

[128] As cited in *Harbord,* 443.

be no green men in the 80th Division when we hit the firing line. If any man in this division is killed because he hasn't been properly drilled in every big and little detail of modern fighting, I shall feel personally responsible for his death. I want the men to realize this; to know that when they are asked to work harder still, until they think they cannot go any harder, that there's good reason for it all, and that reason is their own safety.[129]

Cronkhite also said:

While [our soldiers] haven't the look of war-worn veterans, the Divisional review proved that the men of the 80th Division are real soldiers. They marched exceedingly well, they carried themselves well, and they looked well. They looked like men who are well-trained... There are many things, of course, which have to be improved and corrected.[130]

-Getting Ready to Get Over There-

As this crisis played itself out in northern France, our division received a sufficient number of Selectees at Camp Lee to bring it back up to full strength. Of the 132,000 men in the March draft, approximately 10,000 were scheduled to report to Camp Lee and the Blue Ridge Division. Of this total, Virginia was called upon to furnish 2,178, West Virginia 1,514, and Pennsylvania 6,296. The Virginians began arriving March 29, 1918, followed in the ensuing days by the entire contingent. They were temporarily assigned to the 155th Depot Brigade, then swiftly distributed throughout the division. The previous policy of allocating the new arrivals among the organizations according to their geographical complexion was abandoned, partly because of the relatively low literacy of the Virginia recruits.

In our "Old Virginia Never Tires Regiment," many of these new fillers in fact came from Pennsylvania and they naturally looked upon us "old timers" as veterans of long-standing, which we exploited to the fullest. In order not to ossify the training of the more experienced Blue Ridgers, "veterans" like myself and most of my platoon, the new recruits were put in separate barracks and given special instruction under selected officers and N.C.O.s. These men showed the same spirit of we "originals" had displayed and, by the end of the month, were considered to have progressed far enough to permit their being absorbed into the companies of the regiment.

---

[129] As cited in Stultz, 107.

[130] As cited in *Ibid*, 121.

By the end March, 1918, as the Germans were chewing on the British during *Friedensturm*, "Joe Latrinsky" told us every day that the 80th Division was leaving Camp Lee for France *tomorrow*. We called any rumor, and there were many, a "Joe Latrinsky." We'd say things like, "Well, according to Joe..." "Joe Latrinsky" was therefore a mythical soldier who "knew all"—he was our version of the Germans' "Baron von Münchhausen," you know, the Prussian Hussar officer who could run 1,000 miles an hour, ride on cannon balls, etc.

In the early part of April, orders were in fact received to "prepare to move on short notice" and our months of tedious training with *Ersatz* equipment drew to a close. The time was now spent in checking and re-checking and checking again to see that every man in the organization was fully equipped for overseas duty. We were issued everything except helmet and gas mask, which we were told we'd get "Over There." Company property was carefully marked and labeled and for many days the division was "on its toes" awaiting the signal to move.

The last few days in camp were marked by daily inspections and the men were fully equipped before leaving (*viola*). Two new wool uniforms, two pairs of boots, new underwear, socks, shirts, towels, toilet articles, and a score of other soldier necessities, were issued before leaving. Each man was allotted a barrack-bag as cargo. The barrack-bag was made of heavy blue denim with about a seventy-five pound capacity, which weight was cited as the limit a soldier could obtain storage for in the ship's baggage compartments. Most of the boys placed their knitted garments in the bag and a plentiful supply of soap, as rumor had it that soap was scarce in France. Chocolate bars and smokes were also packed. Examples of the activities taking place can be found in the following log entries from various commands of the division:

April 2: Each man will take 120 rounds of ammunition overseas.

April 6: Supply officers will at once draw all articles to complete Equipment "C," except clothing, vehicles, and animal equipment.

April 8: Articles of equipment to be issued each enlisted man embrace a total of forty items and sixty pieces...

April 9: Record cards will be made for each officer and man prior to departure for port of embarkation.

April 15: A sufficient number of Red Cross sweaters are available to equip each man in the division.

April 16: Only O.D. blankets will be taken overseas, and one will be issued each enlisted man before leaving camp.

April 22: Certain specified stores will not be taken away from camp by organizations leaving.

April 25: Warehouses of division property will open for business at 7:30 A.M., daily, except Sunday. Officers are required to have their complete equipment, except revolvers, by 1 May.

April 29: Cotton breeches, O.D. coats, and long overcoats now in hands of organizations, will be thoroughly cleaned and turned in between 2 and 7 May.

April 30: Stencils for marking boxes and crates have been issued; a white patch, bearing rank, name, and organization of soldier, will be sewed on barracks bags.

May 1: O.D. service coat will be worn at and after retreat, and when officers and men are on leave or pass.

May 2: All organizations have been issued overseas allowance of small arms ammunition.

May 3: Instruction manuals and publications specified for retention by officers and non-commissioned officers for use enroute and overseas.

May 6: Armament of each M.G. company will include twenty-four rifles, to be drawn from camp ordnance officer not later than 7 May. Only ten rounds of rifle ammunition, caliber .30, will be carried in belt of each enlisted man ordered overseas; balance of allowance will be transported in baggage of organization.

May 10: All authorized clothing and equipment of soldiers left behind will be turned in to base hospital, if men are there.

May 13: The Secretary of War directs that, owing to the increased military program, clothing in the hands of troops must be kept at a minimum.

May 14: All organizations will take with them overseas twenty-four rounds of caliber .45 ammunition for each revolver actually in their possession, and twenty-one rounds of ammunition for each pistol actually in their possession. Upon termination of the voyage, box respirators will be collected, boxed, and turned over to the "Quartermaster, Port of Debarkation," for return shipment to the medical supply depot, this camp.[131]

A soldier from the 314th Artillery remembered the last crazy days at Camp Lee:

Only a few days remained to complete all necessary arrangements... From that moment till the last man was on board ship, bedlam reigned supreme, an experience which few will soon forget. At least it will long live in the memory

---

[131] As cited Stultz, 133-34.

of all first sergeants, supply sergeants, and company clerks, who, with their scores of assistants, tumbled over each other in an effort to carry out every conflicting order. The greatest confusion centered around clothing, property, sailing lists, and the acquisition of recruits to replace the brave 400 who had been transferred to the infantry scarcely two weeks before. Who will forget the frantic efforts to box and promptly mark property, most of which we were never to see again; the midnight loading details or the accurate turning in of equipment which would never check, in order to satisfy the demands of an ever-hounding system of accountability?[132]

On May 6, between the Second and Third phases of *Friedensturm*, Brig. Gen. Charles S. Farnsworth, commander of our very own 159th Inf. Brig., was promoted to major general and transferred to Camp Philip Sheridan, Alabama, to command the 37th (Buckeye) Division, which would later play a significant role in the Meuse-Argonne Offensive (the Buckeye Division was moved to Camp Lee after we left for France). Col. George H. Jamerson, commander of the 317th Infantry, was promoted to replace him and he would hold command the brigade until he was incapacitated in Oct., 1918, during the bone-crushing and war-ending Meuse-Argonne Offensive. Col. Howard Perry thence took command of the 317th Infantry and held it until Oct., 1918, when he relieved for cause. Col. Ora E. Hunt, commander of the 320th Infantry, was promoted to command the 165th Inf. Brig., 83rd (Ohio) Division, which was forming at Camp Sherman, Ohio. He was replaced by Lt. Col. Ephraim G. Peyton, the regimental X.O. Peyton would perform well in combat.

On May 16, we learned that Brett's 160th Inf. Brig., along with a few other division units, would depart Camp Lee first and embark for France from Norfolk, Virginia. Farnsworth's 159th Inf. Brig., with the remainder of the division units, would leave Camp Lee second, and embark for France from New York. The first units to in fact depart Camp Lee by train were H.Q. and M.G. Companies/319th Infantry, as well as 1/319th Infantry and twenty-five men from G/319th Infantry, which left for Norfolk at 2:00 A.M., May 17. They were followed by the brigade H.Q. company and 2/320th Infantry, who departed at 5:00 P.M., 2/319th Infantry, less a detachment from G/2/319th Infantry, H.Q., Supply, and M.G. Companies/320th Infantry, 1/320th Infantry, and the 315th M.G. Battalion, which entrained on May 17-18. 3/320th Infantry remained at Camp Lee until May 25, when it joined the rest of its brigade loading up at Norfolk. Capt. Ashby Williams, commander of E/2/320th Infantry remembered:

---

[132] Stultz, 136.

> *It was 5:00 P.M. on May 17, 1918 that my command was lined up in front of the "Upper Barrack" at Camp Lee, Virginia, preparatory to leaving for the Great War. The men, in full equipment, and the officers completely togged up for foreign service, had previously taken part in a battalion parade. As we passed out 31st Street and along Avenue B, on the way to the train, soldiers had lined both sides of the way and cheered us as we passed. Some people whom I knew called to me as I marched at the head of my column and bade me Godspeed. The men were, for the most part, silent. They were wondering, no doubt, how many of us who had started out on that great journey would ever return. And I confess, for my own part, that a lump came in my throat as I answered those who called to me and the tears would not keep back. I remember Mrs. McQuillen, mother of one of my lieutenants, who came to tell him good-bye; she strove hard to keep back the tears as I shook hands with her. Reverend Mr. Nelson was at the train and insisted upon my stepping aside to take a snapshot of me togged up in my foreign service equipment. We were soon aboard the train, men and packs and everything, including Pete, a black and tan bulldog, the mascot of E/2/320th Infantry.*[133]

The "foreign service equipment" noted by Williams was the infamous "Sam Brown Belt," which was not an Army issue item. One of the most public disagreements between General Pershing, commander of the A.E.F., and General Peyton March, who became the Army Chief of Staff on March 4, 1918, revolved around the British Sam Brown Belt.[134] The Sam Brown Belt is an over-the-shoulder leather pistol belt that was designed by Capt. Samuel Brown of the British Army while serving in India during the 1870s. All British officers wore the leather belt/strap and Pershing liked it. He thought that it "set the officers apart" and ordered all A.E.F. officers to wear one.

The problem was that it was not an Army issue item and the Army refused to make it one (that's why all of our officers had to purchase them from local leather makers in either Petersburg or Richmond). General March in fact ordered Pershing to retract his requirement for

---

[133] *1/320th Infantry*, 5. Capt. Ashby will be promoted to command 1/320 while in France. I was one of the soldiers who "cheered them as they passed."

[134] Peyton March commanded the artillery brigade of the 1st Division in France and then that of the entire A.E.F. before he was promoted to the rank of full general to act as Army Chief of Staff from March 1918 until June 1921, when he retired from the Army. As Chief of Staff, he reorganized the Army structure and abolished the distinctions between the Regular Army, the Organized Reserves, and the Army National Guard during time of war. He created new technical branches in the service including the United States Army Air Corps, Chemical Warfare Corps, Transportation Corps, and Tank Corps. He also centralized control over supply.

the Brown Belt, and Pershing refused. With that, it became a "who's in charge here?" fight. The Army Chief of Staff or Mobile Army commanders? Like most other officers in the Army at the time (with exceptions like Brig. Gen. Douglas MacArthur of the 42nd Infantry Division), March believed that officers, N.C.O.s, and E.M. should all wear the same issue gear—that officers should not be allowed to wear a "better grade" of uniform—that only the rank device should be worn to establish a military hierarchy.

But Pershing would not relent, and all officers in the A.E.F., Marines included, were expected to wear the leather Sam Brown Belt and not the issue canvas pistol belt. In my opinion, the issue canvas pistol belt, which was designed to carry the M1911 Browing Auto Pistol and its holdster, a canteen, ammunition pouch, and first aid pouch, was in fact superior to the Sam Brown Belt. It was durable, easy to manufacture, and carried the weight better. I wore a Sam Brown Belt after the war as an officer in the Organized Reserve (more on that later), but do know of some company grade officers who loved them.

Upon arrival to Norfolk, Doughs from Brett's 160th Inf. Brig. boarded four transport ships. H.Q. and M.G. Companies and the 1st Battalion of the 319th Infantry, embracing 48 officers and 1,832 men, went aboard the U.S.S. *Madawaska*, which was formerly the German liner *Koenig Wilhelm II*. A remainder of the 27th Infantry Division, whose overseas movement had begun a week earlier, also boarded the *Madawaska*. 2/319 and 3/319, (less three officers and twenty-five men of Company G and two officers and eighty-nine men of Company H) with a strength of forty-eight officers and 1,663 men, embarked on the U.S.S. *Zeelandia*, a converted Dutch passenger boat. Two officers and forty-two men of the 315th M.G. Battalion also boarded the *Zeelandia*.

Brig. Gen. Lloyd M. Brett and 160th Inf. Brig. H.Q., which numbered 5 officers and 20 E.M., a detachment of 2/319th Infantry, consisting of 5 officers and 114 E.M., 2/320th Infantry, comprising thirty-two officers and 1,116 E.M., and the bulk of the 315th M.G. Battalion, composed of twenty-five officers and 617 E.M., embarked at Lambert's Point on the converted Italian liner *Duca d'Abruzzi* (named after Luigi Amedeo, the Italian Duke of Abruzzi, a cousin to the King of Italy and a well-known Artic explorer who almost married an American heiress). The *Duca* was an older vessel which had plied between Mediterranean and South American ports prior to the war. H.Q., Supply, and M.G. Companies of the 319th Infantry and 1/320th Infantry, totaling 51 officers and 1,631 E.M., went aboard the U.S.S. *Rei d'Italia* (King of Italy), another converted Italian ship, at Lambert's Point. The 305th Signal and Sanitary Battalions were loaded aboard the U.S.S. *Mercury*, formerly the North German Lloyd Liner *Friedrich*

Barbarossa, which was named after one of the Medieval Holy Roman Emperors of the German Nation.[135] Capt. Ashby Williams of E/2/320th Infantry, aboard *Duca d'Abruzzi*, remembered:

> *The Duke d'Abruzzi was an old Italian liner which we understood had been engaged for a number of years in commercial traffic between the Mediterranean Sea and South American ports. She was a dirty old ship of about 400 feet in length, with enough staterooms to accommodate the officers and some of the sergeants and fitted up below the main deck with tier upon tier of canvas bunks for the men. The men's quarters would have been fairly comfortable but for the fact that they were below decks and lighted and ventilated only by the portholes, which had to be closed and kept closed a night to keep out the heavy seas and to prevent the lights from shining out for the benefit of lurking submarines.*[136]

Loading the brigade's 5,200 troops consumed the greater part of the day and night of May 17. At noon, May 18, the convoy sailed out of Hampton Roads and into the North Atlantic. Crowds which had gathered on shore cheered, and the harbor craft sounded a noisy *bon voyage* with their sirens and whistles. The embarkation at Lambert's Point, is described by a member of the 320th Infantry:

> *The system of boarding the transport was very efficient; we were loaded by detachments and companies, the passenger lists of each detachment and company being given to an officer at the gang plank, and each man, in single file, approached the gang plank, giving his name. Each man was checked off and handed a card bearing the section of the ship and the number of the bunk he was assigned to, and was met at the top of the gang plank by a guide who escorted him to his quarters. Our entire battalion was placed on board...exactly one hour after arriving at the Port of Embarkation.*[137]

The convoy which transported Brett's 160th Inf. Brig. to France consisted of nine vessels, all carrying troops, with the exception of one laden with naval stores. The other transports were the *Calamares, Pocahontas, President Grant* (with units from the 27th Infantry Division aboard), and the *President Lincoln*. All ships were fantastically camouflaged with painted

---

[135] *314th M.G.*, 16-17.

[136] *1/320*, 5-6.

[137] As cited in Stultz, 141.

designs and false funnels. Escorting them were the U. S. destroyer *Huntington* and a small torpedo boat destroyer.

A heavy fog settled as the convoy passed between Capes Charles and Henry, Virginia, and by the time the anchor was cast to the bottom several miles off shore, the fog thickened to almost an impenetrable veil. Throughout the rest of the day, the fog was in fact so dense that the convoy could not be assembled. But finally, at midnight May 18, with the *Rei d'Italia* still missing in the mist, the signal "Follow Me in Column" was given by the escort cruiser and the voyage began. Five additional destroyers joined the convoy several days later and remained as a part of the escort with the exception of the time they refuelled in the Azores. The efficiency of the U.S. Navy escort vessels was remarkable. Capable of thirty knots, their fleetness enabled them to provide maximum protection and to permit the transports to maintain an uninterrupted twelve knots along their zigzag course.[138]

In the meantime, news of Brett's 160th Inf. Brig.'s departure had quickly become known in Petersburg, Hopewell, and Richmond. Theoretically, civilians were presumed to be unaware of troop movements, and the movement of the 160th Inf. Brig. by night had been calculated to promote secrecy. However, such a long expected event was impossible of concealment, and thousands of relatives and friends of those of us assigned to Jamerson's 159th Inf. Brig. poured into camp during the weekend of May 18-19. So much for operational security! It always seemed that we in the ranks, those who had their kiesters on the line, knew far less that the average Dick at home in the Shenandoah Valley.

Although our cantonment had become accustomed to holiday crowds, we had never witnessed such an invasion! Long-isolated company streets and barracks, supposedly quarantined, were engulfed by eager mobs of civilians who flowed in and then made way for other multitudes to follow. "Dead lines" established at the inception of the quarantine had previously been respected, but nothing short of a barricade would have restrained the host of humanity seeking a parting word with their loved ones. Sentries were simply ignored. Marvellously had the American people accepted war-time restrictions, imposed by no law, but to individual families, Army rules separating them from their men in uniform were non-existent.

At 1:00 P.M. on the afternoon of May 20, 1918, Doughs from Jamerson's 159th Inf. Brig., as well as the 315th M.G. Battalion, boarded a troop train for Hoboken, N.J. Like other units, the 318th Infantry left Camp Lee in five sections, at fifteen minute intervals, all sections rejoining just outside Washington, D.C., where the Red Cross and Y.M.C.A. provided every soldier with hot coffee, biscuits, and cakes. By and large, this was the first experience most of the men had

---

[138] Stultz, 145.

with traveling in troop trains. While many thought it was a rather loathsome trip—sleeping in a day coach with three men to a seat—it was nothing compared to what we experienced with train cars labeled "*40 Hommes ou 8 Chevaux*" (fourty Men or eight Horses) in France.[139]

On the day of our departure, the 318th Infantry and 313th Artillery Regiments were staffed as follows (you'll note that a Medical Officer, an Intelligence Officer, and a Personnel Officer were added to the T.O.):

---

[139] *40 Hommes ou 8 Chevaux* is pronounced "Oams oh Chev-voo."

318th Infantry Regiment, 80th Division

Col. Ulysses G. Worrilow, Commanding
Lt. Col. James M. Love, Executive Officer
Medical Officer: Maj. Clyde W. Sample
Adjutant: Capt. Senius J. Raymond
Supply Officer: Capt. Ernest L. Nunn
Intelligence Officer: Lt. Reginald Davey
Personnel Officer: Capt. Corvan Fisher
Headquarters Co.: Capt. Charles J. Houser
Machine Gun Co.: Capt. Louie Cuthbert

1st Battalion: Maj. Robert J. Halpin
A Co.: Capt. Clarence E. Goldsmith
B Co.: Capt. James S. Douglas
C Co.: Capt. William A. Taliaferro
D Co.: Capt. Vivian T. Douglas

2d Battalion: Maj. Charles Sweeny
E Co.: Capt. Edward H. Little
F Co.: Capt. John Crum
G Co.: Capt. Charles C. Griffin
H Co.: Capt. Grover E. Moore

3d Battalion: Maj. Henry H. Burdick
I Co.: Capt. Richard P. Williams, Jr.
K Co.: Capt. Robert M. Dashiell
L Co.: Capt. Lincoln MacVeigh
M Co.: Capt. Louis J. Koch

313th Artillery Regiment (L), 80th Division

Col. Charles Herron, Commanding
Lt. Col. Otto Brunzell, Executive Officer
Medical Officer: Maj. Albert Baggs
Adjutant: Capt. John Paul
Operations Officer: Capt. George Anderson
Supply Officer: Capt. Walter Buford
Veterinary Officer: Capt. George Zinkham
Recon Officer: Capt. Emory Niles
Headquarters Co.: Lt. Gregory Tappan
Chaplain: Lt. Gladstone Yeuell
Radio Officer: Lt. William Coulburn

1st Battalion: Maj. Frank Dunnigen
A Co.: Capt. Joseph Peppard from Kansas City, Mo.
B Co.: Capt. Robert Perkins from Richmond, Va.
C Co.: Capt. George Penniman from Stevenson, Md.

2d Battalion: Maj. John Nash
D Co.: Lt. Eban Cross from Baltimore, Md.
E Co.: Capt. Frank Crandall from Westfield, N.Y.
F Co.: Capt. Robert Barton from Winchester, Va.

As the troop trains sped north through small Maryland and Pennsylvania towns, the station platforms were crowded with cheering people. Somehow, word that our brigade was bound overseas had preceded us. Dawn ushered us into New Jersey, where no hamlet seemed too small to contribute its delegation of waving citizenry—each flag-bedecked factory window held cheering humanity. The spontaneity of the greetings appeared all the more remarkable because passage of a troop train was an everyday occurrence to communities along the route to America's chief embarkation port.

Upon arrival at the Jersey City railroad center about 8:00 A.M., May 21, we immediately marched aboard ferry boats and a long-unexplained wait ensued ("hurry up and wait"). Our last substantial meal had been at noon the previous day and company mess sergeants combed the area for food for we hungry, vociferous soldiers. Post cards were surreptitiously purchased and hastily written to home addresses, with friendly bystanders agreeing to mail them. Weeks later, the men were chagrined to learn these final messages had not been delivered until after their arrival overseas. Alas, "Support the War Effort!"

Just before noon, orders were received for all hands to be aboard, and shortly thereafter, we started to sail north into New York Harbor. For most of us it was our first glimpse of New York City and we all gave it a careful once-over from afar. Our enthusiasm was considerably dampened, however, when a terrific driving rain drenched us as we continued our journey further up the bay. After our ferry boats proceeded a bit, a large number of large ocean liners (i.e., troop transports) came into view. Every one of us immediately forgot the discomforts of the rain and speculation ran rife as to which vessel we would get on. From all sides were heard remarks like: "Ya, the big guy is that old German boat. Gee! I wish we'd land her!" or "Look at that little shrimp! Oh boy, won't she roll!" I for one get horribly sea sick. I learned that when I was fourteen and my dad took me out on the Chesapeake to fish. On the one hand, I really wanted to be on one of the bigger ships (less roll), but I knew that it would be targeted by German U's first. The safest one to be on, I thought, was the smallest one. But a journey on one of those would be would have been horrendous for me. So I nervously awaited my fate.

Our ferry pulled into a pier once belonging to the North German Lloyd Line where we disembarked in short order. We then sat around a long time inside a warehouse, waiting for further instructions. Finally, about 2:30 P.M., we were told that we were fortunate enough to draw the S.S. *Leviathan*, formerly *Das Vaterland*, one of the biggest, fastest, and at the time, most luxurious liners afloat. When I heard that she was fast, I was relieved. "Thank you, God," I said to myself. He was taking care of good ole Joe Riddle.

Shortly after "Uncle Sam" entered the war, the German crew, knowing that *Das Vaterland* would be seized, damaged its machinery, especially the boilers. But the liner had been repaired by us, renamed *Leviathan*, and was now operated by the U.S. Navy and used for the transport of troops across the cold North Atlantic to French harbors. Prior to us, it had made but one trip as a transport. Most of the liners were painted in crazy shapes to mask their shapes from hostile U-Boats. Some were painted to look like they were travelling in the opposite direction, some were painted to look like destroyers, some simply had opposing stripes, etc. Some ships even had fake smoke stacks built aboard, to make it look more like a dreaded battleship that a German-U would think twice about attacking.

The 318th Infantry was assigned to the portion of the ship known as "F," "G," and "H" Decks. It might be remarked here that "A" Deck is the section of the ship nearest heaven—nobody knows how far down the lowest portion of the ship's anatomy is, but "G" and "H" Decks represent that intermediate state between heaven and hell which is fringed by the water line and is damnably unpleasant. The ship remained in port until mid-afternoon the following day, taking on ammunition, supplies, and more troops. These troops, while unquestionably most excellent men, were naturally, in our minds at least, of inferior quality to the 318th Infantry. They were therefore assigned to that section of the ship still nearer hell and high water. The "below deck men" consisted mostly of the division's support troops, which proved invaluable while we were fighting in France.

At 3:00 P.M., May 22, 1918, with much tooting of whistles and under the guidance of some three sturdy tugs, *Leviathan* slowly backed into the middle of the Hudson River and started on its long trip, with some 10,000-odd Blue-Ridgers and several thousand sailors aboard. In addition to the crew, there was a grand total of about 13,500 men and women (as luck would have it, there were also some two hundred nurses aboard. But they were, of course, segregated from the rest of us).

Joe Latrinsky told us that some genius war planner, presumably working in the Mid-West, had evolved the idea that, in order to prevent Hun agents from knowing that the *Leviathan* and ships like it were transporting any troops, directed the ship captains to keep all troops below deck until the Statue of Liberty had been passed. This, in spite of the fact that for days any person but a blind person could see that it was being loaded with thousands of Doughboys. So, we didn't get to see the Statue of Liberty—typical Army logic.

The first 24 hours spent aboard the *Leviathan* were as hectic as the first days at Camp Lee. While the officers came on board by one gang plank, everyone else came aboard by another and each had to find their way to the assigned berthing areas from different directions. As a consequence, much time was consumed before the officers were able to locate their men. When they finally succeeded in navigating their way by devious routes to the distant compartments, many were completely lost in trying to get back to their own quarters.

While this confusion was at its height, mess call sounded. All officers had been furnished with a copy of "How to Get to Mess and Back Again" but that didn't do any of the E.M. any good because a liason had not yet been established. Unfortunately, few officers had had a chance to actually study this document, and one could not digest its contents hurriedly. Therefore, one saw "confusion twice co-founded" and darkness had settled over the troubled waters long before the harried officers got their men fed and back to the quarters. Even worse, while in harbor, the water-tight compartment doors had stood open, facilitating traffic to a great extent. Upon weighing anchor, however, these doors were kept hermetically sealed, increasing the perplexities of guides four-fold.

As the infantry brigades of the division headed farther out to sea, Heiner's 155th Arty. Brig. and the remaining specialty units of the division departed Camp Lee and disembarked at the Navy Yard at Norfolk for overseas movement. While the 313th Artillery and the 305th Ammunition, Supply, and Transportation Trains were loaded aboard the transport U.S.S. *Siboney* (named after Siboney, Cuba), which had been built for the Ward Line for passenger service but was recently shanghaied into federal service by the U.S. Shipping Board to act as a trans-Atlantic troop transport, the 314th Artillery and other units were loaded aboard the U.S.S. *Americus*. According to Capt. Donald D. Geary of the 313th Artillery, "the *Siboney* had made but one trip across before this as was consequently quite clean. For the same reason it was much disorganized with a crew badly in need of discipline. It was over-crowded—there must have been 3,200 men on board, counting the crew—and this, coupled with the lack of organization and in inexcusable propensity to roll, no matter how calm the sea, made for a certain amount of discomfort."[140]

Like most other U.S. Navy transports of 1918, ships like the *Siboney*, the *Americus*, the *Leviathan*, or the *Zeppelin* were crewed by four or five U.S. Navy officers, the captain (usually a commander), the engineer, the executive, and the paymaster. The last-named is, in the Navy, in addition to what his title implies, the supply officer of the ship. The *Siboney* was put into commission with these officers—including a few Navy Reserve and Merchant Marine officers and a crew gathered from all parts of the Navy—and sent on its first voyage almost immediately. It had returned to New York for supplies and arrived in Norfolk the same morning that the 313th Artillery, etc., loaded. Oil was being taken on one side while the men and supplies were being

---

[140] As cited in *313th Artillery.*, 8.

loaded on the other. But the need for ships was so urgent at that time and such a situation was excusable.

The next morning the entire convoy of nine transports, the cruiser U.S.S. *North Carolina*, and a destroyer weighed anchor and headed out to sea. The troop transports included the *Americus, Siboney, Mongolia, Huron, Mercury, Tenedores, Mallory, Henderson, Teneriffe*, and the *Von Steuben*. All of the transports had guns. The *Siboney*, for example, sported four five-inch guns and depth bomb on the stern. During the second night, there was a dense fog and the transports crept along in imminent danger of colliding with one another. The *Siboney* followed the *Von Steuben* closely when there was a sudden blast of whistles and lights. Apparently, the *Americus*, which was carrying the 314th Artillery, had lost its place in line and suddenly loomed up out of the fog cutting across the bows of several other transports, including the *Siboney* and the *Von Steuben*. Although they did not collide, it was a close call. Many days later, it was learned that the fog was possibly a blessing in disguise, for that very night, German submarines were busy off the American coast and sank several small ships near the spot where the collision almost occurred.

From the time the troop ships left the U.S. until nearing France, there was little excitement to break the routine. We read, pretended to study military manuals, talked, smoked, napped, and rehearsed our respective duties in case of a submarine attack. Every company had that "set" of men who gambled away their earnings with dice or cards or who "appropriated" chickens, turkeys, apples, and other goodies intended for the officers and sold them to the E.M. At times, the ocean kicked up, and thousands of us, myself included, became horribly and frightfully sea sick. One day it in fact got so bad that I was afraid that I was going to be tossed overboard! Other than that, the only other thing of note was the occasional "abandon ship drill" or watching purposes dart across the white caps. Or at given times, tunes that were played by the bands of the 318th Infantry or the 51st Coastal Artillery. Capt. Ashby Williams of E/320th Infantry, aboard *Duca d'Abruzzi*, remembered:

> *The next day out at sea we were joined by eight other ships, some of them carrying troops as we were, and one laden with naval stores, making a total of nine ships in the convoy. They were, indeed, a curious lot, with their camouflage of paint and false funnels and all that. There was one painted so that it looked like two ships and another fixed up to appear as if going in the opposite direction, and so on, everything to deceive the dreaded submarine torpedo. Al distinctive markings were, of course, effaced, to prevent the Boche from getting identifications, but notwithstanding this we learned the names of*

some of them. There was the Re d'Italia, the slowest ship of the convoy, carrying 1/320. Our escort consisted at first of one American cruiser, the Huntington, so we were informed, and I think, two torpedo boat destroyers. Later on we were joined by five other boats of the latter class. The work of the escort ships was wonderful; they had a speed of as high as thirty knots an hour, and this great speed enabled them to shoot in and out around the flanks and to the front when anything suspicious appeared on the horizon. Their vigilance enabled us to maintain an even and uninterrupted speed of twelve knots along our zig-zag course. On about our fifth day out most of these torpedo boat destroyers left us for a time and we were informed that they and gone to the Azore Islands for fuel oil.[141]

The worry of submarines, of course, was the topic of most discussions. Every precaution that was possible for us to take against them was taken. We always wore our life preservers when awake and kept them close to our heads when we slept. In fact, many men, like myself, wore them all of the time to help keep warm. A submarine watch was organized on every ship and scores of men were posted throughout their ship at all times. We also practiced the "Abandon Ship" drill daily, and it was relatively simple, but did require some practice. Every man was assigned by card to a place on a life boat by which he was to escape in the even the ship was torpedoed. Most men hearkened to the memory of the sinking of the S.S. *Titanic* just a few years before and some even cracked jokes about it. There were "stations" about the ship where each of these small boat-loads was to assemble whenever an alarm was given. The plan was explained to the men as well as possible. When we set out to practice with the command, "All hands! Take station for abandon ship!" was given, bells were rung and confusion reigned. As luck would have it, it seemed as though all the men in the bow of the ship had been given cards assigning them to places in the stern and those in the stern had been assigned places in the bow. Everybody upstairs had a station down below and everybody below had come up. To make matters worse most of us were still unable to go about the ship without getting lost. The drill took us the greater part of the afternoon the first time we tried it, and then many of us never got to our right stations. There was a re-arrangement of some of the assignments after the first experience and as we were called upon to practice twice daily, at sunrise and again at sunset, we gradually became quite proficient and could get to our stations and back with little or no disorder. These occasions, I might add, were further complicated by the rule that you had to bring your life-preserver with you.

---

[141] *1/320 Infantry*, 6.

Aboard the *Zeelandia* with the 319th Infantry, a sailor was actually thrown overboard. Fortunately, he was wearing his life preserver, which saved his life in the icy North Atlantic. When they dropped the lifeboat, it snapped from its moorings and pitched into the sea. Due to the fact that the sailor was now far-behind, the captain of the *Zeelandia* chose to break formation and went back to get him, which, by regulations, he was not supposed to do. Needless to say, it was a very sobering experience for the men of the 319th Infantry and they religiously wore their life jackets for the rest of the voyage.[142] To add one last thing about objects being cast overboard, there is the infamous story of "Pete the Dog," the unauthorized mascot of E/2/320th Infantry, who was unceremoniously thrown overboard—an offering to the "God of Good Order and Discipline." Then-Capt. Ashby Williams remembered:

> *There was much to do and no time was lost on board ship. Reveille in the morning, breakfast and drill and exercise on the promenade deck. It was during one of these exercises that Pete, the mascot of Company E, came to grief. He was tired of being cooped up below decks and wanted some exercise and slipped out and began to run around with the men. Unfortunately, General Brett got a glimpse of him and he asked me whose dog it was and how it happened to be on the ship. I told him that it belonged to the men of my company and no one seemed to know how it got aboard. Later some official correspondence between General Brett and myself in regard to a "black and tan bulldog, named Pete." The next day at dinner General Brett said to me: "If that dog lands in France it is going to be very hard with a certain captain aboard this ship." I had no doubt who that captain was, and I knew also that there were strict orders against landing dogs in France. The next day, therefore, "Capt. X" was "Officer of the Day" and I told him that I thought it was his duty to dispose of Pete, as I did not have the heart myself to do it, although Pete was crippled from many fights and had the mange and was not much good anyway. The next day, therefore, "Capt. X" him to the infirmary and tried to chloroform him, but Pete seemed to "smell a rat" and would not be chloroformed. "Capt. X" then tied an iron to his neck and threw him overboard. That night I told General Brett that Pete had been disposed of and the manner of his taking off. The general turned pale and would not eat any more supper but excused himself and went to his state room. Whether he was ill or whether the story of the dog's death had turned his appetite I do not*

---

[142] *319th Infantry*, 13.

know; but I think it was the latter, because he was a gentleman of great sympathy and kindness of heart and I know it hurt him to think that he had had anything to do with injuring any living creature.[143]

Capt. Williams had other positive reminiscences of General Brett, a man who would prove to his weight in gold to the division and the Army once we were committed to combat:

By far the most interesting part of the ship was the dining salon. It easily held the sixty-odd officers aboard the ship. There was a life-sized painting of the Duke d'Abruzzi, that famous nobleman who almost married one of our American heiresses, for whom the boat had been named. General Brett sat at a table at the upper end of the salon, with his back to that portrait. Maj. Rothwell was at his right and Maj. Holt at his left with Maj. Eby, the brigade adjutant, at the foot of the table. I sat next to Maj. Rothwell with Lt. Ray Miller on my right, and Lts. Vandewater and Benny Weisblatt across the table from us. The three lieutenants were the general's aides. This was, indeed, a happy party. Poor Benny Weisblatt never ate anything except a boiled egg now and then or some soup. We had lots of fun at his expense, but he took it always in good part. We consoled him by telling him that he wasn't seasick but homesick, as he had left a brand new wife in the States and that anyway they only cure for seasickness was dry land. Maj. Eby, at the foot of the table, always ordered a second helping of every last dish; it was a pleasure to watch him eat. He always had time, however, to wedge a joke or two, which he never failed to enjoy immensely. Maj. Rothwell, a quiet gentleman, always told his jokes without a smile but they were good. Unfortunately he had stayed on deck a good deal and the sun and wind had peeled the skin off his nose and turned it red, and he was thereby brought under slight covert suspicion in certain quarters. But General Brett was the life of the table. His comments upon people in history, and his stories of the Indian Wars, and his long experience in the Army, always entertained and delighted us. As I look back upon this boat trip I have nothing to be so glad of as the fact that I had the opportunity of becoming really acquainted with General Brett. He was always the gentleman, always the soldier, in the highest sense. He was a pleasure and a benefit and an inspiration to me. He got the best out of life so that his long service enriched and ennobled his character. He knew men's

---

[143] As cited in *1/320*, 9.

rights and he knew men's duties and he knew what men could stand. The highest compliment I can pay him is to say that on many occasions when problems have confronted me I thought what General Brett might or would have done, and have been benefitted by the thought.[144]

We should have never put Brett in the position where he had to order the removal of Pete the Dog—and that's why he was so upset. We were told straight on that we could not adopt pets or mascots, etc. But somebody decided to do it anyway and it placed Brett in a horrible position.

It is his job, as any officer, to enforce Army regulations—all of them—all of the time, equally and fairly.

If we would have followed said regulations, that poor dog would not have been "sacrificed at the alter of military discipline."

Lesson learned.

After several days out to sea, reports ran rife of German submarine activity in our area and as such, the course of the *Leviathan* and the other ships of the convoy were constantly changed. So much so, in fact, that I'm surprised we didn't end up in Australia! We zigzagged back and forth, back and forth. Lights were not permitted after dark except in the innermost wards of the ship and none of us were permitted on deck after sundown. During our last night out to sea, due to a report of the torpedoing of a nearby merchant vessel, all officers were required to stand on alert throughout the night. But nothing happened and the convoy of destroyers (which arrived during the night of May 28) played about like a lot of happy children. The fact that we were not torpedoed and sent to the bottom of the sea is a testament to the U.S. and British Navies.

On the ships that carried units of Brett's 160th Inf. Brig. (*Duca d'Abruzzi*, *Zeelandia*, etc.), however, the submarine threat was real. On Decoration (or Memorial) Day, while the men on the *Zeelandia* were attempting to eat their chicken dinners, the "abandon ship" alarm drill bell was sounded, which was not unusual. What was unusual, however, was that a shot was fired. With that crack, the men, with their pie desserts in hand, rushed with even more vigor to their life boat stations. Some of the men of the 319th Infantry actually saw the low silhouettes of the German U-Boats as their escorting destroyers wailed away at them. A cruiser then dropped depth charges and everything calmed down. As they headed back to their berthing areas, however, the six-inch guns on the *Zeelandia* again opened up as a whole pack of German U's came upon the convoy from the rear. The *Zeelandia* instantly took evasive action in order to

---

[144] As cited in *1/320*, 10.

avoid a torpedo hit. Because of the angle of the threat, the guns were pointed almost parallel to the outer decks and when fired, the concussion not only removed the campaign hats of many-a-man, including Capt. Charles Ryman Herr, commander of F/2/319th Infantry, but also broke several windows. With these shots, the men backed away from the railing and lay prostrate against the cold and slimy deck. Then-Capt. Ashby Williams of E/2/320th Infantry, sailing on *Duca d'Abruzzi* remembered:

> *I noticed a constant ridge under the water in front of the big liner on our right, much as if some huge fish were plowing his way toward the boat. I was suspicious of it and I called the attention of an officer who was standing near me, to it. The liner on our right passed over it, and immediately began to toot her whistles as a signal of distress. In a moment or two every ship in the convoy, as well as the torpedo boat destroyers of the escort, opened fire behind us. It was the submarines. Instantly every ship in the convoy put on full steam ahead. The torpedo boat destroyers darted in and out amongst us firing as they went. Now and then one of them would hover over a suspicious place and drop depth bombs, those terrible things that sink under water and then explode, crushing and destroying with their concussion anything in a wide radius and carrying terror to the heart of the submarines. These ships fire on the periscope, destroying it and blinding the submarines, and then rush on it and drop bombs, much the same fashion as a man would knock another down with his fist and then jump on him with his feet to make sure that we was dead. We learned afterwards that there were ten submarines that took part in the attack and that our war vessels sunk two of them. But however many there were, they over-shot their mark and were taken by surprise by our ships and subjected to such a fire that not a single torpedo reached its mark; for which we, of course, were profoundly thankful. That was the first time we had ever really been in the presence of death and I think it is no discredit to say that every man's heart was in his mouth.*[145]

We in the 318th Infantry sighted land at about noon on May 30, 1918, after a little more than a week out to sea. I remember seeing a French observation dirigible with "Welcome" written across it and several bi-planes patrolling the coastline, looking for enemy submarines. Shortly thereafter came a sudden "boom" from the forward gun, followed in rapid succession by

---

[145] As cited in *1/320th Infantry*, 11.

a number of other "booms." It was evident to all that there were a number of submarines about. There was danger around a plenty, but all hands conducted themselves with sangfroid. At the first "boom" one man cried: "Mark Number Nine!" Another: "Set 'em up on the other alley!" Our liner put on all speed and made for the now-distant harbor and the foam began rising over the bows of the convoy. Several conning towers could now be seen with the naked eye, but the transport's speed, the accuracy of the gun crews (picked crews from the Navy), and the quick work of the destroyers, prevented any disaster. Though it is not definitely known, it is reported that two British destroyers sank two enemy U-Boats, with depth charges.

Thank you Royal Navy!

By 1:30 P.M., after a rather thrilling finish, the anchor was dropped in the beautiful harbor of Brest, and we had our first glimpse of the great medieval French city which was built along *L'Estuaire de L'Elorn en Provence Bretagne*.[146] We had been lucky to come over on the *Leviathan* and fortunate in seeing the largest French naval base during the day and one felt at home at once by seeing practically every ship in the harbor flying the American flag. Another touch of home, especially for we Southerners, was added when enormous barges, manned by some of America's Sable Sons, came alongside to coal the ship. Owing to their enormous size, the *Leviathan* had to anchor in mid-harbor and unload from that point.

We landed in France just a few days after the Germans had broken the French line along the Aisne and were headed toward the Marne, Chateau-Thierry, and Paris.

1/318th Infantry was assigned the unenviable task of unloading the ship and it was a no-joke job. We worked all night in an atmosphere heavily laden with coal dust, stirred up by our Negro stevedores. Once morning broke, the regiment disembarked and was ferried ashore on lighters. We then marched about three miles north to *Caserne Pontanezen*, one of the oldest military bases in France. It was used as a concentration point for Comte de Rochambeau's expeditionary force to America in 1778 during the War for American Independence and, some years later, by the Emperor Napoleon I for his proposed invasion of England in 1805.[147] On our march there, shouldering our M1917 Enfields, carrying our packs, and wearing our particular Doughboy Campaign Hats, cocked in our particular jaunty fashion, we were accompanied by crowds of French children who pestered us for money, food, or "*Cigarettes pour Papa*." They called us "Sammies" after one of our monikers, "Uncle Sam." We didn't really like to be called

---

[146] *Brest* is pronounced "Bres" and *L'Estuaire de L'Elorn en Provence Bretagne* or "The Estuary of the Elorn in Brittanny" is pronounced "Les-tu-air-ee day Lay-lorn en Pro-vens Bret-tan."

[147] *Caserne Pontanezen* or "Barracks of Pontanezen" is pronounced "Cas-ern-ah Pon-tan-ah-zen"; it is one of the oldest military bases in France.

"Sammies" by the French because it reminded us of our own black "Samboes" in the States. But we also didn't like being called "Yanks," either, as that denoted those of us north of the Mason-Dixon Line. Needless to say, what really caught our eyes were the wounded French soldiers (called *Poilu* or "hairy one") who stood up and saluted as we passed.[148] Some were missing arms, others legs, others, eyes. Humbled by the experience, we marched into the ancient barracks.

Living conditions at Camp Pontanezen were not the best. Water was very scarce and cooking facilities were meager. One soldier from the 317th Infantry remembered:

The camp at Brest was under canvas, and the ground available was quite limited and inadequate at that time. The sanitary conditions you would term reasonably fair because the troops made them so... The surroundings as a whole were quite pleasing in a way, by reason of so many points of interest. Pontanezen Barracks, with its great walls and ancient gates...and the old court yard or parade grounds were points of manifest interest, because Napoleon during his great career had equipped several armies in this identical old place.[149]

There were benefits to Camp Pontanezen, however. One was the strawberries that grew wild in the area. The other was that we were introduced to two of our most welcome allies—*Vin Blanc* (white wine) and *Vin Rouge* (red wine). Because most of us were young and came from families with which the consumption of alcohol was strictly *Verboten*, let's just say that we imbibed a little too much with the substance, which the French drank like water.[150] To be honest, drunkenness and alcoholism became a problem and many of us continued to be infected with it once we returned home—many switching to American Rye Whiskey until Prohibition kicked in during the 1920s.

While at Pontanezen, the officers and non-coms of the division were allowed to go into Brest with considerable freedom. The E.M. were allowed to go also, but under tight restrictions. We had yet to exchange our Yankee dollars with the French *Franc*, but the French didn't mind it at all. Brest was gay and the streets were crowded in spite of the war. In the course of a few blocks, one saw different kinds of uniforms, more decorations and medals and more-peculiar looking people than could be imagined to exist—esp. for a person from Old

---

[148] *Poilu* is pronounced "Pole-ee-u."

[149] As cited Stultz, 162.

[150] *Verboten* or "forbidden" in German is pronounced "Vehr-boat-en."

Virginia. The cafes with their chairs and tables on the sidewalks were a great novelty to us, as that custom prevails in America only in small cigar stores.

It was here at Pontanezen and in Brest where we made our first attempts at speaking French. In the back of our handy-dandy *Manual for N.C.O.s and Privates of Infantry of the A.U.S., 1917*, there is a good English-French dictionary. Because the manual was small, like our *Infantry Drill Regulations*, most N.C.O.s and E.M. kept a copy of "the Manual" in the upper-right pocket of our tunics. Few indeed were successful at first at "speaky *français*," although we soon learned enough of the common words to get along in the stores and restaurants. Those who remembered a smattering of it from school had had a better start, but most of the others quickly caught up and began speaking for themselves. It was a favorite amusement at first to engage a native in conversation, and it gave one a great feel of superiority to be able to make him understand a few words if someone else could not. These early dialogues were not highly intellectual. They ran something like this:

Doughboy: "*Bon jour, monsieur*," with a Virginia or Pennsylvania accent.

Frenchman: "*Bon jour, monsieur*," with a regional French accent.

Doughboy: "*Beaucoup soldats, ici.*"

Frenchman: "*Oui, oui*," followed by several paragraphs in which only the term "*les Boche*" was distinguishable.

Doughboy: "*Oui, oui! Boche pas bon!*"

Frenchman: "*Oui, oui*," followed by several more paragraphs at an accelerated rate in which nothing was distinguishable.

Doughboy: "*Oui, oui!* Say, aren't we getting along just fine!"[151]

We gradually created a "Blue Ridge Division Speak" of terms in which we Doughs used during and well-after the war. It consists of a fair sprinkling of French and English (and I mean British-English and not American-English) expressions, as we also spent time with the English and Welsh in Artois and Picardy. For instance, when we were later billeted in French towns or villages, we'd head to the local store to try to buy some sundry items. We'd use what little French we knew and they'd use what little English they knew, and that became our language. *Comprendre*? The conversation went something like this:

Doughboy: "Any *tabac*?"

Frenchman: "*Pas tabac; fini* yesterday."

Doughboy: "*Chocolat*?"

Frenchman: "*Chocolat, fini.*"

---

[151] "*Les Boche*" ("Lay Bosh") is a French pejorative for Germans. We used it a lot, as well as "Hun" or "Heiney."

Doughboy: "Well then, *beaucoup comme ca*," pointing to a box of crackers, "*Combien?*"

Frenchman handing them out: "*Deux francs.*"

Like declaring "check" in chess, either party could say, "*Non comprendre,*" which has a fairly international meaning and quickly ended the exchange. In fact, when I simply wanted to tune somebody out at home after the war, I'd simply say "*Je non comprendre.*" Other French terms that we held fast to were "*tout suite,*" which came from "*tout de suite,*" which means "right quick." We'd generally say it: "toot sweet," as in "Move out, toot sweet!" or "Get out of here, toot sweet!" We also used "*beau coup,*" which means "a lot." Sometimes we'd say, "Too coo" for "too much." For example: "There are *beau coup Boche* in that thar *Bois*!" or "Too coo machine guns, get out of here toot sweet!" or "Too coup artillery!" or "Too coo! Too sweet!" which means, "Too much enemy! Get out of here right now!" We yelled that a lot in *Bois d'Ogons*. Other words or terms that we used were "*finis*" for "finished," "*allez*" for "get up/time to go."[152]

We fully expected to work closely with the French, but we rarely if ever saw them. If we did, we saw them in passing, usually at night, and usually manning artillery pieces. Language and cultural barriers do matter when it comes to a real acquaintance and we seldom met a Frenchman who could speak any English. Most of us at first looked on them more or less as curiosities—part of the foreign scenery. As the novelty wore off, however, it changed to an attitude of more or less tolerant amusement. Our admiration for them was founded more on what we knew they had done rather than on what we saw in them, while those of our men who did not know what they had done, did not respect them at all. In our everyday life of passing them on the roads or in the villages, we admired their whiskers, laughed at their strange uniforms, perhaps exchanged a limited greeting, or gave them a few cigarettes—but that was about it. We did not pretend to understand them and they were hardly a factor in our lives. It might have been different if we had been able to know a few of them by individual name and reputation. When a *Poilu* pointed to a scar and said "*Blessé Verdun,*" for example, we would have the same interest about the same way as though he had shown us a shell casing from Verdun. If we would have been able to hear the whole story of his experiences as to how he got wounded, it would have been a different matter.

While at Pontanezen, various details were constantly called for to dig water mains, to unload and sort out baggage at the docks, to perform guard duty or to accomplish the thousand and one little tasks, which marked the inevitable routine of camp life. All told some

---

[152] *Beau coup* is pronounced "Boe-coo," *finis* is pronounced "Fee-nee," *allez is* pronounced "All-lay."

four or five days were spent at this unpleasant location—getting our land legs back and adjusting to the new continent. One soldier from the 317th Infantry remembered:

> *It has been stated before that this camp at Brest was supposedly for rest, but very little so-called rest did the troops get [because] orders were issued for a practice march. It turned out to be…comparatively short…and the men really enjoyed it after being on the water so long…The line of march took us through numerous small French villages, and it was a curiosity to our troops then, as it always will be, the mode of living of the French people… We saw our first French train that morning, and it caused a ripple of laughter to go…down the column, because it was so small and so insignificant looking, and seemed entirely incapable of carrying passengers. The high shriek of its tiny whistle made us think of our Christmas toys.*[153]

On June 2, H.Q./318th Infantry, 1/318th Infantry, and Supply/318th Infantry departed Pontanezen by train and arrived in Calais, where the division, minus the 155th Arty. Brig., was to be concentrated and prepared for movement to the front.[154] As such, the 318th Infantry was the first unit of the division to assemble at Calais, followed by the 317th Infantry. We in 1/318th Infantry were followed on June 4 by 3/318th Infantry and M.G./318th Infantry and on June 5 by the 2/318th Infantry. This particular trip was our first experience with the famous French *40 Hommes ou 8 Chevaux* (or "Forty Men or Eights Horses") cars, and the novelty helped tide over the many discomforts of French railway travel. There was considerable discussion as to how everybody, plus rations and equipment, could be crammed into the allotted space, but after many trials, men, rations, and equipment were piled upon each other and we actually did it. We literally all packed together standing—there was no room to sit down—and each man was held up by the other. It being the first experience of this kind, a journey which otherwise would have been torturous, was made interesting by speculation as to the regiment's destination. One soldier from the 319th Infantry remembered his first experience with the "40 and 8s" this way:

> *A French military train, to the American, is something fearful and wonderful to behold. The common box car used for transporting troops is small and so light that two men can easily shunt it around by hand on the tracks. These little cars standing high on their trucks, the wheels of which are often built with steel spokes, elicited many hearty laughs from the men accustomed to*

---

[153] As cited in Stultz, 162.

[154] *Calais* is pronounced "Call-lay."

> *seeing the heavy American trains...On this trip, thirty to thirty-five men were crowded into each car, together with their equipment and two days' rations for each man, but it is not yet believed that fourty Doughboys could possibly be put into such a small space. The discomforts of this long ride made it a memorable one indeed.*[155]

Our first trip in the 40 and 8s made us remember a part from the *I.D.R.* In fact, Getz, who had a near-photogenic memory, would often repeat things from it verbatim. Although we all had a copy in our left breast pocket, it was usually Getz who got the location close and Corporal Ward, our fearless squad leader, would usually read it aloud. In this case, it was: "Paragraph 624: The training of the infantry should consist of systematic physical exercises to develop the general physique and of actual marching to accustom men to the fatigue of bearing arms and equipment."

This was certainly one of those times of "fatigue of bearing arms and equipment."

Getz then said: "And what about that part about malleable formations?"

Meanwhile, the ocean liners that brought Brett's 160th Inf. Brig., Heiner's 155th Arty. Brig., most of the M.G. battalions and the trains, etc., docked south of Brittany at the famous French ports of Saint-Nazaire or Bordeaux during the first week in June 1918.[156] Lt. Edward C. Lukens of 3/320th Infantry remembered:

> *We anchored inside the [anti-submarine] nets, and knew the submarine peril was at an end. We had to await the turn of the tide before going up the river, which we did the next morning. We had to await the turn of the tide before going up the river, which we did the next morning. I shall never forget that first glimpse of France. The country was green and pretty, and the people along the banks waved their hands and cheered as we steamed slowly past.... About twilight we reached the dock, at the new American port a few miles below Bordeaux, a piece of American itself planted in France. There were big Baldwin locomotives, American flags flying, American soldiers, white and black, and civilian employees, mountains of supplies, and work moving busily on all sides. Mingled in the scene were French soldiers, French civilians, and a swarm of non-descript Orientals known as "Annamites."*[157]

---

[155] As cited in Stultz, 167.

[156] *Saint-Nazaire* is pronounced "San Naz-air" and *Bordeaux* is pronounced "Bore-dough."

[157] As cited in Lukens, Edward C. *A Blue Ridge Memoir* (Baltimore, Maryland: Sun Print, 1922), 11. Hereafter cited as "*3/320th Infantry.*" "Annamites" are people who live in the Mekong Delta of French Indo-China.

Most of the men of the 160th Inf. Brig. stayed at "Camp 1, Base Section 1" in ugly barracks made from pine boards and heavy tar paper. Like at Pontanezen, there were few conveniences at Camp 1, as fresh water and food were inadequate and insufficient. The men were then loaded aboard 40s and 8s like we in the 159th Inf. Brig. had and were also shipped north to Calais, to join us in the 159th Inf. Brig. and the 80th Division H.Q.[158] Then-Capt. Williams of 2/320th Infantry remembers:

I shall never forget that afternoon we glided into the inner harbor between the rows of mines that had been planted to protect us against the submarines. The sun was just going down over the waters to the west. It was like a great ball of fire, purple and red and pink and gradually shading off into the blue of a cloudless sky… We anchored in the inner harbor for the night and in the morning steamed up the Loire River and tied to one of the docks of St. Nazaire. It was a beautiful spring day, warm and sunny; so different from the cold winds we had encountered almost throughout the trip.[159]

Another soldier from the 320th Infantry remembered:

The weather was extremely warm, and we suffered very much from the heat, as this camp was situated very close to the sea and the grounds were very sandy and hot. During our stay of three days…we employed the long hours of daylight by cleaning up generally. A sea bath was enjoyed, and many of our athletes participated in a field meet held by the men stationed at St. Nazaire. It was here that we received our first lesson in "stripping," for all athletic equipment had to be salvaged. Our excellent assortment of football and baseball equipment, the fruit and work of months of labor, was a great loss, although at this time we did not see the need of these articles. Later days proved the loss of this equipment was a serious one. We did not find this camp much of a rest one, as everyone worked very hard while there, details being constantly sent to the docks to unload the large ships which were arriving daily with supplies and equipment for the A.E.F.[160]

As we Blue Ridgers regained our land legs at *Brest* and *Calais*, the German Army continued to drive the Allies back between *Soissons* and *Rheims* along the famous *Chemin des*

---

[158] *319th Infantry*, 14.

[159] As cited in *1/320th Infantry*, 11-12.

[160] As cited Stultz, 172.

Dames and were looking to take Paris from the east, up the Marne Valley, just like they almost had done in 1914. But unlike 1914, this time the French lines had collapsed and on June 4, 1918, Pershing agreed to send the American 2nd, 3rd, 28th, and 42nd Divisions to help stop the Huns along the Marne at *Belleau, Vaux*, and *Chateau-Thierry* while the 1st Division fought it out at Cantigny.[161] When the German High Command learned of this—and shocked and disappointed that thousands-upon-thousands of American Doughs were actually entering France through the U-Boat screen—Hindenburg resolved to hit Americans esp. hard. He not only wanted to crush our morale (which would have been hard to do), but, more importantly, he wanted to also raise the flagging morale of his own men (Germany, Austria, Hungary, and Bulgaria were starving at this point).

Ready or not, we were going to get involved in this war sooner rather than later.

---

[161] *Belleau* is pronounced ""Bell-oo" and *Vaux* is pronounced "Voo."

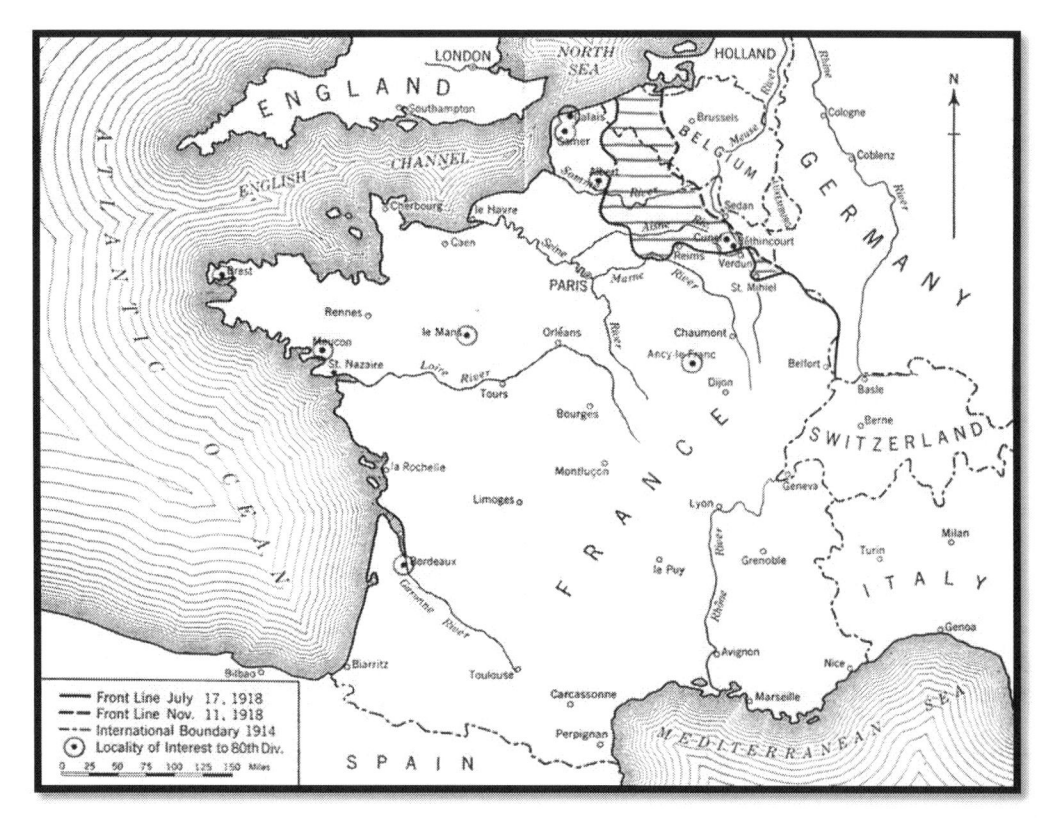

Front lines and "Areas of Interest of the 80th Division." *A.M.B.C.*

Bell-shaped tents at "Rest Camp No. 6" near Calais.

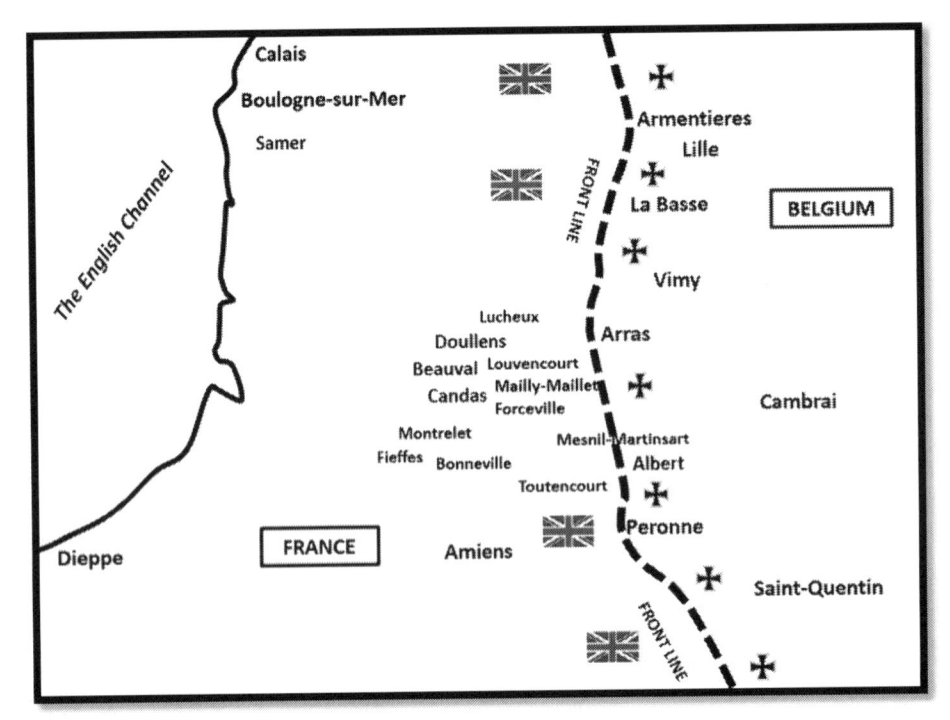

Training with the Tommies in Picardy. The 80th Division was located near Albert.

Washing day (L) and platoon leaders censoring letters (R).

Sharpening bayonets (L) and "80th Division Reconnaissance Car" is representative of the many types of vehicles the division fielded in France. We generally called them "Specials."

Standard gear of a Doughboy in France. This soldier is armed with an Enfield Rifle and carris a British respirator bag. Across the top of his pack is an extra blanket. On his pack he carries his anti-shrapnel helmet and beheath it is his intrenching tool.

An 80th Division signal station in action (L). Comunications are key to victory in modern war: "The fustest with the mostest." A Dough Boy with a Y.M.C.A. doughnut (R). And no, we were not called "Doughboys " because of the donuts we ate from time to time—as far as I know, anyway.

British Maj. Gen. Julian Byng commanded the British Third Army in Picardy. The 80th Division was attached to his command and participated in the Somme Offensive, 1918.

"A camouflaged camp in the front lines one mile from Albert, 7-26-18."

French rifle grenade *tromblon* trainer (L) and the tromblons used in action (R).

French "*Renault*" F.T. light or "*Mosquito*" tank (L) and a French "*Schneider*" medium tank (R).

French *Saint-Chamond* heavy tank (L) and British Mark V heavy tank.

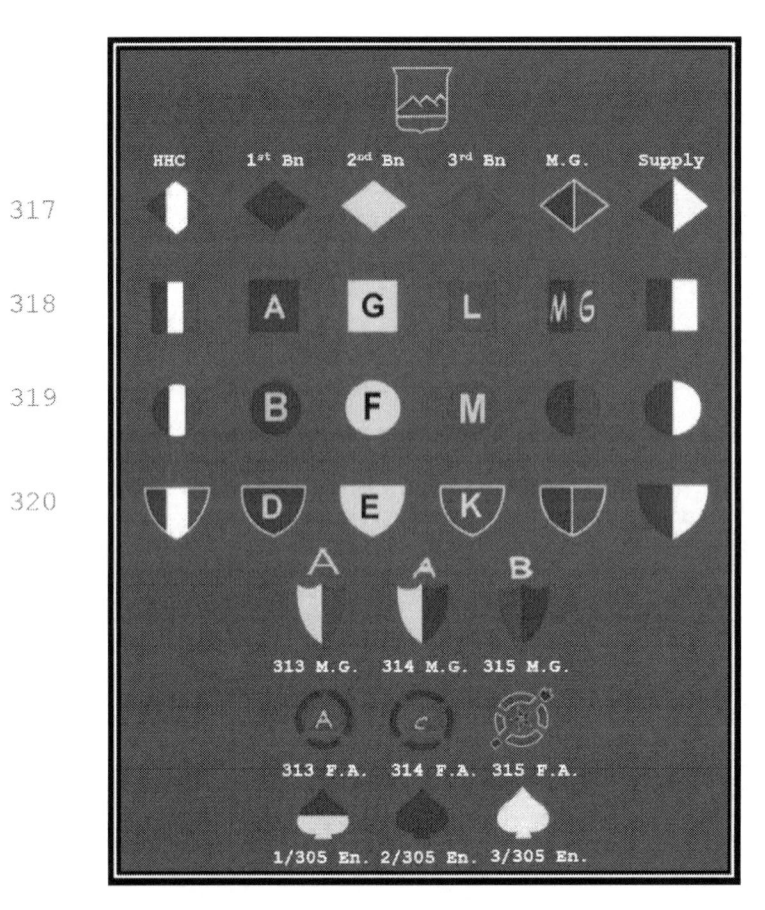

80th Division battalion designs that were painted on our helmets. The infantry regiments are along the top, followed by the M.G. battalions, the artillery regiments, and then the engineer battalions.

Resperator bag of J.C. Wisinger. The designs denote that he was a member of 3/305th Engineers, 80th Division.

Chapter 11
Training with the Tommies (June 8-July 21, 1918).

Upon its arrival in France, the 80th Division was credited with having a strength of 26,851 men out of the authorized 27,500. Approximately 12,000 were in or around *Brest* or *Calais*, about 7,500 were in *Saint-Nazaire*, and some 7,250 were in *Bordeaux*. Their movement to *Calais*, the division's concentration point, entailed unusual problems, since some units were partitioned among various transports arriving at widely separated ports. The inadequate French railroads were already overburdened and required time to transport troops to their designated cencentraion areas. As such, several days elapsed before the infantry brigades were united at *Calais*. Of the three combat brigades, only Jamerson's 159th Inf. Brig., my brigade, had landed intact at Brest. While the bulk of Brett's 160th Inf. Brig. arrived in *Saint-Nazaire*, 900 officers and men of the 320th Infantry were landed at Bordeaux and were housed in "Camp Genicart" for a short time. In the case of Heiner's 155th Arty. Brig., the 314th Artillery (L), a detachment of the 315th Artillery (H) and the 305th T.M. Battery had entered France through Brest, while brigade H.Q., the 313th Artillery (L), the bulk of the 315th Artillery (H), and the 305th Ammunition Trains had arrived at *Bordeaux*. The 313th and 314th M.G. Battalions also landed at *Bordeaux*, and the 315th M.G. Battalion at *Saint-Nazaire*. Of our four ambulance companies, one was unloaded at *Brest* and the other three at *Bordeaux*.[162] One soldier from the 305th Sanitary Trains remembered:

> *A few days later, we left [Bordeaux] and marched to the railroad to take the train for the training area near Switzerland…A French passenger train coach is divided into compartments, furnished with wooden seats, each compartment holding eight men and communicating with the outside by a small door…We were issued rations to supply us for the three days' trip. Each squad, which filled a compartment, was given enough hard-tack, corned beef hash, etc., to give each man his allowance for that time… We were now touring sunny France, and it was some tour. All went well until nightfall when we prepared to sleep, when it was discovered that the compartment was rather crowded, containing, as it did, eight men and eight packs. The only way to go to sleep was to fall asleep in the position we occupied all day long, that is, sitting up…During this three day train ride…we left the train just once. A welfare organization was serving…hot coffee to the troops passing through. Some of the boys did not leave the train at all…The second night on the train,*

---
[162] Stultz, 170.

we ran into a thunder storm and the rain came down in torrents. No lights were visible in the surrounding country and the number of tunnels, curves, etc., seemed to indicate we were passing through a mountainous section of France. The train often stopped entirely, would back for half a mile, then go forward, and we were off again...About 11:00 o'clock on the second day, we reached Dijon...About 2:00 P.M., on June 20, we reached our destination—the point on the railroad next to Vitry—and after a long six-mile march through the town of Vitry and through Chauvirey-le-Chatel, we reached Chauvirey-le-Viel at 5:00 P.M. The French inhabitants came out to see the newly arriving Americans. A drizzling rain was falling. We entered the yard of the chateau, the largest house in the town...The madame at the chateau came to the door and I had a glimpse of the interior of the house. It was furnished in rich style, with deer heads and marble stairways. I thought, "This is not half bad. I can stay for quite a while in a mansion fixed with deer heads and marble stairways." But the madame came out...walked over to the barn and climbed up to the hay-loft. I thought, "Why the hay-loft?" I wasn't left long in doubt. Sergeant... ordered the first forty-two men of the company to climb the ladder and look around our future home. In the meantime, the cooks were preparing supper, and we passed our first night in the interior of France sleeping on the floor and listening to the sounds of the cows and chickens below.[163]

After a journey of some 48-hours from Brittany in the 40s and 8s, Jamerson's 159th Inf. Brig. assembled at the historic port city of Calais—the closest point between England and France—and was marched through the city to a British Army post known as "Rest Camp No. 6." This post, located on the English Channel, was a small city of over-crowded bell-shaped tents. The grounds were covered with sand from three to 6" deep, making walking very laborious, and giving the area the appearance of a mini Sahara. The weather was hot and dusty and the inadequate British faire of crackers and jam was well-flavored with sand. Sandbags were carefully arranged about the tents to a height of two feet, to afford some protection from air raids, which were unpleasantly frequent in that locality. On our second night there, for example, the booming of 75mm anti-aircraft cannon (which the British called "Archies") and the blowing of "air raid" sirens in the port city awoke us all. I remember how the white shafts of the searchlights picked up the German planes in the sky. Luckily for us, the Archies drove the aerial

---

[163] As cited Stultz, 170-71.

raiders off before they succeeded in dropping their "eggs" into our camp. One "egg" fell on a house in the city, however. One soldier from Spalding's 305th Engineers remembered:

> *We went to bed that evening, wondering whether by any chance we could hear any firing from the line, twenty-five miles away, and whether the next great German smash would be for the Channel Ports, and, if so, would we be in the melee. Remember, this was before the middle of June, and the Hun had never seemed stronger. About 10:00 P.M., a sudden, furious thundering came from somewhere, and on the heels of that, some sharp whistle blasts—the aeroplane alarm. We crouched, hearts palpitating, in our tents, scared faces looking into other scared faces, wondering whether the Hun air raiders could destroy the city and all of us in one night, or whether it would take two. But minutes passed, and we were not summoned before the dread tribunal. And gradually most of us fell asleep, not hearing another alarm or two later on that night. The next morning we learned that no firing from the line had reached our ears—that the commotion was made by anti-aircraft guns; that air raids were of nightly occurrence.*[164]

A soldier from the 320th Infantry, who arrived to Rest Camp No. 6 several days after the men from Jamerson's 159th Inf. Brig. remembered:

> *The Boche must have learned that we arrived in Calais that day, because he came over to pay us a visit that night…The country round about was literally filled with anti-aircraft guns, and when the Boche came over they opened up like a thousand Fourths of July. Many a man hugged the floor of his tent that night and thanked the British for that twelve inches below the surface of the ground. Some of us had the hardihood, also the curiosity, to peep out of the fly of the tent to see the flashes of the guns that lit up the sky and the search-lights playing upon the specks high above the earth. I realized then that the camp at St. Nazaire was really a rest camp.*[165]

Each infantry unit of the 80th Division rotated through this camp for about three days, during which time we reunited with our blue denim barracks bags, containing many cherished articles, and extra equipment, which had previously been located at an unknown storage depot. But just like the Army, as soon as we started to assimilate the sundry items, we were ordered to

---

[164] As cited in Stultz, 172.

[165] As cited in *Ibid*.

discard our barrack bags, which contained all of our extra clothing, personal belongings, etc., and to turn it all in as "surplus equipment." One soldier from the 317th Infantry remembered:

> *During the afternoon, instructions were given making it necessary for officers' bedding rolls to be cut down to fifty pounds, and requiring large portions of company property to be left behind, never to be seen again. All of our athletic goods had to be stored away that had been so carefully packed and preserved back at Camp Lee, but even with all this, our spirits were high and nothing seemed to dampen them.*[166]

Each soldier was only able to retain the authorized essentials allowed in his field pack. Both the bags and the officers' surplus baggage were subsequently shipped to a large warehouse in Boulogne for cold storage. Much of the property was in fact returned to its owners after the war's termination—remarkably—either in France or in America, but many of the troops never recovered their possessions. We all stood there in total disbelief at the order, especially our company commanders and supply sergeants, who remembered all too clearly their frantic efforts during the last month at Camp Lee to fully equip their organizations, stood by in dumb and impotent astonishment at this ruthless confiscation of so many fruits of their labor.

At Calais, we were introduced to the infamous British Ration, which most of us thought was disgusting. Unlike Americans, who like "three squares," the British eat more, but smaller meals. This is why 4:00 P.M. "tea time" is so important to them. One soldier from the 305th Engineers highlighted our dislike of British rations and the austere living conditions of the so-called "Rest Camp":

> *If the "Tommies" lived on the rations we did, they were uncommonly small eaters. The meals were paralyzing small, and outside of our own kitchens there was absolutely nothing to be had. This state of affairs was not new in France—it was the normal condition that we encountered everywhere. But getting up from a meal totally unsatisfied, with a hard day's work ahead, was no fun. Water was equally scarce in this region. All the water we had was hauled from a long distance in a water-cart, and we drank, washed, and shaved from our canteens. We had to get along without bathing.*[167]

---

[166] As cited in Stultz, 174.

[167] *Ibid*, 172.

-British Gear-

We were next ordered to exchange our M1917 Enfields and bayonets for (what we thought were) superior "Short Magazine, Lee-Enfield Rifles" (S.M.L.E.s) so we could better operate with the British. While our sweet Enfields fired a .30-06 round, the S.M.L.E. fired a .303 caliber round. The preferred characteristic of the S.M.L.E. (or "Smiley") was that it held ten rounds in an internal magazine rather than five, as did our M1917 Enfields. We were also issued U.S.-made British-style "Brodie" or "Anti-Shrapnel" Helmets that looked like upside-down salad bowls or pie pans, British gas masks, woolen wraps that were called "putties" to replace our pea-green canvas leggings, and wool "overseas caps" to replace our signature broad-brimmed campaign hats.[168] With our "combat kit" now complete, we looked almost like our British "associates" (again, we weren't allowed to call them "allies"). Then-Capt. Williams of E/2/320th Infantry remembered:

> *So far as outward appearance went, all we needed to make us full-fledged Britishers was a little touch of the "lingo" and a few brass buttons on our clothes. But on the inside, I believe, there was almost without exception among the men an utter contempt for everything that was British. There seemed to have been no reason for that feeling. Everything that we got from the British was good—the guns, the masks, the rations, the quarters, the service—everything was good. In fact, many of us marveled at the wonderful machinery of the British government that seemed to reach and supply in good time and good order every corner where there were British troops. Rather, I think, the dislike of the Americans for the British was a feeling of competition every strong man feels when he meets another strong man and measures strength with him, as it were. And this feeling of competition was aggravated. No doubt, by the inclination of the average Britisher to regard anything that Britain and Britishers do as a little better than can be done by anybody else in the world. The Americans were willing to compete with their British friends, but they did not relish the idea of losing their identity by disguising themselves with British equipment. There was a report going the rounds one time that British clothing*

---

[168] The "Brodie" or "Kelly" Helmet was invented by Englishman John L. Brodie in 1915. Easier (and cheaper) to manufacture than the French Adrian Helmut and designed to better protect a soldier from shrapnel bursts from above, the Brodie had many nick-names: Tommy Helmet, Kelly Helmet, Doughboy Helmet, the M1917 Helmet (U.S.), Anti-Shrapnel Helmet, Tin Hat, Dishpan, Tin Pan, Wash Basin, Soup Bowl, and Salad Bowl. We preferred the terms "Tin Hat" or "Dishpan." The overseas cap, which looked much like a French *Bonnet de Police*, could be worn under the helmet.

was going to be issued to our men. I think this would have been more than our American boys could have stood, and I believe there would have been serious trouble, and I should not have blamed them very much. Even worse, there was a rumor making its way through the ranks that we were even to be uniformed by the British, as our American ones were substandard.[169]

According to the *M.M.T.*:

1205. Helmets. Steel helmets made their appearance in the European war in 1915, as a protection to the soldier's head against rifle, machine gun and shrapnel fire. So successful were they that they are being furnished to all troops on the battlefield. Already several millions have been supplied. Where heretofore head wounds accounted for over twenty per cent of the casualties in trench warfare, the percentage has been reduced by the wearing of helmets to about one half per cent. While the helmet does not afford complete protection against rifle and shrapnel fire, it has been found that hits result only in severe concussion, where before fatal wound resulted. These helmets are painted khaki color.

We were instructed to paint colored shapes on the right side of our helmets to help field-grade officers better identify our units. Someone from each platoon painted our newly assigned battalion symbol. The 317th Infantry was assigned a horizontal diamond, the 318th Infantry a square, the 319th Infantry a circle, and the 320th Infantry a shield. Within each regiment, the 1st Battalion was red, 2nd Battalion was white, and the 3rd Battalion was blue. Each company then painted its letter in the center of the shape with white paint. The helmet symbol of the H.Q. company of each regiment had red, white, and blue vertical stripes (like the French flag), the symbol of the M.G. company of each regiment was painted blue and red in two vertical stripes, and the symbol of the supply company of each regiment was red and white in two vertical stripes. For example, my company, B/318th Infantry, had red rectangles with a white "B" in the center. Some men even painted the division symbol on the left side or front of their helmet. The M.G. battalions of the division had shields painted half-and-half, the artillery regiments had circles, and the engineer battalions had spades. The divisional shoulder patches did not come out until 1919, as we were waiting to go home.

As well as the new helmets and gas masks, the designated A.R.-men (four per platoon), myself being one of them, drew British-made Lewis Gun A.R.s. The Lewis Gun was invented by

---

[169] As cited in *3/320 Infantry*, 19.

U.S. Army Col. Isaac Lewis in 1911 and it was initially manufactured by the Automatic Arms Company of Buffalo, New York. Yes, you heard that right: it was an American gun. But due to various stupid and short-sighted reasons (we heard jealousy between the inventor and the Army Chief of Ordnance), our Army chose not to purchase the weapon, instead choosing to rely upon the *Bénet-Mercié* or the *Chauchat* (*infra*). The British were interested in the design, however, and in 1913 the Birmingham Small Arms Company of England started production. The Belgians also liked the design, purchased several patents, and put them to good use in 1914. At first, neither the British nor the Belgian Army knew how to properly employ this new A.R., thinking that it was simply a small M.G. or a souped-up rifle. But as the war wore on and as the capabilities and limitations of the M.G.s manifested themselves, the Lewis Gun grew more and more important—especially at the platoon level. Why the U.S. Army did not purchase these gems from the Automatic Arms Company of Buffalo, N.Y., not only remains a mystery me, but must also be remembered as one of the Army's greatest mistakes. The U.S. Navy and its corps of Marines was smart enough to buy lots of them, however, and put them to good use.

The Lewis Gun weighed about thirty pounds, was air-cooled, and fired a British .30 cal. round from a fifty-round drum magazine. The weaknesses of the gun are that the drums are not easy to carry and the gun out-right seizes up once 1,000 rounds are fired (twenty magazines). As such, two A.R. teams were taught to always act in concert, which means to never fire at the same time, but alternate, and fire three to five round bursts. According to a British training pamphlet *Notes on the Tactical Employment of Machine Guns and Lewis Guns*, the A.R. was to be a supplement to, and not a substitute for, the M.G. They believed that the A.R. should cover areas not covered by the M.G. They also believed that the Lewis should not be carried in the first wave of an attack. Once we were committed to combat, attacking up an axis of advance in which enemy contact was not only highly probable but imminent, we tended to lead with our bomber and assault squads and the A.R.s and R.G.s would come in behind. One of the British trainers, and I don't remember his name, told us that, and I'm paraphrasing here: "The A.R. should be viewed as a submarine. It should pop up unexpectedly, deliver a decisive blow, and then exfiltrate rapidly."

I always tried to remember that during our attacks…especially the part about moving every now and then lest one will be taken out.

-Poison Gas Training-

As far as poison gas training at Rest Camp No. 6 was concerned, British trainers put the fear of God into us about the horrors of chemical warfare. It was only later that we discovered that with the masks on, gas attacks really aren't that bad. The British never forgot those first gas attacks in 1915 in which no masks were had, however, and the traumatic damage that was done. But now, in 1918, every man-jack had a mask—even horses and mules!

In my opinion, gas training at Camp Lee and in France with the British was over-done—we were taught to be scared to death of it and as such, were made far-more nervous about it than necessary. One does not necessarily need to make a soldier scared to make him pay attention to training. The fear will come on its own in combat. What's needed in training is the ability to work through the inevitable and powerful fear by building confidence in one's training and soldier skills. Freezing in battle—and it will happen—can mean a death sentence for all involved. Granted, a soldier can also do everything right and still get blown to pieces, but freezing or doing the wrong thing will almost certainly lead to one's demise.

In fact, I can't remember one death from my entire battalion by gas. Injury? Yes. Death? No. There were some nasty eye and lung injuries and some back and neck burns, but no deaths. It really came down to the time it took to get the mask seated properly on a sweaty, scared face with shaky hands. The British told us that we had "just six seconds" to get our masks on before we were "knocked out cold." That turned out to be a lie. There were times during our big push up the Meuse-Argonne when we all got a quick whiff of the stuff. Some men chose to put on their masks, others simply closed their eyes and held their breath for thirty or so seconds until the threat passed.

-Artois-

The 80th Division, less Heiner's 155th Arty. Brig., was assigned to Maj. Gen. George W. Read's American II Corps to be trained by the British. These instructors were made up of officers and non-coms whose original units had been decimated as the result of many severe campaigns (ending with *Friedensturm*). The 80th Division was assigned to *le Secteur Samer en la province française d'Artois* to be trained by the surviving members of the British 16th (Royal Irish) Division.[170] The Royal Irish Division had been almost wiped out during *Friedensturm* and was

---

[170] *Le Secteur Samer en la province française d'Arois* is pronounced "Lay Sec-tear Sam-air en la province frawn-say Dar-twa."

now rated by the Allies as a training outfit. It retained only its command and staff to direct the training cadres composed of surviving officers and men of units belonging to the British 14th, 16th, 34th, 39th, and 59th Divisions. The Royal Irish Division was being utilized to train American divisions, like ours, until it could be reconstituted.

Province d'Artois was historic bloody ground. It was home to the "Field of the Cloth of Gold" where King Edward III of England bested King Philip VI of France at the Battle of Crècy in 1346 and where King Henry V of England beat Charles d'Arbret of France at the Battle of Agincourt in 1415, the latter battle inspiring Shakespeare to later pen:

We few, we happy few, we band of brothers;
For he to-day that sheds his blood with me
Shall be my brother; be he ne'er so vile,
This day shall gentle his condition;
And gentlemen in England now-a-bed
Shall think themselves accurs'd they were not here,
And hold their man-hoods cheap whiles any speaks
That fought with us upon Saint Crispin's Day!

Samer is about ten miles southeast of *Boulogne Sur Mer*, which is just south of *Calais*. *Samer* itself is a typical little *boulognais* market town, reputedly dating back to the Roman colonization of Gaul, and boasting a population of perhaps 500 remaining inhabitants and a hundred or more stone and brick structures grouped around the usual French square.[171] The central building, of course, is an ancient church flanked by small shops. Along the broad side streets entering the square, pleasant houses—some large and comfortable—were surrounded by walled-in gardens. The walls were vine clad and embowered with tumbling masses of ramblers. These abodes afforded the most desirable billets for officers. In the immediate vicinity were numerous large farm houses, called *château*, some ancient and all set in the shade of noble groves of horse chestnuts and trellised with roses. In the surrounding stables and barns, troops had been billeted in many wars. Green meadows spread about them. Along every road and byway, tall poplars ranged like ranks of plumed grenadiers. The whole country-side was aflame with color that June, the sky never more azure, the sun never more golden and soft. In the air of Samer, there was the tang of the sea whose white-caps were just visible from the hill-sides. Artois was indeed woven of Nature's Gold.[172]

---

[171] *Boulognais* is pronounced "Boo-long-ay-es."

[172] *Boulogne Sur Mer* or "Boulogne-by-the-Sea" is pronounced "Boo-long Sue Mair" and *château* or "castle" or "estate" is pronounced "Shat-toe."

After a short train ride to the south, we disembarked at Samer and marched another ten km to our billet in *Village Cormont* (1/318). One soldier from 1/320th Infantry remembered:

The march was with heavy packs, consisting of three blankets, one shelter-half, underwear, extra pair of shoes, helmet, slicker, one hundred rounds of ammunition, and a rifle. There was also an overcoat... After the first kilometer, one began to suspect that someone had illicitly slipped a grand piano in our packs; on the third, the shoulder straps began to feel like violin strings; and after the fourth we trudged through the hot dust silently cursing each by each and altogether those five kilometers which still separated us from our destination. It was dusk when the men finally marched into the village of Hesdigneul, hungry, tired and sleepy, but mostly tired.[173]

Regimental H.Q. and Supply Company/318th Infantry was just a few km northwest of us at *Bernieulles*, 2/318 was at *Rolet* and *Bout Haut*, and 3/318 was at *Enguinehaut* and *Thubeauville*. Our 318th M.G. Company was at *Hubersent*.[174] These were all small, picturesque French farming villages only a few kilometers apart from one other. In my opinion, the term "bucolic" most probably came from an area like this as it was quintessentially agricultural and, for lack of a better term, bucolic. The other infantry regiments of the division were similarly billeted and the M.G. companies of the division were sent to R.M.G.C. schools, building upon what they had learned from British M.G. trainers at Camp Lee. Because Samer was about ten km from Boulogne, which was a major British base, it received almost nightly attacks from *Boche* aerial raiders. As such, all lights were screened at night and all troop movements were carefully planned with a view to possible trouble from above. It was a long time, however, before all men overcame the conviction that each passing plane was actually hovering directly overhead, just waiting to pounce.[175]

We were, according to the Army, "billeted" at *Cormont*. According to the *F.S.R.*, there are four types of housing for soldiers: cantonment, billet, camp, or bivouac. A cantonment is an area built to specifically house soldiers, a place like Camp Lee. It includes barracks, common buildings, mess halls, etc. A billet is the use of public or private buildings for the housing of

---

[173] As cited in Stultz, 174.

[174] *Village Cormont* is pronounced "Veal-aaj Core-mon," *Bernieulles* is pronounced "Bern-ee-ules," *Rolet is pronounced* "Role-let," *Bout Haut* is pronounced "Boo-hut," *Enguinehaut* is pronounced "En-gene-hut," *Thubeauville is pronounced* "Tube-oh-veal," and *Hubersent* is pronounced "Who-bears."

[175] *Etaples* is pronounced "Ae-top-la."

troops. A camp is when soldiers live under semi-permanent tents, and a bivouac is where they are "on the ground without shelter."[176] The billet is the most unfamiliar to the American soldier because of the 4th Amendment to the U.S. Constitution which states: "No Soldier shall, in time of peace be quartered in any house, without the consent of the owner, nor in time of war, but in a manner to be prescribed by law." Granted, soldiers were billeted in our beloved South during the late-War of Northern Aggression, where Southerners weren't really considered U.S. citizens at the time (because they didn't want to be), but France wasn't the U.S., either. In France, billeting soldiers was normal. A billet is the housing of soldiers in civilian-owned and occupied homes, buildings, barns, stables, etc. In France, in fact, each house has a sign that lists the number of officers or E.M. that were allowed to be billeted there. With this system, and in our experience, most of the men were billeted in barn lofts or stables and all of the officers were billeted in homes at the low price of one Franc per day. The billet of an E.M., however, was nothing more than floor space upon which to spread his blanket roll. Then-Capt. Ashby Williams of E/2/320th remembered:

> *To "billet" a man means to find him a place to lay his head down, usually in a stable or a loft. This was the first time our men had ever been billeted. They had "camped" at Camp Lee, "bunked" on the boat, and "bivouacked" at Calais, and now they were to be "billeted." There was something about the billeting in the lofts on the hay and among the cattle that didn't sit well on the average American, especially on most of our men who had come from refined homes and had been accustomed to the best all their lives. But you cannot down the spirit of the American soldier, as I always said, and I recall distinctly how they went into the barns making a noise like a cow, trying, I suppose, to make the best out of a bad situation…In France, every residence and every outbuilding is a legal billet, to be used by the government for the purpose of quartering troops, providing that only a sufficient space must be left for the owner of the premises and his family, and necessary animals. An officer's billet is always in the residence of the owner, and must be a room with a bed, with bed clothing, furniture, etc., for which the owner is allowed one franc a day during the time the room is occupied. On the other hand, the billet of his E.M. is nothing more than floor space upon which he may spread his blankets.*[177]

---

[176] *F.S.R.*, Para 232.

[177] As cited in *1/320th Infantry*, 20.

Cantonment Samer had been most-recently occupied by the Portuguese Division (Portuguese troops were trained and outfitted by the British—while most of them fought against the Germans in Africa, an entire division was sent to fight on the Western Front). After their infamous attack near Merville in March 1918, the Portuguese Division was sent to the Samer Region to conduct what we call "Recovery Operations." Upon our arrival, we found that the Samer Cantonment had been pretty much trashed by the Portuguese.

Portuguese soldiers shouldering Lewis Guns in France.

Once we got established, intensive training under the British 16th (Royal Irish) Division, and later the British 34th Division, was begun. The training given by the British was thorough and comprehensive. At first, we resented being trained by the British, but as time went on, we learned to really respect them and their training methods. Many of us in fact believe that this effective British mentorship is at least partially responsible for our successes in the Meuse-Argonne from Sept. to Nov., 1918. The subordinate units of the 80th Division were located as follows:

Division H.Q.: Samer
Divisional Troops: Halinghen
305th Trains Brigade H.Q.: Dalle
314th M.G. Battalion: Frencq
H.Q., 159th Inf. Brig.: Parenty
317th Infantry H.Q.: Doudeauville
1/317: Hodicq
2/317: Gregny et Bazinghem
3/317: Grandal
M.G. Company: Hubersent
318th Infantry H.Q.: Bernieulles
1/318: Cormont
2/318: Rolet et Bout Haut
3/318: Enguinehaut et Thubeauville
M.G. Company: Hubersent
313th M.G. Battalion: Le Turne
H.Q., 160th Inf. Brig.: Le Brunquet
319th Infantry H.Q.: Desvres
1/319: Desvres
2/319: Menneville
3/319: Courset
M.G. Company: Hubersent
320th Infantry H.Q.: Chateau l'Enfer
1/320: Hesdigneul
2/320: Questrecques
3/320: Hesdin l'Abbe
M.G. Company: Hubersent
315th M.G. Battalion: Frencq
H.Q., 305th Engineers: Widehem
1/305: Widehem
2/305: Halinghen et Haut Pichot
305th Field Signal Battalion: Samer

At first, we thought that the British (and especially, the French) lacked "pep"—that they were resigned to stay on the defensive for infinity and beyond. They in turn thought that we lacked discipline, that we were "big mouths," "babe's in the woods," or "amateurs." I can say that at this time, we certainly were amateurs but our style of discipline was just different than that of the European, as we weren't nearly as deferential. I think Capt. Ashby Williams of E/2/320th Infantry summed it up best when he said:

> *Our men seemed at first to take at once a violent dislike for everything that was British. It is difficult to analyze the reasons for this first impression. It was doubtless due in large part to the fact that the British Tommy had been at the game a long time and he assumed a cocksure attitude toward everything that came his way—perhaps to the fact that most of the Britishers with whom the men came in contact were old soldiers who had seen service and had been wounded in the fighting line and sent back to work in and about the camp and they looked with some contempt on these striplings who had come to win the war. Perhaps it was due to the fact that on the surface the average Britisher is not after all a very loveable person, especially on first acquaintance. At any rate our men did not like the British. Most of all they did not like the British ration which was very much smaller than the American ration and also very different. But the British had been at the game a long time and they knew how it was played. They had resolved war into a business. There were ample mess facilities, baths, tents, and everything else that could be gotten or might be reasonably expected to make the soldiers comfortable and sanitary. Most of the Americans had been imbued with the idea that we must rush into the war and whip the Germans and have the thing over with, and they could not understand what they thought were the slow, methodical and business-like methods of the British...But we soon learned to like them. After you break the outside crust on an Englishman you find inside one of the finest fellows in the world. A few touches of Scotch and a few well-chosen words will usually break the crust between soldiers, and the British officer is a soldier through and through, we learned afterwards. The men also afterwards in the experience they had with British soldiers on the front and under fire gained them a profound respect, not to say a real affection.*[178]

---

[178] As cited in *1/320th Infantry*, 16-17.

Of course, our attitudes were unfair because the French and British had repeatedly attacked the strong German lines in 1915, 1916, and 1917 without gaining anything. Who could blame their depression and sense of defeat?

As for myself, I can't say that I ever disliked our British cousins. What I can say, however, is that their "I'm inherently superior to you not only because I'm English, but also because I've survived the war thus far...and you haven't" got old really quick. Not so much the second part, but the first part. The second part we hoped to change. We chomped at the bit to get at the "Hun with the Gun" and give 'em a what fer. In retrospect, if the positions would have been switched, we would have been far more arrogant and dismissive to the British than they to us. Combat does something to a person, something we didn't quite appreciate at that particular time. The fact that the British even addressed us in a civilized manner should be commended, esp. considering what they, the French, the Belgians, and the Germans, yes, even the hated Hun, had been through. You can read it in a book or see it in a picture, but until you've actually experienced it, you'll never get it.

I hope you'll never get it.

Nevertheless, we grew to respect the British and in fact began to change how we did things in the 80th Division. For example, the division Q.M., Maj. Robert J. Halpin, did not like how the U.S. Army divided gear and equipment into separate "Ordnance" and "Quartermaster" departments. He preferred a consolidated system, like that of the British, which is what we all assumed would make the most sense (but remember, there's the right way, the wrong way, and the Army way). Halpin was therefore pleased to learn that what the British defined as "Ordnance" included many articles that the American Army classed as Q.M. supplies. Both ordnance and Q.M. items were therefore handled from the same dump, with a total personnel of about sixty. Halpin remembered: "The British instruction and training period proved of great value to the division in many particulars, especially in regard to organization of rail-heads, supply of troops, development of efficiency in handling horse transport, and the employment of most effective methods in waging trench warfare... The policy of having ordnance and quartermaster supplies all controlled by the division quartermaster, as is the case in the British system, proved successful."[179] Maj. Gen. James Harbord, who would command the A.E.F.'s all-important S.O.S., remembered how difficult it was to "supply the troops" in France. He writes:

The Ordnance Department had one of the most difficult tasks that confronted our country in the World War. It was charged with securing, storing, distributing, and maintaining ordnance material in France on a scale far

---
[179] As cited in Stultz, 258.

greater than American had known in its previous experience. American industry was not ready for the tremendous demand for ordnance material, notwithstanding what it had done for the Allies. Its manufacturing facilities had to be reconstructed before munitions from America began to arrive for us in Europe. There were numerous changes in types and no standard of supply could be adopted. This was due to the continually increased schedule of troop arrivals; to the accelerated program of military offensive; and the fact that American troops shot away ammunition in battle, in proportion to the numbers engaged, far more than the Allies, whose standard early was adopted by the Ordnance Department.[180]

On the Q.M. Corps in the A.E.F., Harbord, continues:

The Q.M. Corps did a great business in baking bread, roasting coffee, and running laundries. It received from America 545,599,461 pounds of flour and 132,864 pounds of coffee. There came from America some 15,188,706 pounds of salt, 30,226,884 pounds of lard, 50,895,166 pounds of sugar, and other components of the soldier ration in corresponding quantities. It operated bakeries in the Advance Section with a daily capacity of 1,846,000 pounds of bread; in the Intermediate Section of 600,000 pounds, in the Base Sections of 507,000. The Q.M. Corps ran twenty refrigeration plants and a dozen ice plants, to the added comfort and health of the American soldier. The largest of these was that at Gièvres which had a 5,200-ton capacity. Gardens at fifty-eight points in France raised 75,000,000 pounds of green vegetables for soldier food, by soldier labor, in this department... The Q.M. Corps used 282 officers and 1,398 men in operating: 134 mobile disinfectors, forty stationary, 257 improvised disinfectors, 79 hot-air disinfectors, 545 stationary baths, 517 portable baths, and twenty-one mobile baths, in bathing and delousing treatment of the A.E.F. personnel between the Rhine and the U.S.[181]

Then-Capt. Williams of E/2/320th Infantry was also complementary of the British Army, particularly how it treated its soldiers as human beings and not as simple automations. We're glad that officers from our own Army learned from this, as a few too many thought that all one

---

[180] As cited in Harbord, 494.

[181] As cited in *Ibid*, 500; *Gièvres* is pronounced "Jev-rah."

had to do to make a soldier was to "give him a rifle and some rations and a couple of blankets and send him out to fight." Williams remembered:

> *It was here again that the American officers were struck with the genius of the British organization in its consideration for the natural needs and wants of men even in the military service. There seems to be an impression in certain American circles that all you have to do to make a soldier is to give a man a rifle and some rations and a couple of blankets and send him out to fight. But the British government knows, and its system carries that knowledge unfalteringly into practice, that a soldier is still a human being, that he needs an occasional bath, that he needs amusement once and a while, that wherever possible (and it is almost always possible to some extent) he should have certain of the comforts of home, such as a table and a bench at meal time, and many other things that make him a real human being first of all and then a soldier.*[182]

The first schedule of bugle calls in the Samer training area, announced June 10, prescribed reveille at 5:40 A.M., drill at 7:25, recall at 11:30, mess at noon, drill at 12:55 P.M., recall at 3:30, parade at 5:00, retreat at 5:15, supper at 5:45, and taps at 9:30. All drill formations and duties were omitted on Sundays and holidays. Reveille formations were under arms, followed by ten minutes of vigorous physical drill. For thirty minutes prior to parade, platoons were run through a snappy close order drill, without rest. Each battalion was ordered to stage at least two parades each week, with their regimental bands playing. All guard mounts were informal, meaning we simply stood a post and got relieved without superfluous ceremony.

Detailed regulations stressed saluting, with particular reference to the correct procedure by mounted men and for officers traveling in motor cars. The authorized contents of the infantry pack were also stipulated, and beginning June 17, the "full pack" was ordered to be made up and worn daily when marching from billets to training grounds and back. The pack was to be carried for longer periods as the training progressed, until unit commanders were satisfied that their men could carry the pack under any conditions. British gas masks were worn during some training periods, with the time increased from day to day until a continuous period of one hour had been attained. The drill schedule was relaxed on June 15 to allow the troops one afternoon each week for bathing and cleaning equipment. One soldier from the 305th Engineers remembered:

---

[182] As cited in *1/320th Infantry*, 29.

[Widehem] was well-stocked with British instructors. They were proficient in the use of the rifle, the bayonet, and the gas mask. There could be no doubt about it; they admitted it themselves. The rifle instructors called their art "Moosketry," and laid great stress on the importance of knowing the name of every screw and gadget from the bayonet boss to the butt-trap hinge pin. Second to this was knowing the proper answer to the great English musketry joke: "What is the weight of the pull-through?" The gas mask instructor taught the boys to get into their masks in six seconds. After this was accomplished (we could all do it before we left Camp Lee), he ran games such as leap frog, ducks and drakes, etc., to accustom his class to wearing the masks while exerting themselves. The bayonet instructor had more to show than the others. He had quite a lot of pep in his points and withdrawals. Part of his Spiel was, "Classes, 'shun," "Classes, hup," "At the bloomin' 'Art—Point," "At the bloody throat, point." His favorite stunt was withdrawing with so much snap as to "Throw the oil bottle out of the butt-trap." Three classes were held in the mornings. In the afternoons, we went on hikes wearing tin hats. This was hard at first. We could go out with our masks in the carry position, but would wear them all the way back. A little double-time was sprung on us occasionally, to see that we were keeping in condition.[183]

The British program also emphasized instruction in signal and liaison duty, including visual signaling, message forms, and codes and ciphers, so a fifteen-day course in signal training was inaugurated. The signal platoons from each H.Q. company and four signalers from each rifle of company of the four infantry regiments were assigned to these schools. In addition, eight men from each infantry brigade H.Q. attended the schools. Signal supplies were scarce, however, and the importance of conserving them was stressed.

-Extended Order Combat Training-

While in *Artois* with the British, our training advanced to a series of maneuvers and terrain exercises, which continued without interruption, save during actual battle, until the regiment passed to the command of S.O.S. in March, 1919. The motto in various commands of the A.E.F.

---
[183] As cited in Stultz, 193; "'art' is "heart."

seem to have been: "When in doubt, maneuver." We were taught to attack "in fours" in "the two-wave formation." In general, this means that each battalion would be deployed with two companies up and two in support (i.e., two waves). At the company level, this meant two platoons up, followed by two in support. At the platoon level, this meant the Bomber, Assault, A.R., and R.G. squads would advance in "clumps," usually in that order. In other words, a division attack axis would consist of an eight-platoon front—about a kilometer in width—followed by eight platoons, followed by eight more platoons. We would attack in waves of platoons and each platoon was organized around four squad-sized "clumps."

Unlike at Camp Lee, where we devoted much of our training time on the ranges, in France we spent most of our training time on extended order drill (i.e., platoon-level infantry battle drills), small arms practice, and hand grenade (i.e., bomber) instruction. In the attack, the British emphasized the importance of A.R.s, R.G.s, and hand grenades. The French-made *Viven et Bessières* (V.B.) Rifle Grenades that we used were fired from "grenade dischargers," "grenade cups," or, as the French called them "*tromblons.*" A bullet was fired into the V.B. Grenade, which was seated in the cup, detonating the launching device, and hurling the grenade at distances from fifty to two hundred meters.[184] A rifle grenadier must always fire his R.G. with the butt of his rifle planted into the ground and never from his shoulder, due to the monster kick of V.B. Grenade. Generally, we fired white phosphorus (W.P.) Smoke V.B. Grenades to mask targets, like German M.G. nests, while A.R.s and rifles laid down suppressive fire.

What worked best for the Allies (and the Germans) in the attack was to advance in "clumps." While A.R.s and R.G.s suppressed a target, a tank, if available, was to plow through the enemy wire lines, straddle the enemy trench, and enfilade the enemy with M.G. or cannon fire. If no tank was available, which was usually the case, the bomber squad was to lead the advance with wire cutters and get as far forward as they could. Once they were stopped, the platoon leader would direct the A.R.s and R.G.s to maneuver to their left or right in order to lay suppressive fire. Once done, the bombers would then advance to within twenty yards of the target and throw as many hand grenades as possible. In fact, they were taught to carry at least twenty hand grenades in sandbags and strap them around their necks. As the bombers blew up the target, the assault squad, the largest squad of the platoon, was to sweep through the objective using their rifles, bayonets and/or intrenching tools (hit the Hun where his neck meets his body and split a major artery). If 7mm M.G.s, 37mm I.G.s, 81mm mortars, or 75mm field guns could be brought forward to add further fire power to the A.R.s and R.G.s, then all the better. It sounds simple in concept (as all things should be in war), but nearly impossible to

---

[184] *Viven et Bessières* is pronounced "Vee-ven ae Bess-ee-air" and *tromblons* is pronounced "Trawm-blawn."

execute while under enemy artillery, gas, M.G., or rifle fire! According to the *I.D.R.*, this was the "Army Way" to train troops in these types of exercises:

> *356. After the mechanism of EXTENDED ORDER DRILL has been learned with precision in the company, every EXERCISE should be, as far as practicable, in the nature of a maneuver (COMBAT EXERCISE) against an imaginary, outlined, or represented enemy. Company extended order drill may be conducted without reference to a tactical situation, but a COMBAT EXERCISE, whatever may be the size of the unit employed, should be conducted under an assumed tactical situation.*

The British also had us practice defensive trench tactics and offensive trench raids day and night in some mock trenches (they usually called such raids "stunts"). They taught us how to eat, sleep, and relieve ourselves while in the trenches, how to stand post, how to go "over the top," how to repel attackers, how to position A.R.s, R.G.s, and M.G.s, how to take out enemy M.G. nests with grenades and supporting weapons—everything. They taught us to dig "cross-shaped" foxholes in contested areas—usually once an attack has stalled. These "mini-forts" offered 360-degree defense and could be loaded with M.G.s, I.G.s, etc. We soon leaned on their every word and wanted to get closer to them but you could tell that they had grown harsh from their time in the lines. They'd say, "No, Yank, that's not how you do it!" or "That's right, Yank, you're getting it! etc." The English also said that they preferred that we used the term "Tommy Atkins" over "John Bull" and that's what we called them here on out: the "Tommies." (We called Scots, "Scotties," Irish, "Paddies," and Germans, "Huns," "Krauts," "Heinies," or "Sons-a-Boches.") Then-Capt. Ashby Williams of E/2/320th Infantry remembered the time with his British partners during this phase of the campaign:

> *I remember he took me to the right flank of the support and showed me the "T" trenches that had been dug off from the line which, he explained, were to be used for flanking fire if the enemy should attempt to penetrate down the valley from Ayette around his right flank, and showed me the wire defenses, erected perpendicular to the line of supports, to prevent the Boche from encircling and cutting off the rear, which was a famous German trick. He showed me the sink pits that were constructed to drain the water from the trenches. He showed me the M.G. emplacements to the flanks covering every avenue of approach with a definite sector of fire. I recall that there were some old aeroplane hangars about 400 yards in front of the right flank of the support line, which*

the colonel had decided to tear down for fear that if the Boche should come over he could use them as cover.[185]

Another soldier from the 320th Infantry remembered:

[The British] instructors were excellent, and interest and enthusiasm were kept at a high pitch. During our period of training...the 2-wave formation was mastered, the mysteries of the Lee-Enfield, the Lewis Automatic Gun, the hand and rifle grenade were delved into, and gradually, before anyone realized it, every company was a trained fighting machine. We held various competitions, including field meets, shooting matched and drills, and before the 4 weeks of training had ended our English tutors were prophesying that we were a match even for the Huns.[186]

As we trained in the field, officers and N.C.O.s were selected to attend specialty schools at *Village Bout de Haut*.[187] These British schools were exemplary. One soldier from Spalding's 305th Engineers remembered:

This was an interesting time, since we had learned that we were a combat division...so we took a lively interest in our training here and went at it with fitting enthusiasm. Schools for this and that and the other were established, and all of us attended one or the other of them. I was assigned to the school of musketry and gas, and I may say that the "Tommies" made the most affable and competent instructors that we had yet had. I have only the warmest memories of our special class. The American army system of teaching is to give a man something to do that he doesn't like, careful pains being taken to rob the subject in hand of anything that might prove in the slightest way interesting to the hapless victim, to give him all he can stand of it, to continue it until he is crazy, to drive him to it...to furiously antagonize him in every possible way...Exactly opposite were those British schools, which had a careful, systematic, varied program, interspersed with rest, smoke and play periods; not too much of anything at one time, never being kept at one thing until it became tiresome, and the hours of study being quite short. As a result,

---

[185] As cited in *1/320th Infantry*, 35.

[186] As cited in Stultz, 194.

[187] *Village Bout de Haut* is pronounced "Veal-aag Boo Dee Who."

we worked our heads off and absorbed more in a week than we normally did in a month.[188]

In my opinion, aside from attending these schools and practicing Extended Order Drills, the most important training we received during this period was officially described as the "Use of Cover." It consisted of dropping quickly, crawling so as not to be seen, and making the best possible use of the dips and waves in the ground that would not only stop a bullet or shell fragment, but would also mask one's forward movement from the enemy. Time after time, the Tommy Atkinses shouted at us to "Get flatter, mate! The Hun with the Gun will getcha!" Sometimes the training was elaborate, with actual M.G. fire shot over our heads from one of the flanks. Other times it simply consisted of a lane in which the platoon guide would "man an enemy M.G. position" and shout at us when he saw us, including the platoon leaders, who was expected to participate in the training with the men. In my opinion, this "fire and movement" training is incredibly important. Do it over-and-over again, as it builds up one's body and confidence. Use smoke to help mask your forward movement and try to get within twenty yards of your target in training. From there, throw a fake grenade and charge! If the P.G. has his helmet on, he'll be alright.

Use Of Cover.

I.D.R. 152. The recruit should be given careful instruction in the individual use of cover. It should be impressed upon him that, in taking advantage of natural cover, he must be able to fire easily and effectively upon the enemy; if advancing on an enemy, he must do so steadily and as rapidly as possible; he must conceal himself as much as possible while firing and while advancing. While setting his sight he should be under cover or lying prone.

I.D.R. 153. To teach him to fire easily and effectively, at the same time concealing himself from the view of the enemy, he is practiced in simulated firing in the prone, sitting, kneeling, and crouching positions, from behind hillocks, trees, heaps of earth or rocks, from depressions, gullies, ditches, doorways, or windows. He is taught to fire around the right side of his concealment whenever possible, or, when this is not possible, to rise enough to fire over the top of his concealment. When these details are understood, he is required to select cover with reference to an assumed enemy and to place himself behind it in proper position for firing.

---

[188] As cited in Stultz, 199-100.

I.D.R. 154. The evil of remaining too long in one place, however good the concealment, should be explained. He should be taught to advance from cover to cover, selecting cover in advance before leaving his concealment. It should be impressed upon him that a man running rapidly toward an enemy furnishes a poor target. He should be trained in springing from a prone position behind concealment, running at top speed to cover and throwing himself behind it. He should also be practiced in advancing from cover to cover by crawling, or by lying on the left side, rifle grasped in the right hand, and pushing himself forward with the right leg.

I.D.R. 155. He should be taught that, when fired on while acting independently, he should drop to the ground, seek cover, and then endeavor to locate his enemy.

I.D.R. 156. The instruction of the recruit in the use of cover is continued in the combat exercises of the company, but he must then be taught that the proper advance of the platoon or company and the effectiveness of its fire is of greater importance than the question of cover for individuals. He should also be taught that he may not move about or shift his position in the firing line except the better to see the target.

At first, many-a-Dough were so clumsy in dropping to the ground that he would put his knees to the ground first, like a cow, before taking the prone. That will get you killed. You have to actually dive into the ground like Ty Cobb would. After a few days of "diving into the dirt," we actually got pretty good at it, especially crawling forward under a smoke screen. Even our fattest Doughs, fully kitted-out, including his pack, were but a foot from the ground. Another thing we practiced was firing from the kneeling position. Firing from the hip does not need to be practiced (as you won't hit anything unless it's right in front of you) and standing fire, in combat, will hit nothing. Too much is going on. Firing from the prone is nice, as it's supported, but we rarely saw a target with our "weasel in the dirt." Kneeling, however, gave us the support we needed to hit a target and gave us at least a modicum of cover (although Hun M.G.s generally swept their cones about a foot from the ground).

We also practiced "digging in" while under fire. According to Army Regulations, there were three types of hasty entrenchments: the lying trench, the kneeling trench, and the standing trench:

M.M.T. 1143. Hasty intrenchments include trenches dug by troops upon the battlefield to increase their fighting power. They are usually constructed in the

> *presence of the enemy and in haste and embrace three forms viz:—the lying trench, the kneeling trench, and the standing trench.*
>
> *M.M.T. 1144. Lying trenches give cover to men lying down. When intrenching under fire the rifle trench can be constructed by a man lying down. He can mask himself from view in about ten to twelve minutes and can complete the trench in forty to forty-five minutes. A good method is to dig a trench eighteen inches wide back to his knees, roll into it and dig twelve inches wide alongside of it and down to the feet, then roll into the second cut and extend the first one back. Conditions may require men to work in pairs, one firing while the other uses his intrenching tool. Duties are exchanged form time to time until the trench is completed. The height of the parapet should not exceed one foot. This trench affords limited protection against rifle fire and less against shrapnel.*
>
> *M.M.T. 1145. Time permitting, a lying trench may be enlarged and deepened until the kneeling trench has been constructed...*

As with any war, our tactics and training evolved with time and the G-5 Section of Pershing's A.E.F. staff (Training and Doctrine) constantly published letters or pamplets to help the division and brigade commanders get better results with fewer casualties.

-New S.O.S. Equipment and the Care of Draft Animals-

While in *Artois* with the British, the 80th Division drew its full allotment of transport. Rolling kitchens, general service wagons, limbers, combat, and water carts, all of the British pattern, were issued with the full complement of draft animals. In this connection, it is not inappropriate to state that the wonderful success achieved by the 80th Division in the American First Army horse shows in February 1919, was the direct result of the instruction in the care of animals and transport received from the British in June and July, 1918, as well as the fact that many of us came from "horse country" in Virginia. According to the Army's *Manual of Sanitary Training, 1917*:

> *357. An N.C.O. is designated as stable sergeant or corporal to take immediate general charge of the forage and stables. He his held responsible for the proper policing and sanitary condition of the stable, picket line, and ground pertaining to them. Two or more men, called stable police, are detailed for the purpose of policing, removing manure, feeding, etc. under the direction of the stable*

sergeant. Usually horses are groomed twice daily, at morning and at evening stables, under the supervision of the 1Sgt. and a commissioned officer. The stable police, after grooming their own horses at morning stable, clean out the stalls and police the stable, under the direction of the stable sergeant. The bedding is taken up, that which is most soiled being separated for the manure heap, and the remainder put on the litter racks or spread upon the ground to dry. At or before evening stables, the stable is policed, the bedding is laid down and fresh straw spread on top of it; the bed must be soft and even, with the thickest part toward the manger; where horses eat their bedding, the old litter should be placed on top of the new straw.

358. Grooming is always done at the picket line, except in stormy weather. Stable call is the first call or warning call for stables, and precedes assembly.... The horses are then tied on the picket line, if not already there, and are groomed under the direction of the platoon leader. Each man habitually grooms his own horse, except that the horses of sergeants or commissioned officers, who may, at the discretion of the company commander, have their horses groomed by enlisted members of the platoon... Each horse should be groomed not less than twenty minutes, and as much longer as may be necessary. [When the platoon leader believes the horses under his charge to be properly groomed, he commands] Stand to Heel and each man stands one yard behind of and facing his horse... If, when the horses are inspected, the officer finds any of them not properly groomed, he will direct that these horses be left at the picket line and groomed under the supervision of an N.C.O. detailed for that purpose.

360. The guiding principles of feeding are:

(1) Feed in small quantities and often.

(2) Do not work the animal hard immediately after a full meal... Very little hay, if any, is fed in the morning when hard work follows, but about one-third of the ration should be fed at noon, and the remainder at night. Dust must be well-shaken from the hay before it is placed in the manger... Two and a half ounces of salt should be given each week, preferably lumps of rock salt, secured in or near the manger... Grazing should be encouraged at every spare moment, both in camps and during halts on the march... The daily allowance of oats, barley, or corn is twelve pounds to each and nine pounds to each mule; of that

hay, fourteen pounds to each animal; the allowance of straw for bedding is one hundred pounds a month to each animal.

362. Horses must be watered quietly and without confusion; the manner in which tis duty is performed is often a good test of discipline of a mounted command. Horses are to be led to and from water at a walk. At the drinking place no horse should be hurried or have his head jerked from the water… Horses should be watered before feeding or not until two hours after feeding. The rule is to allow water in small quantities… A horse will rarely drink freely very early in the morning.

As well as draft animals, Maj. J. W. O'Mahoney 305th Transportation Battalion, which had a H.Q. and six companies, also drew several makes and models of motored vehicles, mostly Fords from the States or Dennis-Karrier or Pierce-Arrow trucks from England. Too many didn't run right, however, if at all, and they lacked the spare parts to make them operate correctly. The practice of "cannibalization" and "improvisation" was therefore used, in which especially creative mechanics would use trucks that did not run as spare parts for those that could if fixed with said cannibalized parts. In this way, the 314th M.G. Battalion, our division's two-company mobile M.G. outfit, was finally made motorized as it received several Ford or G.M.C. one-ton motor trucks that the men called "Mountain Goats" or "Specials." The Specials transported the men, M.G.s, ammunition, and the gear of the battalion, enabling the division commander to make this unit a "flying" defensive unit, acting much like cavalry.[189]

Like in other areas where we were located, potable (i.e., drinkable) water in *Artois* was extremely scarce. It was drawn from deep wells and usually hauled a considerable distance to the billeting centers. All water for drinking was chlorinated. Small streams, not available to all, provided the only bathing facilities. Several detachments marched to the Channel Coast and swam in the sea for their "bath." As for food, British rations were penurious in comparison to American ones, and were universally rejected both because of their nature and meagreness. Fortunately, however, many of the companies were able to procure occasional extras, including fresh meat, eggs, strawberries, and vegetables. Certain varieties of food, tobacco and other articles were also obtainable from British canteens in a number of the larger villages. Members of the division were permitted to purchase on the same basis as the British troops—a privilege denied civilians and members of the French and Belgian Armies. One soldier from the 305th Engineers remembered:

---

[189] *314th M.G.*, 24.

There was a little valley near our billet where the mess sergeant set up his kitchen. He had all the equipment, but during our ten days stay he couldn't borrow, beg or steal enough rations to make a square meal. We could hardly get up enough steam to climb back to our billets after meals. We learned all about the British field rations. We will not describe British "Bully Beef," but will leave it buried in our memories. It should have been buried long before we came to sense its presence. The British make slabs of white tile and call them "Army Biscuit." The French make the same stuff in a red shade and use it for putting roofs on barns. British jam is delicious, but a spoonful of jam per day will not sustain a soldier under intensive training. The tobacco issue was regular, if nothing else: two packages of "Ruby Queen" cigarettes or a package of "White Cloud" cut plug. The pipe tobacco was rank, but we know that it was not the worst obtainable, for "White Cloud" had taken many prizes at British expositions. Competition could not have been very keen. As a delightful smoke, "Ruby Queens" are slightly inferior to corn-silk makings, and slightly better than the "Indian Tobies" which grow on Catalpa trees. "Ruby Queens" had taken twenty-one gold medals. They must have been displayed as a fertilizer or a fumigator...The scarcity of drinking water encourages the men, if such encouragement was needed, to patronize the village estaminets. These are found in every French community, the center of their limited social contacts. In the Samer area, American and British soldiers were permitted to visit them, if off duty, from 10:30 A.M. to 1:30 P.M., and from 5:30 P.M. to 9:00 P.M. Spirits were prohibited but wine and beer were permitted. The rum ration of the British soldier—never issued except in foul weather at the direction of a senior officer, and then only in the presence of an officer—was denied the Americans. Contrary to general belief, fully one-fourth of the British troops refused the rum ration, even though at least six rations would have been required to produce intoxication. British officers' clubs and canteens were open to the officers of the division. However, the presence of ten American divisions in the British zone severely taxed facilities, resulting in sharp limitation of the individual officer's allowance of supplies, particularly of Scotch whisky. An influx of American troops inevitably was followed by price boosts in the estaminets and shops.[190]

---

[190] As cited in Stultz, 197.

Almost overnight, *vin blanc* went from two to five francs and *champagne* from seven to twenty-two francs. We later found that every time Americans took billets in a town, the village crier would make his rounds immediately, making official announcements. These we construed to be notices to shop keepers to run prices up, and whether he said that or not, the result was the same. We still regarded French money as so many cigar coupons and handled it rather carelessly, so the rise in prices was to some extent due to our own prodigality.

A month had elapsed since we had left Camp Lee and all were impatient for the first mail to arrive. The brief, crowded stays at ports had afforded opportunity for the men to write home only in hastily scrawled notes. Now in the Samer area, we had sufficient leisure time to swamp the company officers censoring out-going mail. The official post-office of the division was established June 11, and it was designated "A.P.O. 756." American troops were allowed to post letters, if they bore an officer's signature, at any British post office in the field, those in the Samer area being situated at Samer, Desvres, Parenty, Frencq, and Questrecques. During this time, the first pay-day in France was also celebrated by the division.

-Army Life in *Artois*-

Life in the Samer Training Area of *Artois* was found to be pleasant in many respects. The surrounding country was beautiful. A fertile region, wheat appeared to be the dominant crop, with strips of *colza*—known to the American farmer as "rape"—interspersed among the waving wheat. Early morning and late evening, a procession of old men, women and children, carrying their tools and small baskets of bread and wine, could be seen wearily wending its way between the villages and neat farms. It was not unusual for groups of Doughs, during the long evenings, helping the owner of their billets in harvesting and storing his hay and grain. At this point, there was little to remind us of the war except the raiding planes and sometimes the faint rumbling of distant guns.

All of the area's towns were ancient and had narrow streets with squat stone houses that were roofed with red or gray tile and hidden behind massive iron gates. Many of their *mairie* (town halls) were in old *châteaus* (estates where the old aristocracy lived and collected land rents). Any of them could be characterized as a typical French village. All were beautiful from a distance. They were devoid of unsightly suburbs, such as surrounded American towns. Instead, the fields were cultivated to the town's very entrance, and the trees and hedges bordering the highways were neatly trimmed. An accurate word picture of these French villages was best explained by an officer from the 320th Infantry:

An American's idea of a town is well-defined streets, even rows of buildings, trim little shops, and the like. Nothing like this is true of a town in northern France. A French town from a distance is beautiful, but at close range it is horrible. Unlike our American towns, a French town is merely a collection of farmers and farm buildings, with their out-buildings and cow lots and all the rest. The Frenchman is very reclusive; he likes to make it difficult to reach his home and fireside, so that in order to get into the front door in a small French town, you invariably have to go around through the back yard. The average Frenchman in the small towns will also invariably have the manure pile near the front door. It is hard to understand this custom of the French, because they are undoubtedly the most artistic people in the world. The farms and forests and cities of France are beautiful, but about their own front yards and their own habitations they are not artistic; they are quite the contrary. At least this is true of the small towns of France.[191]

-Venus's Disease-

Since much of the *Samer* area had not been previously occupied by too many troops, except for some shot-up Portuguese units, no baths were available and latrines had to be dug. Although cases of influenza developed daily in nearly every British unit, no cases were reported in our division. General health conditions in the command were excellent and only forty-one cases of communicable disease were reported during June, and twenty-one of these were mumps. A number of cases of minor illnesses were sent to the British field hospitals during this period. Two members of G/2/319th Infantry were killed by the premature explosion of a grenade during a training exercise. Just prior to the division's departure from the area, sanitary and water squads were formed under medical officers. The personnel of the former was selected from E.M. not thoroughly fit for full duty. It was during our stay in this area that we were introduced to our first "cooties," or lice, which in subsequent months became our personal plague and gave birth to the nightly practice of "shirt reading."

My company, B/1/318th Infantry, was billeted in *Cormont* with the other companies of the battalion (H.Q., A, C, and D). My platoon was billeted in the loft of a barn that was owned by a small family on the outskirts of *le village*. The family consisted an older father, mother, and a

---

[191] As cited in Stultz, 198.

daughter who was around ten years old. Their son, *Henri*, had been killed while fighting along *Chemin des Dames* in 1915. Once our training for the day was complete, many of us Doughs would eat and make merry in the local cafés and some* would visit the local brothels, which, unlike in the U.S., was not illegal.

The Army was smart enough not to totally eliminate this form of barter. It did, however, try to limit it. It did so by punishing soldiers who caught venereal diseases (they are called "venereal diseases" after Venus, the Roman goddess of copulation), by providing prophylactics to soldiers, by examining the girls who plied the trade, and by trying to scare the Bejesus out of us through incessant briefings about what would happen if one were to in fact lay with a prostitute, no matter how pretty she was. While gonorrhea was pretty easy to treat (a few shots of penicillin), syphilis was not. According to Col. Moss's *M.M.T.*:

> *1466. Syphilis and gonorrhea (clap) are diseases whose germs are usually caught from prostitutes or whores, or from husbands who have caught the germs from prostitutes or whores...The syphilis germ will grow first where it is rubbed in, causing an ulcer, called a chancre, and after that it travels through the entire body. No place is sacred to its destructive power and it lives as long as the patient does. It is the cause of much insanity, palsy, apoplexy, deafness, blindness, and early death [!] In mothers it causes miscarriages and in children it causes stillbirths, freaks, deformities, feeble minds and idiots; also, deaf and dumb, palsied, stunted; sickly and criminal conditions. A syphilic person is always dangerous although apparently well. He often has a sore mouth and his spit is as dangerous as that of a mad dog. The bite of such a man will develop a chancre and any pipe, cup, or tooth pick which he uses, or his kiss, will give syphilis [!]*

According to Army Regulations, a soldier who suffered from the symptoms of venereal disease (V.D.) were to report the problem to his chain of command *at once*. If it became a recurring problem, he would face the wrath of the company top sergeant. Again, according to the *M.M.T.*:

> *1467. Venereal diseases cause more misery than any others and most of the doctors would have to go into other professions to earn their living if these diseases did not exist...When a young man is "sowing his wild oats" he is really planting in his own body the syphilis and clap plants, and the harvest will be greater than any other crop. He will reap it in days of bed-ridden misery, and possibly sudden death. He will reap it in bitter hours by the bedside through the*

illness and death of his wife or in their long years of ill health. He will reap it in little white coffins, idiot babies; blind, deaf, and dumb, sickly and stunted children. And it will cost him lost wages and hospital and doctor fees. Yes, the wild oats crop is a bumper crop. King Solomon was wise when he warned his son against the harlot "for her end is bitter."

The best way to avoid venereal disease is to keep away from lewd women, and live a clean moral life. It is said by medical authorities that sexual intercourse is not necessary to preserve health and manly vigor, and that the natural sexual impulse can be kept under control by avoiding associations, conversations, and thoughts of a lewd character.

However, persons who will not exercise self-control in this matter can greatly lessen the risks of indulgence by the prompt use, immediately upon return to camp or garrison, of the prophylaxis prescribed by War department orders and which all soldiers are required to take after exposing themselves to the danger of venereal infection. Men who immediately after intercourse urinate and wash the private parts thoroughly with soap and water will lessen the chances of infection. Drunkenness greatly increased the risk of infection.

On June 29, 1918, the 318th Infantry passed in review before His Royal Britannic Highness, the Duke of Connaught. Because of this review, gossip (without which there is no army) had it that we were going to fight alongside the British, otherwise so important a personage as the duke would not have reviewed the regiment. All of us felt that after the long period of training at Camp Lee and in Artois, we were overly prepared for service "up the line," and were very anxious to get a crack at *les Boche*.

-With the Artillery at Redon-

While the 159th and 160th Inf. Brigs. and the special troops of the 80th Division trained with the British in Artois, subordinate units from Heiner's 155th Arty. Brig. (i.e., the 313th, 314th, and 315th Artillery as well as the 305th Ammunition Train and the 305th T.M. Battery) disembarked at Brest on June 8 and were sent to Redon, which is just south of Rennes, in Brittany. General Pershing had directed that our artillery camps and ranges be organized at *Coëtquidon* (where *l'École Spéciale Militaire de Saint-Cyr* is located) and *Meucon*, in Brittany, and at *Sougé*, near

Bordeaux.[192] Heavy artillery (i.e., howitzer) training centers for corps and army were established at *Libourne, Limoges, Clermont,* and *Angers*. At these camps, American artillerists were to receive their training according to the French system and with French instructors. As the American Red Legs began to pour into France with unanticipated speed, however, all could not be accommodated on the few available ranges. It therefore became necessary to utilize the zones of *Courtine, Ornans, Redon, Bordeaux, Rennes,* and *Poitiers* for the initial training of American artillery units while waiting for assignment to one of the ranges. In this disposition, the 155th Artillery Brigade was ordered to *Redon*. One soldier from C/1/314th Artillery remembered his journey from Brest to Redon:

> *On June 12, we entrained for Redon, a distance of 192 kilometers. It took us fourteen hours to make this short run. Upon reaching Redon we were billeted on the outskirts of the town, in Chateau-du-Buart, an imposing castle of the Middle Ages, beautifully situated in a large park of century-old trees…We were the first American troops billeted here, and the natives could not do enough for us.*[193]

Rich in history, Brittany (*Bretagne* or "Place of the Britains" or *Armorica* "Place by the Sea") derived its name from a great influx of Celtic-speaking peoples from Britain centuries before the Kingdom of France even existed. In the center of Brittany, there are two plateaus partly covered with unproductive moor land and dominated by wild ranges which, while they nowhere exceed 1,150 feet in elevation, possess the aspect of high mountains. In this region, the French-run American artillery training centers were located.[194]

It was reported to me that *Redon* itself was a sleepy little town of some 6,000 souls about forty miles northwest of *Saint-Nazaire*, above the confluence of *Rivière Oest* and on the canal from *Nantes* to *Brest*. In the heart of *Brittany, Redon* grew up around a monastery that was founded in the 9th Century. In the 14th Century, one of its powerful feudatory abbots, *Jean de Treal*, surrounded *Redon* with walls, remnants of which were still to be seen in 1918. At high tide, the little port was accessible to small draft vessels. Its population was principally engaged in boat building, tanning, brewing, and the manufacture of agricultural implements. Along

---

[192] *Redon* is pronounced "Ray-dawn," *Rennes* is pronounced "Ren," *Coëtquidon* is pronounced "Koe-key-doan," *l'École Spéciale Militaire de Saint-Cyr* is pronounced "Lay-coal Mil-it-tee-air Spec-ee-all day Sawn See-air," *Meucon* is pronounced "Mew-kawn," *Sougé is pronounced* "Sue-shay," and *Bordeaux* is pronounced "Bore-doe."

[193] As cited in Stultz, 329.

[194] *Bretagne* is pronounced "Brew-tang."

Redon's streets were many sturdily built timber houses of the 16th Century, rich in wood carvings, etc. One soldier from Goodfellow's 315th Artillery remembered:

> *Redon was a typical small French town—houses, narrow streets, market place, public square, church, abundance of cafes and the ever present canal... For the next two months we perfected ourselves in our respective military duties, and at the same time learned something of the French customs. During this time games were indulged in, baseball being the most popular... Another popular sport was the bathing. Two afternoons a week, an organization in charge of an officer would go down to the canal for a swim. Always there would be onlookers, and sex did not seem to matter in the scheme of things. Now, there is no issue of bathing suits in the army, and at first the boys were a bit embarrassed, but after the first blush of modesty had worn off no one minded at all impersonating nymphs... "The battle of Redon" was one of the easiest battles fought by the 315th Artillery. Work for officers and men in the morning, some work and much athletics in the afternoon, and no work and beaucoup sentimental happenings in the evening. Every evening, from 7:00 to 8:00 o'clock, the regimental band in all its glory would assemble at the public square and render a variety of compositions, from a "Hot Time in the Old Town" to the sob stuff. The French especially enjoyed this music, and this was their first opportunity to hear music in four years. In France dancing was "defendu" during the war, and this was a double treat to lovers of poetry, music and motion.*[195]

When the war began in 1914, it was an accepted fact the French excelled all other nations in artillery ordnance and training. Development of the quick-firing French 75mm field piece in the late-1890s, for example, at once rendered the field artillery of other countries obsolete. Delaying adoption of the improved weapon until Germany had committed herself to entirely new—and inferior—equipment, France thereby gained a start of at least a decade on her most probable adversary. Even though other armies quickly adopted ordnance that was similar to the "French 75," France enjoyed a major advantage in her experience. Most students of military history have in fact attributed the survival of France in 1914 to her marked superiority in this field. By comparison, the American three-inch field piece, the type used for training purposes at

---

[195] As cited in Stultz, 330-31.

Camp Lee, was considered outmoded. It was therefore natural that America should look to the French for artillery ordnance and instruction.

Beginning June 20, about one hundred officers and N.C.O.s were sent from each artillery regiment of the division to Coëtquidon for specialized training in radio, firing charts, M.G., telephone, signalling, sanitation, camoflague, and ordnance. The courses were practical and thorough, and the details returned praising their French instructors. Training in this area, unlike that in the British zone, was never hindered by hostile air attacks.

Shortly after the brigade's arrival at *Redon*, details were sent to *Calais* to procure horses. These details usually numbered three officers and two hundred men from the 314th Artillery. After an absence of two weeks, they returned on July 2 with more than 2,000 animals requisitioned by the French government from French farmers. The horses were issued from *Saint-Nicolas* to the various units, with the 313th and 314th receiving about 250 each, the 315th Artillery 1,450, and the horse battalion of the 305th Ammunition Train its entire ration. The animals were in poor condition, however, and were far below U.S. Army standards, because, like everything else, Franch was tapped out. When we entered heavy combat in the fall, it was almost imposible to keep the poor beasts fit for duty and we lost most of them.[196]

But they were all that was left.

Vivé la France!

As soon as enough horses were obtained and each artillery regiment received adequate gun equipment, mounted drill began, half of each day being devoted to road work in the form of battery problems. The first trucks for the motor battalion of Lt. Col. Orlo C. Whitaker 305th Ammunition Train were received on June 27, and on July 3 the big 155mm howitzers began to arrive for Col. Goodfellow's 315th Artillery.

The various schools in Redon were conducted by French officers who had seen action and their methods of fire would soon show gratifying results. At this time, Heiner's 155th Arty. Brig. was probably at the highest level of morale and proficiency achieved since its inception—the men were well fed and in good health and the weather was ideal. One officer from C/1/314th Artillery remembered:

> *Redon, for most of us, will always be a place of pleasant memories... It was here that we made acquaintance with the famous 75mm field piece, receiving our materiel, which consisted of four 75s and four French caissons on July 6. Officers and N.C.O. schools for the study of "the 75" had already been started, and under both French and American instruction the mysteries of the gun were*

---

[196] As cited in Stultz, 329 and *313th Artillery*, 13.

soon mastered. In an incredibly short time we had succeeded in developing three complete gun crews for each piece. During this time, the "Instrument" and "Signal" details were receiving special instruction in the use of the fire control instruments and the establishment and maintenance of communication. Horses were received and the battery was soon fully equipped... Although the days were long and the schedule exacting, our evenings were spent in promenades along country roads which were beautiful.[197]

After several weeks' training, the entire artillery brigade was assembled in Redon on the Fourth of July and passed in review before *Général de France Albert Gérard Léo d'Amade*, late of Morocco and Gallipoli, and, at the time, Command of the Tenth Training Region and responsible for American artillery instruction. *Général d'Amade* spoke briefly to the officers of the brigade and administered the usual French salute to General Heiner, the brigade commander. One soldier from the 315th Artillery remembered:

After the French general's speech, he came up to General Heiner and presented him with two resounding kisses, one on each cheek. It was very amusing to see the expression on General Heiner's face. At first he threw up his hands as if to ward off a blow, but then remembering, he recovered himself and submitted graciously to the symbol of the Frenchman's binding friendship. Somewhat awkwardly done on the part of the representative of the Franco-American alliance, but it must be considered that the habit of receiving kisses from "un Homme" is not taught in United States Drill Regulations.[198]

-Chateau-Thierry and the Move to Picardy-

While units of the 80th Division trained for front-line service in *Artois* and *Bretagne* in July, the Germans were thrown back along the Marne with heavy losses. As was already stated, the American 1st, 2nd, 3rd, 28th, 42nd, and 77th Divisions were involved in helping to staunch this German drive, the one that was supposed to win the war for the Hun, at places like *Chateau-*

---

[197] As cited in Stultz, 330.

[198] *Ibid*, 331.

Thierry, *Bois Vaux*, and *Bois Belleau* (Belleau Wood).[199] Maj. Gen. James Harbord, in command of the American 2nd (American Indian) Division at Bois Vaux and Belleau remembered:

> *The instructions from the French [corps commander] were that we must "hold the line at all hazards." That was the order I transmitted to the [Marine Brigade]. The companies were hardly more than in place when a message from the same general suggested that I have a line of trench dug several hundred yards back of them, "just in case." My reply was that, with the orders our men had, they were prepared to die if necessary to hold the line, but if started to digging trenches they would know it could have but one purpose and that my orders were not to be taken as given… So, I said: "We will dig no trenches to fall back to. The Marines will hold where they stand." They did.*[200]

With emboldened statements like, "We will dig no trenches to fall back to. The Marines will hold where they stand," these battles brought notoriety to the units involved, especially the Marines of Brig. Gen. Frank Lejune's Marine Brigade, 2nd Infantry Division. Due to Army censorship rules, individual units or divisions were not allowed to be reported. It was, however, decided to allow the use of the term "Marines," and all we heard about in the press was that the "Marines Stopped the Hun at Belleau Wood."

What also helped the Marines' cause was that the Secretary of the Navy, Josephus Daniels, witnessed the battle first hand and made it his top priority to highlight the Marines' fighting in France to buttress the Navy Department, which had actually received little recognition for winning the Battle of the Atlantic. Daniels later wrote: "The Marines fought according to American methods: in successive waves, passing over the bodies of their dead comrades, and plunging ahead until they too, should be torn to bits. In all the history of the Marine Corps, there is no such battle as that one, fighting day and night without sleep, often without water, and for days without hot rations. They lost ¾ of their companies." To this day, the 5th and 6th Marine Regiments share the symbol of the Army's 2nd (Indian) Division to commemorate their time with it during the Great War for Civilization.

During the battle, Harbord and Lejune did not ask for an artillery prep during the counter-attack at Belleau Wood. They did this for two reasons: surprise and they did not want to churn up the attack route with even more shell holes and craters. Although it was a controversial decision, the Marines did take their objective (but with heavy loss—like the British at Bunker

---

[199] *Chateau-Thierry* is pronounced "Chat-ow Tee-air-ee," *Bois Vaux* is pronounced "Bwa Voe," and *Bois Belleau* is pronounced "Bwa Bell-low."

[200] As cited in Harbord, 283.

Hill). Either way, with the battle won, Harbord was promoted to major general and assigned to command the Army's important S.O.S. in France and Britain and Lejune was given command of the 2nd Infantry Division.

It was also during this fight that the American 3rd Division became known as the "Rock of the Marne Division" and the 28th (Red Keystone) Division became known as the "Iron Division" for their stand along the south bank of the Marne in the vicinity of *Chateau-Thierry*. Of particular note to us was the action of the 3rd Division's motorized M.G. battalion—the 7th M.G. Battalion (mot.). Major John Mendenhall's 7th M.G. Battalion was rushed ahead of the infantry brigades of the 3rd Division in its Specials in order to hold the town of *Chateau-Thierry* long enough so the infantry to come up—just like Buford's cavalry had done for the damned Yankee army at Gettysburg. We took great interest in this and wondered aloud how our own M.G. battalions would operate with us once we were thrown into battle.

On July 5, 1918, my beloved 318th Infantry, minus our M.G. company, which was left at *Hubersent* for further training with the M.G. battalions of the division, marched back up to *Samer* and entrained for a 24-hour-long journey to a new training area in French Picardy. Along the way, we noticed that the new area, closer to the front, had numerous aerodromes with aeroplanes flying to and from the front lines. All around the aerodromes were giant sausage-like dirigibles to impede enemy air attacks. There were also countless ammunition and supply dumps stacked high with bullets, H.E., shrapnel, gas, and mortar rounds, hand grenades, rifle grenades, barbed wire, timber, and duckboards for the trenches.

We were later told that all wells in the area were mined for destruction in case of a retreat and every tree along the main roads were mined for destruction in such a way as to fall across the road and form a barrier for *les Boche*. Trenches were numerous and barbed wire was everywhere. All was ready for a retreat that never came. One month later, in fact, we found the Hun promenading *tout de suite* the other way.[201] One soldier from the 319th Infantry, who soon followed us south, remembered:

> *July Fourth, "Iron Rations" were issued, consisting of little round crackers and bully beef, and correct is the name "Iron Rations," as the crackers would make good shrapnel for the Hun. At 9:00 A.M., we entrained for Bouquemaison—we always moved on holidays, and all along the route a friendly aeroplane kept a watchful eye, in order that the train might not be bombed by enemy planes. A continuous roar of distant cannon cheered us up*

---

[201] *Tout de suite* or "at once" in French is pronounced "Too de Swee." Sometimes we would simply say, "Toot-sweet."

all along the way—a barrage was being put over somewhere, but not the kind we were used to on the Fourth of July in the good old U.S.A.[202]

The air of mystery surrounding this particular movement was referred to by a soldier of Col. Peyton's 320th Infantry when he stated: "The day after the Fourth of July, we got orders to move. These orders always had a certain amount of mystery and uncertainty about them—they seldom stated where we were going, only that we would entrain at a certain time and place, so that officers and men were usually much wrought up at the time of moving and rumors began to circulate as to our destination."[203] A soldier from Lt. Col. Spalding's 305th Engineers noted how they were treated by the British when they departed the Samer Training Area: "Dozens of 'Tommies' gathered around, wished us 'best o' luck,' which caused us no small concern. We didn't know where we were headed, but 'the Tommies' had a pretty good idea, having seen many take the route ahead of us." As we departed Samer, the commanding general of the British 39th Division reported the following about us to Marshal Foch and General Pershing: "Spirit excellent; men of excellent physique, keen and intelligent; material is excellent and I feel they will make a good fighting division." [204]

The de-training point for us was at Candas and while H.Q./318th Infantry and 2/318 were billeted in Bonneville, 1/318 (my unit), was quartered in Montrelet, and 3/318 and Supply/318 were posted in Fieffes, *Province Picardie* (Picardy).[205] I don't know who had a hand in all of our training and preparation before we were thrown into battle—Wilson, Pershing, or Foch—but I certainly do appreciate it to this day. Given the dire circumstances, we could have easily been off-loaded at Brest and sent to the front in a piecemeal fashion—getting chewed to bits, by the way.

We were only at *Bonneville* for a couple of weeks and we pursued very much the same type of training we had in Samer—only this time it was under the supervision of a battalion from the King's Regiment, British 66th Division. Not that we didn't like the Irishers, but we really liked the Tommies from the King's Regiment. While in *Bonneville*, we could actually hear the guns from the front. Their rumblings could be heard every night and, at times, even during the day. Air raids here were of no less frequent occurrence than in the *Samer* area. For example, on

---

[202] As cited in Stultz, 204.

[203] *Ibid*, 204.

[204] *Ibid*, 205.

[205] *Candas* is pronounced "Cawn-dah," *Bonneville* is pronounced "Bone-ah-veal," *Montrelet* is pronounced "Moan-tra-lay," *Fieffes* is pronounced "Feef-ayes," and *Province Picardie* is pronounced "Prov-awns Peek-are-dee."

the night of July 12, a German aviator, attempting to destroy the railroad passing through *Fieffes*, bombed a supply train of 3/318th Infantry, killing twelve horses. This was the first hostile act against our regiment, and, although no men were hurt, the explosions, coming as they did in the "wee sma'" of the night, took us somewhat by surprise and caused a panic in at least one man that I heard about. An English sentinel from the King's Regiment apprehended the scared Blue Ridger a few minutes later, about a mile away and still going strong. From here, we were moved closer to the front, near *Albert*.[206]

Upon our arrival in the zone just west of Albert, *Province Picardie*, we were spread throughout the rear areas of Maj. Gen. Julian Byng's British Third Army, which was centered around Beauval. From these points, the infantry regiments of America's Blue Ridge Division would be sent into the front lines or "Up the Line." In the north, General Brett's 160th Inf. Brig. was attached to the British IV Corps for training and operations around Louvencourt. In the south, General Jamerson's 159th Inf. Brig., my brigade, was attached to the British V Corps for training and operations around Toutencourt (the two "courts").[207] Subordinate units of the 80th Division, minus the 155th Arty. Brig., were located at the following places in Picardy by July 5, 1918:

Division H.Q.: Beauval
305th Trains Brigade Headquarters: Beauval
305th Engineers: Beauval
H.Q., 159th Inf. Brig.: Doullens
317th Infantry: Doullens
318th Infantry: Bonneville
1/318: Montrelet
2/318: Bonneville
3/318: Fieffes
H.Q., 160th Inf. Brig.: Lucheux
319th Infantry: Haute Visee
1/319: Crouches
2/319: Bouquemaison
3/319: La Souich
320th Infantry: Sus-St. Leger
1/320: Sus-St. Leger
2/320: Beaudricourt
3/320: Ivergny.

---

[206] *Albert* is pronounced "Al-bear."

[207] Byng was later elevated to "First Viscount of Vimy" (pronounced Vye-count) and became the Royal Governor of Canada. He had led Commonwealth troops at Gallipoli and Vimy Ridge. *Beauval* is pronounced "Boo-val," *Louvencourt* is pronounced "Loo-von-core," and *Toutencourt* is pronounced "Too-ten-core."

-Albert-

Beauval and *Doullens* were the two largest towns in the British 66th Division's area, and in these the troops found facilities for purchasing supplies and enjoying their leisure. [208] For the first time since Camp Lee, the infantry brigades of the 80th Division were united in a comparatively small area. Due to a scarcity of billets, however, several unfortunate comapnies had to pitch pup tents in orchards (i.e., "establish a bivouac"). Frequent rainfall made the experience for them a little more difficult. But we in the 318th Infantry were lucky because we were billeted in Doullens, a fairly sizeable town. Here we found many comforts: supplies of wine, chocolate, and oranges were still plentiful and the stores and cafes afforded luxuries not again obtainable for several weary months. Doullens was an important military center during the French Revolutiony and Napoleonic Wars (1790-1815), and the ancient moats and great masonry and earthen walls were still well preserved. Local tradition reported the existence of a subterranean passage that connected Doullens with Arras, reputedly built by Napoleon. While long since abandoned, the Doullens end of the tunnel was occupied by civilian refugees. One officer from Col. Peyton's 320th Infantry remembered:

> *Beaudricourt was another of those country towns of northern France, beautiful without, but unsightly and unkempt within…I remember when Sunday morning came and I could examine the billets intended for the men. I found them so dirty and so unsightly that I decided not to occupy them at all, and selected a permanent orchard lot where they pitched tents, two rows on either side and two at the back, making a quadrangle with open front… My best impressions of Beaudricourt will always be of a quiet, dirty little French country town, with old stone buildings and narrow, crooked streets, and hedges and cow-lots; of the quiet and happy little home in which we lived, facing upon the stable court-yard; of routine days training men to fight, and of policing areas to meet and satisfy the eye of unexpected visitors from higher up.* [209]

While in *Picardie* (Picardy), the British Army rendered the infantry and S.O.S. battalions of the Blue Ridge Division yeoman service by obtaining and transporting supplies for us. Rations were drawn at the British rail-head and all transport equipment for the battalions was furnished by them. Transport for an infantry battalion, as originally assigned by the British, consisted of

---

[208] *Doullens* is pronounced "Due-long."

[209] As cited in Stultz, 218.

four general service (G.S.) wagons, ten double limbers for ammunition transport, two water carts (big barrels hauled by a mule—sometimes called "water buffaloes"), four rolling kitchens, one medical cart, and one officers' mess cart, or twenty-two vehicles with about sixty animals total, including several officers' mounts and ten pack mules.

"On the fourth day of Christmas, my true love gave to me, four G.S. wagons, three double limbers, two water carts, and one wa-ter buf-fa-lo!"

Like those received by our artillery brigade, many of the draft animals were old and worn and the harness and equipment was barely serviceable. British transport standards were consistently sought and stressed in the American Army, but no official provision whatsoever was made for the maintenance of these standards. Not even essential supplies for the care and preservation of British equipment was issued.

Everything else had to be purchased, with great difficulty, out of organizational funds, even soap, curry-combs and horse brushes, while the supplies necessary for the care of leather, steel bits, chains, stirrups, and the brass of the heavily mounted British harness, were almost impossible to obtain in the usual French stores. Nor did the methods applied to the use of the horse transport allow the animals and equipment to be properly rested and cared for, since they were constantly in use, not supplemented by motor transport. All these handicaps imposed upon the services of supply (S.O.S.) required a vast amount of labor and exactions. In comparing the American and British supply systems, the following comment was made by Maj. Robert J. Halpin, our division Q.M., which sort of conflicts with the impressions of other soldiers about "American Regular Army policy":

The British policy of seeing that everything possible is done for the comfort of the fighting men seems to be exactly the same as the American Regular Army policy of teaching officers that their first and greatest duty is to look out for the comforts and needs of the enlisted personnel. This policy is so well emphasized by the British higher command that we found this training most valuable for the American national Army officers, who had little previous experience in caring for the needs and welfare of the enlisted personnel.[210]

On July 6, under instructions from the British Third Army, orders were issued by division H.Q. enumerating precautionary measures to be employed in view of probable enemy aerial bombing and contact with the civilian population. These provided for the screening of lights, the extinction of unconcealed fires during darkness, and the shading of headlights on

---

[210] As cited in Stultz, 220.

motor vehicles. Local fire orders for Beauval assigned troops to assist the French firemen in case of an attack. Regulations forbade soldiers leaving billets for any purpose unless in proper uniform and the men were required to be in their billets by 9:30 P.M. Cafes were open to the troops only from 10:30 A.M. to 1:30 P.M. and from 5:30 P.M. to 9:00 P.M. Prophylaxis treatment against V.D. was ordered given any man found drunk. Commanding officers were charged with taking necessary precautions against damage to fruit trees, crops, or land, and use of any land not assigned to the division, was banned. Troops living under canvas were directed to protect themselves from aerial bombs by a digging a parapet at least three feet high and two feet thick. We were also warned to be on the alert against persons inquiring for military information and were urged to watch for paper balloons, reportedly being used to transmit information from behind the lines. The posting of letters in civilian post-offices by soldiers was forbidden. American II Corps H.Q. decreed that no leaves would be granted to members of of the corps.

Because the division was now well within the sound of the enemy's guns and air raids were more frequent, one platoon from each rifle company was charged with firing at low-flying enemy planes and battalion parades were discontinued because of danger from the air. Gas masks were required to be worn daily (except Sunday) by all officers and E.M., starting with a sixty-minute period and increasing to ninety minutes on the sixth day. All motor cars except the six assigned to division and brigade H.Q.s, were ordered pooled.

One night, we heard the drone of a monster new type of German bombing plane, called a *Gotha*, which was driven by three powerful engines and crewed by fifteen men.[211] Several large British airdromes and aviation bases were at *Candas, Gert-Vallant*, and *Bonneville*, and they were the object of almost nightly enemy attention. Many of the pilots and observers were Canadian or other British "Commonwealth Soldiers" (e.g., Australians, New Zealanders, South Africans, etc.). The dromes also never failed to attract groups of curious American Doughs, people like Getz and I, who were frequently treated to the spectacle of the British flyers taking off in their frail craft (sometimes called "motorized kites" because they were made of wood and cloth and had a motorized propeller attached to them—a far-cry from the aircraft of today) or the signal of an approaching German plane. Occasionally, when enemy aerial activity was curtained, venturesome officers and men would accept the invitation of some friendly pilot to accompany him on a short flight behind the lines. There were no parachutes in those days. Needless to say, I did not want to go up in one of those flimsy suicide devices.

---

[211] *Gotha* is pronounced "Go-ta."

Under capable British instructors, emphasis continued to be placed upon rifle and bayonet practice, bombing, gas defense, and extended order drill. The instruction included the deployment of platoons for attack and defense, simple maneuver problems for platoons and companies, and tactical problems for battalions prepared by regimental commanders. Practice marches were also required of battalions, with rigid march discipline.

...And the beat goes on...

Col. George R. Spalding's 305th Engineers, billeted at *Beauval*, also embarked upon a strenuous schedule of training. In addition to barbed wiring and trench drill, their instruction included rifle and bayonet practice and the usual gas training. Practically every morning, the engineers marched to the rear of the British lines where they engaged in their daily duties, returning in the evening for a total march of about fifteen miles a day. We depended on them to "clear the way," either in obstacle clearance, the building of roads, the repair of bridges, etc. The signal platoons of the 305th Field Signal Battalion and of the infantry regiments also received a varied and comprehensive course in signal training under British instructors. The schedule included map and lamp reading, how to operate and or maintain the "buzzer" (a military field telegraph), British "Fuller Phones" (Morse code tappers), "Popham" Signalling Panels (for aircraft), radios, and telephones. The British system of signalling was largely discarded for the American system after the troops left the British zone, however. The following account of these training activities by a soldier from Maj. E. E. Kelly's 305th Signal Battalion:

> *At Beauval, we received Signal Corps instructions from the British "Sigs" and learned our "Acks," "Beers," and "Tocks." In a former brickyard we practiced the International Code and planned real maneuvers. After hiking three or four miles across country with Lucas lamps strung from our shoulders, we flashed messages from hill to hill. In groups of four, we went to the New Zealand-British front to get our first experience of being under shell fire. This front was a quiet one, yet the German artillery made things quite interesting and exciting... We learned to make fast friends with the fighting men of the islands of the Pacific, and during rest periods and at mess the broad-hatted fighters told us much about New Zealand... Under the supervision of a British officer, we were taught the care and handling of horses.*[212]

---

[212] As cited in Stultz, 222.

-Division Call Signs-

While in Picardy, every battalion and brigade of the division was issued a "call sign" or "code name." Effective July 15, use of the "Potomac Code" was required for transmitting all confidential messages between the division and the American II Corps H.Q. or other American divisions and secret code was ordered used for all confidential messages within the division, down to battalions. On July 17, a secret memorandum by division H.Q. assigned each organization down to battalions a code name. Use of these names was required in all official correspondence within the division. The need for this precaution was stressed in a letter from the American II Corps H.Q. dated July 11, which cited British authorities as reporting that recent movement of American troops had been a matter of open discussion in villages where the soldiers were billeted. In many cases, even the destination of units was declared known to civilian inhabitants before the troops moved. We in the 80th Division were assigned code names that started with the letters "H." In this way, when talking on a field phone, an officer didn't say his actual unit, but simply used its code name. I have included some of the pertinent call signs that I remember our officers using during the next coming weeks:

80th Division H.Q.: HAMILTON
317th M.G.: HIBBARD
159th Inf. Bde.: HAROLD
317th Inf.: HARPER
318th Inf.: HAMMOND
1/318: HAVER
2/318: HATFIELD
3/318: HANSCOM

If the division commander or his designate wanted to talk with General Jamerson or the 159th Inf. Brig., for example, he'd say something like:

"HAROLD, this is HAMILTON, over."

"HAMILTON, this is HAROLD, over."

"HAROLD this is HAMILTON, execute Plan GREEN, over."

"HAMILTON this is HAROLD, WILCO, over."

"HAROLD this is HAMILTON, out."

Proper phone or radio procedure is critical. The British-trained signalmen of the Blue Ridge Division stressed this time after time. If one didn't say, "over" or "out" then the other person may not get the complete message and in a combat zone, complete messages were sometimes the difference between life or death or even mission accomplishment. Phone lines could also be cut quite easily. They were, in fact, cut most of the time. The Germans, on the defensive for so long, had so many advantages over us in this arena, having short and protected lines of communication, enabled them to deploy reserves quickly and decisively. According to American doctrine and practice, the division's 305th Signal Battalion was tasked with running phone lines from division H.Q. to the brigades but no further. The regiment was responsible for communicating with its battalions and brigade H.Q. with their own signal detachments. Runners were used to communicate between battalion, company, and platoon.

To conform more closely to the British T.O. while in the Albert zone of operations (which was far-more battalion-centric than the U.S. Army at the time) and to thereby ensure complete harmony, seconds-in-command were appointed in each battalion, the following officers being designated: 1/318, our very own Capt. James S. Douglas, Jr. of Company B, 2/318, Capt. Edward H. Little of Company E, and 3/318, Capt. Richard P. Williams, Jr. of Company I. A few days later, General Cronkhite ordered each brigade staff to add an assistant to the brigade adjutant in order to correspond to a British staff captain. Capt. Richard P. Williams, Jr., of I/3/318 was accordingly transferred to the 159th Inf. Brig. H.Q. and Capt. Louis J. Koch of M/3/318 became the executive officer for 3/318.

-The British Defensive System-

Byng's British Third Army's twelve divisions held the front along the west bank of *la rivière Ancre* from just north of Amiens, opposite Albert, to a point slightly beyond Arras.[213] Its frontage embraced about 25 miles, with the British V, IV, and VI Corps in the order named from south to north. The British V Corps, with headquarters at Naours, had the British 38th and 21st Divisions in line on the right and left, respectively, with H.Q. at Lealvillers and Rancheval.[214] While the 38th (Welsh) Division had the 113th and 115th Inf. Brigs. in line and the 114th Inf. Brig. in reserve, the 21st Division had the 62nd and 110th Inf. Brigs. in the line and the 64th Inf. Brig. in reserve.

The British IV Corps, in the center of the army line, with H.Q. at Marieux, had the British 37th and 42nd Divisions as well as the New Zealand Division. In the 42nd Division, the 125th Inf. Brig. was on the right, the 127th Inf. Brig. was on the left, and the 126th Inf. Brig. was in reserve. In the New Zealand Division, the 1st Inf. Brig. was on the right, the 2nd Inf. Brig. was on the left,

---

[213] *La rivière Ancre* is pronounced "La riv-ee-air Awnk" and *Arras* is pronounced "Are-aas."

[214] *Naours* is pronounced "Now" and *Lealvillers et Rancheval* is pronounced "Leave-vee-air ae Rawn-chav-awl."

and the 3rd Inf. Brig. was in reserve. In the British 37th Division, the 111th Inf. Brig. was on the right, the 112th Inf. Brig. was on the left, and the 63rd Inf. Brig. was in reserve. The British 62nd Division, with H.Q. at Aultue, had its three Infantry brigades, the 185th, 186th, and 187th, at Vauchelles, St. Leger, and Henu. The British 63rd (Hood's Naval) Division was held in reserve.

Then came the British VI Corps on the northern edge of the army front, with the British 2nd Division on the right, the famous British Guards Division in the center, and the British 59th Division on the left. All brigades of the 2nd Division, the 5th, 6th, and 99th, were up the line. In the British Guards Division, the 1st, 2nd, and 3rd Guards Brigades were also in the line, while the 176th and 177th Inf. Brigs. of the 59th Division were in the line with the 178th Inf. Brig. in reserve. In this corps, the 3rd British Division formed the reserve, with H.Q. at *Bavincourt*, and the 8th, 9th, and 76th British Inf. Brigs. at Sombrin, Le Souich, and Sus-St. Leger. Opposite Byng's Third British Army was the German Seventeenth Army, with the 3rd Naval Division, the 16th Reserve Division, and the 183rd Infantry Division of the XIV Reserve Corps opposite the V British Corps, the 111th Infantry Division and the 2nd Prussian Guards Reserve Division opposite the IV Corps, and the 234th Infantry Division and 21st Reserve Division opposite the British VI Corps.

To avoid a possible repetition of the disaster which befell the British Fifth Army in March with *Friedensturm*, Byng's army, with the aid of innumerable engineer battalions of Chinese and others commanded by officers unfit for combat service, had undertaken the construction of an elaborate and layered defensive system. In the past, the Belgian, British, and French Armies were rightly fixated on offensive and not defensive operations. But since the shock of *Friedensturm*, the one that almost drove them into the Channel, the British had built up their defenses until the Americans could be thrown into battle.

Like the Germans, the British defenses when we got there were some twelve miles deep and the successive defense works were designated as the Green, Purple, Brown, and Red Lines. The Green Line was the outpost line, nearest to the enemy, and, within the British V Corps sector, it was a little east of *Mesnil-Martinsart* and just west of Albert. The Purple Line was the Main Line of Resistance (M.L.R.) in case of a general attack and it ran just east of *Mailly-Maillet*. The Brown Line skirted east of *Forceville*. The final line, the Red Line, passed east of *Louvencourt*.[215] The Brown and Red Lines were planned as rallying points for the army and were intended to delay an advance if worst came to worst, certainly until Army Group reserves arrived. We dared not allow them past the Red Line, as we would have no organized defense beyond it.

"Don't let them pass the Red Line!"

---

[215] *Mesnil-Martinsart* is pronounced "May-nee-Mar-tan-sar," *Mailly-Maillet* is pronounced "May-lee-May-yet," *Forceville* is pronounced "Fors-a-veal," and *Louvencourt* is pronounced "Lou-von-core."

The Green (Outpost) Line was expected to repel a local attack or probe. In case of a general attack, the garrison of the Green Line, which was but four hundred yards behind the Huns' outpost line, was to punish the enemy as long and as much as possible before it withdrew to the Purple or M.L.R. Units from the Purple Line could be sent forward to help stabilize the Green Line. The Brown and Red Lines would stand ready as fallback/rally points in case of an emergency. We Blue Ridge Men were initially placed in the Red or "end-of-the-line" Line and were eventually rotated forward to the Brown, Purple, or Green Lines to gain real-life battle experience without getting our hats handed to us.

In accordance to General Byng's directive, the 318th Infantry and 314th M.G. Battalion were attached to the British V Corps's 17th (Northern) Division in the south, near Albert. The 317th Infantry and 313th M.G. Battalion were attached to the British IV Corps's New Zealand Division in the center. Under the British VI Corps in the north, the 319th Infantry Regiment was attached to the British 2nd Division, and the 320th Infantry and 315th M.G. Battalion went to the famous British Guards Division. In accordance with this general scheme, the British V Corps issued G.O. 3817 on July 5, 1918, relative to the action of our regiment in case of an attack. Extracts from the order are as follows:

In case of attack on the 3rd British Army front the 318th American Regiment will be prepared, on receipt of orders from V Corps H.Q. to:

1. Occupy the Brown Line, allotted by V Corps.

2. Support the Green Line.

3. The 318th American Regiment will reconnoiter the ground in preparation for the above.

4. In case of an attack on the 3d British Army front, the 318th American Regiment will, on receipt of orders from V Corps H.Q., occupy tactical localities in the Brown Line within the V Corps boundaries with:

A. One battalion in each British divisional sector.

B. Three companies of each battalion in the line and one company in reserve.

5. The route will be from BONNEVILLE to BEAUQUESNE. Dry weather tracks will be used as far as possible.

Upon receipt of this order, great activity commenced, and the battalion and company commanders spent days making reconnaissances and working out defensive schemes. When it was learned where each battalion was assigned to a particular sector of the line, the respective regimental H.Q. companies were positioned where they could best aid the regimental commanders' command and control of the entire unit, even though the British were actually "large and in charge."

-Breaking the Monotony-

Despite the need of units for skilled N.C.O.s and specialists, the A.E.F.'s need for officers, especially lieutenants, was even greater. Pershing called upon each division to send a large quota of candidates to the O.T.C. at Langres. In response, Cronkhite, on July 9, instructed his subordinate commanders to send a total of one hundred and twenty-five N.C.O.s to the rigorous course, reporting at Langres on July 30. Each infantry regiment was required to furnish twenty-five candidates, the remainder being drawn from the other units. At the same time, each brigade commander was called upon to select five officers to attend the "Army School of the Line" for two months, beginning on July 15. Those showing ability as staff officers were to be retained as a part of the next staff class, the remainder to return to their commands. Other school details included two officers to the Aerial Observers' School at Tours, mess sergeants to the British Third Army "School of Cookery" at Marconelle, one man from each Infantry regiment to armourers' school and two men from each battalion to the "School of Farriery." Their absences were partly offset by the return of officers and men detailed to various schools from the Samer Training Area. [216]

The Yanks and the Tommies soon became on the best of terms (our uniforms were almost identical for crying aloud!) and entered into friendly competition in many sports. Amongst others, the British V Corps staged a boxing contest at Toutencourt, in which this regiment took third place in spite of the handicap of boxing under regulations very different from those to which our men were accustomed.

On Sunday, July 14, Bastille Day, Pershing ordered that the great French holiday would be celebrated by American soldiers as "a day for competitive platoon drill within the regiments."[217] After an all-day competition in the rain, the following platoons from my regiment were declared winners in their respective battalions: 3/D/1/318; 2/H/2/318; 4/M/3/318. Further competition of these three proved 4/M/3/318 the over-all winner. On July 20, 1918, the Blue Ridge Boys held a division-level field-meet north of Doullens, in which all units of the

---

[216] *Tours* is pronounced "Tour" and *Marconelle* is pronounced "Mar-soan-el."

[217] Bastille Day (pronounced "Bass-teel") (or *La Fête Nationale*—the National Celebration) is the French national holiday that commemorates the French Revolution. On July 14, 1789, rebel citizens of Paris, backed by troops, stormed *la Bastille*, freed its political prisoners, and seized the king's arms.

division had contestants. Maj. Gen. George W. Read, commander of the American II Corps, the division and brigade commanders, as well as most other officers of the corps and division acted as spectators. The following were declared winners:

Rifle Platoon: 317th Infantry

Signal Platoon: 319th Infantry

Band: 320th Infantry

Pioneer Platoon: 319th Infantry

One-Pounder Platoon: 319th Infantry

Transportation Platoon: 317th Infantry

Clearly, Col. Cocheu's "Pittsburghese" 319th Infantry Regiment had some strong leaders and soldiers, but we in the "Virginia Never Tires Regiment" didn't come out too shabby, either. For example, for "Best Rifle Platoon," our very own 3/D/318 came in second as did our transportation platoon, part of our supply company. Because I was neither a competitor nor an officer, I did not see the match. On July 23, Cronkhite stressed the importance of platoon level operations to us when he wrote: *"An army, like a chain is only as strong as its weakest links. The platoon is the link in the fighting chain of today…The 80th Division MUST be successful, and its success rests upon its platoons."*[218]

Cronkhite and the Army chain of command was very prescient when they said: "The platoon is the link in the fighting chain today." Under British tutelage and then when committed to combat, we quickly learned that the platoon was in fact the only real level that could actually operate as a unit. As such, every officer, no matter the rank, was essentially a hopped-up platoon leader. The primacy of the platoon also raised the bar not only for lieutenants, but also for N.C.O.s and E.M., as we were the platoon. It would be us, and not Jamerson or Cronkhite, who would be the ones to break the German lines.

-The Great Allied Offensive of 1918-

As was already stated, on July 15, 1918, the Germans launched their last go-for-broke phase of *Friedensturm* between Soissons and Rheims along *les Chemin des Dames* (soon to be called "the Marne Salient"). *Die Stosstruppen* knew that they would be facing the Americans now, too, soldiers not exhausted from four years of war and who had every military resource at their

---

[218] As cited to Stultz, 225.

disposal—especially food. The Germans also knew that they no longer held numerical superiority—that this was all or nothing. As such, *der Kaisers Feldgrau* armies advanced across the same fields with the same reckless abandon as they had in 1914, but, like in 1914, they were met by a fleshy wall of French *Poilu* and American Doughs, and were stopped dead in their tracks.[219] At the time, there were 26 American divisions in France, each twice the size of a European division (i.e., a total of 52 French, British, or German divisions). Besides the seven divisions in the line or near the Marne Salient, five were holding quiet sectors in the east, five, like us, were behind the British lines, five were in training areas, two in depots, and two had just arrived. As such, seventeen were available for service at the front (including us). It was well that we were on hand, for Allied reserves were down to the danger point.

On July 18, with the Germans once again stopped along the Marne, *Maréchal de France Ferdinand Foch* ordered the armies of the Associated Powers to assume the offensive. Unlike "Papa" Joffre or *Maréchal de France Henri Petain*, who wished to wait until 1919 when we Americans would have arrived in enough strength to launch a decisive bone-crushing counter-attack, Foch resolved to attack now, while the "Hun with the Gun was on the Run" after his failed *Friedensturm*. Foch would do it with the forces that were on-hand at the time and feed American divisions into the line as they arrived from the training areas. This resolution to attack is what led us to our destiny in the Meuse-Argonne. For others in the A.E.F., it meant the great Aisne-Marne Offensive that eventually collapsed the German Marne Salient between Rheims and Soissons in July-August, 1918.[220] *Reichskanzler Georg, Graff von Hertling* later said: "On July 18, even the most optimistic among us understood that all was lost."[221] *Generalfeldmarschal Paul von Hindenburg*, Germany's General-in-Chief, wrote: "We had been compelled to draw upon a large part of the reserves which we intended to use for the attack in Flanders. This meant the end of our hopes of dealing our long-planned decisive blow at the English Army."[222]

Foch's targets would be the salients or "bulges" in the line, starting with the one between Soissons and Rheims. This particular attack would be known to history as the Aisne-Marne Offensive (because we pushed from the Marne River in the south to the Aisne River in the north, evening the line and killing or capturing thousands of Germans, which was our principal goal).

---

[219] *Feldgrau* or "Field gray" is pronounced "Feld Grough." It is actually a deep forest green with just a hint of gray.

[220] *La Meuse-Argonne* is pronounced "La Mewz-Are-gone" and *Aisne-Marne* is pronounced "Ayn-Marne."

[221] *Reichskanzler* (Imperial Chancellor) Georg, Graff von Hertling is pronounced "Ryks-kanz-ler Gay-org, Groff von He-art-ling." As cited in *A.B.M.C.*, 56.

[222] *A.B.M.C.*, 57.

The best way to attack a salient is by attacking its base and then encircling the enemy soldiers in the tip of the bulge. Foch intended to send a million men and five hundred tanks, which consisted of British Mark Vs or French Saint-Chamonds, Schneiders, or Renault FT-17 "Mosquito" Tanks.[223]

Once the attack was launched, using several American divisions, German forces in the sector, lacking reserve troops and tanks, completely collapsed and retreated. Col. Samuel Rockenbach, commander of the A.E.F.'s Tank Corps, chose to use the French Renault Mosquitoes because he wanted to "swarm" the enemy. He proposed to send as many of these little armored caterpillar tractors forward as possible, overwhelming German anti-tank capabilities with too many targets. Thus the term "swarm." I actually preferred the French Schneider tank, however, because most of its firepower was on the sides, where it would straddle an enemy trench and hose it with enfilade M.G. fire. According to the *M.M.T.*:

> *1204. Tanks. The so-called "tanks," first used by the British Army in the battle of the Somme in September, 1916, are in reality armored caterpillar tractors carrying machine guns and capable of traversing rough ground, smashing down trees and entanglements, and passing across the ground between the opposing trenches over the shell holes made by the opposing artillery. The machinery, guns and crew are contained in an armored body and the two tractor belts extend to full length on either side, being so arranged that the tank can climb a steep slope. From the meager data obtainable it would appear that the tanks carry from four to six machine guns in armored projections built out from the sides. These are provided with revolving shields permitting two guns to fire in any direction at one time. The principle of the tractor is similar to that of those manufactured in the United States and used commercially in reclamation work. The addition of the armored body and guns makes the "military tank." These "tanks" have proven of great value in village fighting, by smashing down barricades and driving machine guns from their positions in cellars and houses. They have also been used with some success in destroying obstacles. The power of these new engines may be judged from their ability to smash down trees six inches in diameter and by means of cables to uproot trees*

---

[223] *Le Saint-Chamond* weighed 23 tons, had a crew of 9, and was armed with a 75-mm field gun and 4 *Hotchkiss* M.G.s; *le Schneider* weighed 13.5 tons, had a crew of 6, and was armed with a 75-mm field gun and 2 *Hotchkiss* M.G.s; *le Renault* weighed but 7 tons, was crewed by a driver and a gunner, and was armed with either a 37-mm field gun or a Colt-Vickers M.G.

as large as fifteen inches in diameter. These "tanks" are proof against rifle and machine gun fire, but are unable to withstand even light artillery.

Included in the Aisne-Marne Offensive were the newly-organized American I and II Corps, which consisted of eight divisions: the 1st (Big Red One), 2nd (Indian), 3rd (Rock of the Marne), 4th (Ivy), 26th (Yankee), 28th (Red Keystone), 32nd (Red Arrow), 42nd (Rainbow), and 77th (Statue of Liberty) Divisions, among the first formations to reach France during the spring-summer of 1918. These divisions, as part of the French Tenth Army, fought and slogged their way north from Chateau-Thierry and Bois Belleau, along the Marne, all the way up through Fismette, on the south bank of the Aisne, between Soissons and Rheims.[224]

On July 17, seven bombs were dropped in the main street of Beauval by a Hun plane seeking the warehouses and railroad station a quarter-mile distant. The only casualties were civilian, three women and one man killed and a small home demolished. A baby buried in the ruins miraculously escaped injury. Capt. Robert Luce, regimental dental surgeon of the 305th Engineers and other members of the regiment also had narrow escapes. It was later reported that the aeroplane was shot down near Doullens. On soldier from the 317th Infantry remembered:

First time Boche planes were actually over our heads. Air raid about 11:00 P.M., awakened by anti-aircraft guns. Plane flying very low, circling above our billets and shooting tracer bullets at searchlights and anti-aircraft batteries that were located on the edge of the town (Doullens). Instead of taking to cover in the shallow trenches dug in the garden in back of the school building, or going into the shelters built in the basement for this purpose, the whole outfit piled out into the street to see what was going on—a distinctive characteristic of the Americans, and one that contributed largely to our success. This inquisitiveness went so far that one non-commissioned officer stuck his head out thru the skylight with a lighted candle to get a better look at the plane... Air raids were frequent during our stay in the "back areas," but were not as bad as often described. At least, this was true in our case; other outfits whose luck was different might estimate them differently... It is a weird experience at first to hear the motors whirring overhead and try to figure which sounds are "Jerry" and which are British; then to hear the low boom of the "Archies" and the rattle of M.G.s, punctuated by the heavy boom of the "eggs" themselves. A person is a

---

[224] *Fismette* is pronounced "Fis-met."

little nervous, wondering how close they are going to drop, but the space we occupied was such a small proportion of the space available that we could hardly imagine our luck being bad enough to get them. After the first two or three fairly distant raids, most of the men would merely wake up, curse a little, and go back to sleep.[225]

Throughout the rest of the month, changes in the officer personnel of the 318th Infantry continued. Due to some leadership concerns, Maj. Robert Halpin, commanding 1/318th Infantry, was reassigned as division deputy Q.M. In his place was put Capt. Senius Raymond, who was the regimental operations officer. Almost all of the men preferred Raymond more, as he was far more down-to-earth, practical, brave, and fit. Maj. Halpin was just a little too nervous and brainy to be a line officer. As division deputy Q.M., however, he performed outstandingly. Capt. Corvan Fisher, our adjutant, was transferred to the American II Corps, which was deployed further south, in Lorraine. Capt. Vivian Douglas of D/318th Infantry was sent to the prestigious Army General Staff College in Chaumont, Pershing's H.Q. He was replaced by Capt. Earnest Nunn, who had been our regimental supply officer. In the Army, most officers came to feel "like a rolling stone, which perhaps may gain no moss, but certainly acquires a lot of polish!" But for us E.M., we not only grew moss, but trees!

---

[225] As cited in Stultz, 419.

Rolling to Picardy in a 40 or 8. High living!

The 320th Infantry disembarks in Picardy to fight alongside Byng's British army.

"Chateau Henencourt: A half mile from the Jerry lines in the Arras Sector near Albert. 9-22-18."

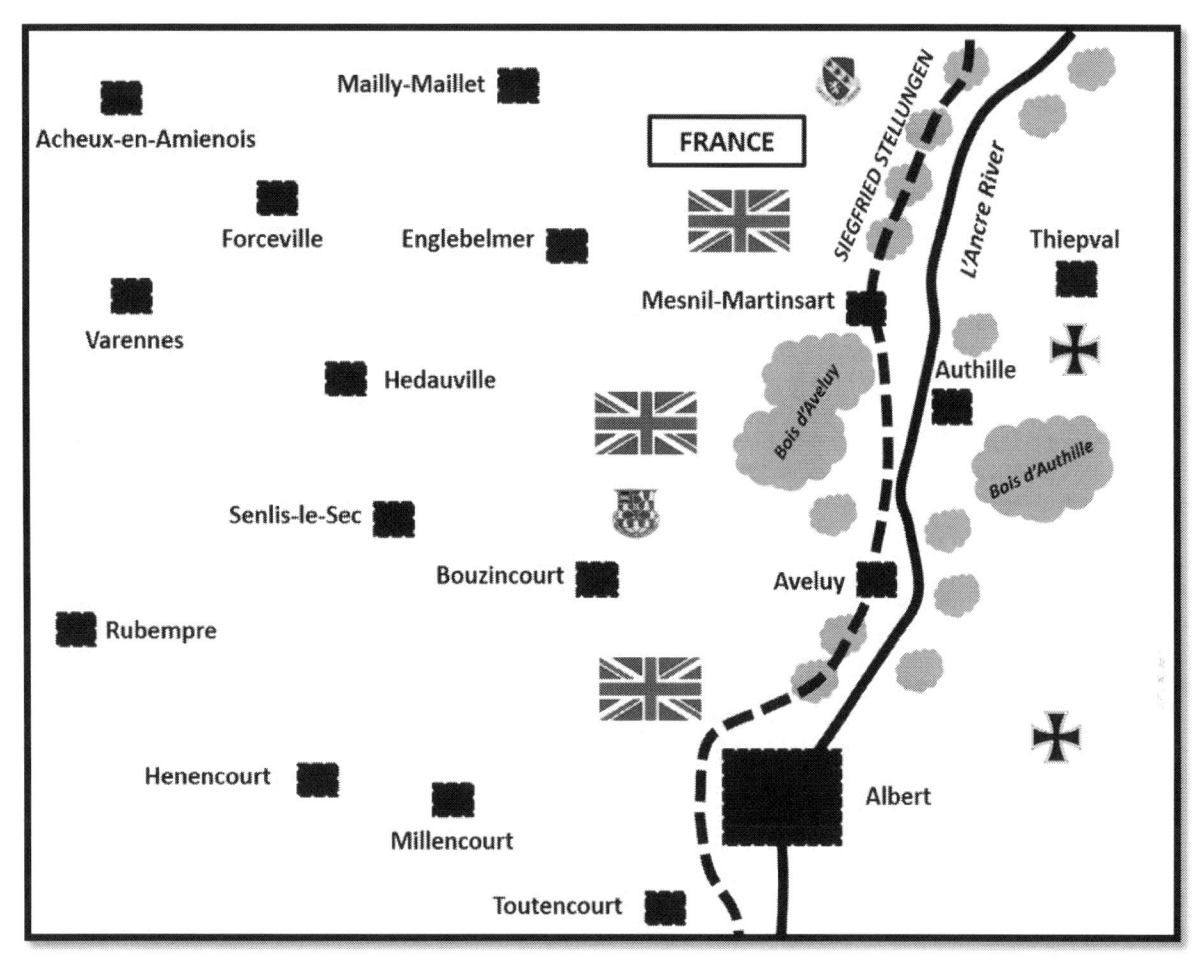

159th Inf. Bde. Area of Operations in Picardy, July-Aug., 1918. The 317th Infantry is in the north and the 318th Infantry is in the south.

"From the top of this hill we could see our shells exploding in the German lines. 7-22-18." Looking across the flat and fat farmland-turned-battlefield of northern France (L) and the Ancre River, just north of Albert (R).

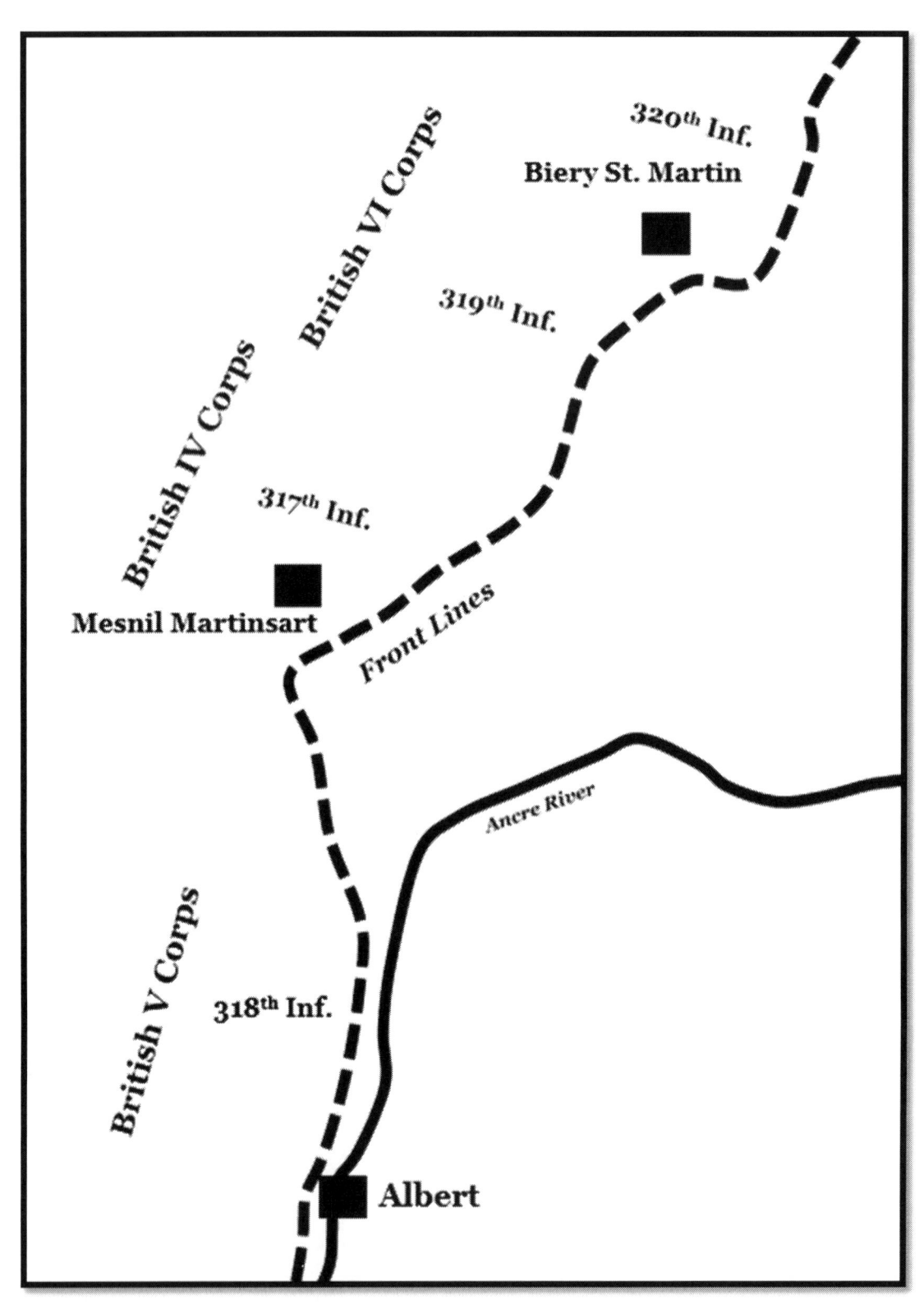

80th Division positions "Up the Line" with Byng's British Third Army at Albert, France, Aug., 1918.

Chapter 12
Up the Line with the British in Picardy (July 22-Aug. 18, 1918).

<u>July 22-26, 1918</u>.

On July 22, 1918, the 318th Infantry and other units of the division passed at last from a long (too long!) period of training in the back areas to our first experience "Up the Line." The transition was effected gradually.[226] In general terms the training of American combat units serving with the British in France was divided into three phases, as follows:

A. Training behind the lines.

B. Training in the lines by attachment of individuals, of platoons, and of battalions, to British units.

C. Training in the lines by attachment of regiments to British units. Our division, however, never reached the third phase because we were pulled out of the line to reinforce the American 1st Army at *Saint-Mihel* (*infra*).

"Old Virginia Never Tires" placard attached to one of our Supply/318th Infantry wagons. Each division had hundreds of this type of G.S. wagon.

I've included extracts from a letter to Maj. Gen. Adelbert Cronkhite from the Adjutant-General, American II Corps, dated July 15, 1918, which outlined the conditions of the service of the division while in the line with the British from July 22-Aug. 19, 1918:[227]

---

[226] In the final analysis, the long training period was the right thing to do. Units cannot be "over trained." The fear was that if we Americans were sent into combat too soon, we would have been eaten up and spat out by the Hun and all of the training and equipping that had gone into us, would have been for naught. When we were finally unleashed in the summer-autumn of 1918, however, it was decisive.

[227] As cited in *318th Infantry*,

1-1

FIRST ARMY.

SECOND CORPS.

AMERICAN EXPEDITIONARY FORCES.

15 July 1918.

It is contemplated that the units of your division, in case there be no further interruption, will complete the first phase of training with the British [Phase "A"] on 22 July, 1918. Under present agreements between British and American General Headquarters, the tactical control of your organizations will rest with the British commanders of higher units during Phases "B" ad "C" and at any time in case any emergency arises. In brief, Phase "B" covers service in the line by battalions, and phase "C" by regiments. In view of the situation now existing on your front, the exact time and method of passing from Phase "B" to Phase "C" cannot be laid down, and detailed arrangements as to the service must be determined to a considerable extent by circumstances as they arise. It is understood between these headquarters and the British authorities that in general American organizations shall serve with their organization complete and in accordance with the general principles established by American methods of training and table of organization. The regiment when serving as an organization will have with its headquarters, supply, and machine gun companies. All units will invariably serve under the command of their own officers. The normal method of attachment in the line will be by first sending up officers and enlisted men for short periods of about 48 hours; then by complete platoons for periods not exceeding three days; then by complete companies for similar periods; and finally by battalions and regiments, the total time to aggregate from five to six weeks.

2-2

It is, however, desirable that if conditions permit the attachment by platoon be limited to tours of 48 hours, the attachment of companies be eliminated, and that Periods "B" and "C" be merged where practicable. The situation at the time may be such that variation from either of the above methods will be advisable, in which case the question shall be taken up with these headquarters.

It is probable that all your units may not be in the line at the same time and that in executing the part allotted to you of the defensive scheme of the British Army to which you are attached, it will be necessary for you in case of a hostile attack to utilize under your command a part or all of your division, depending upon the disposition of your units at the time...

Lorries and busses will report at 1 P.M., 23 July, 1918, for American personnel and proceed to H.Q. British 17th Division at TOUTENCOURT. A similar number of empty Lorries and busses will be at the disposal of 318th American Regiment on 25 July, 1918, for the second party for attachment.

British 17th Division will make all arrangements for Lorries and busses to proceed from TOUTENCOURT to the debussing point, and will supervise the debussing on both dates and the embossing on both dates and the embossing of the returning party on 25 July, 1918.

During this period, each platoon of each American battalion will be attached as a platoon to a company of the British 17th Division. These attachments will be synchronized as far as possible with the British reliefs except that no American platoon will be in the line for more than 4 days.

Further guidance for our "Up the Line" rotation came from the American II Corps H.Q. on July 15:

> *Under present agreements between British and American G.H.Q., the tactical control of your organizations will rest with the British commanders of higher units during Phases "B" and "C"; and at any time in case any emergency arises. In brief, Phase "B" covers service in the line by battalions, and Phase "C" regiments. In view of the situation now existing on your front, the exact time and method of passing from Phase "B" to Phase "C" cannot be laid down, and detailed arrangements as to the service must be determined to be a considerable extent by the circumstances as they arise. It is understood between these H.Q. and the British authorities that in general American organizations shall serve with their organization complete and in accordance with the general principles established by American methods of training and tables of organization. The regiment when serving as an organization will have with it its H.Q., Supply, and M.G. Companies. All units will without exception serve under the command of their own officers...The normal method of attachment in the line will be by first sending up officers and enlisted men for short periods of about 48 hours; then by complete platoons for periods not exceeding three days; then by complete companies for similar periods; and finally, by battalions and regiments, the total time to aggregate from five to six weeks... It is, however, desirable that if conditions permit the attachment by platoon be limited to tours of 48 hours, the attachment of companies eliminated, and that Periods "B" and "C" be merged where practicable. The situation at the time may be such that variation from either of the above methods will be advisable, in which case the question shall be taken up with these H.Q...It is probable that all your units may not be in the line at the same time and that in executing the part allotted to you of the defensive scheme of the British Army to which you are attached, it will be necessary for you in case of a hostile attack to utilize under your command a part or all of your division, depending upon the disposition of your units at the time. A representative, from G-3, whose H.Q., will, in consultation with your H.Q. and the H.Q. of the British 3rd Army, arrange the necessary details for the inauguration and carrying out Phases "B" and "C"...Upon completion of Phases*

> *"B" and "C," the division will be at the disposal of the Commander-in-Chief, American E. F., and instructions concerning it will be issued later.*[228]

As per above, the 318th Infantry moved to the forward zone of Rubempre and, for the first time, entered the "Precautionary Gas Zone" (in which the gas mask must always be kept on the person). The soldiers of the division, myself included, arrived in the "forward areas" in high spirits, feeling sure that at last we were to have a chance at *les Boche* and do our share in bringing about ultimate victory. The rifle range was located just outside Rubempre on the side of a steep hill, and we did quite a lot of "charging" on the back trenches, where the British had "Chinese Coolies" digging trenches and putting up barbed wire entanglements. While here, we gained actual hands-on knowledge about the anatomy of the trench. Trenches had several parts: revetments, latrines, dummy trenches, communication (or approach) trenches, firing trenches, look outs, overhead cover, etc. One soldier from the 319th Infantry remembered his advance into the forward area this way:

> *Excitement ran high early July 22, when call to arms was sounded at 4:00 A.M., and a hike of 25 kilos was made to La Cauchie…where we were finally billeted in an old English camp. Frequent practice trips were made to old trenches nearby for further training purposes, and every day we were getting nearer the front and by this time well used to the continuous roar of the big guns. We were now carrying our gas masks in the "Alert" position, as we were in the "danger zone." The move from Bouquemaison to Cauchie, a shell torn town not far from Arras, was accomplished on foot. Not many will soon forget that hike along the Arras road on a hot, sultry July day, with the sun beating down on the men struggling with their heavy packs. It was not without interest, however, as the hike took the company past innumerable aeroplane sheds with their bombing planes going to and from the lines, past the immense sausage observation balloons they had so long seen from afar, and countless ammunition dumps stacked high with powerful explosives, gas shells, grenades, barbed wire, dugout timber and duck boards for trenches… All wells along the road were mined for destruction in case of retreat, and every tree on the Arras road was cut and mined in such a way as to fall across the road and form an impassable barrier to the Boche in case of necessity. Trenches were numerous and barbed wire was everywhere. All was ready for the retreat that never*

---

[228] As cited in Stultz, 225.

came. One month later found the Boche promenading "tout de suite" the other way.[229]

A soldier from the 320th Infantry similarly remembered:

We left Beaudricourt at 9:00 A.M. in the forenoon of July 22, marching with light packs, the heavy rolls being carried on trucks. At half-past one we reached our destination, Bavincourt, about one kilometer to the left of the great Doullens-Arras Road, and about fifteen kilometers from the British front—not within range of the guns, but within the area of active operations of the Boche aeroplanes… Bavincourt was just behind the British lines and had been used apparently for three or four years for the quartering of fighting troops and therefore had barracks, horse lines, dugouts…gun shops to which disabled Artillery came to be repaired, and machine shops for work of all kinds. And besides, when the big Doullens-Arras road was under fire, the main line of traffic to and from the front was through Bavincourt. It was a busy, busy place. My men had a fairly comfortable situation in six low frame buildings, about twenty feet wide and about fifty feet long, which had been erected by the British three or four years before. There were deep trenches along the sides of these buildings, into which it was assumed the men would jump in case of an air attack… Within fifty feet of these buildings, there was also an immense dugout, perhaps forty feet deep, hewn out of the chalk that underlies the soil of northern France, and said to be large enough to accommodate an entire battalion of 1,000 men… The officers were quartered in the up side of the town in little long buildings, some in the shape of Nissen Huts and others with quaint little low mansard roofs… We secured from the British "Town Major" some cots with wooden frames and canvas bottoms, and on these, with the assistance of our bedding-rolls, we made fairly comfortable beds. We secured from him also some tables and benches for our mess. It was here again that the American officers were struck with the genius of the British organization in its consideration for the natural needs and wants of men, even in the military service. There seems to be an impression in certain American quarters that all you have to do to make a soldier is to give a man a rifle and some rations and a couple of blankets and send him out to fight. But the British government knows, and its system carries that knowledge unfalteringly into practice, that a soldier is still a human being,

---

[229] As cited in Stultz, 226-27.

that he needs an occasional bath, that he needs amusement once in a while...a table and a bench at mealtime.[230]

During this time, we slept in our bivis that were dug into the ground about 15", with our pup tents stretched over them. This was done to insure safety from the enemy air attack. We enjoyed the stay here very much and regretted to leave, but, oh, boy, when it rained, the mud! Just about two miles southwest of us was a nice little town called Talmas.[231] According to Col. Moss, the "Principles Governing Selection of Camp Sites" is as follows:

M.M.T. 1230. The following basic principles govern in the selection of camp sites:

(a) The water supply should be sufficient, pure, and accessible.

(b) The ground should accommodate the command with as little crowding as possible, be easily drained, and have no stagnant water within 300 yards.

(c) There should be good roads to the camp and good interior communication.

(d) Camps sites should be so selected that troops of one unit need not pass through the camp of another to reach their own camp.

(e) Wood, grass, forage, and supplies must be at hand or obtainable.

(f) In campaign, tactical considerations come first in the selection of camp sites, capability of defense being especially considered, and, as a result, troops may have to camp many nights on objectionable ground.

(g) However, sanitary considerations must always be given all the weight possible consistent with the tactical requirements. Through no fault of their own, troops occupying an unsanitary site may suffer greater losses than in the battles of a long campaign.

For us, point (f) "tactical considerations come first in the selection of camp sites, capability of defense being especially considered, and, as a result, troops may have to camp many nights on objectionable ground" was the rule of thumb and point (b) "no stagnant water within 300 yards," especially with all of the shell craters, was almost impossible.

As we settled in around Rubempre, the regiment's M.G. Company finally joined us but was attached to the brigade's 314th M.G. Battalion for training. The M.G. sections were critical to our future success. As was already stated, they were armed with water-cooled M1915 Colt-Vickers 30.06 M.G.s, sometimes called "American Vickers." They were taught how to move

---

[230] As cited in Stultz, 227-28.

[231] *Talmas* is pronounced "Tall-mass."

forward with the infantry and to deliver direct "grazing fire" or indirect "plunging fire," how to establish "interlocking fields of fire" in the defense (in which they'd become the principal weapon system on the line), and how to draw up range cards, etc. Remember, M.G.s are meant to fire "up and down" in a straight line at different ranges ("moving the cone") and not "side-to-side" like sometimes stupidly shown in the movies. Because their guns, ammunition, and gear were carried in mule-towed Baltic carts, we generally and affectionately called the M.G. sections the "Jack-Ass Artillery."

On July 25, during a gas attack, seven N.C.O.s of I/3/320th Infantry were disfigured when a noxious German shell landed directly in their bivy while they were asleep. The members of this detachment were 1Sgt. Walter I. Barnhart, Sgts. Charles J. Johnson, Victor R. Mowry, and George T. Smith, and Cpls. Warren J. Cassidy, Edward J. Donnelly and George Gemperlein. The gas wounds appeared in the form of burns on the body, in the eyes, and in the lungs. The advance parties from the 317th and 318th Infantry, however, returned from their front line baptism without casualties.

On July 26, 1918, the popular commander of 2/318, Maj. Charles Sweeny, was assigned as our regimental operations officer and Maj. Jennings Wise took his place as commander of 2/318. On that same day, we finally received the green light to start sending platoons forward to operate with the British in the front lines. The concept of the operation was as follows:

1. "Phase B" will start on 28 July, 1918 and be completed no later than 7 August, 1918.

2. During this period, each platoon of each American battalion will be attached to a British company in the line.

3. Particular attention will be paid to instruction in patrolling; patrols from American troops will be sent out with experienced men from the British Army.

4. Each American platoon will bring two Lewis Guns.

5. Pioneer platoons of the Regimental H.Q. Company will be attached to field companies from the Royal Engineers, under arrangement between the Royal Engineers and the American 305th Engineer Regiment/80th Division.

6. The Sappers and Bombers Platoon of H.Q. Company, 318th Infantry Regiment (equal to the British Light Trench Mortar Battery) will be divided into two parties of one officer and 24 E.M.

7. No Stokes Mortars will be brought.[232]

---

[232] As cited in *318th Infantry*, 42-43.

In accordance to this order, units from my regiment were attached to the British front-line divisions as follows: platoons from 2/318 and sections from the regiment's signal and medical platoons reported to the British 17th (Northern) Division July 27-31, platoons from 3/318 and sections from the regiment's signal and medical platoons reported July 31-August 1, and platoons from 1/318th Infantry and sections from the regiment's signal and medical platoons reported August 8-12, 1918. While my battalion waited our turn "Up the Line" with the British Northern Division, schools for teaching the tactical use of all weapons in the attack continued and all training was aimed at keeping the aggressive spirit. In fact, the very idea of us being thrown into the defensive occured to no one. All knew that it was President Wilson's desire to have the American Army posted in Lorraine along the Moselle River and to attack straight into the Germany until the Kaiser screamed, "Uncle Sam!"

We rehearsed our "square formations" as best we could. Remember, everything in the American Army was based on fours. Each platoon, a "combat group," consisted of four squads. The 1st Squad was the "Bomber Squad" that had twelve "bombers," or soldiers armed with hand grenades. The 2nd Squad was the "Assault Squad," which had seventeen men who were extra-adept with the rifle and bayonet, the 3rd Squad was the "A.R. Squad" with sixteen soldiers and four A.R..s, and the 4th Squad was the and the "R.G. squad," which consisted of eight soldiers and four R.G.s. I belonged to the 3rd Squad or the A.R. Squad. Led by a corporal, the A.R. Squad had two A.R. teams of one automatic rifleman (A.R.), one assistant gunner (A.G.), and two ammunition carriers (A.C.s) per team. My four-man team consisted of A.R. Joe Riddle (me), A.G. Albert Getz, and A.C.s Boss Atkins and Wort Wise. We A.R. men were armed with British Lewis Guns and the A.G.s and A.C.s were armed with British S.M.L.E.s and carried several drum magazines to "help feed the pig."

It is my understanding that it was Maj. Gen. Charles Summeral, the officer who was sent over on the Baker Commission to represent the artillery branch and who later commanded an artillery brigade, an infantry division, and, later, a army corps, who pushed Pershing for the four A.R.-teams-per-platoon concept. The Germans, who were known masters of the M.G. (in fact one can not even imagine the war without a German Maxim M.G. crew rattling away from a fortified position), were not that interested in utilizing A.R.s. They had one, the L.M.G. 15 or "Bergman Gun," which was invented by Theodor Bergmann Waffenbau, but just didn't use it much.

It was also reiterated to us before we went "Up the Line" that the Germans were dug-in with elaborate "Skeleton Key" trench formations. These formations were constructed in late 1917 far-behind the forward Hun lines. Collectively, this network was called *das HINDENBURG*

STELLUNG or "the Hindenburg Line" and it had at least four belts, each with a code-name that was drawn from a character from *das Nibelungenlied* ("Magic Mist People's Legend") that Richard Wagner made famous with his "Ring" operas. Examples of the code-names are "*SIEGFRIED*," the great Germanic warrior-king-of-kings, "*KRIEMHILDE*," his wife, and "*BRUNHILDE*," their Valkrie nemesis. Once completed, the Germans pulled back to the Hindenburg Line in early 1918 in order to better concentrate their forces for *Unternehmen Friedensturm*. Granted, during the late-offensive, they constructed new lines, like the ones here at Albert, but *HINDENBURG* was out there, with its skeleton key angles.[233]

The biggest reason why the German defensive lines were so hard to take, aside from being well-planned out and resourced, was because of how their M.G.s (and their cones) were positioned. On the inside of each "box" of the key was a fortified M.G. nest or dug-out, which fired across the front of another M.G. position. In this way, they had "interlocking fields of fire." Parallel to the M.G. cone of fire was a line of wire that was to "channel" the enemy (i.e., us) right into the barrels of said M.G. So, as we got caught up on a wire, trying to cut, dig, or bite our way through, a Hun M.G. would simply squirt cones of enfilade fire into us, cutting us in two. Add to that the mortars and artillery which preceded the M.G.s and you'll get the gist of it. Between the M.G. nests or dug-outs were Hun riflemen in a linear trench, who took long or short-range shots from multiple angles. The "school solution" to breach this type of line was to get a tank to blast through the defensive wire, straddle a trench, and then blast it with enfilading M.G. fire. Around it would sweep the bomber and the assault squads.

If no tank was to be had, which was usually the case, the bombers, equipped with sharp wire cutters, would get as close to the enemy position as possible. Once it was stopped, the platoon leader would order the A.R. and R.G. squads to move to the left or right of the bombers and lay down suppressive fire. While the A.R.s shot into the targeted M.G. nest embrasure, the R.G.s would lay down smoke, masking the enemy gunners' sight.

Sometimes we would lead with the assault squad, however, and once they were pinned, the Bombers would either move through them or to their left or right.

Either way, once the platoon leader determined that fire superiority was achieved, he would lead the attack. The bombers would charge forward to about twenty yards from the enemy trench, take a knee, and hurl all of their grenades.

---

[233] *HINDENBURG STELLUNG* is pronounced "Hin-den-burg Schtel-lung," *das Nibelungenlied* is pronounced "Daws Neebel-oon-gun-leed," *Siegfried* is pronounced "Zig-freed," *Kriemhilde* is pronounced "Cream-hild-ah," and *Brunhilde* is pronounced "Broon-hil-da." Das *Niebelungenlied* or "Legend of the Magical Mist People" is an ancient Germanic story about the warrior king-of-kings *Siegfried* (Peace Through Victory) who died at the hands of his supposed friends with a knife in the back. Many have called him the "German Achilles."

Boom!

Boom!

Boom!

After that, the assault squad, led personally by the P.L., would push forward and take the position with rifle and bayonet. As the P.L and the assault and bomber squads swept over the objective, the P.G. would follow, bringing up the A.R. and R.G. squads to help hold it.

If fire superiority could not be achieved by his own weapons, the platoon leader was to wait for supporting weapons, like M.G.s, I.G.s, or even 75mm Field Guns to come forward to reinforce the A.R.s and R.G.s. Under no circumstances was the platoon leader order the charge until fire superiroty was achived.

But due to the terror of combat, this didn't always happen.

Once a platoon-sized hole in the enemy line was made, the company, battalion, and regimental commanders would send the rest of their respective commands through the breach like milk through a straw. If there was no tank support, then we Doughs would have to take out three M.G. positions on our own. Once through the first line, we'd then have to defeat enemy infantry platoons launching counterattacks against us! Once those were repelled, we'd have to breach another skeleton key line that was in a "lazy-W" formation. "Wash, rinse, repeat" most of us said.

Given this gruesome situation, how many of us were going to make it home?

The first units to move "Up the Line" from America's Blue Ridge Division were platoons from Spalding's 305th Engineers. They were sent up to repair or construct portions of the British trench system from which the Germans could frequently be seen in their trenches on the other side of desolate "No Man's Land." Reconnaissance and night wiring parties were also sent out regularly, and in general they performed the same duties as the British troops holding the sector. The Engineers were under fire almost daily and quite often experienced heavy shelling, particularly B/305th Engineers near Senlis, D/1/305th Engineers at Bayencourt, and F/2/305th Engineers that was in a sector known as "Pigeon Wood."[234] During this period, the engineers were brigaded with Australian and New Zealander troops (called British Commonwealth Troops), who often staged trench raids to keep the enemy off its kilter, as the Scots would say. One Blue Ridge engineer remembered:

> *We were now getting within hailing distance of the well and most unfavorably known Western Front. Far across the flat country, we could see the British balloons and could always hear the rumble of the ever active artillery. After*

---

[234] *Senlis* is pronounced "Soan-lee" and *Bayencourt* is pronounced "Buy-yen-core."

some more training, we marched out, fully equipped, straight for the front, the regimental band giving us a send-off. After a hard march, a battalion of us pulled up…less than five miles from the front, with the observation balloons directly over our heads. Arras was a few kilometers north, and Amiens about fifteen km south. Another German push was imminent, and we worked at a huge, complex system that formed the second line of defense, digging new trenches, wiring, revetting, making sumps and shelters, and various other tasks. Far away, the German balloons could easily be seen. Several times we saw them burned by some enterprising British aviator, but the Germans were no less skilled at that game and managed to keep the score at least even. One morning, while we were all busy on the top of a hill in front of Louvencourt, there was a long, wailing whistle and a terrific thump, and I had seen my first shell burst in a corral about five hundred yards off. There was a great hustle and bustle while the "Tommies" removed all horses from it, several more shells exploding harmlessly inside it. Every night, we listened to the rumble and roar of a barrage somewhere, but still felt that we were not seeing war. Even the guns, while not far ahead, were hidden from us. The closer we drew, the more eager we became, and not a man of us but wanted to get into the front trench within the shortest possible time.[235]

July 27-31, 1918.
On the night of July 27/28, 2/318th Infantry was the first battalion of our regiment to enter the lines by platoons with the "trench garrison" of the 17th British (Northern) Division between Mesnil-Martinsart and Albert.[236] For whatever reason, the men of the Northern Division decided to call us in the 318th Infantry "Squirrels" and each battalion was code-named a different squirrel: 1/318 was called the "Red Squirrels" (we had red rectangles on our helmets), 2/318 the "Grey Squirrels," and 3/318 the "Flying Squirrels." I think the color of squirrel aligned with the color of shape we had on our helmets. I don't think they were being insulting, but sardonic, as they no doubt heard some of our "Joe Latrinskys" tell stories of hunting squirrels in the Blue Ridge. As a unit, we rarely ever called ourselves the "Red Squirrels," however, as we were mostly wedded to our helmet shapes and colors. I know that I never did! I aint no squirrel! All that I

---

[235] As cited in Stultz, 221.

[236] Pronounced "Law-awn" and "Mez-nee Martin-saw."

know is that we in 1/318th Infantry preferred to be called the "Red Squares," 2/317th Infantry the "White Diamonds," etc.[237] The Northern Division, the English Tommies who gave us our sardonic "Squirrel" moniker, had three Infantry brigades, the 50th, 51st, and 52nd Brigades, which were organized as follows:

50th Inf. Brig.

    6th Battalion, Dorsetshire Regiment

    7th Battalion, East Yorkshire Regiment

    7th Battalion, Princess of Wales's Own Regiment

    7th Battalion, York and Lancaster Regiment

    10th Battalion, Prince of Wales's Own Regiment

51st Inf. Brig.

    4th Battalion, Queen's Own Regiment

    7th Battalion, Lincolnshire Regiment

    7th Battalion, Border Regiment

    8th Battalion, South Staffordshire Regiment

    10th Battalion, Sherwood Foresters

52nd Inf. Brig.

    9th Battalion, West Riding Regiment (Duke of Wellington's)

    9th Battalion, Northumberland Fusiliers

    10th Battalion, Lancashire Fusiliers

    12th Battalion, Manchester Regiment

British regiments and brigades were organized differently from American ones. To them, "the regiment" was the ceremonial, administrative component of the army that didn't actually deploy. What "the regiment" did do, however, was raise, equip, and train fighting battalions to be attached to deployed or "field" brigades, which were equivalent to our brigades, just a little smaller. For example, while our American 159th Inf. Brig. had six battalions, the 50th British Inf. Brig. had five: the 6th Battalion, Dorsetshire Regiment, the 7th Battalion, East Yorkshire Regiment, the 7th Battalion, Alexandra, Princess of Wales's Own, and the 7th Battalion, York and Lancaster Regiment, and the 10th Battalion, Prince of Wales's Own Regiment. Each battalion, although acknowledging their existence within the 50th Inf. Brig., saw it as a temporary condition. When we met the Tommies, they'd say that they were with the "Princess of Wales's Regiment," etc. At first we were confused as we thought that they had three battalions in the

---

[237] Young, Rush, S. *Over the Top with the 80th, by a Buck Private* (N.P., 1933). Pvt. Rush was also a member of B/1/318th Infantry.

Princess of Wales's Regiment, but soon learned that they were simply one battalion from the Princess of Wales's Regiment, which was currently assigned to the 50th British Inf. Brig., etc. It is a very interesting system, actually. And when the Tommies say "7th Battalion," it doesn't necessarily mean that there are seven battalions floating around either, but that it's the seventh battalion from that regiment to be activated for war. If the 7th Battalion got wiped out (which sometimes happened during the Great War), then the regiment, headquartered somewhere in Britain or Ireland, would raise, equip, and train the new 8th Battalion. This of course wasn't always the case because some regiments did deploy multiple fighting battalions during a war, but it is a general rule. Our American system is actually more bureaucratic, regimented, and mathematical.

The 320th Infantry, the northern-most unit of the 80th Division posted along the line, was paired with the famous British Guards Division, a top-notch unit. Then-Capt. Asbhy Williams of the 320th Infantry remembered:

That night the Grenadier Guards were relieved by the Coldstream Guards, the former having completed its six days' tour in the forward zone. There was great rivalry (friendly, of course) between these Guards. To hear them tell it, the Coldstream Guards were raised "during the Time of King Solomon." They called the Grenadier Guards "the Infants" because they were "only raised during the time of Charles II." The discipline and efficiency of the Guards were wonderful. A soldier only answers, "Sir," when spoken to by an officer, no matter what is said to him, unless in time of war other words are necessary for military efficiency and then he uses as few words as possible. Colonel Thorne said that in time of peace, for example, if a guard were asked what he thought of a parade he would only answer, "Sir," and denote by his tone and expression whether, in his opinion, the parade was good or bad. And they were manly, calm men, every one five feet eleven or over and all with mustaches. It was very fortunate for our men—and our officers—that they should have been under the instruction of the best organizations in the British Army.[238]

Another soldier from the 320th Infantry remembered:

One American platoon was joined to each British company, so that a company was with a battalion, and the battalion was spread over an entire brigade. It was an ideal arrangement by which we could get the experience of doing the job

---

[238] As cited in *1/320th Infantry*, 38.

instead of merely observing it, while at the same time avoiding as yet the independent responsibility for the defense of the sector. Each platoon spent part of its tour in the reserve or support, and part in the front line...We joined the Coldstream Guards lieutenant, who was attached to us as adviser, in the old Hun dugout, which was indeed worthy of admiration, both for its safety and comfort...The Americans have suffered from their failure to expend enough labor on protection. Perhaps it was to our advantage that we never got the dugout habit, or we might not have been so successful in the later open warfare, but there were times when we might well have done more...Each man slung over his shoulders a pair of sand-bags filled with food, carried his arms and ammunition as well, and then for a long haul through the mud and darkness to the front line, with the potential shelling always a mental factor even when they were not actually dropping near us. Then long stretches of trench, with the bulky bags bumping on the curves, before we reached the right platoon; then back again to the sunken road, wondering several times if we were on the right track. No casualties, not terribly dangerous, but exhausting, nerve-wearing, generally mean. The fights we were in, we will talk about the rest of our lives, but the thought of some of our night working parties arouses all that is ugliest in our dispositions...The next night found us in the front line, having relieved two platoons of L/320 with little trouble. At last our own outfit was holding its own little section of the long ditch we had heard so much about, and there was not a man who did not feel proud to be there, and feel that he had now reached the point when his life was worthwhile. The men were in the game now, and were willing to play it hard, and every man was determined to show the veteran "Tommies" that we were just as good, if not better. Nevertheless, it was their first night at the front, and many of them were nervous, peering out across "No Man's Land" in readiness for advancing Boche... The evening after the relief had taken place, a patrol to inspect our barbed wire entanglements was decided upon. The necessity was not very great, but we decided it would be well to get used to patrolling before a necessity arose for some more difficult patrol, and the wire was about the nearest objective available. There was a vast difference in one's state of mind about being in the front trench, and being in "No Man's Land." There had been a sort of hoodoo thrown about the latter that it was well to get rid of at once, for in reality it was often safer to be out in front than in some places far behind. Later, in the autumn drives, the hoodoo disappeared, because half the time you didn't know what was "No Man's Land" and what was within your front positions; but in the trench warfare, it seemed to have an especial "spookiness" about it...We notified the platoons on our flanks, so that they would not fire if they saw us, and crawled out over the parapet, being careful not to show our forms above the general line of the dirt. There were five of us altogether: four Yanks and a sergeant of the Irish Guards; three had rifles with fixed bayonet and two had revolvers, while each man carried a bomb in his pocket. We traveled on our bellies, wriggling along like snakes.[239]

While "Up the Line," the first thing we learned was to divine the difference between incoming (enemy) artillery and outgoing (friendly) artillery by the noises they made. Our own "friendly" shells flew leisurely over our heads in large numbers when we were close to the front lines, with an occasional enemy "incoming" shell exploding a safe distance behind us by way of variation. Fortunately for us, friendly ones were in great majority, but enough of them were "again us" to give some valuable practice in learning to differentiate between the two. The difference is almost impossible to describe in words, but easy to learn. An H.E. "contact shell" travelling through the air is often compared to the sound of a fast train passing by. We nicknamed them things like "Express Trains" or "Petersburg Locals." Our own shells, outgoing shells, could be heard from early flight and high above our heads. They would give a sort of rhythmic roar, decreasing in volume. Incoming sounds, on the other hand, would increase in sound, and sound as if the express train were rapidly gaining in speed. The apparent speed of the express train, which is the best sound analogy, shows how close you are to where the shell is going to land. If you hear a roar that is ten times too fast for any train in the world—then dive quick! What I can't fully explain is why the shells that landed nearest were often not heard coming until it was too late to duck. I suppose it was because sound travels more slowly than the shell, which has landed while we were still hearing it in flight. At any rate, there is much truth in that old adage: "You never hear the one that gets you."

We also learned to tell the difference between shrapnel (air explosions that dart hundreds of red-hot shards downward) and H.E. (contact ground explosions). The Germans, for reasons unknown to us, burst their shrapnel munitions at an enormous height, so that they rained down over a large area. Because of this, they left plenty of places untouched, much to our advantage. The British also taught us that shrapnel gives one ample time to dive for cover because the air burst is seen before the metal shards actually hit the ground. The decision a

---

[239] As cited in Stultz, 232.

Dough had to make when it came to shrapnel was to either lie down, giving the shrapnel a larger target on the ground but less of a target in height, or to kneel down. I chose to kneel down with my neck in and my "Anti-Shrapnel Helmet" up. I understood that the Brodie Helmet was specifically-designed to give a Dough more protection from shrapnel (thus the name) if it lay parallel to the horizon. For H.E. or ground explosions, however, everyone chose to dive into the earth (you'll note that I said "into," like Ty Cobb) and stay as flat as possible. In our experience, shrapnel attacks were rare. We estimate that we saw perhaps two hundred H.E. shells churn up the ground to every one shrapnel air burst. And when I say "churn," I mean a giant front-end loader dumping a ton of earth onto you.

Sploosh!

If the explosion didn't get you, you may be buried alive.

It was bad.

Without doubt, the most frightening weapon in the Hun arsenal was the infamous "Whiz-Bang" that was fired from German 77mm Field Guns or "Quick Dicks" that were fired from Austrian 88mm cannon. They were named such because they came in so fast: "Whiz...Bang!" I would add a "Boom!" too: "Whiz-Bang-Boom!" And while we had 81mm mortars invented by Sir Wilfred Stoke of of the British Empire, the Germans had comparable *Grenatenwerfers* (Grenade-throwers) or *Minenwerfers* or (Bomb-throwers) that we called "Minnie-werfers."[240] The Minnies, especially, are terrible weapons. Falling slowly from a high angle, their shells dropped more easily into a trench than an ordinary shell, and during the day, one could actually see *Minenwerfer* projectiles sail through the air (in great wonderment and terror, I might add) like giant blank trash cans. Their concussion alone is terrific, not to mention the scattering of their deadly fragments.

After a few hours at the front, almost every Dough got a handle on the different sounds that artillery projectiles made in flight—to know which ones were "coming" and which ones were "going." Sometimes they crossed and the crashes were simultaneous. On the point about "the one that gets you makes no sound": one generally hears the sound of the explosion of the shell before the hissing shriek of its flight through the air has ceased. Whether the victim hears the shell that kills him can hardly be settled without practical test—and then we would have to wait for Eternity to receive the answer. As described by General Harbord after the war: "The high velocity of the French 75s, the German 77s, and the Austrian 88s carried the shells faster during

---

[240] *Grenatenwerfer* is pronounced "Gren-aat-ten-ver-fer" and *Minenwerfer* is pronounced "Me-nen-ver-fur." *Grenatenwerfers* are equitable to our 81mm Stokes mortars and *Minenwerfers* are equitable to our trench mortars.

a short flight or the initial position of a long flight than the rate at which sound waves travel. But as the range increased, the high curve of the trajectory of the shell made its path longer than that of the sound waves."[241] For example, if you were fired upon from a mile away, there would be no warning sound of the shell's approach. At greater range, the sound of the shell is preceded by its arrival. The time of warning usually varied from practically nothing with the "Whiz-Bangs," to perhaps two seconds with the "Quick Dicks," to as many as five seconds with the heavier calibers. This gave some time to throw one's self flat to the ground or to get into a shell hole or bunker.

During the night, the battle front was illuminated by flares or *Véry* Lights from each side to help staunch effective reconnaissance, wiring, or mine-laying patrols. We infantrymen of course conducted all of these types of patrols. They were all dangerous and they were all in "No Man's Land," which was that contested area between the two lines. Reconnaissance patrols were designed to gather information about enemy troop strength, wiring patrols were sent out to fix or string new defensive wire, and mine-laying patrols did just that: laid mines. Of the three, the wire patrol was the most dangerous as we were the most exposed.

Patrols.

I.D.R. 605. A patrol is a detachment sent out from a command to gain information of the country or of the enemy, or to prevent the enemy from gaining information. In special cases patrols may be given missions other than these.

I.D.R. 606. The commander must have clearly in mind the purpose for which the patrol is to be used in order that he may determine its proper strength, select its leader, and give the latter proper instructions. In general, a patrol should be sent out for one definite purpose only.

I.D.R. 607. The strength of a patrol varies from two or three men to a company. It should be strong enough to accomplish its purpose, and no stronger. If the purpose is to gain information only, a small patrol is better than a large one. The former conceals itself more readily and moves less conspicuously. For observing from some point in plain view of the command or for visiting or reconnoitering between outguards two men are sufficient. If messages are to be sent back, the patrol must be strong enough to furnish the probable number of messengers without reducing the patrol to less than two men. If hostile patrols are likely to be met and must be driven off, the patrol must be strong. In friendly

---

[241] Harbord, 282.

territory, a weaker patrol may be used than would be used for the corresponding purpose in hostile territory.

I.D.R. 608. The character of the leader selected for the patrol depends upon the importance of the work in hand. For patrolling between the groups or along the lines of an outpost, or for the simpler patrols sent out from a covering detachment, the average soldier will be a competent leader.

609. For a patrol sent out to gain information, or for a distant patrol sent out from a covering detachment, the leader must be specially selected. He must be able to cover large areas with few men; he must be able to estimate the strength of hostile forces, to report intelligently as to their dispositions, to read indications, and to judge as to the importance of the information gained. He must possess endurance, courage, and good judgment. His instructions should be full and clear. He must be made to understand exactly what is required of him, where to go and when to return. He should be given such information of the enemy and country as may be of value to him. He should be informed as to the general location of his own forces, particularly of those with whom he may come in contact. If possible, he should be given a map of the country he is to traverse, and in many cases his route may be specified.

An example of an 80th Division patrol report during this period is as follows:[242]

---

[242] As cited in Stultz, 242.

                              80th Division
                                 A.E.F.

On the night of 26-27 July, a patrol of seven other ranks (two of
Auckland, and five U.S.A.) left NAMELESS TRENCH at K.23.b.0.2 and
returned to point of departure.

Time of departure 1 A.M. due to return at 3 A.M.

Object: To keep touch between our front line posts, and night posts in
neighborhood of THE POINT (K.23.b.1.7).

On the return journey, the patrol seems to have missed BLIND ALLEY,
and to have got into PIG TRENCH. They were proceeding up the latter,
and were challenged by an enemy sentry at about K.23.b.7.6. The
location of this place is somewhat doubtful. The Patrol Leader (Corpl.
Roper) shot the sentry and American Private Hall dashed in and killed
three with the bayonet. Three machine guns opened up and bombs were
thrown, and it was clear the enemy were in some strength.
The Patrol scattered, and returned to our trenches. Three are missing-
one of our men two U.S.A. It is impossible to say whether the missing
men are killed or now Prisoners of War.

Upon receipt of the orders conferred, they will be delivered with such
military ceremony as the circumstances of service may permit.

                              By command of Major General Cronkhite:
                                                       W.H. WALDRON.
                                                Colonel, General Staff.
                                                       Chief of Staff.

In spite of considerable activity by both sides, during its period of attachment, 2/318th Infantry had but four men killed and five wounded. These were the first casualties of the regiment during the war. Many more would come. It should have been higher but the British trenches were so well constructed with quite a few reinforced dugouts. Platoons from 3/318 replaced the 2/318 and served "Up the Line" from July 31-Aug. 4, 1918. During this period, 3/318 suffered two killed and seven wounded, including Lt. J.F. Clemmer, Jr., who was mortally wounded and subsequently died in a Canadian hospital in Doullens. We actually came out of the experience saying things like, "that wasn't so bad."

In the rear, on the night of July 31, German aerial raiders shellacked Toutencourt, a town about one-half mile from "Camp Kay," where the division's M.G. battalions were located. The attack killed ten civilians, one French soldier home on leave, two British soldiers on sentry duty, injuring a number of others, and killing ten horses. The next day, members of the division's M.G. battalions helped the French bury their horses and a British officer took charge of digging the remains of the dead out of the wreaked buildings.[243]

Aug. 1-9, 1918.

On the night of Aug. 1, members of the 314th M.G. Battalion who were deployed opposite Albert took part in their first M.G. indirect fire barrage in conjunction with the artillery. The British had arranged a raid against a Hun trench and elements of the 314th M.G. were given to mission to provide fire support for the operation. H-hour was set at 9:10 P.M. and the artillery and M.G. barrage was promptly fired, the M.G.s setting their T&Es to match the range and deflection to target according to the British firing charts. In response, at around 1:30 A.M., the Germans returned fire and "completely destroyed some of the British trenches."[244]

The bombardment of one's position is hell on earth. One feels very helpless (and is). The terror of knowing that you could be ripped into pieces or, worse yet, buried alive, weighed heavily upon all of us—all of the time. I for one never had to experience this level of violence. I was lucky. A few men of the division did, however, and it was bad. The British, French, and Germans all experienced it. Because most of our time in France was in conducting attacks, we had to deal with a different set of terror: that of moving in the open—exposed—to rifle, M.G. and artillery fire.

---

[243] *314th M.G.*, 22.

[244] As cited in *314th M.G.*, 22.

From Aug. 7-9, 1918, it was finally our turn "Up the Line." I think being the last to go was the hardest because of all the waiting. "What if" can really wear a person down. Even worse, the British 38th (Welsh) Division had replaced the British 17th (Northern) Division and we had to work with an entirely new group of people, these troops coming mostly from Wales. The 38th Division had a very distinctive shoulder patch, that of a red-winged dragon, the symbol of Wales (the Kingdom of Wales was officially annexed by the Kingdom of England in 1536 and converted into a principality). The "Welsh Division" had three infantry brigades, organized as follows:

<u>113th Inf. Brig.</u>
    13th Battalion, Royal Welsh Fusiliers
    14th Battalion, Royal Welsh Fusiliers
    15th Battalion, Royal Welsh Fusiliers
    16th Battalion, Royal Welsh Fusiliers

<u>114th Inf. Brig.</u>
    13th Battalion, Welsh Regiment
    14th Battalion, Welsh Regiment
    15th Battalion, Welsh Regiment

<u>115th Inf. Brig.</u>
    10th Battalion, South Wales Borderers
    17th Battalion, Royal Welsh Fusiliers
    18th Battalion, Royal Welsh Fusiliers

During our march "Up the Line," I remember singing songs like "Keep Your Head Down, You Dirty Hun" or "Ka-Ka-Ka-Katie" to help keep our minds off the growing rigor of the march. I also remember waiting in a field until it got dark before we started our "final approach" into the trenches. As we started into the pits, however, "the Hun with the Gun" had his observation balloons up and spotted us, because it wasn't long before shells from his artillery batteries were falling at regular intervals all around us.

    "Crrupp!"
    "Crrupp!"
    "Crrupp!"
    "Crrupp!"

This was the first time I was ever been under direct shell fire from an enemy we had come 3,000 miles to fight. The Huns showered us with at least six-inch shells (155mm) and they were dropping a short distance away. It was a horrible feeling and I was soon soaking wet with panic-induced sweat. Even worse, we had our "slickers" on (a slicker is a rubberized rain coat), which made it all the more uncomfortable. It makes no difference how cold a man may be—when artillery attack comes, the blood in his veins immediately boils. This was one way we kept warm in all kinds of weather on the front lines (although most of the time we were "too," viz., too hot, too cold, too wet, too dry, etc.). For me, the fear was gripping. Muscles in my body that I didn't even know I had, tightened. My breathing was rapid, my brain gushed out adrenaline (we called it "war juice" and frankly became addicted to it), and lightning bolts shot up from my feet through my legs and into my guts. That's what fear felt like to me. I'll never forget this first barrage nor that feeling. It wasn't my worst barrage—not by a long shot—but it was my first.

We made our way into the "Tommy Trench" just as the moon rose and I vividly remember that the sky was clear and that the heavens were filled with stars. As we filed through the eathen passages, we could see the Tommies winding their way toward the top of the hill on the other side of the ravine from where we were. Their bayonets glistened softly in the moonlight. Onward they moved in single file to the front line trench. For some, this would be their last march. Shells began to burst farther back behind us. Silvery spheres shot up, exploded, and rained down showers of red, white and green star clusters that floated away softly until they burned out. They were almost beautiful. British *Véry* Flares would go up and explode and a little parachute would open up with a white flare attached to it and float back down to earth making a strange burning sound. As they did so, the ground became almost as light as day. Big searchlights were also trained on the sky looking for enemy planes. From the top of the hill we could also see the muzzle flashes of both Tommie and Heinie artillery for several miles.

The Tommie trenches were dry and in some places very shallow because the ground was so hard to dig up—most of it consisted of white chalk or gravel. The woods were only fragments of trees standing in the underbrush, for they had been torn to shreds by incessant artillery fire. The area also smelled very bad from the unburied bodies, which had been lying around in "No Man's Land" for several days. My platoon from B/1/318th Infantry was integrated with a company from the 15th Battalion, Royal Welsh Fusiliers. Although the Welshmen were very welcoming, I didn't always understand their peculiar accent (remember: "English spoken—American understood"). If I remember right, most of the "Blokes" or "Lads" came from Newtown, Wales and we "Yanks" were matched up with "Tom Joneses" who explained to us their general duties. It was pretty straight forward: keep your head down, watch everything, listen for incoming rounds, sleep with your gas mask out or use it as a pillow, etc. We knew when we were going to attack, but didn't know when they would.

We had to stand guard all night in the trench from the firing step in shifts of two hours each. Being part of the platoon's A.R. squad, my team was matched up with a Tom Jones Lewis

Gun section. Further out were established listening posts. In front of my A.R. position, a dead German had been partly blown out of his shallow grave by a shell, and one foot with a boot on it stood hoisted into the air above the ground.

As the morning sun to our front broke the darkness (we faced east into Hunland), we slowly but surely got a look at our enemy—well sort of. They were along a low ridge that was dug-up with defensive fortifications or pockmarked by shell damage. Between us were rows of tangled barbed wire—some new—some old. The entire country was desolate. Nothing remained of the surrounding villages except piles of stone and brick and cracked and burned timber. The trenches that we occupied were very different from those which we practiced in at Camp Lee, many of them amounting to nothing more than deep ditches connecting shell-holes. We were actually surprised, as we thought that the entire trench system was going to be an elaborate labyrinth of defensive works.

It wasn't.

Across the small river and valley (which was mostly a flooded swamp) at about five hundred yards away, was the German outpost line. Heading up the ridge on the German side of the swamp were more Hun barbed wire entanglements, which were far more dense than ours (they had pulled back to this defensive line while the British were forced to build their works while under fire). Behind the barbed wire was their main defensive line, which was along the "military crest" of the opposing ridge. The military crest is the area just below the crest. One does not want to silhouette his position against the horizon on the crest itself. Therefore, good military units will dig-in along the military crest whenever possible.

The enemy's M.G. positions were well-hidden and defended. I was expecting to *see* the enemy but nothing doing. The only time we actually *saw* the enemy was when they delivered an artillery strike upon us, which was terrifying, when they charged us directly, or when we charged them directly.

The enemy, you see, manifested itself in many forms.

Artillery strikes were of course the worse because they turned men into clouds of red mist or bloody chunks or, at minimum, rattled the teeth from one's gums. Of all of us, I think artillery strikes affected Albert Getz the most. I mean, he just couldn't take it. I had a hard time, too, but I ate all of my fear and just did what I had to do.

As the morning advanced, rolling kitchens from the rear sent a chow detail with some hot coffee and what the Brits called "Slumgullion." It was a terrible job trying to carry the food for over a mile in tin cans. It would almost cut a soldier's fingers through. And between the darned green blow-flies, rats, and smell from the dead, one could hardly eat, even though he was hungry. I couldn't. After a few days, however, we eventually got used to the filth and stress of "the Trench," especially the noises, and began to perform the usual duties, including the digging of new trenches or improving old, the erecting of entanglements with "pig tail" metal rods and barbed wire, and participating in constant and vigilant patrolling of the area. We quickly learned that patrolling wasn't done for "them" (meaning the higher-ups), but for us. Imagine two Prehistoric tribes arrayed against each other and their sole job was to kill the other. Not to win a war, necessarily, but just to kill members from the opposing tribe—meaning you. That's what it was like. That's why we patrolled: to ensure that an enemy raiding party just didn't come upon our squad and wipe us out.

On Aug. 8, the New Zealanders, along with elements of the 317th Infantry of the 80th Division, launched a local offensive against the German salient near Hébuterne. This was the first offensive operation of a subordinate unit of the 80th Division. As the Germans to their front retired to their secondary lines, the 317th Infantry advanced about a mile-and-a-half with their New Zealander compatriots and occupied Puisieux-au-Mont.[245]

Later that same morning, we in 1/318th Infantry experienced our first gas attack. We were awakened by the clarion call of a Klaxon Horns and Welsh sergeants yelling, "Gas! Gas! Gas!"

We frantically put on and adjusted our masks, in the dark, as we were in a dugout. We had a "gas-proof" blanket draped across the entrance to the dugout, but nobody was taking any chances as gas will linger, even in small quantities, in the low areas. We sat still for probably a half hour in our dugout with our nose-pinching masks on before Sergeant Brown decided to risk the "fatal one whiff." He opened his mask, took a sniff, then another, then another. He then walked up to the entrance of the dugout and sniffed around the blanket. He smelled something...but it was faint. He turned and told us that it was safe to unmask as long as we stayed in the dugout.

This first experience taught us a lot: respect the gas, but don't be afraid of it. Taken in small doses, it's okay. When we attacked up the division axes of advance during the Meuse-Argonne in Oct.-Nov., we would sometimes get a "whiff" or two of mustard or phosgene gas that hung in the hollows, but it was nothing too serious.

As we gained first-hand experience in the trenches north of Albert with the Welshmen, New Zealanders, and others, the British attacked with hundreds of thousands of men, supported by hundreds of tanks, and broke through the German lines north of us at Arras using the Germans' own infiltration-style tactics. This means that the British, like the Hun with the Gun

---

[245] *Hébuterne* is pronounced "Heb-u-ten" and *Puisieux-au-Mont* is pronounced "Pews-u-ow-Mon."

during *Friedensturm*, hit one point of the German line with a limited artillery preparation (as not to pound the axis of advance into a morass) and attacked across a narrow front with special attack squads armed with flamethrowers and grenades, avoiding enemy strong points, and heading for the enemy's rear, allowing follow-on forces to deal with the bypassed frontline forces. From where we were near Albert, we could hear the massed artillery and see flocks of friendly aeroplanes heading east. What was later coined the "Black Day of the German Army" (Aug. 8, 1918) by Hindenburg himself, the Tommies kept on going, led by assault troops, tanks, and aircraft.

It was therefore the British and their Commonwealth partners (e.g., Canadians) who really honed the "combined arms concept" to the hilt during the summer-fall, 1918.

But only with the arrival of American forces could they have even contemplated such a massive offensive against the hated Hun.

At this point, Hindenburg informed Kaiser Bill that *das Krieg ist vorbei* (the war is over) and that peace should be immediately be made with the Allies and the U.S. The problem was that the Allies, now seeing blood in the water, did not want a cease-fire, but an all-out victory against Germany and its confederates.[246]

On Aug. 9, the 80th Division's artillery brigade had completed its instruction at Redon and was ordered to march to "Camp Meucon." The T.M. battery was armed with sixteen six-inch "Newton Mortars" which delivered high-angle rounds that we called "G.I. Cans." They were our answer to the German *Minenwerfer*. Heiner's 155th Arty. Brig. travelled 73 km in four days, with the troops camping the first night at Beganne, the second at Muzillac, and the third at Theix. Food and forage was transported by the brigade's 305th Ammunition Train. According one Red Leg, "The weather remained good and the horses stood up well. Only the belligerent stallions issued the 315th Artillery [H] failed to behave, and they ignored all march regulations."[247]

A conspicuous feature of the march was the daily stampede of the horses to water. Considerable ingenuity was required to place the horse battalion of the ammunition train on the road in marching order. While Companies E and F were equipped with horses, but not caissons or ration and baggage wagons, Company C possessed small arms wagons and harness but no mules. The problem was easily solved by consolidation of the equipment. The march demonstrated the importance of proper watering facilities and orderly watering. This was the brigade's first field movement and it provided the best of training.

---

[246] *Das Krieg ist vorbei* is pronounced "Daws Kreeg eest Vor-bye."

[247] As cited in Stultz, 333.

The men found Camp Meucon to be a large, permanent artillery training center, about eight miles north of Vannes. It was equipped with wooden barracks, mess halls, showers, and stables. After two months in pup tents or French billets, the camp's facilities were a refreshing contrast. Here an intensive final training schedule was continued without interruption for three weeks. The range was in excellent condition for both artillery and small-arms firing, and large enough to permit all three regiments to practice at the same time. Instruction was also given to the assembled officers from observatories in rear of the battery positions by one instructor for each battalion, both French and American officers being employed. The firing batteries went on the range almost daily. Service firing began at 7:30 A.M. which necessitated a start two hours earlier on the long, dusty march. Schools in map reading, topography, and telephone communications were conducted for officers and N.C.O.s during the afternoons and evenings. Instruction in one subject or another was constantly in progress, with little time for recreation. The 305th Ammunition Train, which had received all of its equipment except for sufficient caissons and mules, engaged in practice marches and ammunition hauling. Col. Carroll I. Goodfellow's 315th Artillery (H) received the balance of its 155mm Schneider Howitzers and other equipment. An unpopular requirement provided that the men wear gas masks two hours daily and for a four-hour interval one day each week. The value of this drill was later demonstrated atop a small hill near Germont during the bone-crushing and war-ending Meuse-Argonne Offensive. Between assignments to range firing, the batteries remaining in camp held gun drill and horse exercise and furnished camp details. One soldier from the 314th Artillery remembered:

> *Once again, in fact the last time for many months to come, the regiment was quartered in barracks and had regular mess halls with tables and benches...In spite of its fine showers, which never ran when needed, however, and in spite of cots and stables in exchange for picket lines, it does not linger in our memories as one of the pleasantest spots in France. For one thing, there was altogether too much dust and heat; for another, there were too many dead horses around in spite of the valuable assistance rendered by German prisoners. Then, again, watering facilities were totally inadequate and liberties were too few. The ambitions of all, however, were set on an early departure for the front, and we knew that the length of our stay at Meucon depended on the work accomplished.*[248]

---

[248] As cited in Stultz, 333.

August 10-18, 1918.

On the night of August 10, 1918, as our British and Commonwealth "associates" attacked east across Belgium toward Brussels and as our A.E.F. brothers slogged north to the *Vesle* between *Rheims* and *Soissons* (the Aisne-Marne Offensive), another monster *Gotha* bombed *Doullens* from the air and made a direct hit on the post of command (P.C.) of General Jamerson's 159th Inf. Brig. Fortunately, only one officer was in the building at the time and he miraculously escaped injury. The only casualty was a sentinel at the gate, who was wounded in the knee by a machine gun bullet. While the Hun bomber was making its escape, however, British searchlights caught it and held it until a British plane swooped in an shot it down. The *Gotha* crashed in flames near our regimental P.C. in *Rubempré*. One of the bombs that the plane was carrying exploded when it crashed into the ground.

On the night of August 12-13, the 318th Infantry's M.G. company was attached by platoons to the 38th Battalion, R.M.G.C., remaining in line until August 19. Prior to that time, from August 4-10, the sections of the 318th M.G. Company had been attached to the British 38th M.G. Battalion, each for a period of two days. The 159th Inf. Brig.'s T.M. Platoon was attached to the 17th British (Northern) Division in *Bois d'Aveluy* from July 27-Aug. 4, 1918; our new 37mm I.G. section remained in *Bonneville* for further training.[249] The I.G. was a 37mm (1.45-inch) direct fire cannon, capable of crippling German tanks or taking out reinforced M.G. positions. While the French called it a "Cigarette Gun," the British called it a "one-pounder" or a "pom pom" and used it first during the Boar War in South Africa during the 1890s. Sometimes we Americans would also call it a "Cigarette Gun," but I preferred to use the term "Infantry Gun." Like the M.G. sections, the I.G. sections used mule-drawn Baltic carts to help transport the gun and its ammunition to the front.

During the night of Aug. 12-13, 2 soldiers from 3/320th Infantry performed actions that later earned them decorations from "British General Hon. Sir J.H.G. Byng, K.C.B., K.C.M.G., M.V.O, Commanding Third Army": Cpl. J. Johnston and Pvt. L.B. Collier. Their citations read:[250]

> *During the night 12-13 Aug., 1918, in the line opposite Boyelles, Cpl. J. Johnston (No. 1831379), U.S. Infantry, was in charge of a post. The enemy put down a heavy barrage for half an hour and wounded Johnston; when the barrage lifted*

---

[249] *Bois d'Aveluy* is pronounced "Bwa Dav-ah-lee."

[250] As cited in Stultz, 265-66. "K.C.B., K.C.M.G, etc. are prestigious British military associations, like "Knight of the Bath" or "Knight of the Garter."

and enemy raiding party entered the trench and endeavored to capture the post. With the greatest gallantry, although severely wounded, this N.C.O. immediately organized and led a counter attack up the trench with the garrison of his post, and shot the commander of the hostile party. The enemy immediately fled, whereupon this N.C.O. got his party out on the parapet and poured heavy rifle fire into them, causing many casualties. It was entirely due to the coolness and gallantry displayed by this N.C.O. that the enemy's attempt at obtaining identification.

During the night 12-13 Aug., 1918, Pvt. L.B. Collier (No. 1831302), U.S. Infantry, was in the front line opposite Boyelles. The enemy put down an intense barrage for half an hour, under cover of which a hostile raiding party entered the trench and commenced bombing their way down. Casualties were inflicted on the garrison of this man's post, and their numbers were much reduced. A counter attack was instantly organized and the fine example displayed by this man was largely responsible for the ejection of the enemy without further loss.

During the night of Aug. 13-14, 1918, platoons from the 320th Infantry, in the northern part of Byng's British Third Army line near Boiry-Saint-Martin, helped repel a trench raid.[251] Trench raids had become S.O.P. for both armies and although small in scale, were effective in killing the enemy or gaining information. These raids, which were also called "stunts" by the British, generally consisted of a combat patrol of twenty or so men through "No-Man's-Land" at night. The patrol was normally armed with trench knives, grenades, and at least two A.R.s. Said patrol would infiltrate into the enemy line and either grab a prisoner or two from a strong point or take out a strong point.

In 2/318th Infantry, four platoons were assigned to the British 50th Inf. Brig., six went to the 51st Inf. Brig., and six went to the 52nd Inf. Brig. They remained in the trenches until Aug. 14, 1918. During that time, they witnessed a very heavy artillery barrage by the British upon the enemy's trenches and lines of communication on the east bank of *Rivière L'Ancre*.[252] During the concurrent Aisne-Marne Offensive, which was being fought further south, Maj. Gen. Robert Lee Bullard, late commander of the 26th Infantry Regiment and the 1st Infantry Division and now in command of the American III Corps that was operating with *Général de France* Jean Degotte's French Sixth Army, fought hard to keep his casualties as low as possible while also

---

[251] *Boiry-Saint-Martin* is pronounced "Bwa-ree Sawn-Mar-tawn."

[252] *Rivière L'Ancre* is pronounced "Riv-ee-air Lawn-cur."

accomplishing the mission.[253] When Degotte, for example, extolled Bullard to "press forward, regardless of the cost!" Bullard instructed his divisions, which lacked proper artillery support, to instead move ahead at a slow but steady pace, advancing only when enough artillery cover fire was available. Bullard even fought Degotte's order on holding indefensible terrain in the valley of the Vesle, where *Fismes-Fismette* were located. Degotte insisted, however, and the 56th Inf. Brig. of the American 28th (Red Keystone) Division, paid for it with great loss.

We later served under General Bullard during the Meuse-Argonne Offensive.

On Aug. 14, Col. Howard R. Perry's 317th Infantry, operating north of us, participated in a second localized push with the New Zealanders to help collapse a bulge in the line that was created during *Friedensturm*. The offensive lasted four days (until Aug 18) and the officers and men of the 317th learned even more about advancing in small groups or "clumps" while under fire. They stressed to the rest of the division the importance of A.R.s and R.G.s in helping to achieve "fire superiority"—that relying upon M.G.s for direct fire support was helpful, but once M.G.s started squirting targets and moving their cones, they were living on borrowed time because Hun mortars targeted them first.

The war had thus turned a corner with the arrival of the American Doughboys, enabling the British, Belgians, and French to mass their forces on other parts of the line in order to renew the offensive and drive "the Hun with the Gun" back beyond the Rhine ("where the beer flows..."). Our feelings of fraternity with the British troops grew during that hot summer of 1918 whether we liked it or not and most felt that we benefitted from the other: like real allies. During our ten weeks of service on the British front, the 80th (Blue Ridge) Division, which numbered 25,268 troops (short 27 officers and 1,554 men), had engaged in its first combat operations with a casualty list of seven officers and 420 men. Of these, 276 were listed as killed or wounded in action. More than one-half, or four officers and 309 men, were lost during the first eighteen days of August. During this period, the division was also credited with gains of 1,700 yards and earned two silver bands for its colors and an extra bar for the campaign badges of its men for its presence in the Picardy defensive sector and its participation in the Somme offensive.[254] Of this total, the 318th Infantry suffered seven killed and 32 wounded, mostly from 2/318. My company, B/1/318, suffered no casualties. The killed from the 317th Infantry were: Lt. Samuel H. Hubbard (Co. C), Lt. Jay F. Clemmer (I), and Pvts. George M Lang (G), John H. McQuinston (F), John F. Penn (F), David W. Powers (H), and Nathan Pride (I). These casualties served to reflect the

---

[253] *Général de France* Jean Degotte is pronounced "Jen-er-al due Frawnce Jawn Da-go."

[254] As cited in Stultz, 277.

mounting tempo and warned of the toll that would inevitably attend the division's full-fledged participation on the great Allied offensive in the making.

Needless to say, the Blue Ridge Division gained a lot of experience while in the British zone, although many of us failed to appreciate it at the time (we were eager to get into the fight, end the war, and go home). But we did appreciate each other. One soldier from Spalding's 305th Engineers, for example, remembered having the following discussion with a New Zealander: "We never will drive the Germans out of France and Belgium. Since you fellows (Americans) have come, we will be able to hold out against any driving that they can possibly do, but there aren't men enough in the world to break through all the German lines of defense. We will win the war by continued blockade, and when there are so many Americans here that the Germans will know their cause is hopeless."[255] In my opinion, one of the reasons why Pershing turned to the 80th Division time after time in the up-and-coming Meuse-Argonne is because we were well-prepared by the British.

Not to belabor this point, but since the war's end, there has been too much tit-for-tat about who was "most responsible for winning the war." To be clear, nobody really won anything. A few bankers? Sure. But those who participated? No. Could the Allies have beaten the Germans in 1918 without us? No. Could we have beaten Germany alone, without French or British help? Heavens no. Could the Germans have broken through along the Marne in 1918 without U.S. divisions being present? Perhaps. Without the U.S. would the war probably have gone into 1919, all sides simply withering away? Probably. Remember, Germany's "Go For Broke" *Friedensturm* was thrown back mostly by British or French forces. Granted, the U.S. 3rd and 28th Divisions stopped them cold at the Marne, but it is debateable whether the French would have finally stopped the Hun drive on Paris from the east if the Americans weren't there. All that I can say is that the only thing worse that fighting in a war is losing one.

Some of the "Training Take-Aways" of our time "Up the Line" were collected and published by General Cronkhite in various division publications. Edited and truncated, they are replicated below:[256]

1. Tactical exercises held recently have shown the absolute necessity and importance of explicit and detailed instructions being given the company and platoon commanders.

---

[255] Stultz, 278.

[256] As cited in Stultz, 256-57.

2. Platoon commanders are chiefly responsible for transmitting instructions to their units. It is especially important that the scouts and platoon sergeants should be given detailed information and know the general situation.

3. Battalion commanders, as well as company commanders, cannot depend on exercising complete control and the giving of additional orders when troops have moved out and are engaged with the enemy. The execution of the task and its success depends mainly on the initiative and intelligence of the platoon commander.

4. The practice of ignoring simulated hostile fire, and of the consequent careless exposure, leads to the formation of habits that are sure to result in heavy casualties, if not disaster.

5. In the noise, confusion, and excitement of battle, men can be expected to do well only those things that have become a habit as a result of training. It is therefore vitally important that each man receive individual instruction, Not only as to what he is expected to do - as a member of a covering detachment, a patrol, a raiding party, in combat, on defense, etc. - but how to do it.

6. With this end in view, unit commanders will see that all available time is devoted to the study and execution of small tactical problems, involving the operations of patrols and platoons. No error of judgment, or violation of a fundamental tactical principle, should be considered too insignificant to receive immediate correction, with an explanation of the reason why.

7. All ranks must understand that loss of life due to needless exposure is a crime, and no less inexcusable than the loss or failure due to stupidity, lack of interest, and energy.

8. Soldiers will not talk of military matters in the presence of strangers.

9. Should a soldier become a prisoner of war, he shall give my name and rank only. He will not answer any questions, nor talk of military matters to other prisoners of war.

10. In the constant troop movements to and from the front line, special attention was ordered given to the adequacy of traffic regulation and protection, the state of camouflage of exposed routes, and the standards of troop gas and march discipline. The importance of concealment during movements was strongly impressed.

11. The steel helmet will be worn. Officers will wear an issue soldier's coat without insignia or rank.

12. Maps will not be carried exposed to view.

13. Two persons at most, not groups of several persons, may move about together.

14. Assemblages and conferences at observation posts or at points under enemy observation are forbidden.

15. Every possible advantage will be taken of cover. Open country overlooked by the enemy will be avoided. Detour must be made to avoid points exposed to enemy sniper fire.

16. When necessary, reconnoitering officers will requisition guides from Infantry units occupying the sector.

17. Gas casualties are absolutely preventable. The box respirator gives complete protection. Gas officers and N.C.O.s will personally see that their organizations are fully informed regarding all the gas defense measures to the end that any gas situation may be met without casualties.

18. A soldier will always be on the alert for gas signs so that he may give timely warning to his comrades and take proper steps for his own protection.

19. In a gassed area a soldier will not remove my mask except on the order of an officer.

Once again, the primacy of the platoon-sized combat group, with its attachments, was stressed.

It would be up to us.

When firing the M1915 Chauchat Automatic Rifle from a fixed position, we would drop the bi-pod. Note the "banana" magazine for the bullets.

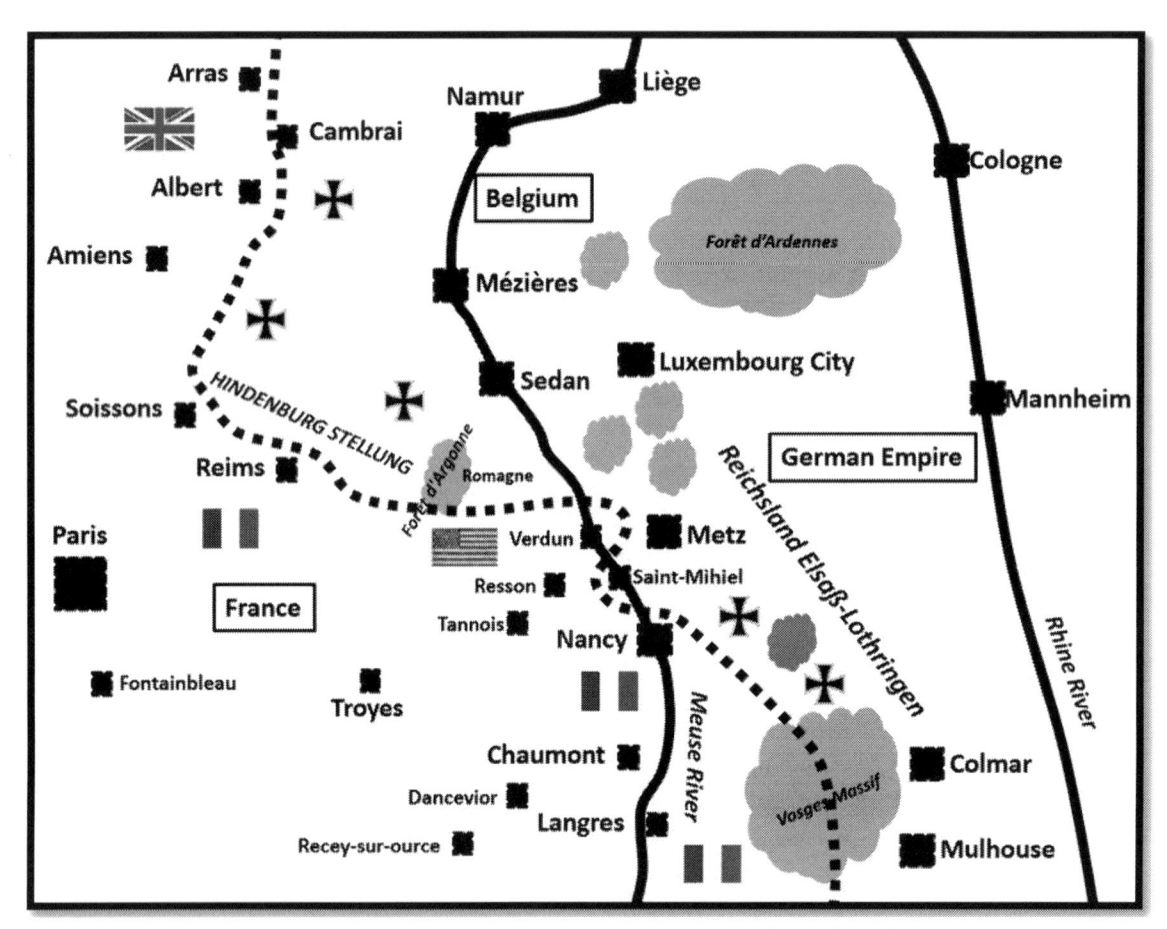

80th Division Area of Operations, July 1918-May 1919. If Pershing's American First Army could break through at Romagne in the Meuse-Argonne and take Sedan, Mézières, Namur, and Liège, it could turn the Germans from their position in France and Belgium.

"Dugout—Senlis. A Yank Home on the front lines." 319th Inf. in camp, 1918.

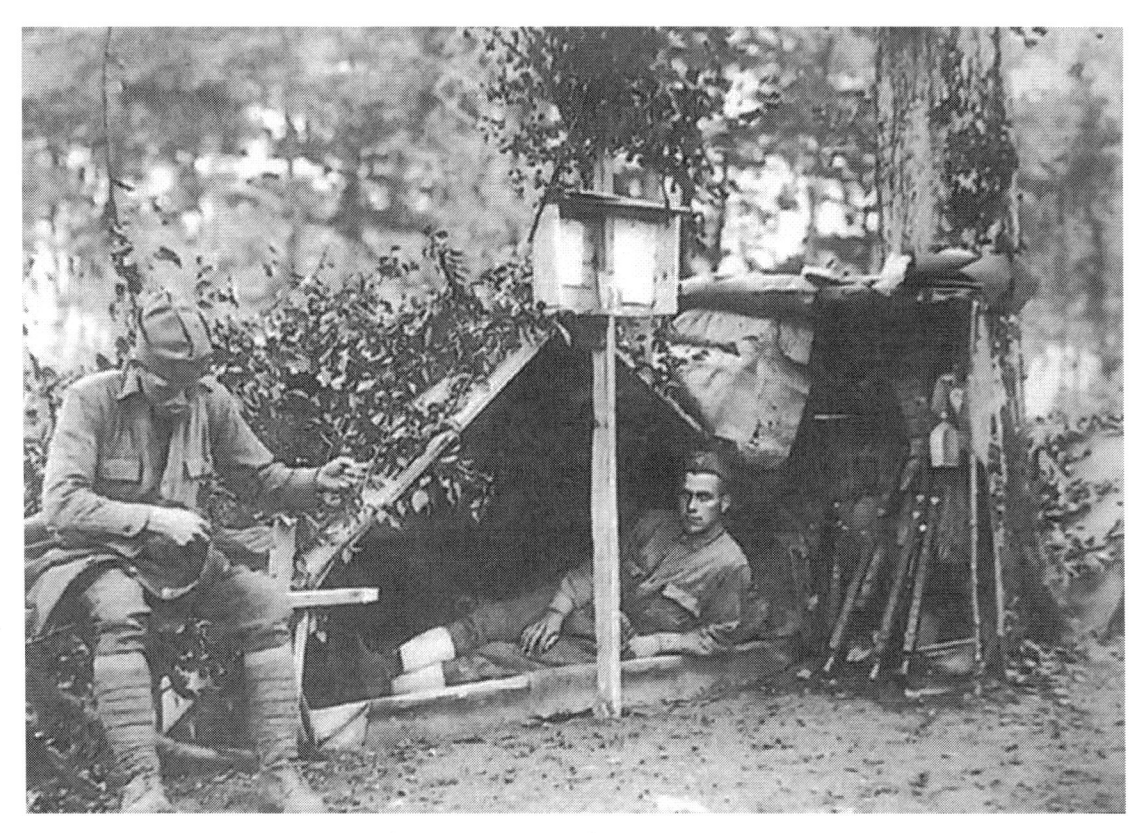

80th Division Doughs in camp, August, 1918.

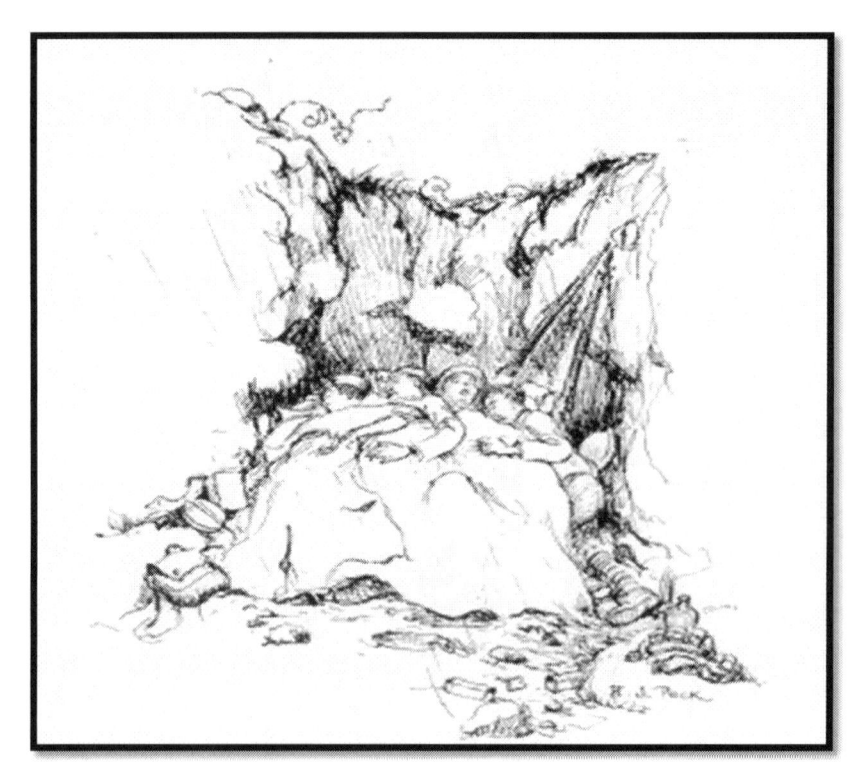

"Home Sweet Home Up the Line."

Camions to the front.

Chapter 13
We Join "Black Jack's" American First Army (Aug. 19-Sept. 15, 1918).

It was always Pershing's desire to take over *le Secteur de Alsace-Lorraine* from the French in order to fight the Germans *mano-a-mano*.[257] He hoped to have three one-million-man American field armies arrayed in Lorraine by spring 1919, attack across the Meuse and the Moselle Rivers into *Deutsches Reichsland Elsaß-Lottringen*, take the heavily fortified city of Metz, its capital, and hold it hostage until the Kaiser's government surrendered to the United States.[258] If it didn't, then we'd drive further east, capturing the Alsatian fortress city of Colmar.[259] If that wasn't enough, then we'd attack across the Rhine River and drive even deeper into Germany until Kaiser Bill gave up, marching all the way to Berlin if we had to!

By late-August, once the French and the Americans collapsed the Soissons-Rheims Salient during the Aisne-Marne Offensive and as the British drove east from Arras toward Namur, Foch allowed Pershing to finally assemble the American First Army in Lorraine. This area of the front was chosen in large part because the lines of communication and supply from French ports back to the U.S. made logical sense. On this front, two possible campaigns presented themselves. First, an offensive against Metz and the coal and iron fields of Briey from which the Hun were obtaining a great portion of their raw material for munitions, and second, a thrust north between *la Meuse et le Fôret d'Argonne* with sights on seizing the important railroad junctions at *Sedan* and *Mézières*.[260] The cutting of these lines of communication would force the German armies in France, Belgium, and Luxembourg to withdraw through *Liège* and *Namur* or risk total encirclement. Either one of these plans required a preliminary operation—the reduction of *le Saillant de Saint-Mihiel*—in order to eliminate the threat of an enemy attack on the flank. The Saint-Mihiel attack was therefore planned in great detail.[261] Its execution on Sept. 12-13, 1918, was as clean cut as any operation attempted by the armies of the Associated Powers. On Sept. 5, Pershing issued the following guidance to his divisions:

> *From a tactical point of view, the method of combat in trench warfare presents a marked contrast to that employed in open warfare, and the attempt by assaulting Infantry to use trench warfare methods in an open warfare combat*

---

[257] *Le Secteur de Alsace-Lorraine* is pronounced "Luh Sec-tour day All-sayce Lore-ayn."

[258] *Deutsches Reichsland Elsaß-Lottringen,* which means "The German Imperial Land, Alsace-Lorraine," is pronounced "Daws Doitsch-es Rikes-laand El-sahs Lot-rin-gen."

[259] *Kolmar* is pronounced "Coal-mar."

[260] *Briey* is pronounced "Bree-yeah," *la Meuse et le Fôret d'Argonne* is pronounced "la Mooz-ah ae luh Fore-et Dar-gone," *Sedan* is pronounced "Say-dawn," and *Mézières* is pronounced "Mez-yayhr."

[261] *Le Saillant de Saint-Mihiel* is pronounced "Luh Sall-ee-ent day San-me-hell."

will be successful only at great cost. Trench warfare is marked by uniform formations, the regulation of space and time by higher commands down to the smallest details*** [sic] fixed distances and intervals between units and individuals*** little initiative ***. Open warfare is marked by*** irregularity of formations, comparatively little regulation of space and time by higher commanders, the greatest possible use of the infantry's own fire power to enable it to get forward, variable distances and intervals between units and individuals*** brief orders and the greatest possible use of individual initiative by all troops engaged in the action.*** The infantry commander must oppose M.G.s by fire from his rifles, his automatics and his rifle grenades and must close with their crews under cover of this fire and of ground beyond their flanks.*** The success of every unit from the platoon to the division must be exploited to the fullest extent. Where strong resistance is encountered, reinforcements must not be thrown in to make a frontal attack at this point, but must be pushed through gaps created by successful units, to attack these strong points in the flank or rear.[262]

In order to flesh-out the new American First Army which was assembling in Lorraine near Saint-Mihiel, Pershing ordered the 80th Division, as well as several other American divisions, to get there by mid-September. We first learned of this grand movement of men and *matériel* in late-August when we were ordered to return our British Lewis Guns and Vickers M.G.s and exchange our beloved S.M.L.E.s with our old M17 Enfields. Like I already said, we really liked being armed with British-issue weapons and thought that they were superior to what the U.S. Army issued us. This was especially true with the Lewis Gun. Boy, could we make her purr! On Aug. 19, Cronkhite issued G.O. #1 to move us from Picardy to Lorraine:[263]

---

[262] As cited in Pershing, 2:358.

[263] As cited in Stultz, 276-77. A "bayonet frog" is a leather strap that connects the bayonet sheaf to a belt.

EIGHTIETH DIVIISON
A.E.F.

19 Aug. 1918

G.O. # 1

1. Horsed transport will be taken by the division. Riding horses will be taken.
2. (a) The following mechanical transport will NOT be taken:
All motor ambulances.
All motor-cycles and side-car combinations.
(b) Motor ambulances, motor-cycles and side-car combinations will be turned into the division Q.M. at Beauval at 4:00 P.M., August 20.
(c) Motor cars with the exception of five to be designated later, will also be turned in to the division Q.M. at the same time and place.
(d) The division will take all ambulance lorries.
(e) All American transmitters in the possession of the field signal battalion will be turned in at H.Q., American II Corps.
3. Separate instructions have already been issued regarding Vickers and Lewis Guns and British ammunition.
4. 3-inch Stokes Mortars and 37mm guns will accompany the division. 37mm Gun and Colt Pistol ammunition in the possession of the division and fifty rounds per 3-inch Stokes Mortar ammunition will be taken. Arrangements are being made to obtain this latter ammunition.
5. The field ambulances handed over to the 80th Division will proceed with the division complete in transport (less motor transport) and equipment.
6. Arrangements are being made to take four days' rations and forage plus one days' iron rations (2 days' rations for consumption on trip, 2 days' for consumption after arrival).
7. American rifles and bayonets (100 rounds per man) will be issued before entrainment.
8. Bayonet scabbards and frogs now in possession will be retained.
9. All British drivers will be replaced by American drivers before move commences and no British personnel will proceed with the Division. All British personnel attached to this division will be sent to Beauval.

OFFICIAL
CRONKHITE
COMMANDING

With plan in hand, we were again loaded aboard the *40 Hommes ou 8 Cheval* rail cars and sent south and east, through *Paris* and *Troyes*. Excessive heat and confinement in the small boxcars marred the routine journey, which proved tiresome, as around forty men were crowded into each car with their rations and packs. After the trains chugged out, some of us, including yours truly, crawled out onto the flat cars expecting relief from the heat. It was worse, in fact, as we were stuck in the pitiless sun and sometimes even rain for two very long days. Soaked to the skin, we suffered from the penetrating chill of the night. Near Paris, late on the afternoon of Aug. 23, one of the trains sideswiped a construction train standing on a spur track. Five Blue Ridgers were knocked from the train and ten others injured their feet and legs. The severely injured were carried by members of the division medical and M.P. detachments to a hospital at Enghien-les-Bains and transferred the next day to "Base Hospital No. 1" in Paris. One died shortly after the accident and two others expired the following day at the hospital. One of the three belonged to the 305th Engineer Supply Battalion.[264]

Per S.O.P., we did not know our destination so speculation ran rife. "Joe Latrinsky" was really chatting it up! Italian members of the division—mostly from General Brett's 160th Inf. Brig.—were reportedly jubilant with a false confidence that we were being sent to Italy, that is, until the trains turned east from the main line short of *Dijon*. Groups of French civilians, mostly women and children, waved enthusiastically from each town or village. On the second day, we traveled through the heart of France, unmatched in charm and beauty, unmarred by war, and quite unlike the shell-wrecked areas of Picardy. Between Paris and Lorraine (named after Charlemagne's son, Lothar), we saw broad fields of wheat, oats, barley, and rye, in every direction. Fat sheep and cattle grazed in meadows still lush with summer grasses. Almost everywhere, one might find cool, sparkling water to drink, and a patch of soft, clean sod on which to rest his bones. Fresh fruit and vegetables, sweet milk and cheese, too, were to be had along the way—the first that the hungry, can-fed troops had seen in many days. After two days, we disembarked at *Recey-sur-ource*, which is just south of *Chaumont* (Pershing's H.Q.) and west of Langres (A.E.F. Officer Training Academy).[265]

This particular section of France was by far the most beautiful that had yet been encountered, well-wooded, and full of game, and with plenty of room in which to move around. By this time the regiment had had sufficient experience in billeting to be able to settle down in a very short time, and training was immediately taken up to get ready for the action which

---

[264] Stultz, 285. *Troyes* is pronounced "Troy."

[265] *Recey-sur-ource* is pronounced "Re-zay-zu Oar," *Chaumont* is pronounced "Shau-mon," and *Langres* is pronounced "Lawn-gah."

everyone realized was soon to come. While at *Recey-sur-ource*, America's Blue Ridge Division received 768 American Chauchat A.R.s and 168 Colt-Vickers M.G.s for its infantry regiments and M.G. battalions, all delivered by truck during the night of Aug. 28-29.[266] The official nomenclature of the Chauchat A.R. was "Automatic Rifle, Model 1915 (Chauchat)." The ones issued to us were of French design but American manufacture and were redesigned to fire a standard American 30.06 cal. round, which is larger than the original French design (thus the big reason why it often jammed). We didn't like the Chauchat, esp. after having a Lewis Gun, and called it the "Sho-sho" or "Chow-chow." Sometimes Getz would say things like, "I gotta take a Sho-sho"—meaning, I have to relieve myself.

The Chauchat or *"Fusil Mitrailleur"* was invented by Col. Henri Chauchat in 1910 and was the most-produced A.R. of the war. The American version, the M1915, fired 240 R.P.M. and had a maximum range of about two thousand yards although an effective range (meaning man plus weapon), at least in my case, about two hundred yards. We could barely see a target out to a hundred yards anyway. While my job was to load, point, fire, and fix jams, my assistant, Pvt. Getz, was to point out targets, help load the magazine, and keep me from running. My M1915 Chauchat did in fact jam from time-to-time. The biggest reason why it did this is because the expended cartridge cases would either get jammed in the bolt receiver or sheared off completely. My understanding is that the original French Chauchat fired far better than our American one because of the smaller round. I don't know this for a fact, as I never actually fired a French Chauchat.

On Aug. 31, 1918, my regiment was ordered to march to Dancevoir, which is just south of Chaumont.[267] It must be remembered that when we say "march" we really meant "struggle." We were like pack mules, weighed down with at least 75 lbs of gear. We A.R.-men had it even worse, because we had to carry even-more-heavy Sho-shos. In general, this is what we had to carry in or on our packs: one overseas service cap (which was sometimes worn under the helmet, esp. if it was cold), three pairs of woolen socks, two O.D. wool shirts, two suits of cotton underwear, one pair of extra ankle boots, one pair of extra wool puttees, one poncho or slicker, two O.D. Army wool blankets (one in the pack rolled with the canvas shelter half and one wrapped across the top of the pack), one O.D. canvas shelter half, one bayonet and scabbard (strapped to right-side of the pack), one "T-Handle" intrenching tool (strapped to the back of the pack), one mess kit, two days of "Emergency" or "Iron" rations, and toiletries, etc., stuffed in our "meat tin."

---

[266] *Chauchat* is pronounced "Show-sha."

[267] *Dancevoir* is pronounced "Dance-ah-vwa."

On our person, we carried or wore our helmet, assigned weapon, at least one hand grenade, one British gas mask with respirator bag, an Army O.D. canvas cartridge belt, canteen, canteen cover, and first aid pouch and packet. That's a lot of gear, but important for each soldier to have. One Dough from the 317th Infantry remembered: "We marched over twenty-two miles that day. At noon, we were told that the village we were to occupy was only 'three kilos away and was all down hill,' but there were many hills to climb and we did not reach our destination until midnight. It was a long hike, but true to the reputation of the company, not a man had fallen out. Men had marched till they could hardly stand, and after this long hike found themselves in the village of Chameroy. Billets were found before morning and occupied."[268]

As we marched through Dancevoir, our march objective for the day, the various platoons of the company took up a step and struck up some old songs like "Hail, Hail, the Gang's All Here" or "Carry Me Back to Ole Virginny." Once we passed through the town, we were encamped as a brigade in our four-man shelter or "pup" tents (about 3,500 tents total), all battalions in sight of each other! By dusk, General Jamerson's entire 159th Inf. Brig. was assembled in a big, open field, some 8,000 strong. This was the first time we had been together since Camp Lee. General Brett's 160th Inf. Brig. was not far away. It was a most-inspiring scene, reminding us of old-time campaigning (like during the days of George Washington or Robert E. Lee) before the time when aeroplanes turned men into moles burrowing into the earth and scurrying about above ground only during times of limited visibility. That night (a "time of limited visibility"), we all went hunting for our old buddies in different companies or battalions. We had plenty of fun, with the boys singing all the old songs after a couple shots of cognac.

According to Army Regulations, to pitch a double shelter tent (to ensure that at least two men in four has a rifle, or, in our case, an automatic rifle), one must perform the following steps with aluminum tent pins, wooden tent poles, and Army O.D. canvas shelter halves:

I.D.R. 793. At the command, pitch tents, equipments are un-slung, packs opened, shelter half and pins removed; each men then spreads his shelter half, small triangle to the rear, flat upon the ground the tent is to occupy, the rear-rank man's half on the right. The halves are then buttoned together; the guy loops at both ends of the lower half are passed through the buttonholes provided in the lower and upper halves, the whipped end of the guy rope is then passed through both guy loops and secured, this at both ends of the tent. Each front-rank man inserts the muzzle of his rifle under the front end of the ridge and holds the rifle upright, sling to the front, heel of butt on the ground beside the

---

[268] As cited in Stultz, 286.

> *bayonet. His rear-rank man pins down the front corners of the tent on the line of bayonets, stretching the tent taut; he then inserts a pin in the eye of the front guy rope and drives the pin at such a distance in front of the rifle as to hold the rope taut. Both men go to the rear of the tent, each pins down a corner, stretching the sides and rear of the tent before securing. The rest of the pins are then driven by both men, the rear-rank man working on the right. The front flaps are not fastened down, but thrown back on the tent. Double shelter tents may be pitched by first pitching one tent as heretofore described, then pitching a second tent against the opening of the first, using one rifle to support both tents, and passing the front guy ropes over and down the sides of the opposite tents. The front corner of one tent is not pegged down, but is thrown back to permit an opening into the tent.*

After this, we constructed our "single sleeping bags" with our wool blankets and ponchos. Again, according to Army Regulations:

> *I.D.R. 796. Spread the poncho on the ground, buttoned end at the feet, buttoned side to the left; fold the blanket once across its short dimension and lay it on the poncho; tie the blanket together along the left side by means of the tapes provided; fold the left half of the poncho over the blanket and button it together along the side and bottom.*

We spent two days encamped at Dancevoir and on Monday, Sept. 2, 1918, we marched to Latrecey, once again entrained, and were shipped to Tannois.[269] The 80th Division was now in the section of the country which Foch had allotted to the American Army, and as such, mostly American troops were in evidence. We were assembling behind the French lines getting ready to complete a switch-out with them. One soldier from Col. Ephraim G. Peyton's 320th Infantry remembered:

> *We understood that we were going down on the American sector. The men were not at all displeased with the prospect, especially because they knew they would then draw the American ration, which was not only a larger ration than the British but better suited to the American taste—not so much cheese and jam and tea and stuff of that sort. Indeed, I think there was a deeper reason than that.*

---

[269] *Latrecey* is pronounced "Lay-tresh-ae" and *Tannois* is pronounced "Tan-wah."

The men wanted to go where there was a distinctly American enterprise going on.[270]

That same day, Maj. Charles Sweeny, our popular regimental operations officer (S-3), was assigned to command 1/318th Infantry and Capt. Edward Little replaced Sweeny as S-3. The regiment remained in bivouac in wooded ravines near Tannois from Sept. 2-7, 1918, the men being required to keep carefully concealed during the day from possible air observation. We were rightly told that the concentration of Pershing's new American First Army for the Saint-Mihiel attack demanded the utmost secrecy in order to maintain the essential element of surprise. No efforts were therefore neglected to conceal troop movements from enemy. Field kitchens were screened to prevent smoke rising above the trees and even these fires at times had to be extinguished on account of their billowing smoke. No other fires or lights were allowed and even the wearing of luminous dial watches was forbidden. Men were prohibited from gathering in groups or from leaving the woods during the day. A strong guard was in fact posted to restrain all unnecessary movement except at night, and American observation planes patrolled actively. Training, restricted to the hours of darkness, was hampered by the constant precautions. I also remember that it rained most of the time we were in *Tannois*, and when it was not raining we knocked down drippings from the bushes as we passed, so that continual rain was well simulated. One soldier from the 320th Infantry remembered: "We camped in the woods about two km from the town of *Nancois-le-Petit* the following five days, in which we rested or rather existed. These five days were dreary ones—it rained the whole time, and our pup-tents became so soaked that they could not repel water any more. Because of this, all of our clothing, blankets, equipment, and sundry items were soaked and the sun refused to shine to dry them…We were a sick and sore crowd, though everyone's morale was of the highest order and eager for the fray, which we hoped would soon arrive."[271]

During this particularly wet and gloomy period, training was continued with our "Sho-shos" on improvised ranges. When totally clean, they fired well—when not—they did not. The necessity for concealment prevented practically all other training, except what could be done entirely in the wet woods or at night. As such, while bivouacked at Tannois, we practiced night operations, especially reconnaissance patrolling, night marches, and the occupation of an attack position.

---

[270] As cited in Stultz, 301.

[271] *Ibid.*, 309.

Night Operations.

558. By employing night operations troops make use of the cover of darkness to minimize losses from hostile fire or to escape observation. Night operations may also be necessary for the purpose of gaining time. Control is difficult and confusion is frequently unavoidable. It may be necessary to take advantage of darkness in order to assault from a point gained during the day, or to approach a point from which a daylight assault is to be made, or to effect both the approach and the assault.

559. Offensive and defensive night operations should be practiced frequently in order that troops may learn to cover ground in the dark and arrive at a destination quietly and in good order, and in order to train officers in the necessary preparation and reconnaissance. Only simple and well-appointed formations should be employed. Troops should be thoroughly trained in the necessary details—e.g., night patrolling, night marching, and communication at night.

560. The ground to be traversed should be studied by day-light, and, if practicable, at night. It should be cleared of hostile detachments before dark, and, if practicable, should be occupied by covering troops. Order must be formulated with great care and clearness. Each unit must be given a definite objective and direction, and care must be exercised to avoid collision between units. Whenever contact with the enemy is anticipated, a distinctive badge should be worn by all.

561. Fire action should be avoided in offensive operations. In general, pieces should not be loaded. Men must be trained to rely upon the bayonet and to use it aggressively.

562. Long night marches should be made only over well-defined routes. March discipline must be rigidly enforced. The troops should be marched in as compact a formation as practicable, with the usual covering detachment. Advance and rear guard distances should be greatly reduced. They are shortest when the mission is an offensive one. The connecting files are numerous.

563. A night advance made with a view to making an attack by day usually terminates with the hasty construction of intrenchments in the dark. Such an advance should be timed so as to allow an hour or more of darkness for intrenching. An advance that is to terminate is an assault at the break of day should be timed so that the troops will not arrive long before the assault is to be made; otherwise the advantage of partial surprise will be lost and the enemy will be allowed to re-enforce the threatened point.

564. The night attack is ordinarily confined to small forces, or to minor engagements in a general battle, or to seizure of positions occupied by covering or advanced detachments. Decisive results are not often obtained. Poorly disciplined and untrained troops are unfit for night attacks or for night operations demanding the exercise of skill and care. Troops attacking at night can advance close to the enemy in compact formation and without suffering loss from hostile artillery or infantry fire. The defender is ignorant of the strength or direction of the attack. A force which makes a vigorous bayonet charge in the dark will often throw a much larger force into disorder.

As we waited in our concentration area, one soldier from the 318th Field Hospital noted that "staying in shape" was always a priority—for all soldiers of the division—combat or support. He writes:

The barracks were located in a forest, and we did no marching in the daytime, but each night after dark we started out carrying a light pack and marched about six miles, afterwards returning to the barracks. On these marches, which were always on roads parallel with the battle line, we could see the artillery in constant bombardment. We were marching on roads about three miles from the front lines and the constant flashing and roar of the artillery reminded us that we had at last arrived in the battle area. On these night marches, we always proceeded in column of twos, for the reason that the road which was of the usual width, was at the same time being used by artillery columns. We used to pass these columns every night, and as there was no light to see the projecting parts of guns and caissons, we always kept well to the right of the road.[272]

On the evening of Sept. 7, 1918, my very own 159th Inf. Brig. was marched further north and east, to be billeted in Resson, which was even closer to the front lines near Saint-Mihiel.[273] From here, we could hear the dueling artillery fire, just like when we were deployed near Albert with the British. For some time, it had been rumored that a drive on the Saint-Mihiel Salient was imminent. The location of America's Blue Ridge Division was southwest of, and about twenty

---

[272] As cited in Stultz, 302-03.

[273] *Resson* is pronounced "Ray-sawn."

km from, the point of the salient, a position from which any part of the sector could be readily reached.

Familiar with British regulations, we quickly discovered an entirely different billeting system in operation in the American sector. Under this system, a "Zone Major" functioned in each divisional training area. He was charged with facilitating relations between American and French authorities and centralizing and expediting the settlement of all claims of the French involving American troops. All billeting arrangements were made by the Zone Major, pursuant to the orders of his S.O.S. section commander. For each town in the divisional area, an acting "Town Major" was appointed by the regimental or separate unit commander. To each Town Major was supplied a dossier of the individual town, with all information necessary to billet troops. Each Town Major also had one interpreter and one clerk, with at least one man on duty at all times. No billet could be occupied without authority from the Town Major. The French interpreter attached to an American unit had the duty of explaining to the officers about French laws regulating the rights of armies in the field, principally those concerning requisitions and other dispositions. He was particularly charged with investigating claims from French civilians and with seeing that American soldiers were not overcharged. Upon an organization's departure from a billet, it was required to leave its acting Town Major behind for twenty-four hours to receive claims. Upon completion of this assignment, he was instructed to leave with the French mayor a complete record of all claims and a description of the condition in which the town was left by the departing troops.

I remember being billeted in Resson for a week or so. I remember getting some mail there and sending a lot home in return. All letters were of course censored by the P.L. before mailing them. We were warned many times about writing things we shouldn't (like locations, troop morale, you know interesting stuff like that). Consequently, some of the letters were all cut to pieces before they were mailed. I also remember that Resson had a beautiful little church—actually the only real place to visit—and I remember the old people of the town kneeling and praying. I imagine they were doing it for their boys who were on the front, though I could not understand what they were saying. There were few young girls there, but no men, only the old and infirm. It was that way all over France—every one able to shoulder a gun was doing his bit. It was actually quite sad. I don't know of any other Western Power who shouldered more of the burden of the war than France.

It was here in Lorraine where Pershing hoped to decisively affect the war's outcome. The coal and iron mines near Metz, the fortress itself and the essential railway systems at Sedan and to the southeast, all made the area protected by the Lorraine front of vital importance to the

Hun—an area he could ill-afford to lose—because on its retention depended her ability to maintain the German armies west of the Rhine. The American Army in Lorraine would, therefore, be able to drive a knife into the ribcage of Imperial Germany!

This new "American Zone" in Lorraine embraced about 8,000 square miles, or a territory about the size of Massachusetts. It was about 50 miles wide in the north, between *Saint-Dizier* and *Toul*, 110 miles deep from *Toul* to *Dijon*, and 100 miles wide at the south from *Dijon* to *Joigny*. Near the center of the zone, at *Chaumont*, a city of nearly 15,000 people, Pershing's H.Q. was established. The town of *Langres*, 30 miles to the south and with a population of about 5,000, was selected as the principal officer school of the A.E.F.

Foch made it a point to place at Pershing's disposal a large territory for A.E.F. lines of communication and military stations and camps for concentrating and training. It was the development of this extensive section of the A.E.F. that had made such an extraordinary demand upon the first contingent of the draft. A vast program was required to prepare for the American divisions. This included the construction of railroad links to connect the lines turned over to the A.E.F. with its ports, the erection of those bases and the great replacement camps near them, the building of depots, hospitals, bridges, and telegraph lines, and the collection of enormous stores of ammunition and supplies. Pershing, foreseeing that American artillery, aeroplanes, and tanks would not be readily available, arranged to purchase large quantities from the Allies. We must remember that the American First Army, throughout its entire service on the front, did not fire one American-made cannon or shell and no American-made tank was made available for battle. On Sept. 8, 1918, the subordinate units of the 80th Division were located as follows:

H.Q., 80th Division: Tronville
305th Trains Brigade: Tronville
305th Engineers: Ligny-en-Barrois
159th Inf. Brig. H.Q. and 313th and 314th M.G. Battalions: Guerpont
317th Infantry H.Q., M.G. Supply, and 3/317: Salmagne
1/317 and 2/317: Loisey
318th Infantry H.Q., Supply, and 1/318: Resson
2/318th Infantry and 318th M.G. Company: Culey
3/318th Infantry: Gery
160th Inf. Brig. H.Q.: Velaines
319th Infantry: Morlaincourt
320th Infantry: Nancois-le-Petit
315th M.G. Battalion: Willeroncourt

Pershing planned to smash the southern end of the Saint-Mihiel Salient with ten American divisions, the 1st (Big Red One), 2nd (American Indian), 5th (Red Diamond), 26th (Yankee), 42nd (Rainbow), 78th (Lightning), 80th (Blue Ridge), 82nd (All-American), 89th (Rolling W), and 90th (Tough Hombre) Divisions along with several French divisions that were placed under his operational control. Pershing also had several American aero squadrons at his disposal. As such, this would be the first real battle for the National Army divisions and everyone held their breath, hoping that our level of training would be enough to carry the day. The worse off were the 89th and 90th Divisions, who had only been in country for a few weeks. We in the 80th Division had been in country for a while and had even participated in some minor operations with British or Commonwealth troops, but we had yet to conduct a whole hog offensive.

The Saint-Mihiel Salient was shaped roughly like a triangle, with its points near *Pont-á-Mousson, Saint-Mihiel,* and *Haudiomont.*[274] It was 25 miles wide at its base, extended 16 miles into the French lines and had remained almost unchanged for four years. Because of its elaborate trench systems, vast barbed wire entanglements, concrete shelters and M.G. emplacements, the salient had withstood several French attacks in the preceding years. It protected the German strategic centers of Metz and the Briey iron ore mines, interrupted traffic on the main Paris-Nancy Railroad, cut the Verdun-Toul Railroad, and threatened the Allied territory in its vicinity, especially west of *la Meuse*. Its reduction was imperative before any great Allied offensive could be launched against the Briey and Metz region or northward between the Meuse River and Argonne Forest, which was in the area south of Sedan, the primary target.

On Sept. 12, 1918, the American First Army launched its first sustained attack into *Saint-Mihiel*. The 80th Division, just arrived, was assigned as part of the Army's reserve, along with the 35th (Santa Fe) and 91st (Wild West) Divisions. I remember that while we waited to be committed to the battle, the training emphasis turned to "rules for the handling and treatment of enemy P.O.W.s." Each chaplain or "Holy Joe" was also instructed to organize a detachment of one N.C.O. and six privates to search for and bury the dead. For the latter, attention was called to the German practice of leaving booby-trapped dug-outs, dumps, trenches, and houses that were timed for explosion after occupation of American troops. Marching troops were cautioned to provide for protection against low flying enemy aeroplanes by means of M.G. or rifle fire, since our aviators were unable to gain air superiority in the region. Commanders of M.G. companies were yet directed to improvise means of centering fire on German aircraft and to train their organizations in this firing, both on the march and from stationary positions. Special

---

[274] *Pont-á-Mousson* is pronounced "Poo-ah Moose-awn" and *Haudiomont* is pronounced "Ud-U-mon."

detachments of riflemen were also formed to combat the Hun aerial raider hazard, indiscriminate firing by individuals being prohibited.

Since transport animals were scarce, their care was stressed, especially to the men who handled them. Two collecting stations for the evacuation of wounded animals when the division was in action, were also established. A number of unserviceable animals received by the 305th Mobile Veterinary Section were evacuated by rail to veterinary stations. Commanders were instructed to have the proper equipment loaded on their combat carts and to ensure that their water carts were completely filled. A redistribution and re-marking of all service wagons was also ordered. Green brassards were prescribed for all scouts, observers and snipers, the arm bands permitting the wearers to pass at will in the zone of operations.

Final plans provided for a main drive against the southern face of the salient with the American I and IV Corps and a secondary blow against the western face with the American V Corps, with holding attacks and raids by the French II Colonial Corps against the tip of the salient at Saint-Mihiel proper. Maj. Gen. Hunter Liggett's I Corps, extending from Pont-á-Mousson westward, had the 82nd, 90th, 5th, and 2nd Divisions in line from right to left with the 78th Division in reserve. Maj. Gen. Joseph T. Dickman's IV Corps continued the line on the west as far as Seicheprey, with the 89th, 42nd, and 1st Divisions in line and with the 3rd Division in reserve. In the center at Saint-Mihiel, was the French II Colonial Corps with the French 39th and 26th Divisions as well as the 2nd French Cavalry Division. On the far left, up near Haudiomont, was Maj. Gen. George Cameron's V Corps, with the American 4th and 26th Divisions as well as the 15th French Colonial Division. The 80th Division was held in reserve.[275] This gave Pershing about 550,000 American and 110,000 French troops, some 1,481 planes, and about 500 French tanks, of which 350 were light and 144 were manned by Americans. About 3,000 pieces of artillery were assembled and over three million artillery rounds were brought into the area. Of the three American corps and the nine American divisions which took part in the attack, two of the corps (IV and V) and four of the divisions had never been involved in offensive combat.

Opposing the American First Army in the salient was an enemy force known to us as "Army Group C." It was composed of eleven divisions. The Hun apparently suspected that an attack by us was being prepared, probably for late September. In anticipation of this offensive, and to shorten their own front line because their reserves on the Western Front were being depleted, the Germans on Sept. 2 began removing *matériel* and on Sept. 11, Hindenburg ordered gradual withdrawal from the salient and the destruction of all things of military value that could

---

[275] *Seicheprey* is pronounced "Sheesh-pray" and *Haudiomont* is pronounced "Hood-u-mon."

not be moved. The main withdrawal, however, had not yet occurred when Pershing's attack began.

The bombardment of Hun positions in the salient began at 1 A.M. on Sept. 12, and was apparently so overpowering that Hun artillery could not reply in kind. At dawn, after four hours of violent cannonade, the infantry brigades of Liggett's I and Dickman's American IV Corps advanced into the salient. Although only a few tanks actually came up in time to assist the troops through the wire entanglements, the advance proceeded according to schedule. The plan provided that the greatest initial penetration should be made by Dickman's corps, the objectives for Sept. 12 requiring a five-mile advance. On the western face of the salient near the center, the artillery preparation was continued until 8:00 A.M., when units from Cameron's American V Corps launched its assault. By nightfall the corps had advanced about two miles, but had not yet reached its assigned objective.

While the attacks on the flanks were progressing, reports indicated that the Germans were in fact retiring from the tip of the salient in front of the French. To cut off the retreat of as many Germans as possible, Pershing, on the evening of Sept. 12, directed that units from the American IV and V Corps be rushed to *Vigneulles*, in the center of the salient. About dawn on Sept. 13, troops from the American IV and V Corps made a junction just northeast of the town, closing the salient. German soldiers who had not retired beyond that point were cut off and captured. At this point of the battle, Pershing ordered the 80th Division to send one infantry regiment and one M.G. battalion to support the French II Colonial Corps, which was conducting "mopping-up" operations deep in the pinched-off salient near Vigneulles.[276] Cronkhite chose Col. Ephraim G. Peyton's 320th Infantry, reinforced by Maj. Prescott Huidekopper's 315th M.G. Battalion. Recently-promoted Maj. Ashby Williams, commander of 1/320th Infantry, remembered being dropped off near *Village Woimby*, along the banks of *la Meuse* north of Saint-Mihiel, and seeing enemy P.O.W.s escorted to the rear by some of our horizon-blue-clad French "associates":

> *At 7:00 A.M. on Sept. 13, 1918, 1/320th Infantry pulled into the town of Woimby on the Meuse River, north of St. Mihiel. We debussed, marched along the plank road traversing the marsh and across the historic Meuse River which, but for a little stone bridge, we would have jumped, and sat down in the rain and had our breakfast, such as it was. I remember I divided my two pound can of roast beef with several officers on the theory that one can of beef only should be opened at a time...This little town had been in the hands of the Boche not more than*

---

[276] *314th M.G.*, 25-26. *Vigneulles* is pronounced "Vig-knee-ell."

twenty-four hours before we reached it and the stone buildings were a pile of debris and labor troops were filling up the great shell holes and opening the roadway so we could pass. Just beyond the town some Germans came out of the woods and gave themselves up.[277]

Lt. Edward Lukens of Maj. German H. Emory's 3/320th Infantry similarly remembered: *We piled out of our trucks in the morning of Sept. 13 near Woimby, on the bank of the Meuse, and after a hasty breakfast of cold "canned Willie" and crackers, started into what had been German territory twenty-four hours before. We had not the slightest idea whether we were one mile or twenty behind the front line, but not a sound of battle was heard. We saw Austrian prisoners coming back in droves escorted by French; and some French artillery shared the roads with us. All along the way we passed signboards printed in German—Boche equipment of all kinds, and in the little villages and hurriedly abandoned camps, their fires were still burning. Some of the boys even had the good fortune to find beer in the dug-outs. At one point was passed a solid belt of barbed wire entanglements at least sixty yards wide, in front of trenches, and I believe this was the Hindenburg Line, which, before the drive, was a reserve position a few miles in rear of the front trenches.*[278]

Col. Peyton's 320th Infantry advanced east across the war-torn salient until it reached the edge of a wooded area near Lavigneville, where the troops rested and the regiment received its orders from the commanding general of the French 2nd Cavalry Division by mounted courier.[279] These orders directed the 320th Infantry to take up defensive positions across a hill to the rear of Lavigneville, entrench for the night and establish outposts. The translated message read:

---

[277] As cited in *1/320th Infantry*, 62. *Village Woimby* is pronounced "Veal-awg Voim-bee."

[278] 3/320th Infantry, 49-50.

[279] *Lavigneville* is pronounced "Lav-veen-ah-veal."

> 1. The line you had to occupy is held now by elements of the 5. Cuirassiers, and of the 26. Division, in waiting for your regiment. Since you hear of a change of plan (I have not yet), the line is slightly held, keep your regiment together and give it a rest. But get liaison with the 5. Cuirassiers and the 26. Division troops, and guard yourself towards south.
> 2. Unhappily, we cannot supply you this evening with food. Let your men live upon the rations they have on them. As for tomorrow, the general commanding the division has been informed of your situation.
> 3. Please send a man on horse-back or with a bicycle as "Agent of Liaison" in case of emergency, and establish a telephone line between your regiment and me.
>
> The Commanding General.

Peyton's position was organized after nightfall, with 1/320 and 3/320 on the right and left of the sector with 2/320 in support, the ground having been reconnoitered by the battalion commanders. Liaison was established with elements of the French 2nd Cavalry and and 26th Infantry Divisions, who were also operating the sector. These dispositions were made to foil any possible Hun counter-attacks which was felt might be made up the valleys between Lavigneville and Senonville. Lt. Lukens of 3/320th Infantry admitted to a deployment screw-up, as maneuvering units in the dark are even more difficult than maneuvering during the day. He writes:

> *Our battalion was to advance over the hill in front of us and take up a position with outposts for the night. It was pitch dark, and no one knew anything about the lay of the land or the distance or position of the enemy. In a general movement on the main front, the direction of the enemy was, as a rule, obvious, but as our mission was to get in behind a retreating detachment of the Boche in the salient, the directions were almost reversed. As this had not been clearly explained to us, it was no wonder that the idea wasn't correctly carried out, but it was lucky that the Boche were well on the run and did not counterattack that night...Companies L and M were in the front of our battalion and established outposts on the wrong side, the rest of the men sleeping peacefully with their backs toward the enemy. Companies I and K thought they were behind them but were actually alongside and contented themselves with a few gas sentries facing*

the Allied lines! The commanders of Companies I and K went to find battalion H.Q.; they couldn't find it nor could they find their own companies when they tried to come back to them; so they slept by themselves in the middle of the field, several hundred yards nearer the enemy than the whole rest of the regiment. Luckily, the Boche were by this time far enough away so that no harm was done, but it gave us a shock when we found out the situation, and many a laugh afterwards.[280]

Following the 320th Infantry, the division ordnance officer established an ammunition dump just south of Woimbey, where some 750,000 rounds of small arms ammunition and about 10,000 hand grenades were placed in small lots under the trees along the main highway. The S.O.S. in France was an amazing organization that should not be underestimated. Its commander, Maj. Gen. James Harbord, remembered:

To effect the distribution of material and ammunition, general storage and supply depots and many small Army depots were constructed across France from the base ports to the front. Twenty-five important shops were erected, equipped and operated for the repair of guns and other equipment. Six large ordnance schools and a dozen small centers of instruction were established to train personnel, and at these nearly 5,000 officers and men were educated in the specialized work of the department. In addition to handling the supplies received from America, sources of procurement in Europe were found and purchase made of artillery, ammunition, T.M.s and shells, M.G.s, tanks, and equipment aggregating half a million tons and more than half a billion dollars in value.[281]

The 320th Infantry's stay in the Saint-Mihiel Salient wasn't long, as word was soon received from the French that the enemy had withdrawn to the east—out of the salient. As such, on Sept. 14, telegraphed orders from the V Corps relieved the 320th Infantry from the French 2nd Cavalry Division and the French cavalry commander ordered the 320th Infantry to return to *Woimbey* no later than 9:00 A.M., Sept. 15, in order to be transported out of the salient by large flat-bed trucks that the French called "*camions*."[282] The French commander further instructed that the return march be made by way of *Lavigneville, Lamorville,* and *Lacroix*, since "that is

---

[280] As cited in *3/320th Infantry*, 50.

[281] As cited in *Harbord*, 495.

[282] *Camions* is pronounced "Cam-ee-awn."

shorter than the one by which you came." His order concluded: "I am very thankful for the way the 320th Regiment, though very tired, did what it had to do and I regret we had not the opportunity of fighting with it against our hated enemy."[283] On departing the salient, one soldier from the 320th Infantry remembered:

> *Reveille sounded at 1:30 A.M., Sept. 14, and at 2:00 A.M. the troops began moving out on their return to Woimbey, a distance of twelve km. This shorter route had been unavailable the previous day. The men crossed the former French and German trench systems at Lamorville, from which the enemy had been driven only the previous night. The town was now only a smoldering ruin, like Seuzey. Congestion of American artillery here hindered the column in passing through. Lacroix, reached about 7:00 A.M., bore numerous but lesser scars of battle. At Woimbey from which the troops had departed scarcely more than twenty-four hours before, they found their transport waiting with a hot meal—their first since leaving Silmont... By this time, numbers of the men were approaching physical exhaustion. Without sleep for two days and on the march with heavy packs for nearly three days, eating only the reserve rations they carried, the troops participating in the bloodless expedition looked back upon it as an assignment rarely equaled in strain by actual combat duty.*[284]

The success of the American First Army in its first offensive at *Saint-Mihiel* (the Aisne-Marne Offensive was under French command) greatly heightened the morale of the Allies and depressed that of the Germans. American casualties were less than 9,000 and we snagged more than 15,000 prisoners of war, about 450 pieces of artillery, and over two hundred square miles of territory, with its remaining French population (an often over-looked fact).

No longer could any German position be considered "impregnable."

The noted railroads had been freed, the threat against the surrounding country removed, and a great obstacle to an advance toward the Briey-Metz-Sedan region had been overcome. American staffs had shown their ability to maneuver large units and the whole American First Army had developed a sense of power which was to be of great value in the difficult days ahead. The ability of the Americans in penetrating the most formidable of wire entanglements so impressed the Allied High Command that select groups of French officers and N.C.O.s were sent

---

[283] As cited in Stultz, 322.

[284] *Ibid.*, 322-23.

to view the strength of the "insurmountable" obstacles through which the American soldiers had made their way.

With the success at Saint-Mihiel and the successful British attacks across Flanders, Foch resolved to collapse the mother of all salients—the one that ran from Verdun in the south to the channel ports in the north—while the Germans were reeling in Belgium from British blows. If this giant bulge could be breached from the south in *la Secteur Meuse-Argonne,* the entire German line in northern France and most of Belgium would be turned. If Foch could get the Americans and the French to punch up through Meuse-Argonne in the south, capturing Sedan, Mézières, and the real prize, Namur, then the Germans would be forced to fall back into Hunland! It would be a classic double-envelopment on a large scale.[285]

But to do so, he'd need American units.

With the "First Team" committed in Saint-Mihiel, that left the 28th (Red Keystone), 29th (Blue and Grey), 33rd (Prairie), 35th (Santa Fe), 37th (Buckeye), 77th (Statue of Liberty), 79th (Cross of Lorraine), 80th (Blue Ridge), and 91st (Wild West) Divisions for the early stages of the Meuse-Argonne Offensive. Most of these divisions, like ours, had at least some combat experience. Others, like the 28th, 33rd, and 77th Divisions, lots of combat experience—so much so that they now consisted mostly of replacements after the Aisne-Marne Offensive (inexperienced E.M. with experienced N.C.O.s and officers). Other American divisions, like the 27th (Orion) and 30th (Old Hickory) were still up north with the Tommies. The rest of the in-country American forces were either depot divisions (i.e., fillers) or were still being trained by British or French cadre. It would therefore be up to us, *les dilettantes,* to launch the decisive offensive of the war.[286]

The German positions to be attacked in the Meuse-Argonne were among the most difficult to assault along the entire front. (Remember, the front stretched from the English Channel down to Switzerland and across northern borders of Italy, Greece, Palestine, Syria, and Iraq. This is why the French, after the defensive victory of Verdun in 1916, never attempted to retake the area in 1917-18). Maj. Gen. Hugh Drum, Pershing's operations officer, said that it was "the most ideal defensive terrain I have ever seen or read about." The area was not cast in the traditional bucolic French theme, either. On the contrary, it reminded many of us, save for the particular French medieval architecture, of Blue Ridge Mountain Country. *La Fôret d'Argonne,* for example, was very Germanic. It was deep, dark, and cut with numerous ravines and *cul de*

---

[285] *Mézières* is pronounced "Mez-ye-air" and *Namur* is pronounced "Nam-U.

[286] "A dilettante" is someone with little real experience or who has superficial interest. One can train for battle all he wants, but it's experience that counts; pronounced "Lays dil-et-awnt."

sacs. It is a place where Hansel and Gretel—crumbs or not—could have easily gotten lost. The irony is that Pershing assigned the most urban of our divisions, the 77th (Metropolitan) Division, to fight in the most-densely-wooded area of the sector. The divisions that should have been sent into it should have been us, the 28th (Keystone) Division, or the 91st (Wild West) Division. On the other hand, the trees and ravines could double for the 30-story skyscrapers on Manhattan or the narrow streets of Brooklyn. The rest of the sector consisted mostly of wooded hills and ridges that were extremely easy to defend, especially given all the time the Germans had to improve their defenses with barbed wire, concrete-reinforced dug-outs and trenches, pre-registered Artillery, etc. And that's exactly what German forces in the area had done over the past three years: improved their position.

All things being equal, we should have never been able to break through the strong German lines in the Meuse-Argonne. But amazingly and against all odds, after a-month-and-a-half of extremely hard fighting, from Sept. 26-Nov. 11, 1918, we did, and the results directly led to the end of the war. And that is something that will never, ever be taken away from us. It surely was one hell of a bloody mess, though—a human tragedy. If the Titans Under the Earth actually need a blood sacrifice to keep them underground, then we certainly placated them during the now-famous Meuse-Argonne Offensive. For those who survived it, it is our responsibility to ensure that the memory of those who were lost stay alive.

Bibliography.

"313th Artillery": Irving, Thomas and Edward Crowell. *A History of the 313th Artillery, U.S.A.* (New York: Thomas Y. Crowell Company, 1920).

"314th Artillery": *History of 314th Artillery* (314th Artillery Veterans' Association, N.D.).

"314th M.G.": *314th M.G. Battalion History, Blue Ridge (80th) Division. Published as a Matter of Record by the Officers and Men of the Battalion* (N.P., 1919).

"317th Infantry": Craighill, Edley, *History of the 317th Infantry Regiment, 80th Division* (N.P., N.D.).

"318th Infantry": *History of the 318th Infantry Regiment of the 80th Division, 1917-1919* (Richmond, Virginia: William Byrd Press, N.D.).

"319th Infantry": Peck, Josiah C. *The 319th Infantry A.E.F.* (Paris, France: Herbert Clarke Printing, 1919).

"2/319th Infantry": Herr, Charles Ryman. *Company F History, 319th Infantry* (N.P., 1920).

"1/320th Infantry": Williams, Ashby. *Experiences of the Great War: Artois, St. Mihiel, Meuse-Argonne* (Roanoke, Virginia: Press of the Stone Printing and Manufacturing Company, 1919).

"3/320th Infantry": Lukens, Edward C. *A Blue Ridge Memoir* (Baltimore, Maryland: Sun Print, 1922).

"A.B.M.C.": *American Armies and Battlefields in Europe: A History, Guide, and Reference Book* (Washington, D.C.: Government Printing Office, American Battle Monuments Commission, 1938).

"A.D.R.": *Drill and Service Regulations for Field Artillery, 1917* (Washington, D.C., Government Printing Office, 1917).

"B.M.G.M.": British General Staff. *Infantry Machine-Gun Company Training Manual, 1917.*

"Bullard": Bullard, Robert Lee, Maj. Gen. (U.S.A., ret). *Personalities and Reminiscences of the War* (Garden City, N.Y., 1925).

"F.S.R.": *Field Service Regulations, U.S. Army, 1914. Text Corrections to December 20, 1916.* (New York: Army and Navy Journal, 1916).

"Harbord": Harbord, James. *The American Army in France, 1917-19* (Boston: Little, Brown, and Company, 1936).

Hunt, Frazier: *Blown in by the Draft: Camp Yarns Collected at One of the Great National Army Cantonments by an Amateur War Correspondent. Forward by Col. Theodore Roosevelt.* (New York: Doubleday, Page, and Company, 1918).

"I.D.R.": *Infantry Drill Regulations, 1917.* (Washington, D.C.: Government Printing Office, 1917).

"*I.N.C.O.M.*": *Manual for Noncommissioned Officers and Privates of Infantry of the Army of the United States, 1917, to be used by Engineer companies (dismounted) and Coast Artillery companies for Infantry instruction and Training* (Government Printing Office, 1917).

"Mitchell": Mitchell, Lt. Col. William A. *Outlines of Military History* (Washington, D.C.: National Service Publishing Company, 1931).

"*M.G.D.R.*": *Drill Regulations for Machine Guns: Infantry, 1917* (Washington, D.C., Government Printing Office, 1917).

"*M.M.T.*": Moss, Col. James. *Manual of Military Training* (Menasha, Wisconsin: Army and College Printers, 1917).

"*M.S.T.*": *Drill and Service Manual for Sanitary Troops, U.S.A., April 15, 1917.*

"*N.C.O.M.A.*": *Manual for N.C.O.s and Privates of Field Artillery of the A.U.S., 1917* (Washington, D.C., Government Printing Office, 1917).

"Pershing": Pershing, John Joseph. *My Experiences in the World War* (New York: F.A. Stokes, 1931), 2 volumes.

"*P.M.*": Ellis, O.O. and E.B. Garey, Majors, U.S. Army Infantry. *Plattsburg Manual: A Handbook for Military Training* (New York, The Century Company, 1917).

"Stultz": Stultz, Sgt. Russell Lee. *History of the 80th Division, A.E.F.* (80th Division Veterans' Association, 1923).

"*T.O.E., 1914*": *Tables of Organization Based on the Field Service Regulations of 1914* (Washington, D.C., War Department, 1914).

Young, Rush, S. *Over the Top with the 80th, by a Buck Private* (N.P., 1933).

About the Author

Author, historian, and Army Major Gary Schreckengost (ret.) is a life member of the 80th Division Association (80thdivision.com) and a Cold War, Homeland, Bosnia, and Iraq War veteran. He is the author of *Wheat's Tigers: The 1st Louisiana Special Battalion in the Civil War* and his other works have been published in *America's Civil War Magazine, World War II Magazine, Field Artillery Journal,* and *Armor Magazine.*

The four books in this series, found on Amazon.com, are:

The 80th Division in World War I, Volume 1: Camp Lee to Saint-Mihiel.
The 80th Division in World War I, Volume 2: Meuse-Argonne to Homecoming.
The 80th Division in World War I: Into the Meuse-Argonne, Sept.-Nov. 1918.
The 80th Division in World War I: The Battle for Bois d'Ogons, Oct. 4-6, 1918.

80th Division Books on Amazon.com

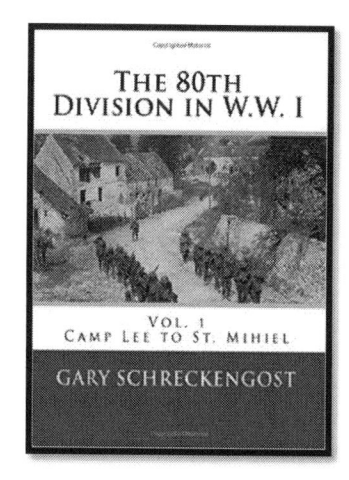

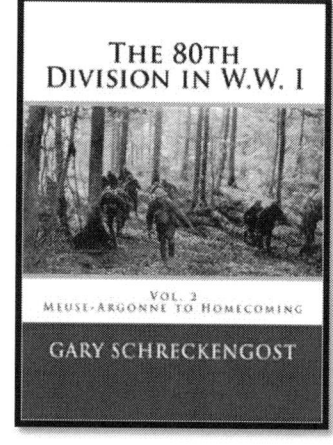

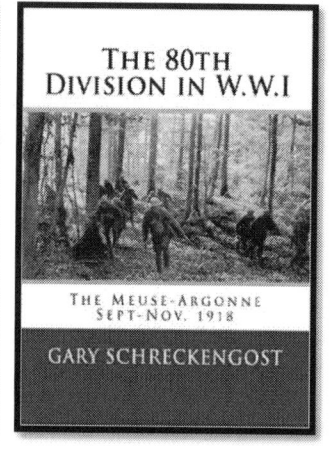

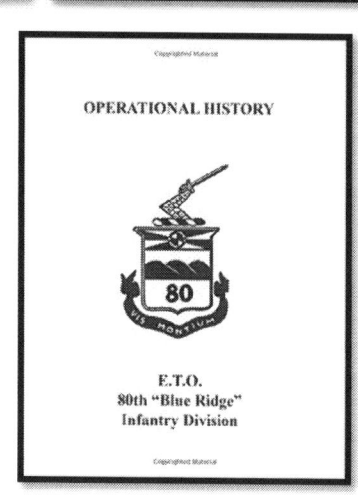

Made in the USA
Middletown, DE
08 October 2018